China's Bilateral Relations with Its Principal Oil Suppliers

China's Bilateral Relations with Its Principal Oil Suppliers

George G. Eberling

LEXINGTON BOOKS
Lanham • Boulder • New York • London

Published by Lexington Books
An imprint of The Rowman & Littlefield Publishing Group, Inc.
4501 Forbes Boulevard, Suite 200, Lanham, Maryland 20706
www.rowman.com

Unit A, Whitacre Mews, 26-34 Stannary Street, London SE11 4AB

Copyright © 2017 by Lexington Books

All rights reserved. No part of this book may be reproduced in any form or by any electronic or mechanical means, including information storage and retrieval systems, without written permission from the publisher, except by a reviewer who may quote passages in a review.

British Library Cataloguing-in-Publication Information Available

Library of Congress Cataloging-in-Publication Data Available

Library of Congress Control Number: 2017955331

ISBN 978-1-4985-5332-2 (cloth: alk. paper)
ISBN 978-1-4985-5333-9 (electronic)

∞™ The paper used in this publication meets the minimum requirements of American National Standard for Information Sciences—Permanence of Paper for Printed Library Materials, ANSI/NISO Z39.48-1992.

Printed in the United States of America

Contents

List of Illustrations and Tables		vii
Abbreviations		xi
Introduction		xiii
1	China and Angola	1
2	China and Brazil	17
3	China and Congo-Brazzaville	43
4	China and Iran	57
5	China and Iraq	73
6	China and Kazakhstan	87
7	China and Kuwait	115
8	China and Oman	129
9	China and Russia	143
10	China and Saudi Arabia	189
11	China and South Sudan	207
12	China and Sudan	223
13	China and United Arab Emirates	249
14	China and Venezuela	265
Conclusion		287

Bibliography 301
Index 329
About the Author 345

List of Illustrations and Tables

LIST OF ILLUSTRATIONS

Figure I.1	China's Daily Oil Consumption vs. Production (1980–2013)	xv
Figure I.2	China's Oil Imports by Source in 2014	xxiii

LIST OF TABLES

Table I.1	China's Bilateral Trade in 2000 and 2014	xx
Table I.2	Proven Oil Reserves	xxii
Table 1.1	Top Five Commodities Traded between China and Angola	4
Table 1.2	Chinese Crude Petroleum Imports from Angola	10
Table 1.3	Chinese Petroleum Gas Product Imports from Angola	10
Table 2.1	Top Five Commodities Traded between China and Brazil	22
Table 2.2	Chinese Crude Petroleum Imports from Brazil	32
Table 2.3	Chinese Oil and Gas Acquisitions in Brazil	33
Table 3.1	Top Five Commodities Traded between China and Congo-Brazzaville	45
Table 3.2	Chinese Crude Petroleum Imports from Congo-Brazzaville	51
Table 4.1	Top Five Commodities Traded between China and Iran	60
Table 4.2	Chinese Conventional Weapons Transfers to Iran	63
Table 4.3	Chinese Crude Petroleum Imports from Iran	65
Table 4.4	Chinese Petroleum Gas Product Imports from Iran	66

Table 5.1	Top Five Commodities Traded between China and Iraq	76
Table 5.2	Chinese Conventional Weapons Transfers to Iraq	79
Table 5.3	Chinese Crude Petroleum Imports from Iraq	81
Table 6.1	Top Five Commodities Traded between China and Kazakhstan	93
Table 6.2	Chinese Crude Petroleum Imports from Kazakhstan	101
Table 6.3	Chinese Petroleum Gas Product Imports from Kazakhstan	102
Table 6.4	Chinese Oil and Gas Acquisitions in Kazakhstan	103
Table 7.1	Top Five Commodities Traded between China and Kuwait	118
Table 7.2	Chinese Conventional Weapons Transfers to Kuwait	121
Table 7.3	Chinese Crude Petroleum Imports from Kuwait	123
Table 7.4	Chinese Petroleum Gas Product Imports from Kuwait	123
Table 8.1	Top Five Commodities Traded between China and Oman	132
Table 8.2	Chinese Crude Petroleum Imports from Oman	136
Table 9.1	Top Five Commodities Traded between China and Russia	150
Table 9.2	Soviet Conventional Weapons and Equipment Transfers to China	160
Table 9.3	Russian Conventional Weapons and Equipment Transfers to China	162
Table 9.4	Chinese Crude Petroleum Imports from Russia	173
Table 9.5	Chinese Petroleum Gas Product Imports from Russia	173
Table 9.6	Chinese Liquefied Natural Gas (LNG) Imports from Russia	174
Table 9.7	Chinese Oil and Gas Deals with Russia	174
Table 10.1	Top Five Commodities Traded between China and Saudi Arabia	193
Table 10.2	Chinese Crude Petroleum Imports from Saudi Arabia	199
Table 10.3	Chinese Petroleum Gas Product Imports from Saudi Arabia	199
Table 11.1	Top Five Commodities Traded between China and South Sudan	210
Table 11.2	Chinese Crude Petroleum Imports from South Sudan	218
Table 12.1	Top Five Commodities Traded between China and Sudan	229
Table 12.2	Chinese Conventional Weapons Transfers to Sudan	237
Table 12.3	Chinese Crude Petroleum Imports from Sudan	241
Table 12.4	Chinese Oil Acquisitions in Sudan	241

Table 13.1	Top Five Commodities Traded between China and the UAE	252
Table 13.2	Chinese Crude Petroleum Imports from the UAE	258
Table 13.3	Chinese Petroleum Gas Product Imports from the UAE	258
Table 14.1	Top Five Commodities Traded between China and Venezuela	268
Table 14.2	Chinese Conventional Weapons Transfers to Venezuela	271
Table 14.3	Chinese Crude Petroleum Imports from Venezuela	275
Table 14.4	Chinese Oil and Gas Acquisitions in Venezuela	276

Abbreviations

AAPSO	Afro-Asian Peoples Solidarity Organization
APC	Armored Personnel Carrier
APEC	Asia-Pacific Economic Cooperation
BBL	Oil Barrel
BOC	Bank of China
BRIC	Brazil, Russia, India, China
CBERS	China-Brazil Earth Resources Satellite
CCB	China Construction Bank
CCP	Chinese Communist Party
CDB	China Development Bank
CITIC	China International Trust & Investment Corporation
CMEC	China Machinery Engineering Corporation
CNG	Compressed Natural Gas
CNPC	China National Petroleum Corporation
CNOOC	China National Offshore Oil Corporation
CNSA	National Space Administration of China
CPA	Comprehensive Peace Agreement
CRBC	China Road and Bridge Corporation
CSCEC	China State Construction Engineering Corporation
CSTO	Collective Security Treaty Organization
DLF	Dhofar Liberation Front
ETIM	East Turkestan Islamic Movement
EXIM	Export Import
FDI	Foreign Direct Investment
FNLA	National Liberation Front of Angola
GCC	Gulf Cooperation Council
ICBC	Industrial and Commercial Bank of China

IEA	International Energy Agency
IMF	International Monetary Fund
KIA	Kuwait Investment Authority
LNG	Liquefied Natural Gas
MOFCOM	Chinese Ministry of Commerce
MOU	Memorandum of Understanding
MPLA	Popular Movement for the Liberation of Angola
NAM	Non-Aligned Movement
NATO	North Atlantic Treaty Organization
NCNA	News China News Agency
NOC	National Oil Company
NORINCO	China North Industries Corporation
OPEC	Organization of Petroleum Exporting Countries
PFLOAG	Popular Front for the Liberation of the Occupied Arabian Gulf
PLA	People's Liberation Army
PLAN	People's Liberation Army Navy
SCO	Shanghai Cooperation Organization
SINOPEC	China Petroleum and Chemical Corporation
SIPRI	Stockholm International Peace Research Institute
SLOC	Sea Lines of Communication
SOE	State-Owned Enterprise
UAE	United Arab Emirates
UN	United Nations
UNCTAD	United Nations Conference on Trade and Development
UNITA	National Union for the Total Independence of Angola
WMD	Weapons of Mass Destruction

Introduction

In *Chinese Energy Futures and Their Implications for the United States*, I examined how China's oil energy needs will likely shape future Sino-American relations under the conditions of dependency or non-dependency. Using Scenario Analysis and the PRINCE forecasting system to estimate the likelihoods of three oil energy futures or scenarios (Competitive Dependency, Competitive Surplus, and Cooperative Surplus), I discussed and evaluated the strategic implications of these energy futures for the United States and determined the most likely oil energy future.

In *Future Oil Demands of China, India, and China: Policy Scenarios and Implications*, I built on this analysis to examine how China's oil energy needs will likely shape future Sino-Indian relations and Sino-Japanese relations.

In this book, I examine China's strategic relations with its principal oil suppliers and what role, if any, oil shapes its strategic relations. Unlike the previous books I wrote, I focus solely on China's relations with its principal oil and gas suppliers and not the comparative relations of India, Japan or the United States. Obviously, as China's thirst for oil grows, so will its political and economic status and influence. Militarily, it is very likely that Chinese naval presence and activity may increase not only in the East China Sea and South China Sea but also in the Indian Ocean and the Persian Gulf—geographic areas which have strategic political, economic and military significance to other oil-consuming nations like the United States, India, and Japan. Beyond the strategic maritime commons, political and economic competition for oil energy resources may evolve on land in the Near East, Sub-Saharan Africa and the Western Hemisphere—distinct geographic areas which are rich in natural energy resources.

Given that (crude or refined) petroleum is a finite strategic commodity, that China may be the world's largest energy consumer of oil in the next twenty years, and that non-organization of petroleum exporting countries (OPEC) oil production is predicted to plateau by 2030,[1] thereby increasing the Near East's strategic importance, it is important to know how China's insatiable thirst for petroleum energy resources shapes its strategic relations with its oil suppliers.

Why is oil so important? Oil has a geopolitical dimension. According to Philip Andrews-Speed and Roland Dannreuther:

> Oil is different from other commodities in the extent to which its production, supply and distribution are marked by geopolitical tensions and sensitivities. To a degree surpassing other commodities, oil excites considerable strategic nervousness and suspicion. And as China is driven to secure ever-increasing quantities of oil from different parts of the world, so anxieties and suspicions of other countries about China's intentions and ambition will grow.[2]

In the international context, Philip Andrews-Speed and Roland Dannreuther opined oil's specialty derives from a number of features:

> Its physical properties make it a liquid fuel with a high quantity of energy per unit of volume and of weight, and ideally suited to past and current technologies for transport; conventional geological resources of crude are becoming increasingly concentrated in a small number of countries, principally in the Middle East, North Africa and the former Soviet Union, and its fungible nature and relative ease with which it can be transported around the world have resulted in a market for oil that is essentially global in nature, through regional hubs.[3]

HISTORICAL OVERVIEW OF CHINA'S OIL ENERGY DEPENDENCY

China was self-sufficient in oil energy resource until 1993 when its domestic oil production began to lag behind its growing oil consumption and the country became a net importer of oil.[4] Figure I.1 illustrates China's daily oil consumption versus production since 1980 including 1993 when it became dependent on foreign petroleum.

Since then, China has been securing petroleum energy resources globally through the acquisition of production sources and facilities in addition to oil products, by actively seeking concessions for oil exploration and production and by establishing energy relationships.[5] As of 2015, China imports petroleum from forty-eight countries and has oil exploration and production operations in forty-four countries.

Despite China's rising use of oil, great potential exists in future energy savings in China's transport sector by further raising fuel efficiency standards in vehicles, replacing old vehicles, changing the structure of the road fleet,

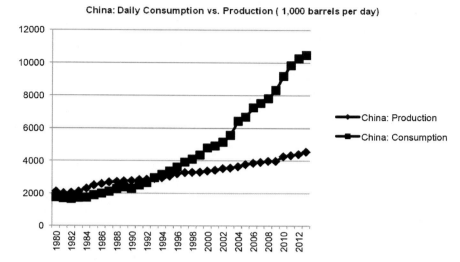

Figure I.1 China's Daily Oil Consumption vs. Production (1980–2013). *Source*: Energy Information Administration, U.S. Department of Energy.

encouraging the use of diesel and hybrid cars, and investing in urban transport systems.[6] In this context, China has taken a number of steps to constrain the rise of oil use in this sector since 2006:

> It has raised the level of purchase tax on large cars, raised the fuel economy standards for vehicle manufacturers, increased state funding for research and development in alternative-fuelled vehicles, and ordered that government departments use vehicles with higher fuel efficiency standards and that departmental vehicles not be available for private use by employees.[7]

However, the argument for an energy-efficient and environmentally friendly transport policy seems to have been subsumed beneath an industrial policy that has championed automobile manufacturing, an urban design policy that has favored multilane highways as the main transport network, and a social policy that, intentionally or otherwise, has highlighted car ownership as a legitimate expectation of the growing middle classes.[8]

Political, Economic and Military Strategies

Since 1993 China has imported crude oil in order to sustain economic growth and development. Moreover, in recent years, China has imported over 1,196,270,000 barrels of crude oil annually. Further, 90 percent of China's oil is imported by tankers originating from the Arabian Gulf and Sub-Saharan

Africa. In addition, approximately 90 percent of China's oil tankers transit from the Indian Ocean to the South China Sea through the Strait of Malacca, a key strategic chokepoint in Southeast Asia, which potentially subjects China to supply disruptions caused by piracy, international terrorism and interdiction by U.S. Naval Forces.[9]

To avoid supply disruptions, China has developed diversification strategies like building oil pipelines from Russia, Central Asia, South Asia and Southeast Asia to China and made port facility agreements with Burma and Pakistan. Moreover, China has modernized its navy and facilitated bilateral dialogues with its neighbors in South Asia and Southeast Asia regarding the deployment of Chinese warships from naval bases in Bangladesh, the Maldives, Myanmar, Pakistan, the Seychelles and Sri Lanka, to protect the vital sea lines of communication (SLOCs) from the Strait of Hormuz and Horn of Africa to the South China Sea. Minimizing supply disruptions by ensuring the safe passage of China's oil tanker fleet transiting through the Indian Ocean region is critical to China's energy security because more than 50 percent of China's imported oil originates from the Near East and Sub-Saharan Africa.[10] Otherwise, China will not able to sustain economic growth and development as well as maintain Communist Party rule.

In addition to diversification strategies, China uses economic strategies to acquire oil. According to Philip Andrews-Speed and Roland Dannreuther, Chinese national oil companies (NOCs) use corporate tactics to acquire the rights to explore for oil and gas or to develop and produce from proven fields:

> Participating in an open tender, possibly in a licensing round; buying a share of a field from an owner seeking to reduce their share or to sell out completely; buying an entire field or suite of fields from a company, or buying a local subsidiary from a multinational company; buying shares in an oil company in order to gain access to assets in a specific country; forming a joint venture with a local company; negotiating directly with the host government or the NOC to gain rights to assets or acreage; and finally a whole company.[11]

Chinese NOCs have pursued every one of these tactics in their overseas expansion in such countries like Sudan, Iran, Kazakhstan, Russia, and Angola. In some cases, Chinese NOCs have received direct and explicit political support from their government that may have been backed by loans from one China's development banks, such as the China EXIM Bank. Such was the case in Angola, Nigeria and Sudan.[12]

In some cases, China overbid for oil projects when the prize was substantial. Such was the case in Angola, Kazakhstan, Saudi Arabia, and Venezuela as well as in the failed bids for Slavneft and Unocal. The bidding strategy is assisted by the NOCs' strong financial positions. Chinese NOCs were able to receive favorable tax treatment from their government in comparison to other sectors and take advantage of low-interest free loans from state-owned policy banks.¹³

In addition to cash and loans, China has drawn on a wider array of instruments gain access to reserves. According to Philip Andrews-Speed and Ronald Dannreuther:

> The contracts to explore and develop oil and gas fields may be explicitly or implicitly linked to the construction of oil refineries or export pipelines within the host country and to long-term agreements to export oil to China. In addition, Chinese oil companies may bring their own service and construction companies. Investments in Kazakhstan and Turkmenistan have also linked in production, export agreements, and pipelines.¹⁴

China has also baited NOCs from the host country to invest in refinery, petrochemical and other downstream projects in China. Saudi Aramco constructed a new refinery in Qingdao in Shandong providence in 2008 while Kuwait Petroleum Company and Qatar Petroleum Company agreed to construct a refinery and petrochemical plants.¹⁵

Chinese NOCs have also undertaken most of their investments in partnership with one or more other companies: Sudan, Russia, Algeria, Libya, Kazakhstan, Uzbekistan, Venezuela, Nigeria, Iran and Myanmar.¹⁶

Lastly, Chinese NOCs has chosen partners NOCs from other developing countries. In Sudan, Petronas of Malaysia and Oil and Natural Gas Corporation (ONGC) of India are partners of China National Petroleum Corporation (CNPC). ONGC also partnered with CNPC in Syria and Sinopec in Colombia and Cote D'Ivoire.¹⁷

Based on the foregoing description, Chinese NOCs have expanded in the international oil and gas arena with increasing determination and speed.¹⁸

China also uses its military to acquire oil. China's defense industry and its military (PLA or the People's Liberation Army) find opportunities to advance its foreign policy interests and improve its military relations with the oil-producing nations. As the United States has often done, China can further their military relations with the oil-producing nations in the wake of successful diplomatic and commercial ties. It is important to note that Chinese foreign military operations are a strategic level activity in support of the larger, foreign, diplomatic, economic, and security agenda established by China's leadership. David H. Shinn opined that:

> The PLA does not engage in freestanding military initiatives conducted by military professionals for military reasons. In other words, the PLA is not an independent actor; it must coordinate its activities with the party and the state bureaucracy. The PLA maintains an ambitious global program of military exchanges and training programs.¹⁹

CHINA'S STRATEGIC PARTNERSHIPS

China's relations with its oil suppliers are based on the extent of overall diplomatic/political, economic/trade, and military/security relations, aid and influence and amount of oil energy resources available in each region. Thus, China's relations with its oil suppliers are best understood through its strategic partnerships. Dawn Murphy opined that:

> Starting in the mid-1990s, China introduced a new diplomatic mechanism called "strategic partnership." These strategic partnerships are established with individual countries and groupings of countries. China's strategic partnerships are not military alliances (or quasi-military alliances).[20]

Evan S. Medeiros further opined on strategic partnerships stating:

> For China, *strategic partnership* has a different meaning from the Western connotation of the term. A partnership is strategic for two reasons: (1) It is comprehensive, including all aspects of bilateral relations (e.g. economic, cultural, political, and security), and (2) both countries agree to make a long-term commitment to bilateral relations, in which bilateral problems are evaluated in that context and, importantly, occasional tensions due not derail them.[21]

Thus, it is beneficial to study China's relations with its oil suppliers in terms of its strategic partnerships, that is, political/diplomatic, economic/trade, and military/security.

China's cultural relations with oil suppliers are also important. China has been very active in promoting the Chinese language and culture. It has established numerous Confucius Institutes in key countries that serve Chinese strategic interests: Azerbaijan, Bangladesh, Egypt, Iran, Myanmar, Nigeria, Sri Lanka, Sudan, Seychelles, and the United Arab Emirates.[22] The institutes seek to improve China's image abroad and assuage concerns about "a China threat" in the context of the country's increasingly powerful economy and military.[23] Many scholars have characterized the institutes as an exercise in adroit Chinese soft power,[24] while others have suggested that the institutes are engaged in intelligence collection.[25] In this book, we examine China's strategic relations with its principal oil suppliers.

PLAN OF THE BOOK

The scale of China's involvement with its key oil suppliers can be measured in multiple ways including but not limited to the amount of energy flowing to

China, the level of bilateral trade and investment, the number of military arms and equipment transferred from and to China, or the level of political-diplomatic or cultural interactions. This book examines China's bilateral relations with its principal oil suppliers based on a five-dimensional framework: political-diplomatic relations, economic-trade relations, military-security relations, cultural relations, and petroleum-energy relations. A five-dimensional approach is comprehensive in nature and offers a complete understanding of China's complex relationships rather than looking solely on more typical perspectives like politics, bilateral trade, and security relationships. More often than not, social science literature focuses on one or more aspects of China's bilateral relations, which does not provide a complete picture of the complex nature of its interstate ties. This book endeavors to bridge this gap and look more substantially at China's bilateral relationships with energy-petroleum relations being the key aspect linking each one of them. The specific bilateral relationships examined are China's relations with Angola, Brazil, Republic of the Congo, Iran, Iraq, Kazakhstan, Kuwait, Oman, Russia, Saudi Arabia, South Sudan, Sudan, United Arab Emirates, and Venezuela.

Political-Diplomatic Relations

The essential building block in the study of contemporary bilateral relations begins with an examination of political-diplomatic ties. Political-diplomatic ties are the foundation for building strategic partnerships and serve to advance China's trade, security, and energy relationships and goals. Political-diplomatic ties cover a swath of items including the finalization of formal documents like treaties, communiqués, agreements, and memorandums of understanding (MoUs), official representation such as establishing diplomatic missions, and high-level bilateral exchanges such official visits and conversations between heads of states or their political lieutenants including cabinet secretaries and ministers or ambassadors and chiefs of missions. The Bandung Conference (1955) and Non-Aligned Movement (NAM) was essential for establishing early Chinese political-diplomatic ties with many countries including its principal oil suppliers because they provided China with an international forum from which to engage in international politics, given that China was not a member of the United Nations and its organs. In particular, the Bandung Conference provided China with the opportunity to engage with participants in one-on-one dialogue to ease their fears on China and its foreign policy, and to understand its support of emerging national liberation movements across the Third World. China effectively used the Bandung Conference to secure diplomatic relations, engage in bilateral trade talks, and strengthen its cultural relations with participants.[26]

Table I.1 China's Bilateral Trade in 2000 and 2014

Country	2000	2014	Change
Angola	$1,876,428,476	$37,081,321,855	20
Brazil	$2,844,986,286	$86,552,743,152	30
Congo	$342,055,454	$6,463,543,848	19
Iran	$2,486,499,369	$51,847,164,049	21
Iraq	$974,903,405	$28,504,710,847	29
Kazakhstan	$1,556,958,492	$22,451,869,160	14
Kuwait	$615,517,283	$13,433,551,380	22
Oman	$3,321,314,018	$25,858,058,961	8
Russia	$8,003,242,457	$95,294,513,380	12
Saudi Arabia	$3,098,263,526	$69,083,739,502	22
Sudan	$890,108,065	$3,449,892,539	4
South Sudan	N/A	$4,395,320,811	N/A
United Arab Emirates	$2,494,504,396	$54,797,218,575	22
Venezuela	$351,242,874	$16,977,833,539	48
Total	$28,856,024,101	$516,191,481,598	18

Source: United Nations Commodity Trade Statistics Database.

Economic-Trade Relations

Equally important to developing political-diplomatic relations are economic-trade ties. Like political-diplomatic ties, economic-trade relations help to build strategic relationships between China and its principal energy suppliers. One aspect unique to China's interstate relations is that its economic-trade relations preceded its political-diplomatic relations with foreign governments and nations.[27] Before establishing diplomatic relations with its key oil suppliers, China established "trade diplomacy."[28] This led to the creation and promotion of bilateral and multilateral economic forums, organizations, entities, and frameworks. Consequently, these economic-trade measures provided the building blocks for comprehensive bilateral economic development such as direct foreign direct investment, financial aid, infrastructure assistance, and strategic trading including precious energy resources. The net effect was the transformation of China from a communist command economy to the socialist market economy; the realization of a new Asian economic superpower; and a global economic rival to the United States in a time span of less than twenty years. Table I.1 illustrates China's rapid economic transformation by comparing its volume of bilateral trade with its principal oil suppliers in 2000 and 2014. China has transformed itself from a regional economic power to an economic superpower.

A review of Table I.1 indicates that bilateral trade expanded by eighteen-fold between 2000 and 2014. The largest change occurred between China and Venezuela. Bilateral trade between these countries increased forty-eight-fold.

Military-Security Relations

China's military-security ties with its principal energy suppliers are an integral aspect of its bilateral relations and serves as building block for developing closer political-diplomatic ties. It also represents hard currency and an extension of China's influence globally. Depending on the nation, China either imported or exported arms and equipment and provided or received military technical assistance. In the case of the former Soviet Union and Russia, it was the latter. The former Soviet Union and Russia provided China with extensive military arms and equipment during the Cold War (1946–1991) and post-Cold War (1991–present) with the exception of the Sino-Soviet split (1960–1989). Soviet and Russia military assistance was profound and laid the foundation for China's military modernization during both periods. China saved Russia's arm industry during the post-Cold War when arms sales dried up as a result of the collapse of the Soviet Union.

China arms sales and military technical assistance with its principal energy suppliers of Africa and the Middle East are deeply rooted in Chinese support for national liberation movements since the 1950s with the exception of Brazil, Venezuela, and Kazakhstan. China did not establish diplomatic relations with Brazil, Venezuela, and Kazakhstan until after it was admitted into the United Nations on October 25, 1971. Therefore, military-security relationships became a natural extension of established political-diplomatic ties for Brazil and Venezuela and not necessarily for security cooperation because the vast geographical distance between Asia and South America. On the other hand, Kazakhstan is an essential partner to China in terms of regional security. As a neighboring country, Kazakhstan contributes to China's national security and vice versa because of not only its close proximity to China but also its geographical location. Kazakhstan is in Central Asia and a member of a regional security framework, the Shanghai Cooperation Organization (SCO), fighting the three evils of separatism, terrorism, and extremism. Beyond regional security, Kazakhstan serves a vital economic partner and major oil and gas supplier to China.

Cultural Relations

Culture has been a primary instrument of Chinese foreign policy since the founding of the People's Republic of China of 1949. China sent cultural delegations throughout the world and conducted sports diplomacy long before establishing political-diplomatic relations. It also sent medical teams, provided scholarships for students, signed hundreds of cultural agreements, exchanged delegations, conducted people-to-people and party-to-party relations, student exchange programs, and prompted bilateral tourism. It also established Confucius Institutes and classrooms throughout the world to promote Chinese culture and language. Moreover, China hosted one of the most successful international expos in its business capital, Shanghai, in 2010. An estimated 83 million people visited the expo's 200 pavilions and covered 5,000 square meters between May and October 2010.[29] Overall, culture is an instrument of soft power and a means of projecting Chinese global political and economic interests especially with those countries which are China's principal energy suppliers.

Energy-Petroleum Relations

China's bilateral energy-petroleum relations with its principal energy suppliers are essential to its national security and economic growth. Since becoming hydrocarbon dependent in 1993, China has aggressively pursued oil and gas resources using soft power diplomacy. Remarkably, China overtook United States and became the largest net importer of petroleum and liquid fuels in March 2014. Its key energy suppliers have the largest proven crude oil reserves in the world making them key targets for China's "Go Out" or "Going Global" strategy to secure critical energy resources. This policy seeks to employ China's foreign reserves by acquiring assets overseas and equipping its domestic firms (such as China's NOCs like China National Petroleum Corporation, China Petroleum & Chemical Corporation, and China National Offshore Oil Corporation) and their management with international experience so that they can take the competition to the home markets of foreign nations and compete better in mainland China's own domestic market. To illustrate, proven crude oil reserves as of July 16, 2016 are shown according to the U.S. Energy Information Administration. See Table I.2.

China's principal key energy suppliers are clearly located in the regions with the largest proven oil reserves such as Africa, the Middle East, Eurasia, and South America. The Middle East holds the majority of proven oil reserves and is clearly the most important region of the world in terms of China's energy security. Nevertheless, China's need for fossil fuels is the determining factor for its growing interactions in these regions.

China has been increasingly reliant on its key energy suppliers to fuel its economic growth, industrialization, and overall process of development. To illustrate their importance, Figure I.2 shows China oil imports by source for 2014. China's key suppliers comprise 93 percent of the total crude petroleum suppliers in the same year.

The top three crude petroleum suppliers are Saudi Arabia, Angola, and Russia. Moreover, the key oil-producing states in the Middle East comprise

Table I.2 Proven Oil Reserves

Region	Country	Billion Barrels	% of World Total
North America	Total	219.8	13.3
Central and South America	Brazil	15.0	0.9
Central and South America	Venezuela	297.7	18.0
Central and South America	Total	328.3	19.8
Europe	Total	12.3	0.7
Eurasia	Kazakhstan	30.0	1.8
Eurasia	Russia	80.0	4.8
Eurasia	Total	118.9	7.2
Middle East	Iran	157.3	9.5
Middle East	Iraq	140.3	8.5
Middle East	Kuwait	104.0	6.3
Middle East	Oman	5.0	0.3
Middle East	Saudi Arabia	268.4	16.2
Middle East	United Arab Emirates	97.8	5.9
Middle East	Total	803.6	48.5
Africa	Angola	9.1	0.5
Africa	Congo (Brazzaville)	1.6	0.1
Africa	Sudan and South Sudan	5.0	0.3
Africa	Total	126.7	7.7
Asia & Oceania	Total	46.0	2.8
World	Total	1,655.6	100.0

Source: U.S. Energy Information Administration, 2014.

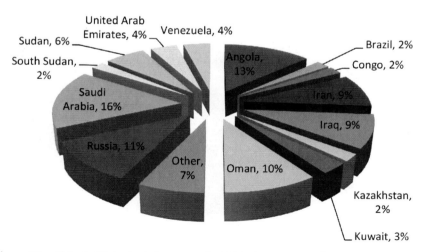

Figure I.2 China's Oil Imports by source in 2014. *Source*: United Nations Commodity Trade Statistics Database.

the bulk of China's suppliers at approximately 51 percent of China's total imports: Iran, Iraq, Kuwait, Oman, Saudi Arabia, and the United Arab Emirates. This book focuses not only on the key oil-producing states in the Middle East but also on those in Africa, Eurasia, and South America. The book examines China's relations with each principal oil supplier based on five criteria: political-diplomatic relations, economic-trade relations, military-security relations, cultural relations, and energy-petroleum relations.

Chapter 1 examines China's relations with Angola, chapter 2 examines China's relations with Brazil, chapter 3 examines China's relations with Congo-Brazzaville, chapter 4 examines China's relations with Iran, chapter 5 examines China's relations with Iraq, chapter 6 examines China's relations with Kazakhstan, chapter 7 examines China's relations with Kuwait, chapter 8 examines China's relations with Oman, chapter 9 examines China's relations with Russia, chapter 10 examines China's relations with Saudi Arabia, chapter 11 examines China's relations with Sudan, chapter 12 examines China's relations with South Sudan, chapter 13 examines China's relations with the United Arab Emirates, and chapter 14 examines China's relations with Venezuela. This book concludes with a summarization of the key findings, discusses China's future outlook and the research impediments, and offers suggestions for further research.

NOTES

1. Jamal S. Al-Suwaidi, "Introduction," in *China, India and the United States: Competition for Energy Resources* (Abu Dhabi, United Arab Emirates: Emirates Center for Strategic Studies and Research), 2008, 5.
2. Philip Andrews-Speed and Roland Dannreuther, *China, Oil and Global Politics* (London, UK: Routledge), 2011, 2.
3. Ibid., 61.
4. Bernard D. Cole, *Oil for the Lamps of China: Beijing's 21st Century Search for Energy* (Washington, DC: Institute for National Strategic Studies, National Defense University), 2003, 15.
5. Ibid., 15–16.
6. Andrews-Speed and Dannreuther, ibid., 31.
7. Ibid.
8. Ibid., 45–46.
9. Flynt Leverett, "Resource Mercantilism and the Militarization of Resource Management: Rising Asia and the Future of American Primacy," in Daniel Moran and James A. Russell, eds., *Energy Security and Global Politics: The Militarization of Resource Management* (New York, NY: Routledge), 2009, 217.
10. Jon. B. Alterman and John W. Garver. *The Vital Triangle: China, The United States and the Middle East* (Washington, DC: CSIS Press), 2008, 6.

11. Andrews-Speed and Dannreuther, Ibid., 80.
12. Ibid., 80–81.
13. Ibid., 81.
14. Ibid.
15. Ibid., 81–82.
16. Ibid., 82.
17. Ibid., 83.
18. Ibid.
19. David H. Shinn, "Military and Security Relations: China, Africa, and the Rest of the World" in Robert I. Rotberg, ed., *China into Africa: Trade, Aid, and Influence* (Washington, DC: Brookings Institution Press), 2008, 162.
20. Dawn Murphy, "China and the Middle East," testimony, June 6, 2013, before U.S.-China Economic and Security Review Commission.
21. Evan S. Medeiros, *China's International Behavior: Activism, Opportunism, and Diversification* (Santa Monica, CA: RAND Corporation), 2009, 82.
22. Confucius Institute Online, "Worldwide Confucius Institutes," accessed January 17, 2014, http://www.chinesecio.com/m/cio_wci.
23. Xiaolin Gao, *Repacking Confucius: PRC Public Diplomacy and the Rise of Soft Power* (Stockholm, Sweden: Institute for Security and Development Policy), 2008, 26.
24. Peter Schmidt, "At U.S. Colleges, Chinese-Financed Centers Prompt Worries About Academic Freedom," *The Chronicle of Higher Education*, October 22, 2010, A8, accessed January 15, 2014, http://chronicle.texterity.com/chronicle/20101022a?pg=8#pg8.
25. Fabrice De Pierrebourg and Michel Juneau-Katsuya, *Nest of Spies: The Startling Truth About Foreign Agents at Work Within Canada's Borders* (Canada: HarperCollins), 2009, 160–162.
26. Muhamad S. Olimat, *China and the Middle East Since World War II* (Lanham, MD: Lexington Books), 2014, 5.
27. Ibid., 11.
28. Ibid.
29. Ibid., 14, 47, 48.

Chapter 1

China and Angola
Political/Diplomatic Relations

Formal Sino-Angolan diplomatic relations were established on January 12, 1983 after China distanced itself from supporting the erstwhile National Union for the Total Independence of Angola (UNITA) rebels and recognized the ruling People's Movement for the Liberation of Angola (MPLA) as the governing party.[1] China and Angola established diplomatic ties by inking the Joint Communiqué on the Establishment of Diplomatic Relations between the People's Republic of China and the People's Republic of Angola (1983).[2]

China's involvement in Angola predates formal relations as it was supporting three major liberation groups in Angola's anti-colonial struggle against Portugal from the early 1960s: People's Movement for the Liberation of Angola (MPLA), National Union for the Total Independence of Angola (UNITA), and National Liberation Front of Angola (FNLA).[3] Political and military assistance alternated between the three rival groups but subsided during China's Cultural Revolution (1966–1976). China's hedging strategy of supporting the three liberation movements was a disaster because the Soviet-backed MPLA came to power and became independent in November 1975.[4] China was engaged in a political and ideological struggle with the erstwhile Soviet Union following the Sino-Soviet split of 1960 and was worried that the Soviets would increase their influence in Angola.[5] Additionally, the MPLA already had established strong links with the Soviet Union which precluded China's support following the Sino-Soviet split.[6] Consequently, UNITA and China found each other by default.[7]

Although China initially supported UNITA, China provided limited funding to the MPLA in 1960. Contact between the MPLA and the Chinese Communist Party (CCP) first occurred at the conference of Afro-Asian Peoples Solidarity Organization (AAPSO) in April 1960. In August 1960, the MPLA received funds from the CCP after an MPLA delegation visited China in

August 1960. The MPLA apparently turned to the Soviet Union to access more advanced weapons technology than those available from China. Nevertheless, the MPLA established official relations with the CCP in 1980, three years prior to China's official recognition of the new Angolan government in January 1983. Party-to-party relations have become a prominent feature in China's foreign relations with Angola since then. The party structure of both countries supersedes that of the government. Lucy Corkin opined stating that "solid relations between the parties would have been a prerequisite to official governmental relations being subsequently established."[8]

Sino-Angolan diplomatic relations developed cautiously given China's long-standing support for the MPLA's enemies.[9] China remained detached when fighting between the MPLA and UNITA resumed in 1992. Consequently, Angola turned toward Taiwan diplomatically yet unsuccessfully in a desperate need for external financing and in defiance of Beijing's "One-China" policy.[10] There were also allegations of Chinese weapons assistance to UNITA via Zaire such as light and medium artillery pieces and Type 72 anti-personnel mines but China denied it.[11]

Diplomatic ties have improved since the end of the Cold War especially in the twenty-first century and are based on an emerging energy trading relationship as evidenced by the fact that Angola is China's largest supplier of petroleum in Africa at approximately 15 percent annually; that China offered Angola a $9 billion loan for infrastructure improvements in return for petroleum; and that China has burgeoning projects such as offshore oil prospecting and exploration and refinery development. Angola also exports to China a lighter or "sweeter" crude oil to import unlike Saudi Arabia's heavier or "sour" crude oil, which is more difficult to refine in terms of time and money.

Bilateral relations have developed through high-level, official visits and exchanges. Since 2002, China and Angola have engaged each other officially no less than twenty-four times.[12] Some of the most important exchanges include: President Hu Jintao and President Jose Eduardo dos Santos (August 2008 and December 2008), and President Xi Jinping and President Jose Eduardo dos Santos (June 2015 and December 2015).[13] Bilateral cooperation has occurred on many levels such as culture, mining, geology, trade, and infrastructure. In 2005, both countries signed cooperative agreements and letters of intent in the fields of economy, technology, energy, mineral resources, and communications.[14] In 2015, both countries sealed eight agreements in economic cooperation, transportation, electricity, and financing.[15] Bilateral cooperation is considered excellent today according to a senior Chinese Ministry of Foreign Affairs official.[16]

China and Angola also inked several treaties, agreements and memorandums of understanding to further cooperation between their countries. These include:

the Cooperation Treaty between the CCP and the People's Liberation Movement of Angola to strengthen friendly relations (October 22, 1988);[17] the Protocol of the Feasibility Studies of building a Party School in Angola (December 22, 1989);[18] the Re-establishment of a Bilateral Cooperation Commission (February 2005);[19] the Memorandum of Understanding Between the Ministry of Land and Resources of the People's Republic of China and the Ministry of Geology, Mines and Industry of the Republic of Angola on Cooperation in the Field of Geology and Mining (2010);[20] and the Treaty of Extradition between the People's Republic of China and Republic of Angola (October 2013).[21]

Bilateral relations reached new heights in November 2003 when the Chinese Ministry of Foreign Trade and Economic Cooperation signed a framework agreement with the Angolan Ministry of Finance which detailed that loans to Angola would extend up to $10 billion. China's Export-Import Bank would also emerge as the primary financier of Angola's national program for reconstruction in December 2004 with its first concessional loan of $2 billion. According to Lucy Corkin, "China Export-Import Bank has become an important foreign policy tool in Beijing's diplomatic arsenal."[22]

China and Angola also maintain diplomatic representation in each other's respective capitals in Luanda and Beijing. Angola also has consulates in Hong Kong, Macau, and Shanghai.[23]

ECONOMIC/TRADE RELATIONS

Sino-Angolan economic relations are robust especially in the twenty-first century. China and Angola established a Joint Economic and Trade Commission in 1988 and China initiated a strategic partnership with Angola in 2010.[24] The Joint Economic and Trade Commission met in December 1999, May 2001, March 2007, and March 2009.[25] Since 2007, Angola has been China's top African trading partner.[26] In 2013, China was Angola's largest trading partner.[27] According to the United Nations commodity trade statistics database, bilateral trade was: $25.3 billion (2008), $17 billion (2009), $24.8 billion (2010), $27.7 billion (2011), $37.6 billion (2012), $35.9 billion (2013), $37 billion (2014), and $19.7 billion (2015).[28] Since 2000, bilateral trade increased almost eleven-fold. In 2012, foreign direct investment (FDI) into Angola from China was $392 million and foreign direct investment stock was $1.245 billion.[29] Angola was the largest recipient of Chinese FDI in Africa and the largest recipient of FDI stock in Africa after Algeria, Nigeria, South Africa, and Zambia in the same year.[30] Chinese FDI historically has been concentrated on natural resources.[31] Chinese FDI played a pivotal role in rebuilding Angola's ravaged infrastructure and oil industry.[32]

In terms of bilateral trade, Table 1.1 shows the top five commodities traded between China and Angola in 2015. Energy commodities, such as crude petroleum and petroleum products, appear to be most traded commodity between the two countries at 99.74 percent. See Table 1.1.

China's energy commodities accounted for the following in terms of trade value in previous years: 99.8 percent (2008), 99.6 percent (2009), 99.9 percent (2010), 99.5 percent (2011), 99.6 percent (2012), 99.7 percent (2013) and 99.8 percent (2014).[33]

Bilateral trade is promoted through several organizations such as the Angolan National Agency for Private Investment, the Industrial Association of Angola, the Angolan Commercial and Industrial Association, the Association of Women Entrepreneurs of Luanda Province, the Chamber of Commerce and Industry of Angola, the Angola Ministry of Commerce, the Forum on

Table 1.1 Top Five Commodities Traded between China and Angola

Commodity	Importer	Trade Value ($)	Percentage (%)
Mineral fuels, mineral oils and products of their distillation; bituminous substances; mineral waxes	China	15,955,366,252	99.74
Natural or cultured pearls, precious or semi-precious stones, precious metals, metals clad with precious metal, and articles thereof; imitation jewelry; coin	China	18,092,668	0.11
Wood and articles of wood; wood charcoal	China	12,457,229	0.08
Salt; sulfur; earths and stone; plastering materials, lime and cement	China	11,051,697	0.0691
Plastics and articles thereof	China	135,407	0.0008
Electrical machinery and equipment and parts thereof; sound recorders and reproducers, television image and sound recorders and reproducers, and parts and accessories of such articles	Angola	555,132,391	15
Furniture; bedding, mattresses, mattress supports, cushions and similar stuffed furnishings; lamps and lighting fittings, not elsewhere specified or included; illuminated signs, illuminated nameplates and the like; prefabricated buildings	Angola	373,392,677	10
Nuclear reactors, boilers, machinery and mechanical appliances; parts thereof	Angola	362,179,862	10
Articles of iron or steel	Angola	253,077,369	7
Iron and steel	Angola	216,630,216	6

Source: United Nations Commodity Trade Statistics Database.

China-Africa Cooperation, the China-Africa Development Fund, the PRC Ministry of Commerce, the PRC Ministry of Foreign Affairs, and the All-China Federation of Industry and Commerce.[34]

China and Angola have inked some important agreements to facilitate trade between their countries. The most notable agreements and notes include: the Trade Agreement (June 12, 1984);[35] an Agreement for Setting Up a Joint Committee for Bilateral Cooperation in Economics, Technology, and Trade (June 12, 1984);[36] the Minutes on the Meeting of the Joint Economic and Technological Commission (December 22, 1989);[37] the Notes Exchange on China Granting Angola General Goods (December 22, 1989);[38] the Credit Accord of RMB 50 million (August 1991);[39] the Framework Agreement on Preferential Credit (October 1997);[40] the General Accord, for Bilateral Economic and Technical Cooperation worth RMB 30 million (October 1998);[41] the Cooperation Protocol, between the Angolan Chamber of Commerce and Industry and the China Council for the Promotion of International Trade (October 1998);[42] Framework Agreement between the Chinese Ministry of Commerce and Angolan's Ministry of Finance to extend loans up to $10 billion (November 26, 2003);[43] Energy, Mining, and Infrastructure Agreements (February 2005);[44] a Technical Cooperation Agreement including a new loan from the Chinese government to Angola for $6.3 million (February 2005);[45] a new Telephone Network Cooperation Contract between Chinese ZTE Corporation International and the Angolan firm Mundo Startel, estimated at $69 million (February 2005);[46] a $2 billion Infrastructure Agreement between Angola and Export-Import Bank of China (October 3, 2007);[47] the Partnership Agreement to Finance the Construction of Social Housing and Infrastructures (April 18, 2008);[48] the Agreement on Economic and Technical Cooperation between the Government of the People's Republic of China and the Government of the Republic of Angola (2010, 2012, and 2013);[49] and the Agreement for Mutual Acceptance of National Currencies (August 5, 2015).[50]

China has been actively involved in Angola's economic development which includes financial aid, infrastructure, and investment especially in the twenty-first century. Some of the largest and most recent infrastructure and development projects include: a $1.02 billion loan for oil from the Export-Import Bank of China implemented through Sinohydro Corporation for the National Rehabilitation Projects Phase 1 (water, electricity, health, education, public works) (2004); a $205 million loan for oil from the Export-Import Bank of China to Luanda Electricity Distribution Company (EDEL) for the National Rehabilitation Projects Phase 2 (telecommunications, health, fisheries, infrastructure, public works, education) (2004); a $2 billion loan for oil from the Export-Import Bank of China implemented by China Road and Bridge Corporation (CRBC) to Benguela Railway Company for the post-conflict infrastructure projects (transport and storage, water supply and sanitation, construction)

(2005); a $1.2 billion loan for oil from the China Development Bank (CDB) implemented by CITIC Group Corporation for agricultural development (agriculture, forestry, and fishing) (2009); a $3.53 billion loan for oil from CITIC Group Corporation and China International Fund for the Kilamba social housing development (2011); a pledge of a $3 billion line of credit from Export-Import Bank of China to Angola in exchange for oil (2011);[51] and China Road and Bridge Corporation and Landscape formed a consortium to construct roads and hydraulic passages and rehabilitate secondary and tertiary roads in Luanda for $690 million (May 2016).[52]

The Export-Import Bank of China, CDB, CITIC Group Corporation, and other Chinese public and private sector agencies and corporations loaned, invested, granted, debt-relieved, or participated in joint ventures totaling $28 billion between 2001 and 2014.[53] There are at least fifty-eight projects to date covering the following sectors: telecommunications, motor and railway transportation, automobiles, utilities, agriculture, health, education, agriculture, fisheries, solar energy, sports, water supply, sanitation, construction, infrastructure, and public works.[54] Most of China's financial assistance was directed toward rebuilding war-torn Angola especially since the West had little interest in reconstructing Angola after the civil war between the MPLA and UNITA ended 2002.[55] China's intention was not perceived as altruistic because it wanted oil and it received it.[56]

China also funded the construction and development of an industrial park outside the capital of Luanda. This park is a special economic zone (Viana Industrial Zone) and is a site for Chinese construction companies to further localize their supply chains. The Viana Industrial Zone was also established for manufacturing. Chinese automobile company Dongfang Nissan established a car assembly plant in this industrial zone.[57]

China's economic assistance has not been without criticism as its activities resulted in the large Chinese presence of mostly low-skilled and temporary workers and shopkeepers in Angola. This resulted in resentment from Angolans and personal attacks against Chinese workers.[58]

Chinese policy banks like China Export-Import Bank, CDB, and China Agricultural Bank have played an important role in Angola's infrastructure development. China Export-Import Bank has been the most important Chinese financial institution lending billions to rebuild Angola after the civil war ended in 2002. China Export-Import Bank's first encounter with Angola was in 1991 when it loaned 50 million RMB for an Angolan government school project. However, it was not until 2002, when the bank's current role took shape. The bank provided development financing in the form of a loan provided that Chinese companies were awarded the infrastructure contract financed by the loan. The loan must have been greater than RMB 20 million and no less than 50 percent of the contract's procurement in terms of equipment, materials, technology, or services must have originated from China. All China Export-Import Bank loans were managed by the Angolan Ministry of Finance. The Chinese Ministry of Commerce (MOFCOM) pre-approved all Chinese companies eligible to tender China Export-Import Bank projects.[59]

China Export-Import Bank has been a political and economic success for China and Angola. The bank has initially assisted in facilitating Chinese companies' investment in Angola in the construction sector and the oil industry. Its loan mechanism has also given rise to Chinese construction companies' prominence in the Angolan market, providing them with a successful market entry strategy with very little previous experience in the same market and guaranteed projects and procurement shipments totaling several billion dollars. Additionally, loans from the bank are a facilitation mechanism for the Angolan government to covert oil revenues directly into construction contracts undertaken by Chinese companies.[60]

MILITARY/SECURITY RELATIONS

Sino-Angolan military relations and cooperation are modest because Angola relies mostly on Russian military equipment. Angola is becoming a more important partner for military cooperation with China because Angola is China's primary source of oil in Africa.[61]

Since 2002, China and Angola have conducted several reciprocal, high-level military visits and port visits. In 2007, China has provided military technical assistance and supplied military equipment to the Angolan armed forces. Angola military personnel also have received training in China.[62] China also plans to establish a naval base at Luanda Port by 2024.[63]

China and Angola have engaged each other no less than eight times since 2002 in terms of military-to-military interactions: four visits to the PRC by Angolan military officials and four visits to Angola by Chinese military officials including one port visit to Angola by Chinese warships according to the Ministry of National Defense of the People's Republic of China, *PLA Daily*, *Xinhua*, and *China Military Online*. China and Angola also have assigned defense attachés at their respective embassies in Beijing and Luanda.[64]

China has modestly supplied Angola with military weapons and equipment. Per Stockholm International Peace Research Institute (SIPRI) Arms Transfers Database, China has delivered twenty-five Type-59 Tanks and forty-five BF6 Diesel Engines in 1975 and 2015, respectively. The dearth of military transfers indicates China is a modest supplier of military arms and equipment. Russia is Angola's top supplier of military arms and equipment. China's total arms sales to Angola are $44.26 million based on the 2016 CPI index. In 2000, total arms sales to Angola were $42.38 million—the difference being $1.88 million over a 16-year period.[65]

Chinese weapons manufacturers more likely than not provided training to the Angolan military to use the military equipment because China supplied Angola with tanks and diesel engines. This is the standard practice when China supplied aircraft, ships, artillery pieces, and other military equipment to other countries. For example, China provided training and donated minesweeping equipment in the wake of civil war which ended in 2002.[66]

CULTURAL RELATIONS

Sino-Angolan cultural relations are good. China and Angola signed a cultural agreement in 1988, a judicial cooperation agreement in 2000, and bilaterally cooperated in health, sports, journalism, and education.[67] Highlights of exchanges and cooperation include: Notes confirming that the Chinese will present Angola with 1,000 tons of wheat for drought-stricken regions (January 12, 1984);[68] Cooperation Agreements between Xinhua News Agency and the Angola Press Agency (January 1986);[69] Cultural Treaty (October 22, 1986);[70] Cultural Accord (December 22, 1988);[71] Implementation Plan for cooperation in culture and education (September 8, 1990);[72] Protocol on Conditions of Chinese Specialists to Angola (September 8, 1990);[73] De-mining training workshop (2000); Judicial training (2000); $300 million in medicine, equipment, and humanitarian aid (2002); $300 million in tuberculosis medicine (2003); Journalist Exchange (2004); Marburg Fever Medicine (2005); Establishment of Anti-Malaria Center (2006); Medical Team Assistance (2007); Medical Equipment (2010); Donation to the Angolan Volleyball Association (2010); Donation to the Angolan Table Tennis Association (2010); Medical Team Assistance (2011); Academic Scholarships (2010–2013); Agreement to Build a School in Angola (2012); Medical Team Assistance (2013); Establishment of the BN Angola CITIC Vocational Training Center (2013); and the Establishment of the China-Angola Friendship School (2013).[74]

China and Angola established regularly scheduled commercial air service between their countries.[75] China also established an individual pavilion at the 2010 Shanghai International Expo where millions of visitors were amazed by Angolan culture, music, and folklore.[76] China also established a Confucius Institute at the Agostinho Neto University in February 2015 to promote the Chinese language and culture.[77]

China also has been sending medical aid units to Angola since 1963 and has sent teams to over 40 African countries to date.[78] China has sent three groups of medical workers to Angola to carry out medical aid since 2007.[79] China also sent medical teams in 2007, 2011, and 2013.[80]

Angola's participation in the 2008 Summer Olympic Games in Beijing serves as evidence of bilateral sports cooperation.

In terms of educational cooperation, Chinese construction-oriented state-owned enterprises (SOEs), China Road and Bridge Corporation (CRBC), and Sinohydro sent groups of Angolan students to China since 2008. Sinohydro sent up to seventy students whereas CRBC sent fifty students to Changsha University to study bridge building. CITIC Construction initiated skills training programs. As of mid-2010, CITIC sent approximately 100 Angolans to China for one to three months.[81]

ENERGY/PETROLEUM RELATIONS

Sino-Angolan oil economic relations are robust and strategic as evidenced by the fact that Angola is China's largest petroleum energy trading partner in Africa and second largest supplier of crude petroleum. Angola exports about 15 percent of China's total annual petroleum and China has oil equity stakes, offshore oil prospecting ventures, an oil refinery project, and oil for credit deals of $2 billion. This $2 billion aid package, funded through the Export-Import Bank of China, includes funds for infrastructure development including the rehabilitation and expansion of MT/BT networks, new generation networks, construction of transmission lines, and the reconstruction of the Ganjelas Hydroelectric Dam.[82] Between 2004 and 2010, the Export-Import Bank of China has extended a total of $10.5 billion in oil-backed credit lines to the Angolan government.[83] In 2011, the Export-Import Bank of China pledged a $3 billion line of credit in return for oil.[84] In 2013 and 2014, respectively, CDB agreed to loan $1.32 billion and $2 billion to Sonangol to expand oil and gas projects to Africa's second largest crude oil producer.[85] China bases the majority of the bilateral relationship on energy cooperation. The share of Angola's crude going to China accounted for 46 percent of total crude exports in 2012.[86] Crude oil is essentially the principal commodity traded between the two countries.

China imported between 12–17 percent of its crude petroleum from Angola between 2006 and 2015 according to the United Nations Commodity Trade Statistics Database. In terms of total trade value, crude oil petroleum imports were approximately 99 percent for the same years. Table 1.2 illustrates China's crude petroleum imports from Angola in thousands of barrels per day, oil imports share, world ranking, trade value, total commodity trade value, and percentage from 2006 to 2015. See Table 1.2. Crude petroleum is the dominant commodity imported from Angola.

Petroleum gas trading plays an insignificant role in their petroleum relations. Table 1.3 illustrates China's petroleum gas imports from Angola in millions of

Table 1.2   Chinese Crude Petroleum Imports from Angola

Year	KBPD	Oil Imports Share (%)	World Ranking	Crude Oil Trade Value ($)	Total Commodity Trade Value ($)	Percentage (%)
2006	471	16	2	10,930,839,396	10,933,295,107	100.0
2007	502	15	2	12,879,534,443	12,888,664,603	99.9
2008	600	17	2	22,358,967,995	22,382,523,829	99.9
2009	646	16	2	14,599,867,180	14,675,830,702	99.5
2010	791	16	2	22,748,976,857	22,815,049,454	99.7
2011	626	12	2	24,809,999,280	24,922,180,492	99.5
2012	806	15	2	33,373,390,248	33,561,896,917	99.4
2013	803	14	2	31,808,646,588	31,972,669,347	99.5
2014	816	13	2	30,893,003,075	31,106,015,046	99.3
2015	777	12	3	15,914,200,706	15,997,249,079	99.5

Source: United Nations Commodity Trade Statistics Database.

Table 1.3   Chinese Petroleum Gas Product Imports from Angola

Year	Volume (MMcf)	Global Share (%)	World Ranking	Petroleum Gas Trade Value ($)	Total Commodity Trade Value ($)	Percentage (%)
2009	1.87	1	15	17,986,580	14,675,830,702	0.12
2010	2.64	1	15	46,758,231	22,815,049,454	0.20
2012	2.27	1	21	57,133,856	33,561,896,917	0.17
2013	4.52	1	19	98,161,316	31,972,669,347	0.31
2014	7.13	<1	20	167,216,131	31,106,015,046	0.54
2015	3.34	<1	21	41,158,324	15,997,249,079	0.26

Source: United Nations Commodity Trade Statistics Database.

cubic feet, global imports share, world ranking, trade value, total commodity trade value, and percentage from 2009 to 2015. See Table 1.3. Petroleum gas product trading did not occur in 2006, 2007, 2008, and 2011.

In terms of China's liquefied natural gas (LNG) imports from Angola, China imported liquefied natural gas (LNG) only in 2013 and 2014—approximately 3 and 13 MMcf, respectively, or 1 percent and less than 1 percent of total LNG imports for the same years. [87] LNG imports are very insignificant.

China's oil and gas acquisitions in Angola appear to be robust. China entered Angola's energy market in 2004 when China Petroleum and Chemical Corporation (Sinopec) formed a joint venture— Sonangol Sinopec International (SSI)—with Angolan Sonangol, with Sinopec becoming the majority shareholder at 55 percent.[88] Sonangol (30 percent) and China's New Bright International Development Ltd. (70 percent) also formed a joint venture, China Sonangol in the same year. Both companies have acquired shares in Angolan oil blocks since 2004; however, China Sonangol became the broker for Angolan oil sales to China.[89] Chinese business companies finalized the following transactions:[90] Government of China-China EXIM Bank provided a $2 billion line of credit for 10,000 bpd supply in 2004;[91] Sinopec signed a Memorandum of Understanding for joint refinery and offshore prospecting in 2004;[92]

China Sonangol acquired a 25 percent interest in Angola's Block 3/05 and 3/05A in 2005;[93] Long-Term Supply Agreement was established between Sonangol and Sinopec in February 2005;[94] a Memorandum of Understanding linked to the study on the oil exploration of Angola's Block 3/05 (formerly Block 3/80) was inked between Sonangol and Sinopec in February 2005.[95] In 2006, SSI secured: a 20 percent interest in Angola's Block 15/06;[96] a 27.5 percent interest in Angola's Block 17/06;[97] and a 50 percent interest in Angola's Block 18/06 for $725 million;[98] Sinopec and China National Offshore Oil Corporation (CNOOC) purchased a 20 percent stake of Block 32 from Marathon Oil for $1.8 billion in October 2008.[99] In 2010, China Sonangol purchased: a 5 percent interest in Block 31;[100] and a 20 percent interest in Angola's Block 32.[101] In 2011, China Sonangol purchased: a 10 percent interest in Angola's Block 19/11;[102] a 10 percent interest in Angola's Block 20/11;[103] and a 20 percent interest in Angola's Block 36/11.[104] In June 2013, SSI purchased a 10 percent stake of Marathon Oil Company's offshore oil block 31 for $1.52 billion.[105]

China and Angola also signed the following agreements in February 2005 to promote energy cooperation: A Cooperation Agreement between the ministries of oil, geology, and mining of Angola and the China National Commission on Development and Reform (February 2005); and a Memorandum of Understanding on the joint exploration of new Angola's proposed oil refinery, Sonaref (February 2005).[106]

Energy cooperation extends beyond the oil and gas sector. In August 2014, China Machinery Engineering Corporation (CMEC), a subsidiary of Sinomach, signed a $990 million contract with the Angolan Ministry of Energy and Water to build the Angola Soyo 750 megawatt combined-cycle power plant. This power plant will generate electricity from Angola's natural gas once built. In June 2015, China Gezhouba Group Corporation, a member company of China Energy Engineering Corporation, formed a joint venture with Boreal Investments Ltd. and Niara Holding and signed a $2.77 billion contract with the Angolan Ministry of Water Resources to build the 2,100 megawatt Caculo Cabaca Hydropower Plant and Dam. In June 2016, China Machinery Engineering Corporation signed a $400 million contract with Angola's Ministry of Energy and Water to design, supply, commission, and operationalize a transport system associated with Lauca. This project also includes the construction of a 400 kilowatt power transmission lines and substations.[107]

SUMMARY

Sino-Angolan relations are strong. While early diplomatic ties were complicated, China has carved out a prominent position in Angola's economy as its largest partner, a major provider of funds and development assistance and the largest operator in Angola's infrastructure projects including the rehabilitation and expansion of MT/BT networks, new generation networks, construction of transmission lines, and the reconstruction of the Ganjelas Hydroelectric Dam.[108] China has been engaged in an infrastructure for oil loans arrangement which has helped to rebuild Angola after the civil war ended in 2002. The infrastructure for oil loan arrangement is the Chinese model for Chinese loans to other resource-rich countries.[109] In Angola's case, China's development and infrastructure aid has been financed directly by the Chinese government through the Export-Import Bank of China, CDB, CITIC Group Corporation, and other Chinese public and private sector agencies and corporations and is a soft power instrument for Chinese foreign policy goal of acquiring natural resources. China Export-Import Bank has had the most success in opening the door for Chinese construction companies in the Angola market.[110] Although the Western oil companies (Chevron-Texaco, Total, and BP) control the oil market in Angola, China's effective use of soft power instruments such as capital investment and financial aid and assistance makes it a fierce competitor for crude oil resources.

NOTES

1. Alex Vines and Indira Campos, "China and India in Angola" in Fantu Cheru and Cyril Obi, eds., *The Rise of China and India in Africa: Challenges, Opportunities and Critical Interventions* (New York, NY: Zed Books), 2010, 195.

2. Ministry of Foreign Affairs of People's Republic of China, "Joint Communiqué on the Establishment of Diplomatic Relations Between the People's Republic of China and the People's Republic of Angola," January 12, 1983, accessed May 26, 2014, http://www.fmprc.gov.cn/mfa_eng/wjb_663304/zzjg_663340/fzs_663828/gjlb_663832/2914_663834/2915_663836/t16465.shtml.

3. Indira Campos and Alex Vines, "Angola and China: A Pragmatic Relationship," working paper presented at the CSIS Conference "Prospects for Improving U.S.-China-Africa Cooperation," (Washington, DC), December 5, 2007, accessed November 2, 2014.

4. Ibid., 3.

5. David H. Shinn and Joshua Eisenman, *China and Africa: A Century of Engagement* (Philadelphia, PA: University of Pennsylvania Press), 2012, 339.

6. Lucy Corkin, *Uncovering African Legacy: Angola's Management of China's Credit Lines* (Farnham, England: Ashgate Publishing Limited), 2013, 2.

7. Ibid.
8. Ibid.
9. Shinn and Eisenman, *China and Africa: A Century of Engagement*, 340.
10. Ibid.
11. Campos and Vines, "Angola and China: A Pragmatic Relationship," 3.
12. Ministry of Foreign Affairs of People's Republic of China, "China-Angola: Activities," (n.d.), accessed August 7, 2016, http://www.fmprc.gov.cn/mfa_eng/wjb_663304/zzjg_663340/fzs_663828/gjlb_663832/2914_663834/2916_663838/.
13. Ibid.
14. Ministry of Foreign Affairs of People's Republic of China, "The President of Angola Meets with Zeng Peiyan," February 26, 2005, accessed August 12, 2016, http://www.fmprc.gov.cn/mfa_eng/wjb_663304/zzjg_663340/fzs_663828/gjlb_6638 32/2914_663834/2916_663838/t185309.shtml.
15. Shengnan Zhao, "China and Angola sign Cooperation Deals," *China Daily*, June 10, 2015, accessed August 12, 2016, http://www.chinadaily.com.cn/world/2015-06/10/content_20955887.htm.
16. Corkin, ibid., 4.
17. Wolfgang Bartke, *The Agreements of the People's Republic of China with Foreign Countries 1949–1990* (Munchen, Germany: K.G. Saur), 1992, 6.
18. Ibid.
19. Corkin, ibid., 175.
20. Ministry of Foreign Affairs of People's Republic of China, "China and Angola," Ibid.
21. Ibid.
22. Corkin, ibid., 1, 5, 78.
23. Campos and Vines, "Angola and China: A Pragmatic Relationship," 4.
24. Zhongping Feng and Jing Huang, "China's Strategic Partnership Diplomacy: Engaging with a Changing World" (Fride and ESPO), Working Paper No. 8, June 2014, accessed November 1, 2014, http://www.fride.org/descarga/WP8_China_strategic_partnership_diplomacy.pdf; and Campos and Vines, "Angola and China: A Pragmatic Relationship," 3.
25. Corkin, ibid., 175.
26. Corkin, ibid., 166.
27. European Commission Directorate-General for Trade, "Angola: EU Bilateral Trade and Trade with the World," April 10, 2015, accessed May 3, 2015, http://trade.ec.europa.eu/doclib/docs/2006/september/tradoc_112456.pdf.
28. United Nations, United Nations Commodity Trade Statistics Database, accessed July 22, 2016, http://comtrade.un.org/db/default.aspx.
29. United Nations Conference on Trade and Development (UNCTAD FDI/TNC) Database, *Bilateral FDI Statistics 2014*, accessed November 1, 2014, http://unctad.org/Sections/dite_fdistat/docs/webdiaeia2014d3_CHN.pdf.
30. Ibid.
31. Lloyd Thrall, *China's Expanding African Relations: Implications for U.S. National Security* (Santa Monica, CA: RAND), 2015, 38.
32. Ibid., 38–39.

33. United Nationst, United Nations Commodity Trade Statistics Database, accessed July 22, 2016, http://comtrade.un.org/db/default.aspx.
34. International Trade Centre, Directory of Trade Promotion Organizations and Other Trade Support Institutions, accessed January 5, 2015, http://www.intracen.org/itc/trade-support/tsi-directory.
35. Bartke, ibid., 6.
36. Ibid.
37. Ibid.
38. Ibid.
39. Corkin, ibid., 174.
40. Ibid.
41. Ibid.
42. Ibid.
43. Ibid., 4, 78.
44. Ibid., 174.
45. Ibid, 175.
46. Ibid.
47. Angola and China's Exim bank sign New Infrastructure Agreement, *Macauhub*, October 3, 2007, accessed August 12, 2016, http://www.macauhub.com.mo/en/2007/10/03/3816/.
48. "Angola: China and Angola to sign New Partnership Agreement to Support Basic Infrastructures," *Macauhub*, April 18, 2008, accessed August 12, 2016, http://www.macauhub.com.mo/en/2008/04/18/4900/.
49. Ministry of Foreign Affairs of People's Republic of China, "China and Angola," (n.d.), accessed October 15, 2014, http://www.fmprc.gov.cn/mfa_eng/wjb_663304/zzjg_663340/fzs_663828/gjlb_663832/2914_663834/; and Austin M. Strange, et al., "Tracking Underreported Financial Flows: China's Development Finance and the Aid–Conflict Nexus Revisited," *Journal of Conflict Resolution*, Volume 61, Issue 5 (2017): 935–963.
50. "China and Angola sign Agreement for Mutual Acceptance of National Currencies," *Macauhub*, August 5, 2015, accessed August 12, 2016, http://www.macauhub.com.mo/en/2015/08/05/china-and-angola-sign-agreement-for-mutual-acceptance-of-national-currencies/.
51. Austin M. Strange, et. al. "Tracking Underreported Financial Flows: China's Development Finance and the Aid–Conflict Nexus Revisited." *Journal of Conflict Resolution*, Volume 61, Issue 5, 2017: 935–963.
52. The Heritage Foundation and American Enterprise Institute, *China Global Investment Tracker Database*, accessed August 13, 2016, http://www.heritage.org/research/projects/china-global-investment-tracker-interactive-map.
53. Strange, et al., ibid.
54. Ibid.
55. Shinn and Eisenman, *China and Africa: A Century of Engagement*, 343.
56. Ibid.
57. Corkin, ibid., 104, 106.
58. Shinn and Eisenman, ibid., 342.

59. Corkin, ibid., 65, 66, 75, 78.
60. Ibid., 84, 95, 119, 155, 164.
61. Shinn, "Military and Security Relations: China, Africa, and the Rest of the World," 165.
62. Ibid.
63. Adam Hartman, "Chinese Naval Base for Walvis Bay," *The Namibian*, November 19, 2014, accessed November 19, 2014, http://www.namibian.com.na/indexx.php?id=20409&page_type=story_detail&category_id=1.
64. United States Department of Defense, Defense Intelligence Agency, *Directory of PRC Military Personalities*, Washington, DC, 2014, 13.
65. Stockholm International Peace Research Institute, SIPRI Arms Transfers Database, http://www.sipri.org/databases/armstransfers.
66. Strange, et al., ibid.
67. Ministry of Foreign Affairs of People's Republic of China, "Angola," October 10, 2006, accessed October 15, 2014, http://www.china.org.cn/english/features/focac/183584.htm; and Strange, et al., Ibid.
68. Bartke, *The Agreements of the People's Republic of China with Foreign Countries 1949–1990*, 6.
69. Ibid.
70. Ibid.
71. Corkin, ibid., 174.
72. Bartke, ibid., 6.
73. Corkin, ibid., 174.
74. Strange, et al., ibid.
75. Shinn and Eisenman, ibid., 342.
76. Muhamad S. Olimat, *China and North Africa Since World War II* (Lanham, MD: Lexington Books), 2014, 17.
77. Confucius Institute Online, Worldwide Confucius Institutes, accessed August 5, 2016, http://english.hanban.org/node_10971.htm.
78. Ministry of Foreign Affairs of People's Republic of China, "Li Keqiang Visits Chinese Medical Aid Unit to Angola, Urging Them to Feel Patients' Sufferings with Their Hearts and Heal the Wounded and Rescue the Dying with Their Excellent Skills," May 9, 2014, accessed August 12, 2016, http://www.fmprc.gov.cn/mfa_eng/wjb_663304/zzjg_663340/fzs_663828/gjlb_663832/2914_663834/2916_663838/t1155439.shtml.
79. Ibid.
80. Strange, et al., ibid.
81. Corkin, ibid., 103.
82. Cyril Obi, "African Oil in the Energy Security Calculations of China and India" in Fantu Cheru and Cyril Obi, eds., *The Rise of China and India in Africa: Challenges, Opportunities and Critical Interventions* (New York, NY: Zed Books), 2010, 184.
83. Lucy Corkin, "China and Angola: Strategic Partnership or Marriage of Convenience?" (Bergen, Norway: Chr. Michelsen Institute), January 2011, Vol. 1, No.

1, accessed November 2, 2014, http://www.cmi.no/publications/file/3938-china-and-angola-strategic-partnership-or-marriage.pdf.

84. Strange, et al., ibid.
85. Ibid.
86. U.S. Energy Information Administration, U.S. Department of Energy, "Country Analysis Briefs: Angola," September 17, 2014, accessed November 15, 2014, http://www.eia.gov/countries/analysisbriefs/Angola/angola.pdf.
87. United Nations, United Nations Commodity Trade Statistics Database, accessed October 10, 2014, http://comtrade.un.org/db/default.aspx.
88. Corkin, ibid., 146.
89. Ibid., 140.
90. Julie Jiang and Chen Dang, *Update on Overseas Investments by Chinese National Companies: Achievements and Challenges Since 2011* (Paris, France: Organization for Economic Cooperation and Development/International Energy Agency), June 2014, 35–39.
91. Ibid.
92. Ibid.
93. Corkin, ibid., 148.
94. Ibid., 175.
95. Ibid.
96. Ibid., 148.
97. Ibid.
98. Ibid.
99. Ibid., 147.
100. Ibid., 148.
101. Ibid.
102. Ibid.
103. Ibid.
104. Ibid.
105. Jiang and Dang, ibid.
106. Corkin, ibid., 175.
107. The Heritage Foundation and American Enterprise Institute, *China Global Investment Tracker Database*, accessed August 13, 2016, http://www.heritage.org/research/projects/china-global-investment-tracker-interactive-map.
108. Ana Cristina Alves, *The Oil Factor in Sino-Angolan Relations at the Start of the 21st Century* (Johannesburg, South Africa: South African Institute of International Affairs), February 2010, accessed October 12, 2013, http://www.voltairenet.org/IMG/pdf/Sino-Angolan_Relations.pdf.
109. Shinn and Eisenman, ibid., 341.
110. Corkin, ibid., 164.

Chapter 2

China and Brazil
Political/Diplomatic Relations

Sino-Brazilian diplomatic relations were established on August 15, 1974. To establish and refresh diplomatic ties, China and Brazil issued the following: the Joint Communiqué between the PRC and the Government of the Federal Republic of Brazil on the Establishment of Diplomatic Relations (1974);[1] and the Joint Communiqué between the PRC and the Government of the Federal Republic of Brazil (May 25, 2004).[2]

The Joint Communiqués are important to China because they stipulate that Brazil would recognize the One China policy, and that the two countries would develop their relations on China's five basic principles of peaceful coexistence.[3]

From 1949 to 1974, China and Brazil did not have diplomatic relations because Brazilian government recognized the Chinese National (*Kuomintang*) government in Taiwan.[4] Brazil was also ruled by a succession of military juntas very closely aligned to the United States.[5] The United States was very influential politically on Latin America and staunchly anti-communist. Thus, it was not realistic to hope that Brazil would develop relations with an Asian communist nation like China.[6]

Although no official diplomatic ties existed before 1974, Brazil did attempt to establish diplomatic relations. In 1961, the moderate regime of Brazilian president Jocelino Kubitschek initiated a policy of normalizing relations with China.[7] Brazil already established diplomatic relations with the Soviet Union, Hungary, Romania, and Bulgaria as part of its broader policy of reaching out to countries beyond the Iron Curtain and in the third world.[8] Kubitschek's successor, President Janio Quadros, sent Vice President Joao Goulart to China in August 1961 as head of the Brazilian commercial and trade delegation.[9] Goulart was the first senior government official from Latin America to visit China since the PRC was founded in 1949.[10] Goulart's mission was also very successful because he was well received by Mao Zedong and other Chinese leaders.[11] However, Brazil's relations with China remained subdued.[12]

Goulart succeeded Quadros as President in September 1961 but was ousted in a military coup in 1964. In conjunction with the military coup, a delegation of Chinese journalists from the News China News Agency (NCNA) and trade representatives were arrested, jailed, and eventually deported on charges of espionage and "fomenting revolution in Brazil."[13] Interestingly, ties with other Communist nations were not severed but in fact intensified.[14]

It is interesting to note that Brazil's decision to have some form of official contact with China in 1961 was primarily motivated by a long-standing Brazilian desire to retain its strategic autonomy despite being at the time a close ally of the United States.[15] Also, at several points during the Cold War, Brazil desired to reduce its dependence on the United States and Western Europe by turning its attention to Communist bloc and nonaligned nations.[16] The 1955 Bandung Conference formed the center of Brazil's political imaginary of strengthening of ties with the nonaligned nations in the Afro-Asian world under the premises of an independent foreign policy.[17] This desire for strategic autonomy remains an important feature in Brazilian foreign policy today.[18] The Kubitschek, Quadros, and Goulart regimes were also more inclined to deal with China on ideological grounds since their governments were politically left wing.[19]

China and Brazil established relations at a party-to-party level despite the lack of formal diplomatic ties. The Brazilian Communist Party sent a delegation to China in July 1953 and was invited to participate in China's eighth Communist Party of China (CPC) congress in September 1956. The Brazilian Communist Party was also the first Latin American political party to establish relations with the CPC. Party-to-party relations constitute an important part of China's overall foreign policy.[20]

Sino-Brazilian ties remained modest into the early 1990s because both countries experienced a series of profound political and economic changes from the outset of formal diplomatic relations in 1974. Brazil was ruled by a military government and was a close ally of the United States; however, it remained on America's side between 1964 and 1985 and only recognized China only after China normalized relations with the United States. During this period, China and Brazil exchanged ambassadors but few ministerial visits occurred.[21]

Bilateral relations in the 1980s progressed slowly but consistently. This period was characterized by many agreements on political, economic, cultural, scientific, and technological cooperation. Both President Joao Figueiredo (1984) and President Jose Sarney (1988) visited China but were overseeing relatively closed economies much like their Chinese counterparts and undergoing major domestic reforms in a global environment that limited their international reach. Despite these limitations, bilateral trade started to gather momentum in the early 1980s.[22]

Before the early 1990s, Brazil was facing many challenges from its military-to-democracy transition.[23] The physical distance between China and Brazil also made it difficult to strengthen their relationship.[24] The differences in geography also meant that both countries had different development priorities.[25] Brazil was regional power focusing on maintaining its regional influence and fostering ties with the United States while China focuses the majority of its attention on domestic consolidation and its relations with the United States and the Asia Pacific.[26] As both countries matured and consolidated, their ties naturally fostered.[27] Ironically, the same policies and factors that kept China and Brazil apart for almost three decades created the conditions for closer ties.[28] The focus on economic reform and domestic stability created the conditions for their new relationship.[29] Brazil was also forced to review its role on the international scene with the Cold War's end and the political and economic changes that occurred globally.[30] Thus, Brazil started to prioritize its relations with East Asia and in particular China.[31]

Sino-Brazilian relations strengthened with the establishment and development of a strategic partnership in 1993.[32] Bilateral high-level visits were more frequent under Chinese president Jiang Zemin in 1993 and 2001 and Brazilian president Fernando Henrique Cardoso in 1995.[33] China and Brazil also complemented their political relations with initiatives to stimulate bilateral trade after Brazil opened up its markets and China's greater economic insertion.[34] China became an important destination for Brazil's soy products (soy grain and soy oil) and iron ore. Their strategic partnership also became more concentrated and well defined in technical, scientific, and technological cooperation as seen by their joint efforts to develop the remote sensing satellites.[35]

Sino-Brazilian relations strengthened in the twenty-first century but not without problems. Bilateral visits increased and more agreements were signed demonstrating bilateral cooperation in diplomacy, trade, science and technology, national security, and energy.

China and Brazil interacted no less than 144 times in terms of high-level visits and exchanges.[36] Some of the most important exchanges include: President Jiang Zemin and President Fernando Cardoso (April 2001), President Hu Jintao and President Luiz Inacio Lula da Silva (May 2004, July 2005, July 2008, November 2008, May 2009, and April 2010), President Hu Jintao and President Dilma Rousseff (April 2011 and November 2011), and President Xi Jinping and President Dilma Rousseff (March 2013, September 2013, July 2014, November 2014, July 2015, and December 2015).[37] The year 2004 was a milestone in Sino-Brazilian relations because Brazil declared China to be a market economy.[38] This recognition occurred during President Hu Jintao's visit to South America in November 2004.[39] Interestingly, it was under

President Lula de Silva (2003–2011) and as part of its international political agenda that Brazil further strengthened its diplomatic relations with China.[40]

China and Brazil also signed numerous agreements to promote political-diplomatic cooperation. These include the following: Treaty of Friendship (September 9, 1945);[41] Agreement on the Installation and Operation of a Brazilian Embassy in Beijing and Chinese Embassy in Brasilia (November 27, 1974);[42] Notes Exchange on the Establishment of Consulates General in San Paolo and Shanghai (August 15, 1984);[43] Memorandum of Understanding on Discussions on Issues of Common Concern (November 1, 1985);[44] Agreement by the Exchange of Notes on the Mutual Installation of Consulates General (May 8, 1991);[45] Agreement on the Maintenance of the Consulate General of Brazil in the Special Administrative Region of Hong Kong (November 8, 1996);[46] Agreement by the Exchange of Notes on the Extent of Jurisdiction of the Consulate General of Brazil in Hong Kong to the Special Administrative Region of Macao (December 15, 1999);[47] Memorandum of Understanding between the Federal Republic of Brazil and the PRC on the Establishment of Sino-Brazilian Commission of High-Level Consultation and Cooperation (July 12, 2004);[48] Agreement on Mutual Exemption of Entry Visas between the PRC and the Government of Brazil on Holders of Diplomatic and Service/Official Passports (August 10, 2004);[49] Memorandum of Understanding for setting up an Exchange Mechanism between China and Brazil (August 31, 2006);[50] Joint Communiqué between the Federal Republic of Brazil and the PRC on the Continued Strengthening of the Strategic Partnership (May 19, 2009);[51] Joint Action Plan between the Governments of the Federal Republic of Brazil and the PRC for 2010–2014 (April 15, 2010);[52] Joint Communiqué between the Federal Republic of Brazil and the PRC (April 12, 2011);[53] Ten Year Plan for Cooperation between the Governments of the Federal Republic of Brazil and the PRC (June 21, 2012);[54] and Joint Action Plan between the Government of the PRC and the Federal Republic of Brazil for 2015–2021 (May 20, 2015).[55]

The signing of important bilateral cooperation agreements typically coincides with high-level state visits. In May 2015, thirty-five documents covering production capacity, infrastructure construction, finance, aviation, agriculture, new energy, telecommunication, and science and technology were inked by Chinese Premier Li Keqiang and President Dilma Rousseff of Brazil.[56] The finalization of numerous documents during one high-level political exchange is testimony of the growing strategic partnership between the two countries.

Both countries have also established diplomatic representation through embassies in their respective capitals in Beijing and Brasilia. Additionally, Brazil has established a Consulates General in Shanghai and Hong Kong while China established Consulates General in San Paulo and Rio De Janeiro.

ECONOMIC/TRADE RELATIONS

Sino-Brazilian economic relations are robust especially in the twenty-first century. In 2013, Brazil was China's largest trading partner in South America and seventh largest trading partner globally.[57] China was Brazil's largest trading partner after the European Union in the same year.[58] Bilateral trade was: $48.6 billion (2008), $42.3 billion (2009), $62.5 billion (2010), $84.2 billion (2011), $85.6 billion (2012), $90.1 billion (2013), $86.5 billion (2014), and $71.7 billion (2015).[59] Since 2000, bilateral trade increased twenty-five-fold. In 2012, foreign direct investment into Brazil from China was $194 million and foreign direct investment stock was $1.45 billion.[60] Bilateral trade ties were established before 1949 but remained limited until the 1990s when the two countries experienced a trade boom.[61] The bilateral trade boom is a function of the growth of China's worldwide trade.[62] Improved access to the Chinese market, as a result of China's entry into the World Trade Organization and subsequent reform of its trade practices, facilitated expansion into the twenty-first century.[63]

In terms of bilateral trade, Table 2.1 shows the top five commodities traded between China and Brazil in 2015. Energy commodities, such as mineral fuels which include crude petroleum and petroleum gas products, appear to be the third most traded commodity between the two countries. Mineral fuels are 12 percent in terms of trade value while the top two commodities, ores, slag and ash and oil seeds and oleaginous fruits have a commodity trade value of 29 percent and 38 percent, respectively. See Table 2.1. While bilateral trading has been strong, Brazil has initiated anti-dumping measures against China since the 1990s to limit the amount of imports in the textile and toy sectors. These measures are designed to protect indigenous businesses and labor-intensive sectors that affect many domestic jobs, and thus, a politically sensitive issue within Brazil. At least eighteen anti-dumping measures have been imposed to date.[64]

China's energy commodities accounted for the following in terms of trade value in previous years: 6.3 percent (2008), 5.7 percent (2009), 11.1 percent (2010), 9.3 percent (2011), 8.9 percent (2012), 7 percent (2013), and 9.5 percent (2014).[65]

Bilateral trade is promoted through several organizations such as the Export Promotion Agency, Foreign Trade Association of Brazil, Bank of Brazil SA, National Confederation of Industry, National Confederation of Trade in Goods, Services, and Tourism, Federal of Associations of Women in Business and Professionals in Brazil, Foreign Trade Studies Center, Brazil Ministry of Foreign Affairs, Brazil Ministry of Development, Industry, and Foreign Trade, Brazilian Service of Support for Micro and Small Enterprises, the People's Republic of China (PRC) Ministry of Commerce, the PRC

Table 2.1 Top Five Commodities Traded between China and Brazil

Commodity	Importer	Trade Value ($)	Percentage (%)
Oil seeds and oleaginous fruits; miscellaneous grains, seeds and fruit; industrial or medicinal plants; straw and fodder	China	16,961,105,993	38
Ores, slag and ash	China	12,800,065,343	29
Mineral fuels, mineral oils, and products of their distillation; bituminous substances; mineral waxes	China	5,316,025,815	12
Pulp of wood or of other fibrous cellulosic materials; recovered (waste and scrap) paper or paperboard	China	2,459,361,635	6
Meat and edible meat offal	China	992,220,682	2
Electrical machinery and equipment and parts thereof; sound recorders and reproducers, television image and sound recorders and reproducers, and parts and accessories of such articles	Brazil	5,586,223,292	20
Nuclear reactors, boilers, machinery and mechanical appliances; parts thereof	Brazil	4,038,237,779	15
Organic chemicals	Brazil	1,666,973,852	6
Optical, photographic, cinematographic, measuring, checking, precision, medical or surgical instruments and apparatus; parts and accessories thereof	Brazil	1,535,442,391	6
Articles of apparel and clothing accessories, not knitted or crocheted	Brazil	1,101,376,613	4

Source: United Nations Commodity Trade Statistics Database.

Ministry of Foreign Affairs, and the All-China Federation of Industry and Commerce.[66]

China and Brazil has inked some important agreements to promote economic and trade cooperation between their countries. The most notable agreements and notes include: Agreement on Good Exchange and Payments (August 21, 1961);[67] Agreement on the Mutual Supply of Commodities (November 12, 1974);[68] Trade Agreement (January 7, 1978);[69] Agreement on Maritime Transport (May 22, 1979);[70] Bilateral Trade Agreement (May 29, 1984);[71] Supplementary Protocol to the Trade Agreement (May 29, 1984);[72] Memorandum of Cooperation in the Iron and Steel Industry (November 13, 1984);[73] Summary of Talks on Trade, Science and Technology, and Sea Transport (December 6, 1984);[74] Protocol on Cooperation in the Iron and Steel Industry (November 1, 1985); Memorandum on China's Purchase of Brazilian Iron Ore over a Period of Three Years (May 18, 1990); Agreement on Economic and Technical Cooperation (May 18, 1990); Agreement aimed at the Avoidance of Double Taxation and Prevention of Fiscal Evasion with Respect to Taxes on Income (1993); Complimentary Agreement to Economic and Technical Cooperation (1993); Air Services Agreement between the Government of the Federal Republic of Brazil and the Government of the PRC (1994); Complementary Agreement to Economic and Technical Cooperation between the Government of the Federal Republic of Brazil and the Government of the PRC (1998); Supplementary Agreement between Brazil and China to Ensure the Quality of Imported and Exported Products (1998); Memorandum of Understanding for Economic Planning on Industrial Cooperation between the Ministry of Development, Industry and Foreign Trade of the Federal Republic of Brazil and the State Commission of the PRC (2002); Memorandum of Understanding for Cooperation on the Railroad Transport of Water (May 2004); Protocol on Quarantine and Veterinary and Sanitary Conditions for Thermally Processed Pork to be exported from the PRC to the Federal Republic of Brazil (2004); Protocol on Quarantine and Veterinary and Sanitary Conditions of Meat Exported from Brazil to China (2004); Memorandum of Understanding on Cooperation in Trade and Investment (2004); Protocol on Quarantine and Veterinary and Sanitary Conditions for Thermally Processed Poultry Meat Exported from the PRC to the Federal Republic of Brazil (2004); Protocol on Quarantine and Veterinary and Sanitary Conditions of Poultry Meat Exported from Brazil to China (2004); Agreement Conceding and Easing Visas for Businessmen (2004); Agreement between the Governments of the Federal Republic of Brazil and the PRC on Strengthening Cooperation in the Implementation of Construction and Infrastructure (2006); Protocol of Phytosanitary Requirements for Brazilian Tobacco Exports to China between the General Administration of Quality Supervision, Inspection and Quarantine of PRC and the Ministry of Agriculture of the Federal Republic of Brazil (2010);[75] Memorandum of Understanding between the Ministry of Foreign Affairs of the Federal Republic of Brazil and the Ministry of Commerce of the PRC on the Establishment of the Working Group on Intellectual Property (2010);[76] Trade Cooperation Agreement (June 22, 2012);[77] Memorandum of Understanding Between the Ministry of Finance of the PRC and the Ministry of Finance of the Federative Republic of Brazil on Bilateral Cooperation in Macroeconomic, Fiscal and Financial Policies (2013);[78] Agreement between the Government of the Federal Republic of Brazil and the Government of the PRC on the Facilitation of the Granting of Visas to Businessmen (July 17, 2014);[79] Memorandum of Understanding between the Ministry of Federal Republic of Brazil of Transport and the National Development and Reform Commission of the PRC on Railway Cooperation (July 17, 2014);[80] Memorandum of Understanding between the Ministry of Development, Industry and Trade of the Federal

Republic of Brazil and the National Development and Reform Commission of the PRC on Investment Promotion and Industrial Cooperation (July 17, 2014);[81] and Memorandum of Understanding between the Governments of China, Brazil, and Peru agreeing to conduct a feasibility study on a proposed Transcontinental Railway Line connecting Peru's Pacific coast and Brazil's Atlantic coast (May 22, 2015).[82]

China has been actively involved in Brazil's economic development which includes financial aid, infrastructure, and investment especially in the twenty-first century. Some of the largest and most recent infrastructure and development projects include: Wuhan Iron and Steel agreed to invest $400 million into MMX Mineracao for a 22 percent share (November 2009);[83]China Investment Corporation (CIC) agreed to invest $500 million into CVRD (Vale) (December 2009);[84] East China Mineral Exploration and Development Bureau (Jiangsu) agreed to acquire Itaminas Comercio de Minerios SA for $1.2 billion (March 2010);[85] Honbridge Holdings acquired Sul Americana de Metais, S.A. (SAM) for $390 million (April 2010);[86] Chery agreed to build a $400 million auto plant in Jacarei (August 2010);[87] Chongqing Grain Group agreed to invest $2.4 billion to develop a soy production complex in the Brazilian state of Bahia (March 2011);[88] ZTE agreed to invest $200 million to build an industrial park and cell phone factory (April 2011);[89] China Northern Railway (CNR) agreed to build a $125 million train manufacturing and modification facility (June 2011);[90] Taiyuan Iron, CITIC, and Baosteel paid $1.95 billion for a 15 percent share in Companhia Brasileira de Metalurgia e Mineracao (CBMM) (August 2011);[91] JAC Motors agreed to invest $100 million to build an auto plant in Bahia for a 20 percent share (August 2011);[92] Huawei inaugurated a $61.5 million electronic production and distribution hub in Sorocaba (April 2012);[93] Syngenta opened a $100 million sugarcane processing plant in Sao Paolo (June 2012);[94] Honbridge Holdings agreed to build a 260-mile iron ore pipeline between the Brazilian states of Minas Gerais and Bahia for $600 million (July 2012);[95] Xuzhou Construction Machinery Group (XCMG) invested $200 million to establish heavy machinery final assembly facility in Minas Gerais (June 2013);[96] China Construction Bank acquired 72 percent of the San Paulo-based bank BicBanco for $723 million (November 2013);[97] and Sany invested $300 million to establish two heavy equipment production factories in Sao Paulo (July 2014).[98]

Key Chinese infrastructure projects in Brazil were backed by loans from the Brazilian Government and Chinese banks and financial institutions such as China Development Bank (CDB), Industrial and Commercial Bank of China (ICBC), China Export-Import Bank, and the Bank of China. The record of success of Chinese firms competing to do public infrastructure projects has been decidedly mixed. China has invested or promised to invest no less than $9.7 billion to date. These Chinese-backed loans include: $201 million from ICBC to Gerdau Acominas for steel mill equipment (November 2005); $300 million from CDB to expand the Telemar Norte/Oi Network (February 2009); $1.23 billion from the Bank of China and China EXIM Bank to Vale build ships to transport iron ore to China (September 2010); $500 million from CDB to develop Brazil's 3G Network (April 2012); $5 billion from China EXIM Bank to finance Vale's purchase of equipment and services (July 2014); and $2.5 billion from the Bank of China to finance Vale's purchase of finance services (July 2014).[99]

China and Brazil have also cooperated in banking and finance. Chinese financial institutions established offices in Brazil since 2000. These include China International Capital Corporation, CITIC Securities, and CDB.[100]

Major Chinese banks have established a physical presence in Brazil. These include: China Construction Bank (CCB), Bank of China (BOC), and the ICBC. ICBC is authorized to offer retail and investment banking services and foreign exchange in Brazil. China and Brazil's central banks also signed a $10 billion currency swap agreement in March 2013. This deal was finalized to enhance bilateral financial cooperation, facilitate trade, and safeguard financial stability of both countries.[101]

MILITARY/SECURITY RELATIONS

Sino-Brazilian military ties have existed since diplomatic relations were established in 1974. Defense ties were initially confined to high-level bilateral visits but since President's Lula's election in 2002 their military-security relationship expanded to include education and training, technology cooperation and transfers, and cyber warfare and communications.[102] Bilateral relations appear to be close even through China is not an arms supplier to Brazil. For example, in May 2009 Brazilian defense minister Nelson Jobim announced that Chinese navy fighter pilots would be trained on the Brazilian aircraft carrier *Sao Paulo*.[133] Defense Minister Jobim noted that the Chinese wanted aircraft carriers for power projection and hoped that naval cooperation between China and Brazil could serve as a gateway for further defense cooperation in other areas.[104]

In terms of education and training, Brazilian military officers and defense officials have been attending PLA academies since the late 1990s. Senior officers graduated from the PLA's most prestigious military university, the National Defense University. Junior officers attended specialized PLA schools such as logistics, artillery, intelligence, and special forces. Some officers attended Command and Staff colleges. Some have taken language training at PLA schools and universities. On the Chinese side, few PLA officers went to Brazil for military education because of the difficulty of finding Chinese officers sufficiently proficient in the Portuguese to attend advanced military schools such as the Brazilian Staff College and strategic level courses.[105]

Defense interactions are still primarily confined to bilateral visits;[106] however, China and Brazil have engaged each other no less than thirty-four times since 2002. Interactions include a Chinese fleet visit to Brazil and a joint Sino-Brazilian maritime exercise in October 2013. Beyond bilateral cooperation, one hundred and thirty Chinese police peacekeepers served in Haiti under a Brazilian General under United Nations auspices.[107] Chinese military officials made eighteen visits to Brazil; received eleven visits by Brazilian military officials; participated in two joint security consultations and joint jungle warfare training while Brazilian National Defense University students visited to China's Navy maritime garrison according to the Ministry of National Defense of the PRC, *PLA Daily*, *Xinhua*, and *China Military Online*. China and Brazil also assigned defense attachés at their respective embassies in Beijing and Brasilia.[108]

China and Brazil signed agreements related to military and security matters. This includes the following: Exchange of Notes on the Establishment of Military Attaché Offices in Each Other's Countries (December 7, 1985);[109] Brazil-China Defense Cooperation Accord (October 2004);[110] and Additional Protocol to the Agreement for Cooperation in Defense Matters between the Federal Republic of Brazil and the Government of the PRC in the Area of Remote Sensing, Telecommunications, and Information Technology July 17, 2014).[111]

CULTURAL RELATIONS

Bilateral cultural ties developed in tandem with economic relations in the early 1950s. Developing cultural relations with Brazil was important to China because of Cold War tensions between the United States, China, and the Soviet Union. These tensions did not provide for formal diplomatic ties initially until after China was admitted into the United Nations in October 1971. Most Latin American countries except Cuba were generally politically and economically aligned with the United States and her allies as opposed to the communist bloc of China and the Soviet Union. Cold War alignments did not prevent China and the countries of Latin America from engaging each other on other levels such as culture, journalism, and literature.

Early cultural interactions were manifested in the form of people-to-people exchanges between China and Latin America in the 1950s. Between 1950 and 1959 more than 1,200 Latin Americans from nineteen countries visited China while China successfully sent sixteen delegates of culture, economy, and trade to Latin America.[112] Of those who visited China, approximately thirty were Brazilians.[113]

Since diplomatic relations were established, numerous agreements, memorandums of understanding, and notes were finalized between China and Brazil. These include the following: Arbitration Convention (December 14, 1911);[114] Cultural Agreement (December 21, 1953);[115] Scientific and Technical Agreement (March 25, 1982);[116] Letter of Intent of Cooperation in Agriculture, Animal Husbandry and Fishery (August 2, 1983);[117] Protocol of Intent on the Promotion of Scientific and Technical Exchange and Cooperation in Public Health (August 18, 1983);[118] Adjustment of Cooperation in the Fields of Pure and Applied Sciences between the National Council of Scientific and Technological Development and the Chinese Academy of Sciences (May 29, 1984);[119] Protocol between the National Council for Scientific and Technological Development and the State Committee on Science and Technology in the Field of Scientific and Technological Cooperation (May 29, 1984);[120] Supplementary Protocol on Cooperation in Science and Technology between the Federal Republic of Brazil and the PRC (May 29, 1984);[121] Agreement on Cultural and Educational Cooperation (November 1, 1985);[122] Protocol on Geological Science Cooperation (November 1, 1985);[123] News Exchange Agreement between the Xinhua News Agency and the Brazilian News Exchange (April 6, 1987);[124] Agreement by the Exchange of Notes on the Research and Joint Production of a Sino-Brazilian Remote Sensing Satellite (April 30, 1988);[125] Memorandum of Understanding for Cooperation in the Field of Social Assistance between the Brazilian Assistance Foundation and the China Association for SOS Children Village (July 5, 1988);[126] Protocol on the Approval of Research and Development of a Sino-Brazilian Earth Resources Satellite (July 6, 1988);[127] Protocol on Cooperation in Industrial Technology and Power (July 6, 1988);[128] Supplementary Protocol on Scientific and Technical Cooperation in the Transportation Sector (July 6, 1988);[129] Agreement on Scientific and Technological Cooperation in the Field of Drugs Preventing Serious Epidemics (July 6, 1988);[130] Agreement on Cooperation in the Field of Traditional Medicine and Medical Science (July 6, 1988);[131] Protocol on Technical Cooperation (July 6, 1988);[132] Cooperation Agreement for Sino-Brazilian TV Land Resources from the Chinese Academy of Space Technology and the National Institute for Space Research of Brazil (August 22, 1988); Memorandum of Understanding on Exchanges and Cooperation in Education (February 25, 1993); Supplementary Protocol on the Approval of Research and Joint Production of a China-Brazilian Earth Resources Satellite (March 5, 1993); Protocol on Key Points for the Further Development of Sino-Brazilian Land Resources Satellites between the Ministry of Science and Technology, Brazil and the National Space Administration of China (September 15, 1993); Protocol on Further Developments to the Sino-Brazilian Earth Resources Satellites and Related Matters, between the National Space Administration of China and the Ministry of Science and Technology of Brazil (November 9, 1993); Protocol between the Ministry of Science and Technology of Brazil and the National Space Administration of China (CNSA) on Cooperation in the Peaceful Applications of Science and Technology of Outer Space (November 23, 1993); Protocol of Cooperation in the Context of Higher Education between the Higher Education Personnel Improvement Coordination Foundation (CAPES), the Ministry of Education and Sports (MEC) of Brazil and the National Ministry of Foreign Affairs of the PRC (January 19, 1994); Supplementary Agreement of Scientific and Technological Cooperation in Agriculture between the Federal Republic of Brazil and the PRC (April 4, 1994); Supplementary Agreement of Scientific and Technological Cooperation in Traditional Chinese Medicine and Pesticides between the Federal Republic of Brazil and the PRC (April 4, 1994); Supplementary Agreement of Scientific and Technological Cooperation in the New Materials Industry between the Federal Republic of Brazil and the PRC (April 4, 1994); Protocol for the Intent of Cooperation in the Chemical and Petrochemical Industries between the Brazilian Ministry of Mines and Energy and the Ministry of Chemical Industries of the PRC (September 5, 1994); Framework Agreement on Peaceful Utilization of Outer Space (November 8, 1994); Memorandum of Understanding between the Ministry of Agriculture of Brazil and the Ministry of Agriculture of China (July 25, 1995); Agreement between the Governments of the Federal Republic of Brazil and the PRC on Technical Safety related to the Joint Development of Earth Resources Satellites (December 13, 1995); Agreement on Plant Quarantine (December 13, 1995); Minutes of Understanding on Strengthening and Expanding Space Technological Cooperation between China and Brazil (December 13, 1995); Supplementary Agreement to the Scientific and Technological Cooperation Agreement and the Economic and Technical Cooperation Agreement between the Federal Republic of Brazil and the PRC in Technical Cooperation (December 13, 1995); Memorandum of Understanding on Cooperation in the Areas of Radio and Television (December 13, 1995); Agreement on Cooperation in Health and Animal Quarantine (February 8, 1996); Supplementary Agreement to the Agreement on Cooperation in Science and Technology in the Areas of Metrology and Industrial Quality (October 29, 1997); Protocol of Cooperation in Space Technology between the Governments of the Federal Republic of Brazil and the PRC (September 21, 2000); Executive Program for Cultural and Educational Cooperation between the Governments of the Federal Republic of Brazil and the PRC for the Years 2001–2004 (November 12, 2001); Implementing Arrangement on the Control of Medicines and Products Related to Health (May 24, 2004); Memorandum of Understanding between the Ministry of Agriculture,

Livestock, and Food Supply of the Federal Republic of Brazil and the General Administration for Quality Supervision, Inspection, and Quarantine of the PRC on the Sanitation and Security of Food with respect to Animal and Plant Products (May 24, 2004); Treaty between the Federal Republic of Brazil and the PRC on Mutual Legal Assistance in Criminal Matters (May 24, 2004); Memorandum of Understanding for the Development of an Application System for the Sino-Brazilian Earth Resources Satellite Program (May 24, 2004); Sports Cooperation Agreement between the Brazilian Ministry of Sports and the General Sports Administration of China (May 24, 2004); Supplementary Accord on Health and Medical Sciences under the Scientific and Technological Cooperation Agreement between the Federal Republic of Brazil and the PRC (May 24, 2004); Memorandum of Understanding between the Brazilian Ministry of Tourism and the National Tourism Administration of China regarding the Facilitation of Travel for Chinese Tourist Groups to Brazil (November 12, 2004); Additional Protocol to the Framework Agreement on Cooperation in the Peaceful Applications of Science and Technology in Outer Space for the Establishment of the CBERS Application System though a Cooperative Structure (November 12, 2004); Memorandum of Understanding on Environmental Protection Cooperation between the Ministry of Environment of the Federative Republic of Brazil and the State Environmental Protection Administration of China (August 17, 2005); Memorandum of Understanding on Forest Biodiversity Conservation Cooperation between the Ministry of Environment of the Federative Republic of Brazil and the State Environmental Protection Administration of China (October 13, 2005); Agreement on Information and Communications Cooperation (March 24, 2006);[133] Protocol between the Ministry of Agriculture, Livestock and Supply of the Federative Republic of Brazil and Quality Supervision General Administration, Inspection and Quarantine of the PRC on Quarantine and Health Conditions (April 15, 2010);[134] Executive Program for Cultural Cooperation between the Governments of the Federal Republic of Brazil and the PRC for the Years 2010–2012 (April 16, 2010);[135] Memorandum of Understanding on the Application Policy of Data and Images produced by the China-Brazil Earth Resources Satellite (CBERS) (2010);[136] Memorandum of Understanding on Cooperation in Space and Agricultural Sciences (2010);[137] Cooperation Agreements on Science and Technology, Agriculture, and Customs (June 22, 2012);[138] Memorandum of Understanding between the Civil Aviation Department of the Presidency of the Federal Republic of Brazil and the Administration of Civil Aviation of China to Strengthen the Full Cooperation of Civil Aviation (July 17, 2014); Memorandum of Understanding between the Brazilian Space Agency and the National Space Administration of China on Cooperation in Data and Remote Sensing Satellite Applications (July 17, 2014); Technical Cooperation

Agreement between the Ministry of Science, Technology and Innovation Holding and Baidu Holdings Limited with the Purpose of Promoting the Development of Services and Internet Technology in Brazil (July 17, 2014); Memorandum of Understanding between the Ministry of Education of the Federal Republic of Brazil and the Headquarters, Confucius Institute of China, on Learning Mandarin in Brazil (July 17, 2014); Memorandum of Understanding between the Ministry of Education of the Federal Republic of Brazil and the Confucius Institute Headquarters of China with regarding the Establishment and Expansion of Confucius Institutes in Universities in the Federal Republic of Brazil (July 17, 2014); Memorandum of Understanding between the Coordination of Higher Education Personnel Improvement (CAPES) of the Federal Republic of Brazil and the China Scholarship Council (CSC) on the Students Without Borders Stage Opportunities Science Program (July 17, 2014); Agreement between the Confucius Institute Headquarters of China and the State University of Campinas (UNICAMP) for the Establishment of a Confucius Institute at the State University of Campinas (UNICAMP) (July 17, 2014); and Technical and Scientific Cooperation Agreement between the Ministry of Science, Technology and Innovation and Huawei's Brazil Telecom Ltd., for the purpose to empower professionals in the following areas: Big Data Processing, Cloud Computers, and Safety (July 17, 2014).[139]

Sino-Brazilian cultural relations are extensive and include a wide variety of areas of cooperation including: agriculture, aviation science, biotechnology, information technology, development of new materials, education, sports, environmental protection, health, tourism, media, crime, and space science and technology based on the finalization of over fifty agreements and Memoranda of Understanding.

In aviation science, China Aviation Industry Corporation II (AVIC II) and Brazil's Embraer established a partnership and produced the Embraer RJ 145 regional jet for fifty passengers in Harbin.[140] The production plant produces about twenty to twenty-five aircraft annually.[141]

In space science and technology, Sino-Brazilian bilateral strategic cooperation is well defined for the joint development of the remote sensing satellites (e.g., CBERS).[142] The CBERS program was first established in 1988 to collaboratively develop weather monitoring and communications satellites and launch them into space using Chinese launch vehicles.[143] Agreements were signed in 1988 and 1995 and three resource satellites were successfully launched in 1999, 2003, 2007, 2013, and 2014.[144] China financed 70 percent of the program cost while the Brazilian government financed the remaining 30 percent.[145]

Cultural and educational exchange and cooperation have been frequent.[146] Chinese art, acrobatics, cultural relic exhibition groups visited Brazil and a number of Brazilian art delegations have visited China.[147] The Central Ballet

Theater of China had a successful commercial tour in Brazil.[148] Cultural festivals were held in each other's country in 2001.[149] In 2003, an exhibition of China's terracotta warriors of the Qin Dynasty and historical relics of the Palace Museum was held in St. Paul of Brazil.[150] In September and October 2013, Brazil and China held the "Cultural Month" activities in each other's country.[151] The two sides have held four meetings of the Joint Cultural Committee.[152] On a large scale, the Shanghai World Expo featured the national pavilion of Brazil and attracted over 2.64 million visitors.[153]

China and Brazil have carried out cooperation in personnel exchanges, providing scholarships for the other country's students, language and culture teaching and exchange of educational information and materials.[154] China received 272 Brazilian students through China-Brazil Science Without Borders Scholarship Program.[155] Bilateral cooperation was also witnessed in broadcasting and media. The film crew of Brazil's Globo TV came to China to shoot a feature program in 2010.[156] The Latin American edition of China Daily was launched in Brazil in 2013.[157]

Tourism has increased since 2000. In 2004, 14,000 Chinese tourists visited Brazil; the number grew to 378,000 in 2010. Conversely, 17,000 Brazilians visited China in 2004 with the number reaching 38,000 in 2007.[158]

In terms of health cooperation, joint initiatives are in progress in the struggle against HIV/AIDS, the production and sale of genetic drugs, Chinese traditional medicine, and in the research for new drugs.[159]

China has also established eight Confucius Institutes across Brazil: University of Estadual Paulista, Business Confucius Institute at FAAP, Universidade Federal de Minas Gerais, University of Pernambuco, Federal University of Rio Grand Do Sul, University of Brasilia, Pontifical Catholic University of Rio de Janeiro, and University of Campinas. Additionally, China established a classroom at the San Paulo Asian Cultural Center. Confucius Institutes promote Chinese culture and foster language training for Brazilian students.[160]

ENERGY/PETROLEUM RELATIONS

Brazil is minor supplier of crude petroleum to China. In this respect, China imported than 2 percent of its crude petroleum annually from Brazil between 2006 and 2015. Despite Brazil being a minor oil supplier, the percentage of Brazil's total commodity trade value of all exports to China was 12 percent in 2015; however, crude oil is not the principal commodity traded between the two countries. Crude oil is the third most traded commodity.

In terms of total trade value, crude oil petroleum imports ranged from 5.3 to 12 percent for the same years. Table 2.2 illustrates China's crude petroleum imports from Brazil in thousands of barrels per day, oil imports share,

Table 2.2   Chinese Crude Petroleum Imports from Brazil

Year	KBPD	Oil Imports Share (%)	World Ranking	Crude Oil Trade Value ($)	Total Commodity Trade Value ($)	Percentage (%)
2006	45	2	15	891,859,201	12,909,495,161	6.9
2007	47	1	16	979,384,161	18,342,070,986	5.3
2008	61	2	14	1,886,871,298	29,863,442,631	6.3
2009	81	2	13	1,610,610,810	28,280,982,512	5.7
2010	162	3	10	4,231,065,030	38,099,447,351	11.1
2011	135	3	12	4,884,777,844	52,386,750,280	9.3
2012	121	2	12	4,653,938,170	52,281,126,771	8.9
2013	106	2	12	3,809,926,513	54,299,122,653	7.0
2014	141	2	12	4,886,818,043	51,675,122,593	9.5
2015	280	4	9	5,307,186,533	44,339,257,109	12.0

Source: United Nations Commodity Trade Statistics Database.

world ranking, trade value, total commodity trade value and percentage from 2006 to 2015. See Table 2.2.

Petroleum gas trading does not play a significant role in their energy relations. China imported less than 1 percent of its petroleum gas products in 2012 and 2015 ranking twenty-eighth and thirty-first internationally during the same years.[161] China did not import petroleum gas products from Brazil during in any other year. Further, China does not import liquefied natural gas from Brazil.

Table 2.3 illustrates China's oil and gas acquisitions in Brazil that appear to be significant. See Table 2.3.

China and Brazil can trace their hydrocarbon energy relationship back to May 2004 when Sinopec and Petrobras signed a strategic agreement of cooperation covering sales, prospecting, production, refining, pipeline, and engineering services.[162] In the wake of this agreement, Sinopec and Petrobras pledged and built the 862-mile Gasene gas pipeline from Rio de Janeiro to Vitoria for $1.3 billion.[163] The pipeline project consisted of three sections and was completed in 2010. CDB funded the second phase of the project, known as Cacimbas-Catu Gas Pipeline (GASCAC) at a cost of $750 million.[164] In May 2009, CDB also agreed to provide Brazil with $10 billion to fund the exploration of oil in Brazil's pre-salt layer reserves.[165] The loan agreement was the first of three transactions that made up the "loans for oil" deal.[166] The second part stipulated that Petrobras would supply Unipec, a subsidiary of Sinopec, with 150,000 barrels of crude oil per day in the first year and 200,000 barrels of crude oil per day in the subsequent nine years.[167] The third part was a memorandum of understanding between Sinopec and Petrobras to cooperate in areas of mutual interest, including oil exploration, refining,

Table 2.3 Chinese Oil and Gas Acquisitions in Brazil

Date	Company	Acquisition
October13	CNOOC and CNPC	Jointly won a 35 PSC (20% share) to develop a pre-salt oil discovery in Brazil's Libra oilfield for $1.4 billion Other partners include Petrobras, Shell, and Total
August13	Sinochem	Agreed to buy a 30% stake in Petrobras' Block BC-10 for $1.5 billion. Other partners include Shell and ONGC
February12	Sinochem	Agreed to buy a 10% stake in five offshore oil blocks in Brazil's Espirito Santo Basin from the London-based Perenco
January12	Sinochem	Acquired a 10% stake in five deep-water gas and oil exploration blocks in the Espirito Santo Basin from Perenco SA
November11	Sinopec	Purchased a 30% stake in Galp Energy's Brazilian unit, which has stakes in thirty-three blocks in seven onshore and offshore basins in Brazil for $5.16 billion
October10	Sinopec	Purchased 40% stake of Brazilian subsidiary of Spanish oil company Repsol YPF for $7.1 billion
May10	Sinochem	Purchased Statoil's 40% stake in Brazil's Peregrino Oil field for $3.07 billion. Statoil will still retain 60% share and remain as the field operator
May04	Sinopec	Signed a strategic agreement of cooperation with Petrobras

Source: CNPC, and Julie Jiang and Chen Dang, *Update on Overseas Investments by Chinese National Companies: Achievements and Challenges Since 2011*, Organization for Economic Cooperation and Development/International Energy Agency, June 2014, 35–39.

petrochemicals and the supply of goods and services.[168] In July 2014, ICBC signed an agreement with Schahin to lease two of the latter's semi-submersible drilling rigs, *SS Pantanal* and *SS Amazonia*, for $1.1 billion.[169] In May 2015, the Export-Import Bank of China (EXIM) signed a bilateral cooperation agreement to loan $2 billion to Petrobras to fund capital investment projects of the company.[170] CDB also signed a bilateral cooperation agreement to loan $5 billion to Petrobras to fund capital investment projects in the same month.[171] Finally, the ICBC signed a similar agreement with Petrobras for $2 billion in October 2015.[172]

Sino-Brazilian energy cooperation extends beyond the hydrocarbon sector. In May 2010, China's State Grid bought seven Brazilian thermoelectric power plants for $1 billion.[173] Exactly two years later, State Grid agreed to purchase 39 percent of the Brazilian power company Neoenergia.[174] In December 2012, State Grid won a contract to build 967 kilometers of power lines and substations to distribute electricity from Belo Monte hydroelectric dam to the southern and southeastern portions of Brazil.[175] In January 2014, State Grid won a $2 billion contract to build 2,092 kilometers of power transmission lines to connect Belo Monte to the Brazilian power grid in connection with Brazilian partners Furnas and Eletronorte.[176] In December 2013, China

Three Gorges Corporation acquired 50 percent of the Santo Antonio do Jari and Cachoeira Caldeirao hydroelectric plants for $380 million.[177] In February 2014, China Three Gorges Corporation acquired a 33 percent stake in the Terra Nova project for $390 million, which is a joint venture with EDP and Furnas for the construction of the Sao Manoel hydroelectric power plant.[178] In terms of wind power, CDB signed a loan agreement with the Brazilian Desenvix to fund the Sinovel wind farm.[179] Chinese corporate investments in Brazil's non-hydrocarbon energy sector appear to be substantial in nature as evidenced by significant investments to develop Brazil's hydroelectric and wind power infrastructure.

China and Brazil have signed agreements related to energy cooperation in Brazil's non-hydrocarbon energy sectors. These include the following: Memorandum of Understanding on Cooperation in the Peaceful Uses of Nuclear Energy (May 29, 1984); Agreement on the Peaceful Utilization of Nuclear Energy (October 11, 1984); Supplementary Agreement to the Scientific and Technological Cooperation Agreement in Electrical Energy, including Hydroelectric Generation (July 6, 1988); Memorandum of Understanding between the Ministry of Mines and Energy of the Federal Republic of Brazil and the Ministry of Water Resources of the PRC on Economic, Scientific, and Technological Cooperation (September 5, 1994); Memorandum of Understanding between the Ministry of Mines and Energy of the Federal Republic of Brazil and the Energy Ministry of the PRC on Technical Cooperation in Coal Fluidized Bed Combustion (September 5, 1994); Memorandum of Understanding between the Ministry of Mines and Energy of Brazil and the Ministry of Water Resources of the Republic of China on Economic, Scientific and Technological Cooperation in Small Hydropower Plants (December 13, 1995); Protocol between the Federal Republic of Brazil and the PRC on Energy and Mining Cooperation (February 19, 2009); and Memorandum of Understanding between the Federal Republic of Brazil and the PRC on Oil, Equipment, and Financing (May 19, 2009).[180]

SUMMARY

Sino-Brazilian relations predate formal relations established in 1974 and can be traced back to 1812 when Portuguese colonial government approached the Manchus (1644–1912) to negotiate bringing Chinese labor from China to work in tea and sugar plantations of Brazil. After the founding of the PRC in 1949, China and Brazil did not have diplomatic ties because Brazil recognized the Chinese National (Kuomintang) government in Taiwan. It was until after China was admitted to the United Nations in 1971 that the normalization of relations occurred. From the outset of normalization in 1974, the bilateral relationship remained modest until the early 1990s as both countries were undergoing a series of profound internal political and economic changes. Bilateral relations strengthened in 1993 when a strategic partnership was formed. What followed was bilateral cooperation in diplomacy, trade, science and technology, national security and energy through the signing of many agreements since 1993. The most important area of cooperation was in science and technology where both nations became involved in the joint development of the remote sensing satellites.[181]

Trade brought the two countries together in the twenty-first century. Trading has been robust since 2000 as evidenced by the fact that bilateral trade increased thirty-two-fold between 2000 and 2014. China became Brazil's largest trading partner since May 2009, replacing the United States after eighty years of economic dominance.[182] China also became an important destination for Brazil's soy products (soy grain and soy oil) and iron ore. Conversely, Brazil became an important destination for China in terms of financial aid, infrastructure, and investment. China has poured no less than $9.7 billion to develop Brazil's non-energy sectors in the areas of agriculture, mining, machinery steel, iron, communications, and construction. Many investment projects were financed by Chinese investment banks and financial institutions like CDB, ICBC, China EXIM Bank, and the Bank of China. These entities have established a physical presence in Brazil offering retail and investment banking services and foreign exchange.[183] The most important transaction occurred when China and Brazil's central banks also signed a $10 billion currency swap agreement in March 2013.[184] This deal was finalized to enhance bilateral financial cooperation, facilitate trade, and safeguard financial stability of both countries.[185]

China and Brazil cooperate in energy matters. Hydrocarbon ties were established in 2004 with the finalization of a strategic agreement of cooperation between Sinopec and Petrobras. Brazil is a minor supplier of crude oil to China providing 2 percent annually. Although a minor supplier of crude oil, China has significant oil and gas investments in Brazil involving China's principal oil and gas companies like CNPC, Sinopec, CNOOC, and Sinochem totaling more than $10 billion.

Beyond hydrocarbons, China invested in construction and development projects associated with Brazil's thermoelectric, hydroelectric, and wind power sectors. These include agreements to build thermoelectric and hydroelectric power plants, transmission lines, and a wind farm. In tandem, China and Brazil signed important agreements, protocols, and memorandums of understanding to cooperate in the peaceful use of nuclear energy and scientific and technical cooperation in hydroelectric and coal energy development.

NOTES

1. Wolfgang Bartke, *The Agreements of the People's Republic of China with Foreign Countries 1949–1990* (Munchen, Germany: K.G. Saur), 1992, 19.
2. Ministry of Foreign Affairs of People's Republic of China, "President Hu Jintao Holds Talks with President Luiz Inacio Lula da Silva of Brazil," May 25, 2004, accessed August 20, 2016, http://www.fmprc.gov.cn/mfa_eng/wjb_663304/zzjg_663340/ldmzs_664952/gjlb_664956/3473_665008/3475_665012/t120311.shtml/.
3. Shixue Jiang, "Demystifying the China–Brazil Relations," China Institute of International Studies, September 29, 2014, 2, accessed November 9, 2015, http://www.ciis.org.cn/english/2014-09/29/content_7270603.htm.
4. Loro Horta, "Brazil–China Relations" (Singapore: S. Rajaratnam School of International Studies), RSIS Working Paper No. 287, March 10, 2015, 1.
5. Ibid.
6. Jiang, "Demystifying the China–Brazil Relations," 2.
7. Horta, ibid., 1.
8. Rodrigo Tavares Maciel and Dani K. Nedal, "China and Brazil: Two Trajectories of a Strategic Partnership," in Adrian H. Hearn and Jose Luis Leon-Manriquez, eds., *China Engages Latin America: Tracing the Trajectory* (Boulder, CO: Lynne Rienner Publishers, Inc.), 2011, 237.
9. Horta, ibid., 1; and Maciel and Nedal, ibid., 237.
10. Jiang, "Demystifying the China–Brazil Relations," 2.
11. Ibid.
12. Maciel and Nedal, ibid.
13. Horta, ibid., 1; Jiang, ibid., 2; and Cecil Johnson, *Communist China and Latin America 1959–1967* (New York, NY: Columbia University Press), 1970, 12.
14. Maciel and Nedal, ibid., 238.
15. Horta, ibid., 1.
16. Maciel and Nedal, ibid., 237.
17. Henrique Altemani de Oliveira, "Brazil and China: From South–South Cooperation to Competition?" in Alex E. Fernandez Jillerto and Barbara Hogenboom, eds., *Latin America Facing China: South–South Relations Beyond the Washington Consensus* (New York, NY: Berghahn Books), 2012, 35.
18. Horta, ibid., 1.
19. Ibid.
20. Shixue Jiang, "A New Look at Chinese Relations with Latin America," *Nueva Sociedad 203,* May–June 2006, 62–78, accessed October 2, 2015.
21. Horta, ibid., 1–2.
22. Maciel and Nedal, ibid., 239.
23. Horta, ibid., 2.
24. Ibid.
25. Ibid.
26. Ibid.
27. Ibid.

28. Loro Horta, "China and Brazil: Commercial Success Amidst International Tensions," (Oakland, CA: Japan Policy Research Institute), Working Paper No. 113, November 2007, accessed October 31, 2015, http://www.jpri.org/publications/workingpapers/wp113.html.

29. Ibid.

30. Oliveira. ibid., 37.

31. Ibid.

32. Zhongping Feng and Jing Huang, "China's Strategic Partnership Diplomacy: Engaging with a Changing World" (Fride and ESPO), Working Paper No. 8, June 2014, accessed August 17, 2014, http://www.fride.org/descarga/WP8_China_strategic_partnership_diplomacy.pdf.

33. Ministry of Foreign Affairs of the People's Republic of China, "Sino–Brazilian Relations," (n.d.), accessed November 10, 2015, http://www.chinadaily.com.cn/english/doc/2004-11/11/content_390572.htm.

34. Oliveira, ibid., 40.

35. Ibid., 41.

36. Ministry of Foreign Affairs of People's Republic of China, "China–Brazil: Activities," (n.d.), accessed August 8, 2016, http://www.fmprc.gov.cn/mfa_eng/wjb_663304/zzjg_663340/ldmzs_664952/gjlb_664956/3473_665008/3475_665012/.

37. Ibid.

38. Oliveira, ibid., 43.

39. Ibid.

40. Alex E. Fernandez Jilberto and Barbara Hogenboom, "Latin America and China: South–South Relations in a New Era" in Alex E. Fernandez Jillerto and Barbara Hogenboom, eds., *Latin America Facing China: South–South Relations Beyond the Washington Consensus* (New York, NY: Berghahn Books), 2012, 13.

41. China–Brazil Business Council, Bilateral Agreements: Acts in Force Signed Between Brazil and People's Republic of China, (n.d.), accessed May 1, 2015, http://www.cebc.org.br/en/data-and-statistics/bilateral-agreements.

42. Ibid.

43. Bartke, ibid.

44. China–Brazil Business Council, ibid.

45. Ibid.

46. Ibid.

47. Ibid.

48. Ibid.

49. Ibid.

50. Ministry of Foreign Affairs of People's Republic of China, "Wu Bangguo Meets with Brazilian President Lula," August 31, 2006, accessed August 20, 2016, http://www.fmprc.gov.cn/mfa_eng/wjb_663304/zzjg_663340/ldmzs_664952/gjlb_664956/3473_665008/3475_665012/t270476.shtml.

51. China–Brazil Business Council, ibid.

52. Ibid.

53. Ibid.

54. Ibid.

55. Ministry of Foreign Affairs of People's Republic of China, "Li Keqiang and President Dilma Rousseff of Brazil Hold Talks, Stressing to Enhance Industrial Investment Cooperation and Upgrade China–Brazil Mutually Beneficial Cooperation," May 20, 2015, accessed August 20, 2016, http://www.fmprc.gov.cn/mfa_eng/wjb_663304/zzjg_663340/ldmzs_664952/gjlb_664956/3473_665008/3475_665012/t1266054.shtml.

56. Ibid.

57. United Nations, United Nations Commodity Trade Statistics Database, accessed August 15, 2015, http://comtrade.un.org/db/default.aspx.

58. European Commission Directorate-General for Trade, "Brazil: EU Bilateral Trade and Trade with the World," April 10, 2015, accessed August 15, 2015, http://trade.ec.europa.eu/doclib/docs/2006/september/tradoc_113359.pdf.

59. United Nations, United Nations Commodity Trade Statistics Database, accessed July 22, 2016, http://comtrade.un.org/db/default.aspx.

60. United Nations Conference on Trade and Development (UNCTAD FDI/TNC) Database, *Bilateral FDI Statistics 2014*, accessed April 19, 2015, http://unctad.org/Sections/dite_fdistat/docs/webdiaeia2014d3_CHN.pdf.

61. Horta, "China and Brazil: Commercial Success Amidst International Tensions;" and Jorge I. Dominguez, *China's Relations with Latin America: Shared Gains, Asymmetric Hopes* (Washington, DC: Inter-American Dialogue), June 2006, 27; and Oliveira, ibid., 36.

62. Dominguez, ibid.

63. Ibid.

64. Oliveira, ibid., 46–47.

65. United Nations, United Nations Commodity Trade Statistics Database, accessed July 22, 2016, http://comtrade.un.org/db/default.aspx.

66. International Trade Centre, Directory of Trade Promotion Organizations and Other Trade Support Institutions, accessed April 19, 2015, http://www.intracen.org/itc/trade-support/tsi-directory.

67. Bartke, ibid., 19.

68. Ibid.

69. China–Brazil Business Council, Bilateral Agreements, ibid.

70. Ibid.

71. Bartke, ibid.

72. China–Brazil Business Council, Bilateral Agreements, ibid.

73. Ibid.

74. Bartke, ibid., 21.

75. Ibid.

76. China-Brazil Business Council, Bilateral Agreements, ibid.

77. Ministry of Foreign Affairs of People's Republic of China, "Premier Wen Jiabao Holds Talks with Brazilian President Dilma Rousseff," June 22, 2012, accessed August 20, 2016, http://www.fmprc.gov.cn/mfa_eng/wjb_663304/zzjg_663340/ldmzs_664952/gjlb_664956/3473_665008/3475_665012/t945181.shtml.

78. Ministry of Foreign Affairs of the People's Republic of China, "China and Brazil," (n.d.), accessed April 12, 2015, http://www.fmprc.gov.cn/mfa_eng/wjb_663304/zzjg_663340/ldmzs_664952/gjlb_664956/3473_665008/.

79. Brazilian Ministry of Foreign Affairs, "Note 161: Acts Signed During the Visit to Brazil by the President of China, Xi Jinping," (n.d.), accessed May 16, 2015, http://www.itamaraty.gov.br/index.php?option=com_content&view=article&id=5716:atos-assinados-por-ocasiao-da-visita-ao-brasil-do-presidente-da-republica-popular-da-china-xi-jinping-brasilia-17-de-julho-de-2014&catid=42:notas&Itemid=280&lang=pt-BR.

80. Ibid.

81. Ibid.

82. Austin M. Strange, et al., "Tracking Underreported Financial Flows: China's Development Finance and the Aid -Conflict Nexus Revisited," *Journal of Conflict Resolution*, Volume 61, Issue 5 (2017): 935–963.

83. The Heritage Foundation and American Enterprise Institute, *China Global Investment Tracker Database*, accessed November 11, 2015, http://www.heritage.org/research/projects/china-global-investment-tracker-interactive-map.

84. Ibid.

85. Ibid.

86. R. Evan Ellis, *China on the Ground of Latin America: Challenges for the Chinese and Impacts on the Region* (New York, NY: Palgrave Macmillan), 2014, 23.

87. Ibid., 95.

88. The Heritage Foundation and American Enterprise Institute, ibid.

89. Ibid.

90. Ellis, ibid., 98.

91. The Heritage Foundation and American Enterprise Institute, ibid.

92. Ibid.

93. Ellis, ibid., 100.

94. Ibid., 41.

95. Ibid., 23.

96. The Heritage Foundation and American Enterprise Institute, ibid.

97. Ellis, ibid., 124.

98. The Heritage Foundation and American Enterprise Institute, ibid.

99. Ellis, ibid., 69; and Kevin P. Gallagher and Margaret Myers, "China–Latin America Finance Database" (Washington, DC: Inter-American Dialogue), 2014, accessed November 11, 2015, http://www.thedialogue.org/map_list/.

100. Ellis, ibid., 122.

101. Ellis, ibid.; and Jiang, "Demystifying the China–Brazil Relations," 2, 5.

102. Horta, "Brazil–China Relations," 13.

103. Ibid., 21.

104. L.C. Russell Hsiao, "PLAN Officers to Train on Brazilian Aircraft Carrier," *China Brief* (Jamestown Foundation), Volume IX, Issue 12, June 12, 2009, 1.

105. Horta, "China and Brazil: Commercial Success Amidst International Tensions."

106. Horta, "Brazil–China Relations," 13.

107. Dominguez, ibid., 28.

108. United States Department of Defense, Defense Intelligence Agency, *Directory of PRC Military Personalities* (Washington, DC), 2014, 14.
109. China–Brazil Business Council, Bilateral Agreements, ibid.
110. Dominguez, ibid., 7.
111. Brazilian Ministry of Foreign Affairs, ibid.
112. Bingwen Zheng, Hongbo Sun, and Yunxia Yue, "The Present Situation and Prospects of China–Latin American Relations: A Review of the History Since 1949," in Shuangrong Hu, ed., *China–Latin America Relations Review and Analysis (Volume 1)* (Reading, UK: Path International Ltd.), 2012, 2.
113. William Ratliff, *China in Latin America's Future* (n.d.), 5. Paper presented at CEAS China Brown Bag Series, the Center for East Asian Studies and the Stanford Center for Latin American Studies, Stanford University, Spring 2009–2010.
114. China–Brazil Business Council, Bilateral Agreements, ibid.
115. Ibid.
116. Ibid.
117. Bartke, ibid., 19.
118. Ibid.
119. China–Brazil Business Council, Bilateral Agreements, ibid.
120. Ibid.
121. Ibid.
122. Ibid.
123. Ibid.
124. Bartke, ibid., 21.
125. China–Brazil Business Council, Bilateral Agreements, ibid.
126. Ibid.
127. Ibid.
128. Ibid.
129. Ibid.
130. Ministry of Foreign Affairs of the People's Republic of China, "Sino-Brazilian Relations," (n.d.), accessed November 17, 2014, http://www.chinadaily.com.cn/english/doc/2004-11/11/content_390572.htm.
131. Ibid.
132. Ibid.
133. Ministry of Foreign Affairs of People's Republic of China, "Zeng Qinghong Holds Talks with Brazilian Vice President Alencar," March 24, 2006, accessed August 20, 2016, http://www.fmprc.gov.cn/mfa_eng/wjb_663304/zzjg_663340/ldmzs_664952/gjlb_664956/3473_665008/3475_665012/t242612.shtml.
134. China–Brazil Business Council, Bilateral Agreements, ibid.
135. Ibid.
136. Ministry of Foreign Affairs of the People's Republic of China, "China and Brazil," (n.d.), accessed November 17, 2014, http://www.fmprc.gov.cn/mfa_eng/wjb_663304/zzjg_663340/ldmzs_664952/gjlb_664956/3473_665008/.
137. Ibid.
138. Ministry of Foreign Affairs of People's Republic of China, "Premier Wen Jiabao Holds Talks with Brazilian President Dilma Rousseff," June 22, 2012, accessed August

20, 2016, http://www.fmprc.gov.cn/mfa_eng/wjb_663304/zzjg_663340/ldmzs_664952/gjlb_664956/3473_665008/3475_665012/t945181.shtml.

139. Brazilian Ministry of Foreign Affairs, ibid.

140. Oliveira, ibid., 47–48.

141. Horta, "Brazil–China Relations," 12.

142. Oliveira, ibid., 41.

143. R. Evan Ellis, "Advances in China–Latin America Space Cooperation," *China Brief* (Jamestown Foundation), Volume X, Issue 14, July 9, 2010, 7; and Horta, "Brazil–China Relations," 21.

144. Oliveira, ibid., 41; Zhiwei Zhou, "Analysis of Brazil and China's Rapid Development and Mutual Policy," in Shuangrong Hu, ed., *China–Latin America Relations Review and Analysis (Volume 1)* (Reading, UK: Path International Ltd.), 2012, 137; and Rui C. Barbosa, "200th Long March Rocket Launches CBERS-4 for Brazil" (NASA Spaceflight.com), December 6, 2014, accessed November 11, 2015, http://www.nasaspaceflight.com/2014/12/200th-long-march-launches-cbers-4-brazil/.

145. Horta, "Brazil–China Relations," 21.

146. Ministry of Foreign Affairs of the People's Republic of China, "Sino-Brazilian Relations," (n.d.), accessed November 17, 2014, http://www.chinadaily.com.cn/english/doc/2004-11/11/content_390572.htm.

147. Ibid.

148. Ministry of Foreign Affairs of the People's Republic of China, "China and Brazil," (n.d.), accessed November 17, 2014, http://www.fmprc.gov.cn/mfa_eng/wjb_663304/zzjg_663340/ldmzs_664952/gjlb_664956/3473_665008/.

149. Ministry of Foreign Affairs of the People's Republic of China, "Sino-Brazilian Relations," (n.d.), accessed November 17, 2014, http://www.chinadaily.com.cn/english/doc/2004-11/11/content_390572.htm.

150. Ibid.

151. Ministry of Foreign Affairs of the People's Republic of China, "China and Brazil," (n.d.), accessed April 12, 2015, http://www.fmprc.gov.cn/mfa_eng/wjb_663304/zzjg_663340/ldmzs_664952/gjlb_664956/3473_665008/.

152. Ministry of Foreign Affairs of the People's Republic of China, "Sino-Brazilian Relations," (n.d.), accessed November 17, 2014, http://www.chinadaily.com.cn/english/doc/2004-11/11/content_390572.htm.

153. Ministry of Foreign Affairs of the People's Republic of China, "China and Brazil," (n.d.), accessed November 17, 2014, http://www.fmprc.gov.cn/mfa_eng/wjb_663304/zzjg_663340/ldmzs_664952/gjlb_664956/3473_665008/.

154. Ministry of Foreign Affairs of the People's Republic of China, "Sino-Brazilian Relations," (n.d.), accessed November 17, 2014, http://www.chinadaily.com.cn/english/doc/2004-11/11/content_390572.htm.

155. Ministry of Foreign Affairs of the People's Republic of China, "China and Brazil," (n.d.), accessed April 12, 2015, http://www.fmprc.gov.cn/mfa_eng/wjb_663304/zzjg_663340/ldmzs_664952/gjlb_664956/3473_665008/.

156. Ministry of Foreign Affairs of the People's Republic of China, "China and Brazil," (n.d.), accessed November 17, 2014, http://www.fmprc.gov.cn/mfa_eng/wjb_663304/zzjg_663340/ldmzs_664952/gjlb_664956/3473_665008/.

157. Ministry of Foreign Affairs of the People's Republic of China, "China and Brazil," (n.d.), accessed April 12, 2015, http://www.fmprc.gov.cn/mfa_eng/wjb_663304/zzjg_663340/ldmzs_664952/gjlb_664956/3473_665008/.

158. Horta, "Brazil–China Relations," 10.

159. Oliveira, ibid., 41

160. Confucius Institute Online, Worldwide Confucius Institutes, accessed November 5, 2015, http://english.hanban.org/node_10971.htm.

161. United Nations, United Nations Commodity Trade Statistics Database, accessed April 20, 2015, http://comtrade.un.org/db/default.aspx.

162. Duncan Freeman, Jonathan Holslag, and Rhys Jenkins, *Chinese Resources and Energy Policy in Latin America* (Brussels, Belgium: European Parliament), June 2007, 25.

163. Ellis, *China on the Ground of Latin America*, 69.

164. Ellis, ibid., and Gallagher and Myers, ibid.

165. Jiang, ibid., 5.

166. Erica Downs, *Inside China, Inc: China Development Bank's Cross-Border Energy Deals* (Washington, DC: The Brooking Institution Press), March 2011, 46.

167. Ibid.

168. Ibid.

169. Gallagher and Myers, ibid.

170. Strange, et al., ibid.

171. Strange, et al., ibid.

172. The Heritage Foundation and American Enterprise Institute, ibid.

173. Ellis, *China on the Ground of Latin America*, 115.

174. Ibid.

175. Ibid., 118.

176. Ibid.

177. The Heritage Foundation and American Enterprise Institute, ibid.

178. Ibid.

179. Ellis, *China on the Ground of Latin America*, 117.

180. China–Brazil Business Council, Bilateral Agreements, accessed May 1, 2015.

181. Horta, "Brazil–China Relations," 1, 2.

182. Ibid., 3.

183. Ellis, *China on the Ground of Latin America*, 122.

184. Jiang, "Demystifying the China–Brazil Relations," 2.

185. Ibid., 5.

Chapter 3

China and Congo-Brazzaville
Political/Diplomatic Relations

China and Congo-Brazzaville established diplomatic relations on February 22, 1964.[1] To establish and advance diplomatic ties, China and Congo-Brazzaville inked the following: The Joint Communiqué on the Establishment of the Diplomatic Relations Between the People's Republic of China and the Republic of the Congo (Brazzaville);[2] the Sino-Congolese Friendship Mutual Non-Aggression Treaty (1964);[3] and the 1987–1988 Exchange Plan between the Chinese Communist Party and the Congolese Party of Labor (April 18, 1987).[4]

Congo-Brazzaville was a former French colony that received its independence in 1960. Congo-Brazzaville initially established diplomatic relations with Taiwan in 1960 but switched political ties to China in 1964. Taiwan severed official diplomatic ties upon China's diplomatic recognition.

As a gesture of goodwill, China provided $5 million in loans as budgetary support and $20 million in interest-free loans to Congo-Brazzaville and became Congo-Brazzaville's principal benefactor in 1960s.[5] Congo-Brazzaville was a small and poor country and depended on French subsidies as a colony and early-on an independent nation.[6] China also used financial aid to develop its influence in Africa especially in small independent countries.[7]

China was instrumental in using Congo-Brazzaville as a base from which to conduct revolutionary activities in Central Africa. In this respect, China assisted Pierre Mulele's guerrillas in the Congo, anti-Portuguese liberation groups in Angola such the MPLA, FNLA, and UNITA, and insurgents in Cameroon.[8] China also established at least three secret training camps from which to conduct the revolutionary activities.[9] China also established a broadcasting station for programming to the Portuguese-controlled territories and white-ruled South Africa.[10] While China ceased supporting revolutionary movements in independent African countries, it continued to use Congo-Brazzaville as a base of operations for supporting African liberation groups in southern and Portuguese Africa until those countries became independent.[11]

China developed a normal relationship with Congo-Brazzaville once the latter was no longer necessary to support African liberation movements. China provided financial aid, medical teams, scholarships, minimal military assistance, and traded commodities. China also provided disaster relief and infrastructure development in the wake of Congo-Brazzaville Civil War (June 1997–December 1999).[12]

Since 2002, China and Congo-Brazzaville have interacted through official, high-level visits and exchanges no less than thirty-six times.[13] Some of the most important exchanges include: President Hu Jintao and President Denis Sassau-Nguesso (September 2005 and April 2010) and President Xi Jinping and President Denis Sassau-Nguesso (March 2013, June 2014, and July 2016).[14] China and Congo-Brazzaville also maintain diplomatic representation in each other's respective capitals in Beijing and Brazzaville. Both countries signed cooperation agreements related to the economics, technology, energy, and mineral resources in February 2005.[15] In June 2014, China and the Congo signed agreements on bilateral cooperation involving economics and trade, infrastructure construction, banking, financing, culture, and other fields.[16] In July 2016, both countries signed bilateral cooperation agreements regarding diplomacy, production capacity, economic technology, agriculture, culture, infrastructure, finance and local communication.[17]

ECONOMIC/TRADE RELATIONS

Sino-Congolese economic relations are strong. In 2013, China was Congo-Brazzaville's largest trading partner.[18] In the same year, Congo-Brazzaville was China's sixty-first largest trading partner.[19] Bilateral trade was: $4.3 billion (2008), $2.1 billion (2009), $3.4 billion (2010), $5.1 billion (2011), $5 billion (2012), $6.4 billion (2013), $6.4 billion (2014), and $3.6 billion (2015).[20] Since 2000, bilateral trade increased almost eleven-fold. In 2012, foreign direct investment into Congo-Brazzaville from China was $99 million and foreign direct investment stock was $505 million.[21]

In terms of bilateral trade, Table 3.1 shows the top five commodities traded between China and Congo-Brazzaville in 2015. Energy commodities, which include crude petroleum, appear to be the most traded commodity. In terms of trade value, 88.3 percent is attributed to energy commodities, which includes crude petroleum and petroleum gas products. Energy-related commodities are most important component of bilateral trade and cooperation.

Table 3.1 Top Five Commodities Traded between China and Congo-Brazzaville

Commodity	Importer	Trade Value ($)	Percentage (%)
Mineral fuels, mineral oils, and products of their distillation; bituminous substances; mineral waxes	China	2,312,119,954	88.33
Wood and articles of wood; wood charcoal	China	210,425,834	8.04
Copper and articles thereof	China	87,625,895	3.35
Ores, slag and ash	China	4,559,469	0.1742
Other base metals; cermets; articles thereof	China	2,509,038	0.0959
Electrical machinery and equipment and parts thereof; sound recorders and reproducers, television image and sound recorders and reproducers, and parts and accessories of such articles	Congo	136,612,065	13
Nuclear reactors, boilers, machinery and mechanical appliances; parts thereof	Congo	128,713,684	12
Articles of apparel and clothing accessories, not knitted or crocheted	Congo	74,815,469	7
Vehicles other than railway or tramway rollingstock, and parts and accessories thereof	Congo	68,151,403	7
Articles of iron or steel	Congo	61,535,890	6

Source: United Nations Commodity Trade Statistics Database.

China's energy commodities accounted for the following in terms of trade value in previous years: 82.7 percent (2008), 86.1 percent (2009), 89.4 percent (2010), 93.1 percent (2011), 93.6 percent (2012), 95.5 percent (2013), and 94.5 percent (2014).[22]

Bilateral trade is promoted through several organizations such as the Congolese Foreign Trade Center, the Brazzaville Chamber of Commerce, Industry, Agriculture, and Trade, the Pointe-Noire Chamber of Commerce, Industry, Agriculture, and Trade, the Congo-Brazzaville Ministry of National Economy and Trade, the Forum on China-Africa Cooperation, the China-Africa Development Fund, the PRC Ministry of Commerce, the PRC Ministry of Foreign Affairs, and the All-China Federation of Industry and Commerce.[23]

China and Congo-Brazzaville have inked some important agreements and protocols to facilitate trade between their countries. The most notable agreements and memorandums include: Agreement on an interest-free loan by China (July 10, 1964); Trade and payments agreement (July 23, 1964); Agreement on economic and technical cooperation (October 2, 1964); Agreement on maritime transport (October 2, 1964); Protocol on economic and technical cooperation (February 6, 1965); Protocol on economic and technical cooperation (June 13, 1965); Protocol on economic and technical cooperation relating to Chinese aid in constructing a textile mill (September 13, 1965); and Protocol on economic and technical cooperation relating to the construction of a broadcasting station (January 17, 1966).[24] Protocol on economic and technical cooperation relating to the construction of a wharf for wooden boats (February 7, 1968); Protocol on economic and technical cooperation relating to Chinese aid for a state farm (August 12, 1968); Protocol relating to the agreement on economic and technical aid, stipulating the construction of a wharf for wooden boats (September 6, 1969); Agreement on economic and technical cooperation (October 10, 1969); Agreement on economic and technical cooperation (October 19, 1972); Protocol on the agreement of economic and technical cooperation relating to the building of the Bouenza dam (December 13, 1972); Protocol relating to the agreement on economic and technical cooperation (March 2, 1975); Minutes of talks on the agreement of economic and technical cooperation (relating to the construction of a "People's Palace in Brazzaville" (May 3, 1977); Agreement on economic and technical cooperation (June 18, 1977); Trade Agreement (September 29, 1978); Protocol on economic and technical cooperation in which China is to send technicians to the Naval Yard of Congo (August 13, 1979); Minutes of talks on transformation of the Chacona small-sized wooden boat-building yard (January 2, 1980); Agreement on Economic and Technical cooperation (July 8, 1980); Summary of talks on the arrangements for economic and technical cooperation (July 8, 1980); Two protocols on economic and technical cooperation (November 26, 1982); Agreement on the establishment of a joint committee for economic, trade, and technical cooperation (February 24, 1984); Contract on technical cooperation (June 27, 1984); Agreement on Chinese Loans (April 18, 1987); Summary of talks on the 1st Session of the Joint Committee of Economic, Trade, Technological Cooperation (April 18, 1987); Document on additional loans to Congo (November 25, 1990); Document on rescheduling the debt Congo owes China (November 25, 1990);[25] Agreement of Economic and Technological Cooperation (September 26, 2005);[26] Agreement of Economic and Technological Cooperation (June 20, 2006);[27] An Agreement on an interest-free loan of 50 million Yuan (2012);[28] A Technical and Scientific Cooperation Agreement (2012);[29] a Memorandum on financing of the reconstruction of the disaster areas of northeastern Brazzaville (2012);[30] an Economic and Technical Cooperation Agreement (2013); Agreements to construct a port at Oyo and an ore port at Pointe-Noire (2013); and Agreement to build a 300-mile road connecting Brazzaville and Pointe-Noire (2013).[31]

China has been actively involved in Congo-Brazzaville's economic development that includes financial aid, infrastructure, and investment especially in the twenty-first century. In this respect, some of the largest and most current infrastructure and development projects include: a $28 million soft loan for post-conflict reconstruction (2000); a $24.1 million loan from the

Export-Import Bank of China implemented through China Road & Bridge Corporation (CRBC) to build a cement factory in Loutete (2002); a $5 million monetary grant to rebuild Congo-Brazzaville's war-torn infrastructure (2003); a $280 million export credit funded by Export-Import Bank of China and China National Machinery and Equipment Import and Export Corporation (CMEC) to build the Imboulou Dam and Power Plant (2004); a $12 million monetary grant to restore the Moukoukoulou Dam (2004); a $56 million grant implemented by China Jiangsu International to construct terminals, a tower, and power control center at Ollombo Airport (2007); a $160 million grant from Export-Import Bank of China implemented by Weihai International Economic & Technical Cooperative Co., Ltd. (WIETC) to renovate the Maya-Maya International Airport in Brazzaville (2007); a $500 million loan from Export-Import Bank of China implemented by China State Construction Engineering Corporation (CSCEC) to build highways linking Brazzaville and Pointe-Noire (2007); a $361 million loan from Export-Import Bank of China implemented by CRBC to construct a highway connecting Owando, Makoua, and Mambili (Highway No. 2) (2008); a $35 million project between Zhongxing Technologies (ZTE) and Congo-Brazzaville to construct a Solar Panel Plant (2011); a $124 million grant from China National Machinery and Equipment Import & Export Corporation (CMEC) for the Congo Obouya-Boundji-Okoyo (OBO) Road Project linking Congo-Brazzaville to Gabon (2011); a $1.1 billion loan from China to Congo-Brazzaville to support the latter's 2013 state budget (2012); a $1.225 billion loan from Export-Import Bank of China to rebuild parts of Brazzaville that were destroyed by a deadly blast at a munitions depot in March 2012 (2012); a $600 million loan from Export-Import Bank of China to finance the reconstruction of the Mpila district in Brazzaville, construction road projects on the border of Gabon, lines of transportation electricity produced by the Liouesso Dam, and the relocation of military barracks (2012); China Development Bank agreed to finance the Mengo Potash Project for $370 million (2013); CSCEC commences the construction of the Brazzaville Stadium Project valued at $520 million (February 2014); CSCEC signs a $540 million contract to undertake the pavement structure upgrading works on the Congo-Brazzaville No. 1 National Highway Project (March 2014); CSCEC signed a $590 million EPC contract to build a commercial center in Brazzaville (June 2014); and China Road and Bridge Corporation signed a $2.3 billion contract to build a new port at Point Noire (February 2016).[32]

Between 2000 and 2013, the China Export-Import Bank, Zhongxing Technologies (ZTE), CSCEC, CRBC, China National Machinery and Equipment Import and Export Corporation (CMEC), China Jiangsu International, and other Chinese public and private sector agencies and corporations loaned, invested, granted, debt-relieved, or participated in development totaling $4.8

billion. There are forty-four projects to date covering the following sectors: communications, education, emergency response, general budget support, government and civil society, social infrastructure and services, public health, transportation and storage, energy generation and supply, agriculture, forestry, fishing, industry, mining, construction, and actions related to debt. Most of China's financial assistance was directed toward rebuilding post-conflict Congo-Brazzaville in the wake of the Congo-Brazzaville Civil War (June 1997–December 1999).[33]

MILITARY/SECURITY RELATIONS

Sino-Congolese military-security relations have been traditionally close even though Congo-Brazzaville relied mostly on Russian or France military equipment during the Cold War and more recently on Ukraine and South Africa. In the twenty-first century, Congo-Brazzaville has been an important partner for military cooperation with China because Congo-Brazzaville is China's largest supplier of oil in Africa after Angola. Previously, Congo-Brazzaville was a base for communist insurgencies in Central Africa during the Cold War. In this respect, China established three secret training camps in Congo-Brazzaville, which served as a base for training freedom fighters and communist subversion.[34] China has also provided military technical assistance and supplied military equipment to the Congolese armed forces. China also trained 425 Congolese military personnel in China between 1955 and 1976.[35] After ending its support for liberation movements in independent African countries, it used Congo-Brazzaville as a base for supporting Africa liberation groups in southern and Portuguese Africa until those countries became independent.[36]

Since 2002, Congo-Brazzaville military officials (Defense Minister and Chief of the Armed Forces) made visits to China in 2003, 2005, 2010, and 2013 according to the Ministry of National Defense of the People's Republic of China, *PLA Daily*, *Xinhua*, and *China Military Online*. In 2000, China and Congo-Brazzaville signed a military cooperation accord to reorganize the Congolese Army.[37] China and Congo-Brazzaville have also assigned defense attachés at their respective embassies in Beijing and Brazzaville.[38]

China has modestly supplied Congo-Brazzaville with military weapons and equipment. Weapons transfers include: fourteen Type-62 Light Tanks (1971), fifteen Type-59 Tanks (1978), and five ZFB-05 Armed Personnel Carriers delivered in 2006–2007 and 2009. The dearth of military transfers indicates China is a modest supplier of military arms and equipment. Russia and France were Congo-Brazzaville's top suppliers of military arms and equipment during the Cold War followed by Ukraine and South Africa since 1991 with the dissolution of the Soviet Union. China's total arms sales to Congo-Brazzaville are $53.48 million based on the 2016 CPI index. In 2000, total arms sales to Congo-Brazzaville were $51.6 million; the difference being $1.88 million over a 16-year period.[39]

Chinese weapons manufacturers more likely than not provided equipment training to the Congolese military given China supplied Congo-Brazzaville with tanks, light tanks, and armed personnel carriers. This has been the standard practice when China has supplied aircraft, ships, artillery pieces and other military equipment to other countries.

China and Congo-Brazzaville have inked some important agreements and protocols to facilitate and advance military cooperation between their countries. The most notable agreements include: Agreement on Chinese military aid (September 14, 1971); Military Agreement relating to the supply of military equipment by China and assistance in the training of cadres (April 30, 1975); and Protocol on the construction of a military academy in Congo (May 12, 1984).[40]

CULTURAL RELATIONS

Sino-Congolese cultural relations are close. China sent medical teams to Congo-Brazzaville between 1966 and 2013, provided scholarships for higher education in 1975, and renewed the 1964 cultural agreement in July 1980 and March 2000.[41] China and Congo-Brazzaville bilaterally cooperated in sports, agriculture, communications, public health, and education.[42] Congo-Brazzaville participated in the 2008 Summer Olympics Games in Beijing hosted by China. Congo-Brazzaville also showcased its culture at Joint-Africa Pavilion (JAP) at the 2010 Shanghai International Expo.[43] Congo-Brazzaville also hosted "Experience China in the Republic of Congo" in 2013. Actors from the China Acrobatic Troupe performed diabolo, bowls topping, and balls playing, demonstrating China's cultural highlights at this venue.[44] Highlights of exchanges and cooperation include: An Agreement of Cultural Cooperation (September 1964);[45] News Exchange Agreement (May 12, 1965); Protocol on cultural cooperation (August 13, 1965); Executive Plan on cultural cooperation (April 14, 1966); Protocol on medical aid (January 24, 1967); Protocol on sending a new Chinese medical team (July 9, 1970); Minutes of talks on the construction of a hospital with Chinese assistance (January 27, 1971); Protocol on China's sending a medical team (April 13, 1974); Agreement on Cultural Cooperation (July 8, 1980); Protocol on the Chinese Government continuing to dispatch medical teams (March 21, 1981); Contract on agricultural technological cooperation (April 28, 1983); Agreement on cultural cooperation between the China Federation of Literary and Art Circles and the Congolese National Union of Writers, Artists, and Artisans

(September 10, 1983); Protocol on China to send medical teams (April 2, 1985); Protocol on China to continue sending medics and paramedics to Congo (December 22, 1989);[46] Document on the provision of agricultural goods by China (November 25, 1990);[47] a $2.58 million grant to renovate the Alphonse Massamba-Debat athletics center; and construct a radio station in Djoue, the Maison Radio and Television Center at PK 13 (Brazzaville), and a foreign affairs building (2003);[48] the 2003–2005 Implementation Program of the Agreement on the Cultural Cooperation Between China and the Republic of the Congo;[49] a $5 million grant from the Chinese Academy of Tropical Agricultural Sciences (CATAS) to build an Agro-Technology Demonstration Center (2006); a $6 million grant to build the China-Congo Friendship Hospital in Brazzaville (2006); $3.7 million in economic aid from the CATAS for anti-malarial drugs, agricultural centers, schools, and training (2006); an agreement to finance the construction of library of the University of Marien Ngouabi in Brazzaville at a cost of $4 million (2007); donations totaling $669,034 in medical equipment to the National Public Health Laboratory (2008); donations totaling $7.4 million to upgrade Congo-Brazzaville health facilities (2009); $1.75 million in scholarships from CRBC for students to study in China (2010); a $73 million interest-free loan agreement for agricultural and medical care development (2010); Donations totaling $173,778 in sports equipment (2011); scholarships to forty-one Congolese students to study in China during the 2011–2012 academic year (2011); $3 million in emergency assistance after arms depot explosion in Congo (2012); a $69 million grant to construct social housing in Mont Mambou (2012); donations of badminton equipment, computer equipment, emergency supplies, emergency equipment, and educational and sporting equipment (2012); scholarships to thirty-eight Congolese students to study in China during the 2012–2013 academic year (2012); $47,500 in emergency assistance from Sinohydro Corporation for Congo-Brazzaville tragedy (2012); a twenty-three-person medical team to Congo-Brazzaville to work and equip the Chinese-Congolese Friendship Hospital (2013); donation of medical equipment to the Chinese-Congolese Friendship Hospital (2013); and China pledged to donate $815 million to address the threat of Ebola (2014).[50]

China also established a Confucius Institute at the University of Marien Ngouabi in Brazzaville.[51] China-Congo bilateral cultural cooperation has been mainly in health and medicine. Like many other African countries, China has sent medical teams to Congo-Brazzaville since diplomatic relations were established in 1964. China has sent medical teams to Congo-Brazzaville in 1970, 1974, 1981, 1985, 1989, 2000, 2003, 2005, 2007, 2009, 2011, and 2013.[52] China has also provided medical aid and equipment including building hospitals in 2006, 2008, 2009, and 2013.

ENERGY/PETROLEUM RELATIONS

Congo-Brazzaville is a significant crude petroleum supplier to China. China imported 2 to 4 percent of its crude petroleum from Congo-Brazzaville between 2006 and 2015, averaging just fewer than 3 percent per year. Thus, crude petroleum factors greatly in the Sino-Congolese trade relationship. China also bases most of the bilateral relationship on energy cooperation. The share of Congo's crude going to China accounted for 43 percent of total crude exports in 2012. In 2015, the total commodity trade value of oil compared to all Chinese imports was 88.3 percent. Thus, crude oil is the principal commodity traded between the two countries.[53]

In terms of total trade value, crude oil petroleum imports ranged from 81.4 to 95.5 percent for the same years. Table 3.2 illustrates China's crude petroleum imports from Congo-Brazzaville in thousands of barrels per day, oil imports share, world ranking, trade value, total commodity trade value and percentage from 2006 to 2015. See Table 3.2.

Although China does not import liquefied natural gas (LNG), it has imported petroleum gas products and acquired oil and gas acquisitions in Congo-Brazzaville. To illustrate, China imported less than 1 percent of petroleum gas products in 2014 or .00002 MMcf.[54]

China's oil and gas acquisitions in Congo-Brazzaville are minuscule. Sinopec acquired two oil exploration and production blocks in March 2005: Marine XII and Haute Mer B (High Sea C).[55]

Energy cooperation between China and Brazzaville includes construction projects. In October 2015, CSCEC signed a $1 billion contract to develop the Jiarou Oilfield Project. The groundwork covers nineteen single projects

Table 3.2   Chinese Crude Petroleum Imports from Congo-Brazzaville

Year	KBPD	Oil Imports Share (%)	World Ranking	Crude Oil Trade Value ($)	Total Commodity Trade Value ($)	Percentage (%)
2006	109	4	6	2,504,116,147	2,791,641,670	89.7
2007	96	3	8	2,307,939,820	2,836,696,112	81.4
2008	88	2	11	3,087,774,289	3,731,701,410	82.7
2009	82	2	12	1,498,116,743	1,738,812,252	86.2
2010	101	2	14	2,791,353,618	3,122,346,533	89.4
2011	113	2	13	4,351,792,763	4,672,291,086	93.1
2012	108	2	13	4,265,568,710	4,555,407,364	93.6
2013	142	3	11	5,455,461,551	5,712,190,624	95.5
2014	142	2	11	5,179,948,135	5,479,017,995	94.5
2015	118	2	13	2,312,119,954	2,617,464,534	88.3

Source: United Nations Commodity Trade Statistics Database.

including a crude oil treatment plant, a gas treatment plant, a sewage treatment plant, a gas-fired power plant, and a transmission and distribution circuit.[56]

SUMMARY

Sino-Congolese relations are traditionally close. Since diplomatic ties were established in 1964, China has been active in Congo-Brazzaville's political and economic development. China used Congo-Brazzaville as a base to train and conduct communist revolutionary movements in Angola, the Democratic Republic of Congo, and Cameroon. It also supported liberation movements in southern and Portuguese Africa.

China developed normal ties with Congo-Brazzaville once it was no longer necessary to support liberation movements. China provided financial support and assistance, medical teams, scholarships, military aid and training, disaster relief, and traded commodities. China was also active in Congo-Brazzaville's infrastructure development providing $4.9 billion in sixty-eight projects in sixteen sectors between 2000 and 2013. Most of China's financial aid was directed toward rebuilding post-conflict Congo-Brazzaville in the wake of the Congo-Brazzaville Civil War (June 1997–December 1999).

China and Congolese-Brazzaville engage in energy cooperation. Crude petroleum is the most traded commodity between the two countries. Congo-Brazzaville is also China's the largest supplier of crude petroleum after Angola. Thus, Congo-Brazzaville is a significant exporter of crude oil to China and plays an important role in China's energy security.

NOTES

1. Ministry of Foreign Affairs of People's Republic of China, "Relations with the Republic of Congo," June 14, 2006, accessed November 8, 2014, http://www.china.org.cn/english/features/wenjiabaoafrica/171414.htm.

2. Ibid.

3. David H. Shinn and Joshua Eisenman, *China and Africa: A Century of Engagement* (Philadelphia, PA: University of Pennsylvania Press), 2012, 474, footnote 61; and Wolfgang Bartke, *The Agreements of the People's Republic of China with Foreign Countries 1949–1990* (Munchen, Germany: K.G. Saur), 1992, 34.

4. Ibid., 35.

5. Shinn and Eisenman, ibid., 295.

6. Alaba Ogunsanwo, *China's Policy in Africa 1958–1971* (London, UK: Cambridge University Press), 1974, 156–57.

7. U.S. Central Intelligence Agency, *Communist China's Presence in Africa* (Washington, DC: U.S. Central Intelligence Agency), June 20, 1969, 7.

8. Shinn and Eisenman, ibid., 296.
9. Ibid.
10. Shinn and Eisenman, ibid.; and Alaba Ogunsanwo, *China's Policy in Africa 1958–1971* (London, UK: Cambridge University Press), 1974, 221.
11. Shinn and Eisenman, *Ibid.*, 296.
12. Ibid.
13. Ministry of Foreign Affairs of People's Republic of China, "China–Congo: Activities," (n.d.), accessed August 8, 2016, http://www.fmprc.gov.cn/mfa_eng/wjb_663304/zzjg_663340/fzs_663828/gjlb_663832/2954_663914/2956_663918/.
14. Ibid.
15. Ministry of Foreign Affairs of People's Republic of China, "President Denis Sassou-Nguesso of the Republic of Congo Meets with Zeng Peiyan," February 25, 2005, accessed August 13, 2016, http://www.fmprc.gov.cn/mfa_eng/wjb_663304/zzjg_663340/fzs_663828/gjlb_663832/2954_663914/2956_663918/t185167.shtml.
16. Ministry of Foreign Affairs of People's Republic of China, "Xi Jinping Holds Talks with President Denis Sassou-N'guesso of the Republic of Congo, Stressing to Deepen Friendship, Strengthen Cooperation and Promote the All-round Development of the China-Congo Relations," June 12, 2014, accessed August 13, 2016, http://www.fmprc.gov.cn/mfa_eng/wjb_663304/zzjg_663340/fzs_663828/gjlb_663832/2954_663914/2956_663918/t1166113.shtml.
17. Ministry of Foreign Affairs of People's Republic of China, "Xi Jinping Holds Talks with President Denis Sassou-Nguesso of the Republic of Congo, Both Heads of State Decide to Uplift Bilateral Relations to a Comprehensive Strategic Partnership of Cooperation," July 5, 2016, accessed August 13, 2016, http://www.fmprc.gov.cn/mfa_eng/wjb_663304/zzjg_663340/fzs_663828/gjlb_663832/2954_663914/2956_663918/t1378212.shtml.
18. European Commission Directorate-General for Trade, "Congo: EU Bilateral Trade and Trade with the World," April 10, 2015, accessed May 3, 2015, http://trade.ec.europa.eu/doclib/docs/2006/september/tradoc_147253.pdf.
19. United Nations, United Nations Commodity Trade Statistics Database, accessed August 22, 2015, http://comtrade.un.org/db/default.aspx.
20. United Nations, United Nations Commodity Trade Statistics Database, accessed July 22, 2016, http://comtrade.un.org/db/default.aspx.
21. United Nations Conference on Trade and Development (UNCTAD FDI/TNC) Database, *Bilateral FDI Statistics 2014*, accessed November 9, 2014, http://unctad.org/Sections/dite_fdistat/docs/webdiaeia2014d3_CHN.pdf.
22. United Nations, United Nations Commodity Trade Statistics Database, Ibid.
23. International Trade Centre, Directory of Trade Promotion Organizations and Other Trade Support Institutions, accessed January 5, 2015, http://www.intracen.org/itc/trade-support/tsi-directory.
24. Bartke, ibid., 34.
25. Ibid., 34–35.
26. Ministry of Foreign Affairs of People's Republic of China, "Hu Jintao Holds Talks with President of the Republic of Congo Sassan," September 26, 2005, accessed August 8, 2016, http://www.fmprc.gov.cn/mfa_eng/wjb_663304/zzjg_663340/fzs_663828/gjlb_663832/2954_663914/2956_663918/t214311.shtml.

27. Ministry of Foreign Affairs of People's Republic of China, "Wen Jiabao Holds Talks with President of the Republic of Congo Sassou-Nguesso," June 20, 2006, accessed August 13, 2016, http://www.fmprc.gov.cn/mfa_eng/wjb_663304/zzjg_663340/fzs_663828/gjlb_663832/2954_663914/2956_663918/t259149.shtml.

28. "Congo, China Sign Cooperation Agreements," *Panapress.com*, September 4, 2012, accessed November 8, 2014, http://www.panapress.com/Congo-China-sign-cooperation-agreements--13-841438-0-lang2-index.html.

29. Austin M. Strange, et al., "Tracking Underreported Financial Flows: China's Development Finance and the Aid–Conflict Nexus Revisited," *Journal of Conflict Resolution*, Volume 61, Issue 5 (2017): 935–963.

30. "Congo, China Sign Cooperation Agreements," ibid.

31. Strange, et al., ibid.

32. Strange, et al., ibid.; and the Heritage Foundation and American Enterprise Institute, *China Global Investment Tracker Database*, accessed August 13, 2016, http://www.heritage.org/research/projects/china-global-investment-tracker-interactive-map.

33. Strange, et al., ibid.

34. Shinn and Eisenman, *China and Africa: A Century of Engagement*, 296.

35. David H. Shinn, "Military and Security Relations: China, Africa, and the Rest of the World" in Robert I. Rotberg, ed., *China into Africa: Trade, Aid, and Influence* (Washington, DC: Brookings Institution Press), 2008, 158.

36. Shinn and Eisenman, ibid.

37. Strange, et al., ibid.

38. United States Department of Defense, Defense Intelligence Agency, *Directory of PRC Military Personalities* (Washington, DC), 2014, 14.

39. Stockholm International Peace Research Institute, SIPRI Arms Transfers Database, http://www.sipri.org/databases/armstransfers.

40. Bartke, ibid., 34, 35.

41. Ministry of Foreign Affairs of People's Republic of China, "Relations with the Republic of Congo," June 14, 2006, accessed November 8, 2014, http://www.china.org.cn/english/features/wenjiabaoafrica/171414.htm.

42. Strange, et al., ibid.

43. Muhamad S. Olimat, *China and North Africa Since World War II* (Lanham, MD: Lexington Books), 2014, 16.

44. "Experience China' opens in the Republic of Congo," *China Daily*, March 22, 2013, accessed August 13, 2016, http://www.china.org.cn/world/2013-03/22/content_28327582.htm.

45. Ministry of Foreign Affairs of People's Republic of China, "Relations with the Republic of Congo," June 14, 2006, accessed November 8, 2014, http://www.china.org.cn/english/features/wenjiabaoafrica/171414.htm.

46. Ibid.

47. Bartke, ibid., 34–35.

48. Strange, et al., ibid.

49. Ministry of Foreign Affairs of People's Republic of China, "Relations with the Republic of Congo," June 14, 2006, accessed November 8, 2014, http://www.china.org.cn/english/features/wenjiabaoafrica/171414.htm.

50. Strange, et al., ibid.
51. Confucius Institute Online, Worldwide Confucius Institutes, accessed August 5, 2016, http://english.hanban.org/node_10971.htm.
52. Strange, et al., ibid.
53. Ogi Williams, "Oil for Development: China's Investments in Angola and the Republic of Congo," *Consultancy African Intelligence*, July 29, 2014, accessed November 8, 2014, http://www.consultancyafrica.com/index.php?option=com_content&view=article&id=1699:oil-for-development-chinas-investments-in-angola-and-the-republic-of-congo-&catid=58:asia-dimension-discussion-papers&Itemid=264.
54. United Nations, United Nations Commodity Trade Statistics Database, accessed August 7, 2016, http://comtrade.un.org/db/default.aspx.
55. Julie Jiang and Chen Dang, *Update on Overseas Investments by Chinese National Companies: Achievements and Challenges Since 2011* (Paris, France: Organization for Economic Cooperation and Development/International Energy Agency), June 2014, 35–39.
56. The Heritage Foundation and American Enterprise Institute, ibid.

Chapter 4

China and Iran
Political/Diplomatic Relations

Sino-Iranian political relations date back to pre-Islamic times; however, formal relations were established on August 16, 1971. Their shared historical experiences of empire and autonomy as well as Western colonial power domination further unite them and form a significant part of their relationship.[1]

Today, their relations are characterized by frequent exchanges. Since 2000, no less than 173 bilateral exchanges and discussions have occurred on common areas of interest that include: defense, nuclear technology, and national security issues.[2] Some of most important exchanges include: President Jiang Zemin and President Mohammad Khatami (April 2002), President Hu Jintao and President Ali Larijani (January 2007), President Hu Jintao and President Mahmoud Ahmadinejad (September 2008 and June 2012), and President Xi Jinping and President Hassan Rouhani (September 2013, November 2013, May 2014, April 2015, September 2015, and January 2016).[3] The January 2016 exchange was strategically significant for both countries because multiple bilateral cooperation documents covering energy, production capacity, finance, investment, communications, culture, justice, science, technology, news, customs, climate change, and human resources were signed.[4] China and Iran have also agreed to strengthen cooperation in energy, transportation, telecommunications, science, technology, industry, banking, tourism, agriculture, mining, and environmental protection.[5] In particular, China and Iran signed a memorandum of understanding with respect to railways and transportation.[6] China has also shielded Iran against international sanctions over its nuclear program.[7] Finally, China and Iran agreed to increase trade by $600 billion over the next ten years.[8]

One of the main pillars of their bilateral relationship is oil and gas. China imports approximately 11 percent of its crude petroleum from Iran making Iran one of its major oil suppliers in the Near East. Because of its reliance on Iranian oil and gas, China has invested into Iran's infrastructure such as dam and ship construction, and seaport and airport development.[9] China is also committed to modernizing Iran's oil and gas sector to secure energy resources.

To establish and advance diplomatic ties, China and Iran inked the following: Joint Communiqué on the Establishment of Diplomatic Relations Between the People's Republic of China and the Islamic Republic of Iran (August 16, 1971);[10] Agreement on the Establishment of General Consulates (September 21, 1988);[11] Memorandum on Mutual Exemption of Visas (May 12, 1989);[12] Memorandum of Understanding on the Establishment of an Official Consultation Mechanism between the Foreign Ministries of China and Iran (November 15, 2000);[13] Treaty of Extradition between China and Iran (September 10, 2012);[14] Treaty on the Transfer of Sentenced Persons (September 10, 2012);[15] Joint Statement Between the People's Republic of China and the Islamic Republic of Iran on the Establishment of Comprehensive Strategic Partnership (January 23, 2016);[16] Treaty of Mutual Legal Cooperation on Legal and Criminal, Civil, and Trade Issues (January 23, 2016);[17] and Memorandum of Understanding for Strategic Cooperation in Customs (January 23, 2016).[18]

China and Iran also maintain diplomatic representation in each other's respective capitals in Tehran and Beijing. Iran also has a consulate-general in Shanghai.

China and Iran first encountered each other at the Bandung Conference in 1955. At that time, China was eager to establish diplomatic ties but found itself on opposite sides of postwar developments after 1945. China criticized Iran's close ties with the United States and the United Kingdom; the Shah's solicitation to topple Mohammad Mossadegh; and Iran's support for military pacts in the region, such as the Baghdad Pact. China and Iran clashed in Oman where China was the main supporter of the Dhofar Liberation Front (DLF), a Maoist-left organization that began in Oman and expanded its outreach to the entire Arabian Gulf. China also established and maintained its contacts with the Iranian Communist Party, Tudeh.[19]

China began to reconcile with Iran in the late 1960s and early 1970s. It ceased its military support to the DLF and in return, Iran recognized China in 1971 and its One China principle. From that point, China and Iran began to strengthen ties especially in energy cooperation. Energy cooperation expanded to nuclear cooperation where China supports Iran's peaceful development and use of nuclear energy. In this respect, China has been heavily involved in negotiations with the international community through the P5+1 framework. Oman, Iran's closest ally in the Near East, has also played a major role by providing office space for American and Iranian diplomats to work out their differences not only on nuclear energy issues but also on security matters.[20]

China maintained its diplomatic ties with Iran even after the Shah was ousted in 1979 in the wake of the Iranian Revolution. Even though Iran punished countries that had established strategic ties with the Shah's regime, China was not included. Iran needed China's support in its confrontation with Iraq during the eight-year period that comprised the Iran-Iraq War (1980-1988). China supported a balance of power between Iraq and Iran by providing them both with weapons.[21]

ECONOMIC/TRADE RELATIONS

Sino-Iranian economic relations are robust. China was Iran's largest trading partner in 2013.[22] In comparison, Iran was China's twenty-third largest trading partner.[23] Bilateral trade was: $27.2 billion (2008), $21.2 billion (2009), $29.3 billion (2010), $45 billion (2011), $36.4 billion (2012), $39 billion (2013), $51.8 billion (2014), and $33.8 billion (2015).[24] Since 2000, bilateral trade increased fourteen-fold. In 2012, foreign direct investment into Iran from China was $730 million and foreign direct investment stock was $2.07 billion.[25]

Trade relations began in the 1980s and expanded in the 1990s. Bilateral trade dipped from 2011 to 2012 because of the sanctions imposed on Iran.[26]

In terms of bilateral trade, Table 4.1 shows the top five commodities traded between China and Iran in 2015. Energy commodities, which include crude petroleum and petroleum gas products, appear to be the most traded commodity. In terms of trade value, 69 percent is attributed to energy commodities, which includes crude petroleum and petroleum gas products. See Table 4.1.

China's energy commodities accounted for the following in terms of trade value in previous years: 86 percent (2008), 80 percent (2009), 72 percent (2010), 76 percent (2011) and 74 percent (2012), 72 percent (2013), and 77 percent (2014).[27]

China is also a major infrastructure project developer in Iran. Over 100 Chinese companies operate in Iran, primarily in dam and ship construction, energy, and seaport and airport development.[28] Projects include small business ventures in fish canneries, sugar refineries, paper mills, construction of Tehran's subway system and the development of a $3 billion oil refinery.[29] Approximately eleven deals involving metals, energy, steels, transportation, and real estate were concluded since October 2005 totaling $7.7 billion. These investments represent 42 percent of China's total investments. Some of the largest investments include: Sinohydro signed a $1.5 billion contract for the Moshampa Dam & Power Plant and Irrigation Network with The Ministry of Energy of Islamic Republic of Iran, Zanjan Regional Water Company (September 2010); Norinco International Co. Ltd. inked a $1.22 billion

Table 4.1 Top Five Commodities Traded between China and Iran

Commodity	Importer	Trade Value ($)	Percentage (%)
Mineral fuels, mineral oils and products of their distillation; bituminous substances; mineral waxes	China	11,002,831,418	69
Plastics and articles thereof	China	2,107,526,319	13
Organic chemicals	China	1,332,687,332	8
Ores, slag and ash	China	1,121,200,138	7
Salt; sulfur; earths and stone; plastering materials; lime; and cement	China	281,097,496	2
Nuclear reactors, boilers, machinery and mechanical appliances; parts thereof	Iran	3,481,260,585	20
Electrical machinery and equipment and parts thereof; sound recorders and reproducers, television image and sound recorders and reproducers, and parts and accessories of such articles	Iran	2,257,685,897	13
Vehicles other than railway or tramway rolling-stock, and parts and accessories thereof	Iran	1,771,436,242	10
Iron and steel	Iran	910,617,753	5
Articles of iron or steel	Iran	895,801,924	5

Source: United Nations Commodity Trade Statistics Database.

construction contract for Tehran Metro 6 Line project with the Tehran Urban & Suburban Railway Operation Company (May 2012); and China Communications Construction Company inked a $500 million construction contract for Iran's North Highway Project (second and third Phases) (October 2015).[30]

China and Iran has inked some important agreements to facilitate trade between their countries. The most notable agreements and memorandums of understanding include: Agreement on the establishment of an air link (April 27, 1972); Agreement on civil air transport (November 18, 1972); Agreement on trade and payments (April 8, 1973); Trade Protocol (September 29, 1974); Notes Exchange on the confirming of the agreement on reciprocal trademark registration (December 15, 1975); 1976 Trade Agreement (June 18, 1976); Trade Memorandum on a new list of goods to be exchanged between November 1, 1977 and October 31, 1978 (November 1, 1977); Memorandum relating to trade in 1980 (November 14, 1979); Memorandum and the agreed minutes of the 5th Session of the Sino-Iranian Joint Committee on Trade (January 4, 1983); Agreement on banking management between the Bank of China and Bank Markazi Jomhouri Islami Iran on procedures for the settlement of payments in connection with the economic, scientific, and technical cooperative projects provided by China (May 12, 1989); Memorandum of Understanding relating to solid ties of industrial cooperation of the basis of mutual benefit (July 31, 1989);[31] Agreement aimed at the Avoidance of Double Taxation (April 22, 2002);[32] Agreement on Maritime Transportation Cooperation (April 22, 2002);[33] Agreement on the Establishment of a Joint Business Council (April 22, 2002);[34] Memorandum of Understanding Between the Government of the People's Republic of China and the Government of the Islamic Republic of Iran on Jointly Advancing Construction of the Silk Road Economic Belt and the 21st Century Maritime Silk Road (January 23, 2016);[35] Memorandum of Understanding for cementing Industrial, Mining, and Investment Cooperation (January 23, 2016);[36] Memorandum of Understanding for providing Funds for the Tehran-Mashrad Express Railway (January 23, 2016);[37] Memorandum of Understanding for cementing Investment Cooperation (January 23, 2016);[38] Memorandum of Understanding for developing Joint Cooperation between the Qeshm Free Zone of Iran and Pilot Free Zone of China (January 23, 2016);[39] Agreement for devising a New Mechanism for mediating and arbitrating Disputes between Chinese and Iranian Traders and Businessmen (May 24, 2016);[40] Agreement to follow up on Exports and Investments between China and Iran (May 24, 2016);[41] and Memorandum of Understanding between Export-Import Bank of China (EXIM) and Iran for boosting Mutual Cooperation and providing Grounds for financing Economic and Infrastructure Projects (August 17, 2016).[42]

Bilateral trade is also promoted through several organizations such as the Asian Cooperation Dialogue, the Iranian Ministry of Finance and Economic Affairs, Iran-China Joint Chamber of Commerce, the China-Iran Business Forum, Iran Chamber of Commerce, Industries and Mines, the PRC Ministry of Commerce, the PRC Ministry of Foreign Affairs, All-China Federation of Commerce and Industry, and the Chinese Chamber of E-commerce.[43]

MILITARY/SECURITY RELATIONS

Sino-Iranian military relations are generally good and are driven primarily by China's dependence on crude oil to sustain its economy and Iran's need for a powerful ally in the Middle East as well as a weapons supplier. China is Iran's largest supplier of conventional weapons and plays a major role in Iran's military modernization. China provided to Iran anti-ship cruise missiles, surface-to-air missiles, combat aircraft (fighters and bombers), and fast attack patrol vessels, as well as advanced technology designed to expand the versatility of Iran's burgeoning cruise missile arsenal, which have "contributed significantly to what has become the central element of Iran's military rearmament—a revitalization of its naval forces."[44] In fact, China has supported Iran's quest to develop its own short-range, medium-range, and long-range missile capability.[45] China and Iran also conducted their first joint military exercise in September 2014.⁴⁶ This exercise was maritime-oriented in nature.⁴⁷ China has also supplied Iran with tanks, air search radars, transport aircraft, and mobile surface-to-surface missile (SSM) launchers and licensed surface-to-surface missiles (including portable SSMs), anti-ship missiles, and armored personnel carriers (APC).⁴⁸ See Table 4.2. China's total arms sales to Iran are $7.85 billion based on the 2016 CPI index.⁴⁹ In 2000, total arms sales to Iran were $6.48 billion, the difference being $1.37 billion over a 16-year period.⁵⁰ Consequently, "U.S. intelligence agencies now estimate that Iran has the ability to shut off the flow of oil from the Persian Gulf for brief periods of time, even with a Western military presence in the region."⁵¹

China is also Iran's principal supplier of WMD technology and assistance including nuclear weapons according to the Pentagon. Preliminary liaisons began in the mid- to late-1980s where both two countries are known to have signed nuclear accords in 1989 and 1991, paving the way for what would become a vibrant and multifaceted nuclear partnership.⁵² China helped to start Iran's nuclear program according to a recent RAND report.⁵³

China's military technology transfers to Iran complicate U.S. Near East foreign policy to bring peace and stability to the region. A recent CRS report stated that "China's military cooperation with Iran has also proven to be a recurring problem in U.S.-China relations."⁵⁴ China's hesitance to sanction Iran considering Iran's resistance to discontinue WMD development is an ongoing political crisis which invites a future military confrontation between Iran and United States unless China decides to act prudently and take steps to de-militarize Iran of its nuclear technology and development.

If a military confrontation occurs between Iran and United States, Iran could retaliate by mining or even attacking ships passing through the Strait of Hormuz. According to General Barry McCaffrey, Iran has three Kilo Class submarines, nineteen other mini-submarines, a significant sea mining capacity, shore-based missile batteries, air defense capabilities, and a small number of high performance aircraft with missiles that could deny the two-mile-wide Strait of Hormuz sea transit zone to safe tanker traffic. Iran could also place the Gulf Cooperation Council/Saudi Gulf oil terminals at risk.⁵⁵

China and Iran maintain defense attachés in Beijing and Tehran and conducted military-to-military exchanges.⁵⁶ According to the Ministry of National Defense of the People's Republic of China, *Xinhua*, and *China Military Online*, both countries have engaged each other through six visits to the PRC by Iranian military officials, two visits to Iran by Chinese military officials including one port visit by PLAN ships, one international security consultation in Moscow, a joint Sino-Iranian maritime exercise, and joint military training (International Army Games). The dearth of data may indicate that China does not wish to reveal its military-security exchanges and interactions publicly. While public data may be limited to memorialize Sino-Iranian military-security interactions, China and Iran cooperate on combating

Table 4.2 Chinese Conventional Weapons Transfers to Iran

Year(s) of Delivery	No. of Deliveries	Weapon Designation	Weapon Description
1986–1990	250	Type-63 107mm (L)	Mobile Rocket Launcher
1990–1994	200	M-7/CSS-8 (L)	Surface-to-Surface Missile
1994–2012	380	C-802/CSS-N-8 (L)	Anti-Ship Missile
1996–2006	1,100	QW-1 Vanguard (L)	Portable Surface-to-Air Missile
1997–2011	150	WZ-501/Type-86 (L)	Armored Personnel Carrier
1999–2015	260	FL-6 (L)	Anti-Ship Missile
2004–2015	165	TL-10/FL-8 (L)	Anti-Ship Missile
2010–2011	50	C-704 (L)	Anti-Ship Missile
2006–2015	50	C-801/CSS-N-4 (L)	Anti-Ship Missile
2006–2015	650	QW-11 (L)	Portable Surface-to-Air Missile
1982–1984	16	F-6/Farmer (S)	Fighter Aircraft
1982–1984	300	Type-59 (S)	Tank
1982–1984	300	Type-59-1 130mm (S)	Towed Gun
1981–1987	300	Type-63 107mm (S)	Mobile Rocket Launcher
1982–1988	6,500	Red Arrow-73 (S)	Anti-Tank Missile
1985–1986	100	D-74 122mm (S)	Towed Gun
1986	5	F-7A (S)	Fighter Aircraft
1986–1988	500	HN-5A (S)	Portable Surface-to-Air Missile
1985–1986	150	HQ-2/CSA-1 (S)	Surface-to-Air Missile
1985–1986	6	HQ-2/CSA-1 (S)	Surface-to-Air Missile System
1985–1986	100	Type-59-1 130mm (S)	Towed Gun
1987	100	C-801/CSS-N-4 (S)	Anti-Ship Missile
1986–1987	7	HY-2 CDS (S)	Coast Defense System
1986–1987	75	HY-2/SY-1A/CSS-N-2 (S)	Anti-Ship Missile
1986–1988	600	PL-2 (S)	Short-Range Air-to-Air Missile
1986–1988	400	PL-7 (S)	Short-Range Air-to-Air Missile
1987	120	Type-59-1 130mm (S)	Towed Gun
1986–1988	500	Type-69 (S)	Tank
1988–1994	100	HY-2/SY-1A/CSS-N-2 (S)	Anti-Ship Missile
1990–1994	30	CSS-8 TEL (S)	Mobile Surface-to-Surface Missile Launcher
1989–1991	8	HQ-2/CSA-1 (S)	Surface-to-Air Missile System
1989–1991	200	HQ-2/CSA-1 (S)	Surface-to-Air Missile
1991	15	WA-021/Type-88 155mm (S)	Towed Gun
1993	25	F-7M Airguard (S)	Fighter Aircraft
1992	106	Type-59-1 130mm (S)	Towed Gun
1995–1998	125	C-801/CSS-N-4 (S)	Anti-Ship Missile
1994–1996	10	Hudong (S)	Fast Attack Craft
1994–1995	9	Y-12 (S)	Light Transport Aircraft
1998	2	Y-7 (S)	Transport Aircraft
1996	5	F-7M Airguard (S)	Fighter Aircraft
1999–2001	3	JY-14 (S)	Air Search Radar
2001–2004	40	C-701/FL-8 (S)	Anti-Ship Missile
1999–2004	6	Crotale (S)	Surface-to-Air Missile System
1999–2004	250	R-440 Crotale (S)	Surface-to-Air Missile
2001–2004	9	China Cat (S)	Fast Attack Craft

Source: SIPRI Arms Transfers Database.

international terrorism. In this respect, China seeks Iran's support to end the training activities of the East Turkestan forces in Afghanistan through Iran's allies, the Northern Alliance. China and Iran also cooperate via the Shanghai Cooperation Organization to promote security cooperation, military cooperation, and energy security.[57]

CULTURAL RELATIONS

Sino-Iranian cultural relations are deeply rooted in history. Both agree the Silk Road has provided a solid foundation for cultural exchanges between ancient China and Iran and it expected to be in the future.[58] Bilateral cultural cooperation spans into several areas such as the exchange of cultural delegations, exhibitions, celebrating national days, celebrating the Chinese New Year, celebrating the Iranian Nowruz (New Year), celebrating independence, the Iran Year in China, and China Year in Iran.[59] Bilateral tourism is under development.[60] Both countries seek to develop this sector through promotions, training guides, and increasing direct flights from China to Iran's major tourist centers.[61] Iran participated actively in the 2010 International Expo in China.[62] China and Iran have signed agreements, protocols, and memorandums of understanding to cooperate in radio, television, and satellite broadcasting, art, journalism, education, sports, and culture. Those inked include: Agreement on the cooperation of information between the Xinhua News Agency and the Pars News Agency (June 13, 1978);[63] Cultural Agreement (August 31, 1978);[64] Agreement on cultural, scientific, and technical cooperation (September 14, 1983);[65] Protocol on setting up a ministerial joint committee for cooperation in economy, trade, science, and technology (March 3, 1985);[66] Executive Plan for cultural cooperation (June 29, 1985);[67] Letter of understanding on cooperation between the sports organizations of China and Iran (July 24, 1987);[68] Agreement on cooperation in the fields of radio, television, and satellite broadcasting (January 25, 1988);[69] 1989–1990 Executive Program for cultural, scientific, and art cooperation (May 12, 1989);[70] Agreement for Mutual Cooperation in Cultural, Scientific, and Technical Fields (1991);[71] Memorandum of Understanding for Cultural and Educational Cooperation (1991);[72] Agreement on Telecommunications and Information Technology Cooperation (April 22, 2002);[73] Agreement on the Implementation of Plans of 2003–2005 Cultural Exchanges (April 22, 2002);[74] Memorandum of Understanding establishing Cultural Centers (2012);[75] Memorandum of Understanding for Cooperation in Cultural, Art, and Educational Cooperation (January 23, 2016);[76] Memorandum of Understanding for Communication and Information Technology Cooperation (January 23, 2016);[77] Memorandum of Understanding for the Establishment of the Silk Road Scientific Fund (January 23, 2016);[78]

Memorandum of Understanding for Media Cooperation (January 23, 2016);[79] Memorandum of Understanding for providing Goods for confronting Weather Change (January 23, 2016);[80] Memorandum of Understanding on Science and Technology (January 23, 2016);[81] Memorandum of Understanding for the Development of Human Resources (January 23, 2016);[82] Agreement pertaining to the Production of LED Lights and Optic Education Projectors and Tools (May 24, 2016);[83] and Memorandum of Understanding to enhance Mutual Interaction and Cooperation, including the Exchange of Cultural and Scientific Documents (June 9, 2016).[84]

China has also established a Confucius Institute at the University of Tehran in August 2008 to foster cultural exchanges and Chinese language training.

ENERGY/PETROLEUM RELATIONS

Oil and gas trading establishes the foundation for the trade relationship given Iran's vast energy resources and China's expanding energy needs.[85] China is Iran's largest oil customer.[86] China imported 8 to 13 percent of its crude petroleum from Iran between 2006 and 2015 inclusive. In terms of total trade value, crude petroleum imports ranged from 66 to 80 percent for the same years. Table 4.3 shows Chinese crude oil imports from Iran in thousands of barrels per day, oil imports share, world ranking, trade value, total commodity trade value, and percentage from 2006 to 2015. See Table 4.3. The decrease in production from 557 kbpd to 440 kbpd between 2011 and 2012 can attributed to price disputes and China's attempts to diversify its oil and gas supplies.[87]

Table 4.3 Chinese Crude Petroleum Imports from Iran

Year	KBPD	Oil Imports Share (%)	World Ranking	Crude Oil Trade Value ($)	Total Commodity Trade Value ($)	Percentage (%)
2006	337	12	3	7,785,934,246	9,958,456,154	78
2007	412	13	3	10,453,414,479	13,301,528,289	79
2008	428	12	3	15,765,832,697	19,594,195,353	80
2009	465	11	3	9,802,270,997	13,286,547,277	74
2010	418	9	3	12,070,150,447	18,300,891,267	66
2011	557	11	3	21,820,145,145	30,332,972,751	72
2012	440	8	4	17,800,741,137	24,869,408,279	72
2013	430	8	6	16,887,584,035	25,389,863,878	67
2014	552	9	6	20,807,333,399	27,506,898,024	76
2015	535	8	6	10,730,613,558	16,034,628,725	67

Source: United Nations Commodity Trade Statistics Database.

Table 4.4 Chinese Petroleum Gas Product Imports from Iran

Year	Volume (MMcf)	Global Share (%)	World Ranking	Petroleum Gas Trade Value ($)	Total Commodity Trade Value ($)	Percentage (%)
2006	39	16	4	499,538,837	9,958,456,154	5
2007	28	10	2	414,509,077	13,301,528,289	3
2008	18	7	5	329,799,273	19,594,195,353	2
2009	47	12	2	558,452,925	13,286,547,277	4
2010	38	6	6	661,948,584	18,300,891,267	4
2011	29	3	8	588,084,528	30,332,972,751	2
2012	7	<1	14	170,586,250	24,869,408,279	1
2013	4	<1	21	97,230,683	25,389,863,878	0

Source: United Nations Commodity Trade Statistics Database.

China also imports petroleum gas products from Iran but not liquefied natural gas (LNG). Table 4.4 illustrates China's petroleum gas imports from Iran in millions of cubic feet, global imports share, world ranking, trade value, total commodity trade value, and percentage from 2006 to 2013. See Table 4.4.

China has burgeoning investments in Iran's oil and gas sector. In this respect, China finalized the following transactions: Sinopec signed a Memorandum of Understanding for a twenty-five-year $70 billion agreement to import LNG in exchange for developing Yadavaran Oil field (October 2004); and CNPC won the tender for Block 3 (May 2005) and signed an agreement with National Iranian Oil Company to jointly develop Iran's North Azadegan Oil field for $1.76 billon, which has estimated reserves of 6 billion barrels (January 2009).[88]

In addition to bilateral cooperation in upstream and downstream activities, China and Iran cooperate in services and maintenance, oil rig construction, and oil tanker construction. In 2002, the China Shipbuilding Industry Corporation delivered to the North Iranian Tanker Company the first of five oil tankers ordered in 2000. China Oilfield Services and Iran's North Drilling Company concluded a $35 million agreement which "includes the repair, management, and maintenance of the Alborz semi-floating platform in the Caspian Seas." The project yielded an increase of daily production to 60 kbpd. North Drilling Company also signed an agreement with CNPC in 2010 to build and supply an oil rig worth $143 million.[89]

CNPC also provides oil field services ranging from geophysical prospecting, well drilling, logging, and perforation to formation testing.[90]

In 2001, CNPC won a service contract from National Iranian Oil Company (NIOC) for drilling nineteen wells and workover of two wells. In 2006, CNPC won the tender of the South Pars project to provide offshore well logging and perforating services with a contract term of three years.[91]

In 2008, CNPC acquired 3D seismic data with improved quality from complex mountains in Iran's Block 3. In addition, well logging project of NIOC South (an NIOC offshore project) and a PTTEP (PTT Exploration and Production Plc) project were newly developed.[92]

China and Iran also signed agreements on bilateral energy cooperation. This includes: Agreement on Oil and Gas Cooperation (April 22, 2002);[93] Agreement on the Peaceful Use of Nuclear Energy (January 23, 2016);[94] and Memorandum of Understanding between the Union of Oil, Gas and Petrochemical Exporters of Iran and the Chinese Petrochemical Industries Confederation to boost Petrochemical Cooperation (May 8, 2016).[95]

SUMMARY

Sino-Iranian relations appear to be strategic. China and Iran engage each other on all levels. Relations date back to pre-Islamic times even though formal relations were established in 1971. China is Iran's largest trading partner and conventional weapons supplier. China also helped to establish Iran's nuclear program and shielded Iran against international sanctions. Moreover, in terms of crude oil trading, China is Iran's principal oil customer. Chinese crude petroleum imports from Iran averaged 11 percent of total annual imports between 2006 and 2013. In terms of total trade value, crude petroleum averaged 74 percent of all commodities imported to China from Iran for the same years. Thus, crude oil plays a very important role of the Sino-Iranian relationship.

Unlike crude petroleum, petroleum gas products do not play a significant role in Sino-Iranian relations. Petroleum gas product imports from Iran have ranged from less than 1 percent to 5 percent of overall annual trade value between 2006 and 2013 inclusive. Nevertheless, China and Iran cooperation in energy extends to service and maintenance, oil rig construction, and oil tanker construction.

NOTES

1. Geoffrey Kemp, *The East Moves West: India, China, and Asia's Growing Presence in the Middle East* (Washington, DC: Brookings Institution Press), 2010, 73.

2. Ministry of Foreign Affairs of People's Republic of China, "China–Iran: Activities," (n.d.), accessed August 8, 2016, http://www.fmprc.gov.cn/mfa_eng/ wjb_663304/zzjg_663340/xybfs _663590/gjlb_663594/2818_663626/2820_663630/ default_2.shtml.

3. Ibid.

4. Ministry of Foreign Affairs of People's Republic of China, "Xi Jinping Holds Talks with President Hassan Rouhani of Iran," January 23, 2016, accessed August 19, 2016, http://www.fmprc.gov.cn/mfa_eng/wjb_663304/zzjg_663340/xybfs_663590/gjlb_663594/2818_663626/2820_663630/t1335157.shtml.

5. Ministry of Foreign Affairs of People's Republic of China, "China–Iran: Joint Communiqué Between The People's Republic of China and the Islamic Republic of Iran," June 5, 2012, accessed June 8, 2014, http://www.fmprc.gov.cn/mfa_eng/wjb_663304/zzjg_663340/xybfs _663590/gjlb_663594/2818_663626/2819_663628/t16315.shtml.

6. Ministry of Foreign Affairs of People's Republic of China, "China and Iran," (n.d.), accessed June 8, 2014, http://www.fmprc.gov.cn/mfa_eng/wjb_663304/zzjg_663340/xybfs _663590/gjlb_663594/2818_663626/.

7. Scott Harold and Alireza Nader, *China and Iran: Economic, Political and Military Relations* (Santa Monica, CA: RAND Corporation), 2012, 9.

8. "China, Iran agree to $600 Billion Trade Deal after Sanctions Lifted," *Radio Free Europe/Radio Liberty*, January 24, 2016, accessed August 19, 2016, http://en.trend.az/iran/business/2530745.html.

9. Kemp, *The East Moves West: India, China, and Asia's Growing Presence in the Middle East*, 75.

10. Bartke, ibid., 86.

11. Ibid., 87.

12. Ibid.

13. Ministry of Foreign Affairs of People's Republic of China, "Iranian President Khatami Meets with Foreign Minister Tang Jiaxuan," November 15, 2000, accessed August 19, 2016, http://www.fmprc.gov.cn/mfa_eng/wjb_663304/zzjg_663340/xybfs_663590/gjlb_663594/2818_663626/2820_663630/t16317.shtml.

14. Ministry of Foreign Affairs of People's Republic of China, "Wu Bangguo Meets with Iranian First Vice President Rahimi," September 10, 2012, accessed August 19, 2016, http://www.fmprc.gov.cn/mfa_eng/wjb_663304/zzjg_663340/xybfs_663590/gjlb_663594/2818_663626/2820_663630/t969867.shtml.

15. Ibid.

16. Ministry of Foreign Affairs of People's Republic of China, "Xi Jinping Holds Talks with President Hassan Rouhani of Iran," January 23, 2016, accessed August 19, 2016, http://www.fmprc.gov.cn/mfa_eng/wjb_663304/zzjg_663340/xybfs_663590/gjlb_663594/2818_663626/2820_663630/t1335157.shtml.

17. President of the Islamic Republic of Iran, "Iran, China sign 17 Documents, MoUs," January 23, 2016, accessed August 19, 2016, http://www.president.ir/en/91427.

18. Ibid.

19. Muhamad S. Olimat, *China and the Middle East Since World War II* (Lanham, MD: Lexington Books), 2014, 50.

20. Ibid., 51.

21. Ibid., 50.

22. Harold and Nader, ibid., 10; and European Commission Directorate-General for Trade, "Iran: EU Bilateral Trade and Trade with the World," April 10, 2015,

accessed May 3, 2015, http://trade.ec.europa.eu/doclib/docs/2006/september/tradoc_113392.pdf.

23. United Nations, United Nations Commodity Trade Statistics Database, accessed August 21, 2015, <http://comtrade.un.org/db/default.aspx>.

24. Ibid.

25. United Nations Conference on Trade and Development (UNCTAD FDI/TNC) Database, *Bilateral FDI Statistics 2014*, accessed June 29, 2014, http://unctad.org/Sections/dite_fdistat/docs/webdiaeia2014d3_CHN.pdf.

26. Olimat, ibid., 57.

27. United Nations, United Nations Commodity Trade Statistics Database, accessed July 22, 2016, http://comtrade.un.org/db/default.aspx.

28. Kemp, ibid., 77.

29. Ibid., 77–78.

30. The Heritage Foundation and American Enterprise Institute, *China Global Investment Tracker Database*, accessed October 17, 2014, http://www.heritage.org/research/projects/china-global-investment-tracker-interactive-map.

31. Bartke, ibid., 86–87.

32. Ministry of Foreign Affairs of People's Republic of China, "President Jiang Zemin Held Talks with Iranian President Mohammad Khatami," April 22, 2002, accessed August 19, 2016, http://www.fmprc.gov.cn/mfa_eng/wjb_663304/zzjg_663340/xybfs_663590/gjlb_663594/2818_663626/2820_663630/t16325.shtml.

33. Ibid.

34. Ibid.

35. Ministry of Foreign Affairs of People's Republic of China, "Xi Jinping Holds Talks with President Hassan Rouhani of Iran," January 23, 2016, accessed August 19, 2016, http://www.fmprc.gov.cn/mfa_eng/wjb_663304/zzjg_663340/xybfs_663590/gjlb_663594/2818_663626/2820_663630/t1335157.shtml; and President of the Islamic Republic of Iran, "Iran, China sign 17 Documents, MoUs," January 23, 2016, accessed August 19, 2016, http://www.president.ir/en/91427.

36. President of the Islamic Republic of Iran, "Iran, China sign 17 Documents, MoUs," January 23, 2016, accessed August 19, 2016, http://www.president.ir/en/91427.

37. Ibid.

38. Ibid.

39. Ibid.

40. "Iran, China sign Seven Commercial Cooperation Documents," *Iran Daily*, May 24, 2016, accessed August 19, 2016, http://www.iran-daily.com/News/151976.html.

41. Ibid.

42. "China's EXIM Bank, Iran ink Finance Deal," *Azer News*, August 17, 2016, accessed August 19, 2016, http://iranoilgas.com/news/details?id=16425&title=China%E2%80%99s+EXIM+Bank%2c+Iran+ink+finance+deal.

43. Olimat, ibid., 57.

44. Ilan Berman, "The Impact of Sino-Iranian Strategic Partnership," testimony, September 14, 2006, before U.S.–China Economic and Security Review Commission.

45. Olimat, ibid., 53.

46. "First China–Iran Joint Military Exercise Attracts Attention," *China Military Online*, September 23, 2014, accessed February 1, 2015, http://eng.mod.gov.cn/DefenseNews/2014-09/23/content_4539380.htm.

47. Ibid.

48. Stockholm International Peace Research Institute, SIPRI Arms Transfers Database, http://www.sipri.org/databases/armstransfers.

49. Ibid.

50. Ibid.

51. Berman, ibid.

52. U.S. Department of Defense, *Proliferation: Threat and Response 1996* (Washington: U.S. Department of Defense), 1996, 14.

53. Harold and Nader, ibid., 8.

54. Christopher M. Blanchard, et al., *Comparing Global Influence: China's and U.S. Diplomacy, Foreign Aid, Trade, and Investment in the Developing World.* CRS Report RL34620 (Washington, DC: Library of Congress), August 15, 2008, 149.

55. Barry McCaffrey, "Iran, Nukes, & Oil: The Gulf Confrontation" (PowerPoint Presentation Seminar for NBC Executives and Producers), January 12, 2012.

56. United States Department of Defense, Defense Intelligence Agency, *Directory of PRC Military Personalities*, Washington, DC, 2014, 16; and Heidi Holz and Kenneth Allen, "Military Exchanges with Chinese Characteristics: The People's Liberation Army Experience with Military Relations," in Roy Kamphausen, David Lai, and Andrew Scobell, eds., *The PLA At Home and Abroad: Accessing the Operational Capabilities of China's Military* (Carlisle, PA: Strategic Studies Institute), June 2010, 479.

57. Olimat, ibid., 54, 55.

58. Ministry of Foreign Affairs of People's Republic of China, "China–Iran: Joint Communiqué Between The People's Republic of China and the Islamic Republic of Iran," June 5, 2012, accessed June 8, 2014, http://www.fmprc.gov.cn/mfa_eng/wjb_663304/zzjg_663340/xybfs _663590/gjlb_663594/2818_663626/2819_663628/t16315.shtml.

59. Olimat, ibid., 60.

60. Ibid.

61. Ibid.

62. Ibid.

63. Bartke, ibid., 86.

64. Ibid.

65. Ibid., 87.

66. Ibid.

67. Ibid.

68. Ibid.

69. Ibid.

70. Ibid.

71. Olimat, ibid., 59–60.

72. Ibid, 60.

73. Ministry of Foreign Affairs of People's Republic of China, "President Jiang Zemin Held Talks with Iranian President Mohammad Khatami," April 22, 2002, accessed August 19, 2016, http://www.fmprc.gov.cn/mfa_eng/wjb_663304/zzjg_663340/xybfs_663590/gjlb_663594/2818_663626/2820_663630/t16325.shtml.
74. Ibid.
75. Olimat, ibid., 60.
76. President of the Islamic Republic of Iran, "Iran, China sign 17 Documents, MoUs," January 23, 2016, accessed August 19, 2016, http://www.president.ir/en/91427.
77. Ibid.
78. Ibid.
79. Ibid.
80. Ibid.
81. Ibid.
82. Ibid.
83. "Iran, China sign Seven Commercial Cooperation Documents," *Iran Daily*, May 24, 2016, accessed August 19, 2016, http://www.iran-daily.com/News/151976.html.
84. "Iran and China sign Memo to exchange Cultural, Scientific Documents," *Iran's Book News Agency*, June 9, 2016, accessed August 19, 2016, http://www.ibna.ir/en/doc/naghli/237338/iran-and-china-sign-memo-to-exchange-cultural-scientific-documents.
85. Harold and Nader, ibid., 10.
86. Ibid.
87. Olimat, ibid., 57.
88. Julie Jang and Jonathan Sinton, *Overseas Investments by Chinese National Companies: Assessing the Drivers and Impacts*, International Energy Agency, February 2011, 39–40; CNPC; and John W. Garver.
89. Olimat, ibid., 56–57.
90. China National Petroleum Company, "CNPC in Iran, Oilfield Services, Engineering and Construction," accessed February 6, 2015, http://www.cnpc.com.cn/en/Iran/country_index.shtml.
91. Ibid.
92. Ibid.
93. Ministry of Foreign Affairs of People's Republic of China, "President Jiang Zemin Held Talks with Iranian President Mohammad Khatami," April 22, 2002, accessed August 19, 2016, http://www.fmprc.gov.cn/mfa_eng/wjb_663304/zzjg_663340/xybfs_663590/gjlb_663594/2818_663626/2820_663630/t16325.shtml.
94. President of the Islamic Republic of Iran, ibid.
95. "Iran, China sign Document to boost Petro-Chemical Co-Op," *Trend News Agency*, May 8, 2016, accessed August 19, 2016, http://en.trend.az/iran/business/2530745.html.

Chapter 5

China and Iraq
Political/Diplomatic Relations

Sino-Iraqi diplomatic relations were established on August 25, 1958. Diplomatic ties were established and advanced by the following: Joint Communiqué on the Establishment of Diplomatic Relations Between the People's Republic of China and the Republic of Iraq (August 25, 1958);[1] Consular Treaty (October 27, 1989);[2] Cooperation Agreement on Personnel Exchange Facilitation (December 22, 2015);[3] and Agreement on Mutual Visa Exemption including diplomatic and service passports (December 22, 2015).[4]

Bilateral political ties were formed in the wake of Abd al-Karim Qasim's violent overthrow of the Hashemite monarchy under King Faisal II. Initial diplomatic ties were strained by internal struggles between Iraqis who supported Egypt's Nasser and Arab nationalism and Qasim, who supported the communists, two Ba'athist coups in 1963 and 1968, and Kurdish insurrections by ethnic nationalists. In addition, Iraq showed a predilection for the Soviets as Iraq and the Soviet Union had diplomatic ties since September 9, 1944, and that the Soviet Union supplied Iraq with weapons and was an effective counterweight to Western and U.S. influence in the Near East. Sino-Soviet rivalry for political and technical influence in the Near East following the 1960 Sino-Soviet split exacerbated matters even further. Iraq also preferred relations with and technical support from the United States over China during the same period. Bilateral relations were also strained when Qasim turned against Iraqi communists and by his views on Kuwaiti independence in 1961. Qasim used communist forces to mobilize support for the military coup and then discarded them violently once the coup was successful. Qasim also viewed Kuwait as part of Iraq as China views Taiwan as part of itself, a perspective which is still viewed today. When Qasim was removed on February 9, 1963 in a violent coup, Soviet-Iraqi relations deteriorated.[5]

China gradually viewed the Soviet Union over the United States as the greatest threat to regional and world stability in the 1970s. Realizing the danger of a Soviet-controlled Iraq, China sought to win Iraq's favor through economic incentives. Both penned an agreement of economic and technical cooperation in 1971 in which China would export sulfur to Iraq while Iraq would export chemical fertilizer to China. There was also a provision for a $36 million interest-free loan to Iraq from China which was repayable beginning in 1984.[6]

While China was unsuccessful in reducing Soviet patronage in the early 1970s, it did receive Iraq's support for a permanent seat in the United Nations and voted in favor to admit China and replace Taiwan.

In 1975, bilateral relations resurged because of Soviet-Iraqi political friction and the Iran-Iraqi peace accord. Relations deepened through economic cooperation and infrastructure development. In this respect, Chinese construction projects were realized in Iraq: a 667-meter Mosul Bridge I connecting the Baghdad-Mosul highway to an international road connecting Mosul to Turkey (1975); a sports hall in Baghdad (1976); a wash and spinning mill in Kifri (July 1978); and the Sherquat highway bridge on the Tigris River in northern Iraq (1978). China and Iraq also penned a trade agreement in 1977 to furnish sulfur and fertilizer to China. China also purchased over 100,000 tons of dates becoming Iraq's largest importer of the agricultural commodity.[7] Sino-Iraqi trade and economic cooperation obviously improved overall bilateral relations.

The Iran-Iraq War (September 1980–August 1988) or First Persian Gulf War provided China with even further opportunities to enhance its political and economic ties not only with Iraq but regionally in the Near East. In addition to providing military support and arms transfers to Iran and Iraq totaling $3.9 billion and $5.52 billion, respectively, between 1981 and 1988 (and fostering goodwill with both governments in the process), the war further augmented China's prestige and relevance to regional regimes.[8] It was only the beginning to what would follow in the Post-Cold War (1989–present).

Tiananmen (June 4, 1989), the First Iraq War (1990), and the Second Iraq War (2003–2011) further enhanced Sino-Iraqi ties in the Post–Cold War period. Iraq felt the West, and in particular, the United States, had no right to interfere in the internal affairs of other countries. China's unwavering neutrality in such matters as opposed to Western intervention through economic sanctions against China in the wake of Tiananmen and economic sanctions against and military invasion of Iraq in First Iraq War and Second Iraq War significantly enhanced political and economic ties between China and Iraq. China pursued a two-pronged policy of pursuing Chinese interests while avoid antagonizing the United States, especially when it came to Iraq.[9] China's adroit use of soft power and emphasis on multilateralism, especially in Iraqi internal matters, had garnered political capital from the world community especially in the twenty-first century. Many saw China as a responsible stakeholder and as an arbiter of goodwill and neutrality.

In the twenty-first century, China and Iraq have engaged each through official, high-level exchanges and visits no less than forty-five times.[10] Some of the most important exchanges include: President Hu Jintao and President Bahr Ul-Uloum (March 2004), President Hu Jintao and President Jalal Talabani (June 2007), President Hu Jintao and Iraqi prime minister Nuri Al-Maliki (July 2011), and President Xi Jinping and Prime Minister Haider al-Abadi (December 2015).[11] The Second Iraq War diminished China's political and economic influence in Iraq as well as the number of bilateral visits and exchanges between Chinese and Iraqi officials. Many prewar agreements were temporarily frozen but not China's ability to participate in Iraq's postwar reconstruction.[12]

Since bilateral ties were resumed, China and Iraq have penned four agreements in the areas of foreign affairs, the economy, technology, and education in 2007. In 2008, China and Iraq signed a memorandum of understanding to establish a mechanism for developing bilateral ties and political consultation, activated conventions in the fields of energy and human resources, and furthered cultural and economic relations. The two sides specifically agreed to develop their trading relationship and encourage Chinese investments in reconstruction, communications, and transportation.[13]

In 2011, China helped lift the United Nations sanctions placed on Iraq in earlier Security Council resolutions.[14] China has also been involved in Iraqi's reconstruction.

China and Iraq have established official diplomatic representation, respectively, in Baghdad and Beijing.

ECONOMIC/TRADE RELATIONS

Sino-Iraqi economic relations are robust. China was Iraq's largest trading partner in 2013.[15] In comparison, Iraq was China's thirty-first largest trading partner in the same year.[16] Bilateral trade was: $2.6 billion (2008), $5.1 billion (2009), $9.8 billion (2010), $14.2 billion (2011), $17.5 billion (2012), $24.8 billion (2013), $28.5 billion (2014), and $20.5 billion (2015).[17] Bilateral trade increased eightfold in seven years. Since 2000, bilateral trade increased twenty-one-fold. In 2012, foreign direct investment into Iran from China was $148 million and foreign direct investment stock was $754 million.[18]

Trade relations began in the 1950s. Bilateral trade was "political" in nature rather than profit-oriented for first three decades (1950–1980). China also provided an interest-free loan of $40 million in early 1971 to "loosen Iraq's dependence on the Soviet Union" and supported the nationalization of Iraq's oil industry in 1972, a move which would strengthen Iraq's control over its natural resources and assist in its ambitious economic development process. This led to development of various infrastructure projects in highways, airports, schools, housing, irrigation, electricity, and education.[19]

In terms of bilateral trade, Table 5.1 shows the top five commodities traded between China and Iraq in 2015. Energy commodities, which include crude petroleum and petroleum gas products, appear to be the most traded commodity. In terms of trade value, 99 percent is attributed to energy commodities, which include crude petroleum and petroleum gas products. See Table 5.1.

In previous years, China's energy commodities accounted for the following in terms of trade value: 95.55 percent (2008), 99.9 percent (2009), 99.96 percent (2010), 99.96 percent (2011), 99.95 percent (2012), and 99.9 percent (2013), and 99.9 percent (2014).[20]

China and Iraq has penned some important agreements and protocol to facilitate trade between their countries. The most notable agreements include: Trade and Payments Agreement (January 1959);[21] 1960–1961 Trade and Payments Agreement (May 1960);[22] Agreement on Civil Air Transport (September 9, 1964);[23] Trade Agreement (September 23, 1964);[24]

Table 5.1 Top Five Commodities Traded between China and Iraq

Commodity	Importer	Trade Value ($)	Percentage (%)
Mineral fuels, mineral oils and products of their distillation; bituminous substances; mineral waxes	China	12,668,861,365	99
Edible fruit and nuts; peel of citrus fruit or melons	China	729,592	0.01
Copper and articles thereof	China	664,731	0.005
Lac; gums, resins, and other vegetable saps and extracts	China	135,982	0.0011
Raw hides and skins (other than fur skins) and leather	China	117,808	0.0009
Nuclear reactors, boilers, machinery and mechanical appliances; parts thereof	Iraq	1,426,319,178	18
Electrical machinery and equipment and parts thereof; sound recorders and reproducers, television image and sound recorders and reproducers, and parts and accessories of such articles	Iraq	1,095,436,659	14
Articles of apparel and clothing accessories, knitted or crocheted	Iraq	423,837,375	5
Articles of iron or steel	Iraq	411,241,536	5
Plastics and articles thereof	Iraq	393,918,688	5

Source: United Nations Commodity Trade Statistics Database.

the Agreement on Air Transport between the Government of the People's Republic of China and the Government of the Republic of Iraq (1969);[25] an Agreement of Economic and Technical Cooperation (June 21, 1971);[26] Protocol on the Development of Economic and Technical Cooperation (December 20, 1972);[27] Protocol on the Agreement of Economic and Technical Cooperation (November 25, 1973);[28] Trade Protocol (February 16, 1974);[29] Protocol on Trade Development (July 6, 1975);[30] Protocol on Economic and Technical Cooperation (July 6, 1975);[31] Protocol on amending the trade agreement (November 30, 1975);[32] a New Agreement of Economic and Technical Cooperation (1976);[33] a Trade Agreement (1977);[34] an Agreement to Import Iraqi Nitrogenous Fertilizers (1980);[35] Air Transport Agreement (February 3, 1980);[36] Trade Agreement (May 8, 1981);[37] Agreement on Economic and Technical Cooperation (May 8, 1981);[38] Protocol on the 1st Session of the Iraq-Chinese Committee of Trade Exchange and Technical and Economic Cooperation (June 14, 1983);[39] an Agreement to Import Iraqi Phosphate, Sulfur, and Palm Dates and Export Chinese Textiles, Industrial, Metal, and Mineral Products (1985);[40] Agreement on Economic and Technical Cooperation (April 26, 1986);[41] Cooperation Agreement on the Economy and Technology (June 21, 2007);[42] Agreement on Economic and Technological Cooperation (December 22, 2015);[43] and Memorandum of Understanding Between the Government of the People's Republic of China and the Government of the Republic of Iraq on Jointly Advancing Construction of the Silk Road Economic Belt and the 21st-Century Maritime Silk Road (December 23, 2015).[44]

Bilateral trade is also promoted through several organizations such as China Council for the Promotion of International Trade, China-Arab States Cooperation Forum, China-Arab States Expo, the Iraqi Business Club, the Kurdistan Investment Board, the PRC Ministry of Commerce, the PRC Ministry of Foreign Affairs, and the All-China Federation of Commerce and Industry.[45]

Chinese companies have also been awarded numerous contracts to develop Iraq's power industry and telecommunications infrastructure. These contracts include: Telecommunications Infrastructure Reconstruction Contract awarded to Zhongxing Telecomm Co. (ZTE) (2004);[46] and a $940 million contract awarded to the Shanghai Heavy Industry Corporation to build a large power plant in Wasit, southeast of Baghdad (October 2007).[47]

Some of the largest contracts include: a $1.01 billion utility contract awarded to China Power Investment Corporation (April 2011); and a $1.08 billion utility contract awarded to China National Machinery Industry Corporation (November 2011).[48]

In summary, Chinese investments in Iraq were $4 billion since November 2007.[49] Compared to Chinese energy investments, this is 27 percent of

China's total investments. China was also heavily involved in the construction sector in Iraq building highways, hospitals, airports, government buildings, and housing projects. China's Sinoma, a leading international cement company, built seven major cement production plants in Iraq. China State Construction Engineering Corporation (CSCEC) teamed with major Emirati construction companies to build high-rise apartment buildings, office buildings, and mass-housing units. China's Chery Automobile Co. Ltd. is supplying automobiles to Iraq via Jordan. BYD Auto Co. Ltd. is showcasing the BYD-M6 minivan. Huawei and M2M Solutions are providing telecommunication services.[50]

China and Iraq teamed up in civil aviation to meet the growing demand of business in both countries as well as tourism. Both are taking steps to establish direct flights between the major cities in China and Iraq. The tourism sector is underdeveloped because of Iraqi violence and instability.[51]

China initiated several assistance projects to further bilateral ties such as building schools, hospitals, roads, and housing units. China also canceled 80 percent of Iraq's debt to China estimated at $8.5 billion. This significantly strengthened bilateral trade ties.[52]

MILITARY/SECURITY RELATIONS

Sino-Iraqi military-security relations have been developing since diplomatic ties were first established in 1958; however, Sino-Iraqi military ties do not appear to be robust. China assigned a military attaché at its embassy in Baghdad through 2013 but pulled the representative out due to ongoing violence and instability; nevertheless, Iraq posted a military attaché to its embassy in Beijing.[53] Per the Ministry of National Defense of the People's Republic of China, *PLA Daily*, *Xinhua*, and *China Military Online*, China and Iraq participated in one educational exchange (mine-clearing course in China) in 2007.

Although military-security interactions appear limited, China and Iraq are cooperating on combating international terrorism. Iraq convened an international conference to address counterterrorism methods in March 2014. Both China and Iraq are victims of terrorism even though the Iraqi government has been accused of nurturing the sectarian violence between the Iraqi Army and a predominately Sunni population. China's main concern is the continuation of Arab-Islamic support for its integrity in Xinjiang Province.[54]

China has been Iraq's largest source of conventional arms after France, Russia, the United Kingdom, and the United States. Chinese arms transfers occurred mostly in the 1980s and recently in 2004. Table 5.2 summarizes the arms transfers from China to Iraq according to SIPRI. See Table 5.2. China's total arms sales to Iraq are $7.92 billion based on the 2016 CPI index. In

Table 5.2 Chinese Conventional Weapons Transfers to Iraq

Year(s) of Delivery	No. of Deliveries	Weapon Designation	Weapon Description
1982–1987	1,000	Type-59 (S)	Tank
1982–1988	650	YW-531/Type-63 (S)	Armored Personnel Carrier
1982–1983	40	F-6/Farmer (S)	Fighter Aircraft
1983–1987	1,500	Type-69 (S)	Tank
1983–1987	90	F-7A (S)	Fighter Aircraft
1984–1988	100	Type-63 107mm (S)	Towed Mobile Rocket Launcher
1986–1987	1,000	HN-5A (S)	Portable Surface-to-Air Missile
1986–1988	5	Type-408C (S)	Air Search Radar
1986–1987	25	W-653/Type-653 (S)	Armored Recovery Vehicle
1988	4	B-6 (S)	Bomber Aircraft
1987–1988	200	HY-2/SY-1A/CSS-N-2 (S)	Anti-Ship Missile
1988–1989	50	Type-83 152mm (S)	Towed Gun
2004	5	Predator (S)	Patrol Craft
2015	20	AR-1	Air-to-Surface Missile
2015	4	CH-4	Unmanned Aerial Vehicle/ Unmanned Combat Aerial Vehicle
2015	20	FT-9	Guided Bomb

Source: SIPRI Arms Transfers Database.

2000, total arms sales to Iraq were $7.84 billion; the difference being $8 million over a 16-year period.[55]

Bilateral cooperation also includes the signing of formal agreements. On December 22, 2015, China and Iraq signed an agreement of bilateral military cooperation.[56]

CULTURAL RELATIONS

Sino-Iraqi cultural ties were established in the wake of diplomatic relations in 1958. The China-Iraqi Friendship Association was established in Beijing in late September 1958.[57] Since 1958, bilateral cultural exchanges have occurred in the fields of the arts, culture, media, higher education, sport, and communications.[58] China and Iraq have also penned numerous agreements and memorandums of understanding to develop further cultural ties between them. These include: Agreement on Cultural Cooperation between the Governments of the People's Republic of China and the Republic of Iraq (April 1959);[59] 1959 Executive Plan on Cultural Cooperation (April 8, 1959); 1960 Executive Plan on Cultural Cooperation (May 15, 1960); 1961–62 Executive Plan on Cultural Cooperation (November 25, 1961); 1963–1964 Executive Plan on Cultural Cooperation (May 25, 1964); 1966–1967 Executive

Plan on Cultural Cooperation (June 4, 1966); Protocol on Broadcasting and Television Cooperation (June 4, 1966); Sino-Iraqi Broadcasting and TV Cooperation Agreement (May 25, 1967); Agreement for Cooperation in Sports (December 8, 1979); 1980–1981 Executive Plan on Cultural Cooperation (May 29, 1980); 1984 Sports Cooperation Plan (September 26, 1983); Protocol on Sports Exchange (January 19, 1985); 1985–1987 Executive Plan on Cultural Cooperation (May 31, 1985); Three-Year Cultural Cooperation Plan (September 28, 1988);[60] Agreement on Cultural Cooperation between the People's Republic of China and the Republic of Iraq (November 28, 2004);[61] a Memorandum of Understanding regarding Cooperation in Education, Sports, and Communication (2009);[62] and a Cooperation Agreement in the Fields of Culture, Education, Media, and Sport (2014).[63]

China has also been providing fellowships for Iraqi students to study in China and granted Iraq $6.5 million for public health and development programs.[64] The Iraqi government is keen on sending students to study abroad, especially in medicine, engineering, information technology, management, economics, biology, physics, and sociology.[65] China also entertained several visits of art troupes and media delegations sent by the Iraqi government.[66] Chinese companies have provided cultural, charitable, and social services in Iraq. CNPC provides social services to orphanages in Basra; scholarships and training programs for students at Basra University; cultural and linguistic programs to its Iraqi employees in southern Iraq; technical programs in oil-drilling skills, management, and teamwork to create a consistent business culture between local employees and Chinese expatriates; and internship opportunities for Baghdad University of Technology to assist in the capacity building of Iraqi engineers and technicians in the oil industry. Huawei Telecom established a communications center at the University of Baghdad and aims to expand its network in Iraq. Iraq participated in the 2010 Shanghai Expo exhibiting cultural relics from carved with cuneiform characters and a model of the Hanging Gardens of Babylon.[67] In summary, bilateral cultural ties have developed smoothly without incident for over fifty-five years.

ENERGY/PETROLEUM RELATIONS

Crude oil trading establishes the foundation for the trade relationship given Iraq's vast energy resources and China's growing energy needs. Iraq has been one of China's largest suppliers of crude oil in the Near East after Iran, Oman, and Saudi Arabia. China imported 1 to 10 percent of its crude petroleum from Iraq between 2006 and 2015. In terms of total trade value, crude petroleum imports ranged from 71 to 99.9 percent for the same years. Table 5.3 shows Chinese crude oil imports from Iraq in thousands of barrels per day, oil

Table 5.3 Chinese Crude Petroleum Imports from Iraq

Year	KBPD	Oil Imports Share (%)	World Ranking	Crude Oil Trade Value ($)	Total Commodity Trade Value ($)	Percentage (%)
2006	21	1	19	463,109,182	653,272,934	70.89
2007	28	1	20	690,304,357	765,796,913	90.14
2008	37	1	16	1,311,305,919	1,381,664,347	94.91
2009	144	4	7	3,294,815,207	3,298,111,051	99.90
2010	226	5	7	6,272,767,556	6,275,191,100	99.96
2011	277	5	6	10,438,936,463	10,443,633,871	99.96
2012	315	6	6	12,649,171,736	12,655,773,459	99.95
2013	472	8	5	17,899,812,009	17,984,764,256	99.53
2014	574	9	5	20,759,577,992	20,761,239,088	99.99
2015	645	10	4	12,668,848,118	12,670,542,082	99.99

Source: United Nations Commodity Trade Statistics Database.

imports share, world ranking, trade value, total commodity trade value, and percentage from 2006 to 2015. See Table 5.3.

Although China does not import liquefied natural gas (LNG), it has imported petroleum gas products and oil and gas acquisitions in Iraq. China imported less than 1 percent of petroleum gas products in 2014.[68]

China's oil and gas acquisitions in Iraq appear to be robust. In this respect, China finalized the following transactions: CNPC signed a 22-year production-sharing contract to develop al-Ahdab field for $1.3 billion in 2004 and CNPC reconfirmed the 1997 deal to develop al-Ahdab oil field in exchange for Chinese cancelation of large portion of Iraqi debt to China (January 2007); Sinopec purchased 100 percent of Addax for $8.8 billion acquiring a 45 percent working interest in Taq oil field and a 26.67 percent working interest in Sangaw North PSC oil field in Kurdistan (June 2009); CNPC and BP inked a technical service contract to expand production of Iraq's Rumaila oil field (January 2010); CNPC and others won the contract to operate the Halfaya oil field in consortium with Total, Petronas, and Iraq's Missan oil (January 2010); and PetroChina acquired a 25 percent interest in West Qurna-1 oil field project from Exxon Mobil (November 2013).[69]

China and Iraq has also penned agreements and contracts associated with Iraq's oil sector. These agreements and contracts include: a 20-year Agreement between CNOOC and Turkish Petroleum Corporation (TPO) to develop upstream capacity at the Missan oil field (2010);[70] a Contract awarded to China Petroleum Pipeline Engineering Corporation (CPPE), a CNPC subsidiary, to build a 300-km pipeline to deliver oil extracted from Missan oil field for export (2010);[71] and Memorandum of Understanding on Oil and Gas Cooperation (December 22, 2015).[72]

In addition to owning stakes in three Iraqi oil fields, CNPC provides a wide range of oil field services such as "seismic data acquisition, well drilling, well logging, and testing."[73] In 2005, CNPC signed a contract with Norway's DNO on drilling 3+6 wells with a "50D" drilling rig. CNPC entered the Iraqi market in late 2005 and provided well logging and testing services to DNO and Addax. In 2006, CNPC completed two seismic data acquisition projects for DNO. In 2009, CNPC deployed seismic exploration and drilling operations in Iraq's Ahdab oil field. In 2012, CNPC renewed well logging, mud logging, and testing operation contracts with the Halfaya and Al-Ahdab projects.[74] Finally, in 2014, CNPC won a bid on general drilling services for Rumaila Oilfield.[75]

The Second Iraq War slowed oil exports to China but in the aftermath Iraq eventually reemerged as a major oil exporter. Chinese investments in the Iraqi oil sector have been instrumental in helping to restore Iraq's energy production.[76] The convergence of mutual interests of petroleum trade will serve to underpin a long-term strategic partnership between China and Iraq.[77] This materialized on December 22, 2015, when the leaders of both countries, Xi Jinping and Prime Minister Haider al-Abadi, decided to elevate their relations and establish a strategic partnership.[78]

SUMMARY

Sino-Iraq relations were established in the wake of the 1958 coup that overthrew the Hashemite monarchy under King Faisal II. Today, bilateral relations are strong and potentially strategic. In every facet (politics, economics, military, culture, and petroleum) China and Iraq are engaged despite U.S. interest and influence in the Near East.

In terms of energy relations, Iraq is one of China's largest suppliers in the Near East after Iran, Oman, and Saudi Arabia. Further, crude petroleum trading dominates their trade relationship. Approximately 99 percent of value of total trade is attributed to crude petroleum. The fact that China and Iraq's interest converge on crude petroleum trading has provided for the establishment of a strategic partnership in December 2015.

NOTES

1. Wolfgang Bartke, *The Agreements of the People's Republic of China with Foreign Countries 1949–1990* (Munchen, Germany: K.G. Saur), 1992, 88.
2. Ibid., 89.
3. Ministry of Foreign Affairs of People's Republic of China, "Li Keqiang Holds Talks with Prime Minister Haider al-Abadi of Iraq, Emphasizing to Enrich

Connotations of China–Iraq Strategic Partnership and Build Upgraded Version of Mutually Beneficial Cooperation," December 22, 2015, accessed August 18, 2016, http://www.fmprc.gov.cn/mfa_eng/wjb_663304/zzjg_663340/xybfs_663590/gjlb_66 3594/2823_663636/2825_663640/t1327531.shtml.

4. "Iraq, China Sign Agreements on Defense, Silk Road Cooperation," *Sputnik News*, December 23, 2015, accessed August 19, 2016, http://sputniknews.com/politics/20151223/1032173543/silk-road-cooperation.html.

5. Muhamad S. Olimat, *China and the Middle East Since World War II* (Lanham, MD: Lexington Books), 2014, 66–67.

6. Scott J. Lee, "From Beijing to Baghdad: Stability and Decision-making in Sino-Iraqi Relations, 1958–2012" (B.A. thesis, University of Pennsylvania), April 1, 2013, 32, accessed September 19, 2014, http://repository.upenn.edu/curej/159/.

7. Ibid., 33–34.

8. Ibid., 57.

9. Yufeng Mao, "Beijing's Two-Pronged Iraq Policy," *China Brief* (Jamestown Foundation), Volume V, Issue 12, May 24, 2005, accessed September 14, 2014, http://www.jamestown.org/programs/chinabrief/single/?tx_ttnews%5Btt_news%5D=30441&tx_ttnews%5BbackPid%5D=195&no_cache=1#.VBaHfZtWZhE.

10. Ministry of Foreign Affairs of People's Republic of China, "China–Iraq: Activities," (n.d.), accessed August 8, 2016, http://www.fmprc.gov.cn/mfa_eng/wjb_663304/zzjg_663340/xybfs_663590/gjlb_663594/2823_663636/2825_663640/.

11. Ibid.

12. Richard Weitz, "China and Iraq: The Return," *Second Line of Defense*, June 22, 2012, accessed September 15, 2014, http://www.sldinfo.com/china-and-iraq-the-return/.

13. Ibid.

14. Ibid.

15. European Commission Directorate-General for Trade, "Iraq: EU Bilateral Trade and Trade with the World," April 10, 2015, accessed May 3, 2015, http://trade.ec.europa.eu/doclib/docs/2006/september/tradoc_113405.pdf.

16. United Nations, United Nations Commodity Trade Statistics Database, accessed August 21, 2015, http://comtrade.un.org/db/default.aspx.

17. Ibid., accessed July 22, 2016.

18. United Nations Conference on Trade and Development (UNCTAD FDI/TNC) Database, *Bilateral FDI Statistics 2014*, accessed June 29, 2014, http://unctad.org/Sections/dite_fdistat/docs/webdiaeia2014d3_CHN.pdf.

19. Olimat, ibid., 72-73.

20. United Nations, United Nations Commodity Trade Statistics Database, Ibid., accessed July 22, 2016.

21. Lee, ibid., 24.

22. Lee, ibid., 27.

23. Bartke, ibid., 88.

24. Ibid.

25. Ministry of Foreign Affairs of People's Republic of China, "Agreement on Air Transport between the Government of the People's Republic of China and the

Government of the Republic of Iraq," June 5, 2002, accessed September 19, 2014, http://www.fmprc.gov.cn/mfa_eng/wjb_663304/zzjg_663340/xybfs_663590/gjlb_663594/2823_663636/2824_663638/t16330.shtml.
  26. Lee, ibid., 32.
  27. Bartke, ibid., 88.
  28. Ibid.
  29. Ibid.
  30. Ibid.
  31. Ibid.
  32. Ibid.
  33. Lee, ibid., 34.
  34. Ibid.
  35. Ibid., 42.
  36. Bartke, ibid., 88.
  37. Ibid.
  38. Ibid.
  39. Ibid.
  40. Lee, ibid., 42.
  41. Bartke, ibid., 89.
  42. Ministry of Foreign Affairs of People's Republic of China, "Hu Jintao Holds Talks with Iraqi President Talabani," June 21, 2007, accessed August 18, 2016, http://www.fmprc.gov.cn/mfa_eng/wjb_663304/zzjg_663340/xybfs_663590/gjlb_663594/2823_663636/2825_663640/t333372.shtml.
  43. Ministry of Foreign Affairs of People's Republic of China, "Li Keqiang Holds Talks with Prime Minister Haider al-Abadi of Iraq, Emphasizing to Enrich Connotations of China-Iraq Strategic Partnership and Build Upgraded Version of Mutually Beneficial Cooperation," December 22, 2015, accessed August 18, 2016, http://www.fmprc.gov.cn/mfa_eng/wjb_663304/zzjg_663340/xybfs_663590/gjlb_663594/2823_663636/2825_663640/t1327531.shtml.
  44. "Iraq, China Sign Agreements on Defense, Silk Road Cooperation," *Sputnik News*, December 23, 2015, accessed August 19, 2016, http://sputniknews.com/politics/20151223/1032173543/silk-road-cooperation.html.
  45. Olimat, ibid., 75.
  46. Weitz, ibid.
  47. Yitzhak Shichor, "China Means Business in Iraq," *China Brief* (Jamestown Foundation), Volume VII, Issue 21, November 20, 2007, accessed September 14, 2014, http://www.jamestown.org/programs/chinabrief/single/?tx_ttnews%5Btt_news%5D=4542&tx_ttnews%5BbackPid%5D=197&no_cache=1#.VBaEWZtWZhE.
  48. The Heritage Foundation and American Enterprise Institute, *China Global Investment Tracker Database*, accessed October 17, 2014, http://www.heritage.org/research/projects/china-global-investment-tracker-interactive-map.
  49. Ibid.
  50. Olimat, ibid., 73–74.
  51. Ibid., 75.
  52. Ibid.

53. United States Department of Defense, Defense Intelligence Agency, *Directory of PRC Military Personalities* (Washington, DC), 2013, 8–20.

54. Olimat, ibid., 80.

55. Stockholm International Peace Research Institute, SIPRI Arms Transfers Database, http://www.sipri.org/databases/armstransfers.

56. "Iraq, China Sign Agreements on Defense, Silk Road Cooperation," *Sputnik News*, December 23, 2015, accessed August 19, 2016, http://sputniknews.com/politics/20151223/1032173543/silk-road-cooperation.html.

57. Olimat, ibid., 78.

58. "Iraq, China Sign Cooperation Agreement in the Fields of Culture, Education, Media and Sport," *Iraqi Daily Journal*, September 13, 2014, accessed September 14, 2014, http://www.iraqdailyjournal.com/story-z9658635.

59. Ministry of Foreign Affairs of People's Republic of China, "Agreement on Cultural Cooperation between the Governments of the People's Republic of China and the Republic of Iraq," June 5, 2002, accessed September 19, 2014, http://www.fmprc.gov.cn/mfa_eng/wjb_663304/zzjg_663340/xybfs_663590/gjlb_663594/2823_663636/2824_663638/t16331.shtml.

60. Bartke, ibid., 78, 88, 89.

61. Economic and Commercial Counselor's Office of the Embassy of the People's Republic of China in Iraq, "Agreement on Cultural Cooperation between the Governments of the People's Republic of China and the Republic of Iraq," November 28, 2014, accessed August 18, 2016, http://iq2.mofcom.gov.cn/article/bilateralcooperation/.

62. Weitz, ibid.

63. "Iraq, China Sign Cooperation Agreement in the Fields of Culture, Education, Media and Sport," *Iraqi Daily Journal*, September 13, 2014, accessed September 14, 2014, http://www.iraqdailyjournal.com/story-z9658635.

64. Weitz, ibid.

65. Olimat, ibid., 79.

66. Ministry of Foreign Affairs of People's Republic of China, "China and Iraq," (n.d.), accessed September 14, 2014, http://www.fmprc.gov.cn/mfa_eng/wjb_663304/zzjg_663340/xybfs_663590/gjlb_663594/2823_663636/.

67. Olimat, ibid., 78-79.

68. United Nations, United Nations Commodity Trade Statistics Database, ibid., accessed August 7, 2016.

69. Julie Jiang and Chen Dang, *Update on Overseas Investments by Chinese National Companies: Achievements and Challenges Since 2011* (Paris, France: Organization for Economic Cooperation and Development/International Energy Agency), June 2014, 35–39.

70. Chris Zambelis, "China's Iraq Oil Strategy Comes into Sharper Focus," *China Brief* (Jamestown Foundation), Volume VIII, Issue 10, May 9, 2013, 11.

71. Ibid.

72. Ministry of Foreign Affairs of People's Republic of China, "Li Keqiang Holds Talks with Prime Minister Haider al-Abadi of Iraq, Emphasizing to Enrich Connotations of China–Iraq Strategic Partnership and Build Upgraded Version of Mutually

Beneficial Cooperation," December 22, 2015, accessed August 18, 2016, http://www.fmprc.gov.cn/mfa_eng/wjb_663304/zzjg_663340/xybfs_663590/gjlb_663594/2823_663636/2825_663640/t1327531.shtml; and "China, Iraq sign Memo to promote Energy Partnership," *Xinhua*, December 22, 2015, accessed August 19, 2016, http://news.xinhuanet.com/english/2015-12/22/c_134942270.htm.

73. Olimat, ibid., 77.

74. China National Petroleum Company, "CNPC in Iraq, Oilfield Services Engineering," accessed February 6, 2015, http://www.cnpc.com.cn/en/Iraq/country_index.shtml.

75. Ibid., accessed August 26, 2016.

76. Zambelis, ibid., 10.

77. Ibid., 13.

78. Ministry of Foreign Affairs of People's Republic of China, "Xi Jinping Meets with Prime Minister Haider al-Abadi of Iraq," December 22, 2015, accessed August 18, 2016, http://www.fmprc.gov.cn/mfa_eng/wjb_663304/zzjg_663340/xybfs_663590/gjlb_663594/2823_663636/2825_663640/t1327529.shtml.

Chapter 6

China and Kazakhstan
Political/Diplomatic Relations

Sino-Kazakhstani diplomatic relations were established on January 3, 1992 in the wake of the dissolution of the Soviet Union.[1] To memorialize their political ties, China and Kazakhstan signed a joint communiqué.[2] In establishing ties with China, Kazakhstan aimed to balance the geopolitical and economic influence of its northern neighbor Russia. Previously, Kazakhstan was part of the Russian Empire (1731–1917) and the Soviet Union (1920–1991). After the breakup of the Soviet Union, Kazakhstan sought political and economic independence from Russia.[3] Nevertheless, Kazakhstan is still somewhat politically and economically dependent on Russia given their military-security relationship and that some of Kazakhstan's exports to Western markets transit through Russia.[4]

As early as the Han dynasty (206 BC–220 CE), China had extensive political and economic relations with Kazakhstan.[5] Most trade interactions were carried out using the Silk Road where caravan traffic carried Chinese silk to the Roman Empire.[6] However, Chinese presence diminished during the Song (960–1127) and Ming (1368–1644) dynasties.[7] It was not until the eighteenth century that significant expansion began under the Qing-Manchu dynasties (1644–1911).[8] Under these dynasties, China expanded westward to include Mongolia, Tibet, and East Turkestan.[9] Due to anti-Qing movements in these conquered regions, China was unable to realize its plans to conquer West Turkestan, the territory of the contemporary Central Asian Republics.[10] After the fall of Qing dynasty in 1911, Xinjiang broke away from Chinese control followed by a brief period of independence between 1944 and 1949 when it was known as the Republic of East Turkestan.[11] With the founding of the People's Republic of China on October 1, 1949, the Chinese government reasserted its sovereignty over Xinjiang using military force and the Republic of East Turkestan was absorbed back into China.[12] Notably, for most of the twentieth century, China had little presence in Central Asia including Kazakhstan because bilateral relations were conducted directly through Beijing and Moscow. Moreover, during the Sino-Soviet split, the Soviet Union used its position in Central Asia to support Uyghur groups and undermine China's control in Xinjiang.[13]

After the collapse of the Soviet Union, China initially sought relations with Kazakhstan to enhance the security of its western border, especially in the face of violent extremism in China's western regions like Xinjiang Province where Uyghur militants such as the East Turkestan Islamic Movement (ETIM) seek the independence of East Turkestan from China. China is particularly concerned about any potential secessionist movements within its borders, especially in Xinjiang, Taiwan, and Tibet, because one secessionist movement in one province or region could inspire multiple secessionist movements in other provinces or regions.[14] Therefore, China has been unwilling to support any secession movements or recognize any South Caucasus breakaway states because the political and economic repercussions would be grave for China.[15] Any secessionist movement such as the ETIM not only threatens the territorial integrity of China, but also could threaten the legitimacy and authority of the Chinese leadership.[16]

Apart from political instability posed by Islamic militants, Central Asia helps China to diversify both its energy partners and trade corridors. Central Asian states abundant in oil and gas resources like Kazakhstan help China's ability to reduce its energy dependence on the Near East. China currently imports almost 50 percent of its oil and gas from the Near East. China became dependent on foreign energy resources (oil and gas) after 1993 after a long history of self-sufficiency. Foreign energy resources are essential to sustaining China's growing economy and modernization program in the wake of economic reforms in late 1978, China's "Go Out" Policy or Going Global Strategy (1999), and the New Silk Road Initiative (2013).[17] The New Silk Road Initiative under Chinese president Xi Jinping underlines the importance of connecting China to the West and the securing of energy supplies, by land to the oil and gas fields of Central Asia and beyond, and by sea through Asia's contested waters in the East China Sea and South China Sea, through the Strait of Malacca, to the Indian Ocean.[18] China's Maritime Silk Road will traverse the Horn of Africa before entering the Red Sea and the Mediterranean.[19] It will include the Chinese cities of Quanzhou, Guangzhou, Beihai, and Haikou. In terms of energy trade corridors, Kazakhstan's geographic location relative to China helps China bypass some major oceanic chokepoints (Strait of Hormuz and Strait of Malacca), potentially dangerous naval interdictions by the Indian Navy and U.S. Navy, and the South China Sea, a potentially dangerous body of water disputed by six countries in Southeast Asia. Kazakhstan, by virtue of being China's northwestern neighbor, also helps China to reduce the transit time to transport vital energy supplies via oil and gas pipelines. Finally, China sought to develop and strengthen economic ties with the Central Asian Republics, of which Kazakhstan is a member. Kazakhstan is China's largest regional trading partner today and has been the most beneficial economically vis-à-vis China.

China, a somewhat ally and rival of Russia in the Central Asian region, has provided Kazakhstan with the unique opportunity to hedge against the erstwhile Soviet Union and present manifestation, Russia. Consequently, China and Kazakhstan have rapidly advanced cooperation in the political, economic, and security spheres especially in Kazakhstan's oil and gas industry.

During the Soviet period (1920–1991), direct interaction between China and Central Asian Republics was extremely limited, as official relations were channeled almost exclusively through the Soviet government in Moscow.[20] After the dissolution of the Soviet Union in December 1991, China was among one of the first countries to recognize the five new independent states of Kazakhstan, Kyrgyzstan, Tajikistan, Turkmenistan, and Uzbekistan.[21] It was a week after the Soviet Union broke up that China formally established diplomatic relations with the successor states.[22] China was initially reluctant to engage the region because of Russian dominance and believed the "Russian factor" would play a positive role in securing regional stability in Central Asia.[23] Since Kazakhstan, Kyrgyzstan, and Tajikistan shared a border with China, China first developed bilateral consultations with these states.[24] Afterwards, China developed diplomatic, economic, military, cultural, and energy ties with Turkmenistan and Uzbekistan. China's engagement of Central Asia is primarily driven by five factors: the economic development of Xinjiang, domestic political stability, regional stability, energy security, and the creation of alternative transport corridor to Europe.[25]

China and Kazakhstan have forged a close political relationship since diplomatic relations were established in 1992 much to the frustration of Russia. Bilateral relations were distinctly political initially but took on more of an economic dimension with significant Chinese investments in Kazakhstan's energy sector.[26]

A key feature of Kazakhstan's regime, which advances Sino-Kazakhstan's political ties, is that Kazakhstan is a state governed by authoritarian presidentialism.[27] While Kazakhstan professes to be a democracy, it restricts the freedom of the press and media.[28] Authoritarian presidentialism is manifested by Nursultan Nazarbayev, who was Kazakhstan's first-elected president in 1991. He has been the country's leader since 1989 and was reelected in 2011. He is considered one of the "ultimate oligarchs" of the former Soviet Republics, who transferred over $1 billion worth of Kazakhstan's oil revenues to his private bank accounts in other countries.[29] His family controls many key enterprises in Kazakhstan.[30] Authoritarian presidentialism is not restricted to Kazakhstan because all Central Asian Republics are characterized by this political trait. China has a certain affinity between Central Asia's authoritarian presidential regimes and its own, and in public, defends them with similar rhetoric.[31]

China and Kazakhstan met no less than 101 times through official, high-level dialogues and exchanges, dialogues, and communiqués between 1992 and 2000. Some of the most important exchanges include: President Jiang Zemin and President Nursultan Nazarbayev (October 1993, September 1995, April 1996, July 1996, April 1997, July 1998, August 1999, November 1999, and July 2000).[32] Since November 2000, both countries have met no less than 211 times.[33] The most important bilateral exchanges include: President Jiang Zemin and President Nursultan Nazarbayev (June 2002 and December 2002), President Hu Jintao and President Nursultan Nazarbayev (June 2003, May 2004, June 2004, July 2005, June 2006, December 2006, August 2007, April 2009, June 2010, February 2011, and June 2012), and President Xi Jinping and President Nursultan Nazarbayev (April 2013, September 2013, March 2014, May 2014, September 2014, April 2015, May 2015, August 2015, December 2015, and June 2016).[34] Specific topics discussed since diplomatic relations were established in 1992 include bilateral cooperation and exchanges in economics, trade, science and technology, air and ground transportation, culture, border security, meteorology, intermodal freight transportation, banking, extradition, energy, anti-trust, environment, seismology, land and river resources, public health, medicine, education, and Xinjiang.[35]

In the wake of bilateral ties, numerous treaties and agreements have been ratified by China and Kazakhstan. These include the following: a consular treaty (1992);[36] Joint Statement on the Foundation of Friendly Relations between the People's Republic of China and the Republic of Kazakhstan (1993);[37] Common Declaration about the Basis of Friendly Relationships between the Republic of Kazakhstan and the People's Republic of China (October 18, 1993);[38] Boundary Agreement (1994);[39] Agreement on Mutual Exemption of Entry Visas between the People's Republic of China and the Republic of Kazakhstan on Diplomatic, Service/Special Passports (February 1, 1994);[40] Joint Statement on Furthering Developing and Deepening Friendly Relations (1995);[41] An extradition treaty (1996);[42] Supplementary Boundary Agreement (1997);[43] Second Supplementary Boundary Agreement (1998);[44] Declaration on the Mutual Relations between the Member States on the Conference on Interaction and Confidence Measures (September 1999);[45] Common Declaration between the Republic of Kazakhstan and the People's Republic of China of Further Improvement of All-Round Collaboration in the 21st Century (November 23, 1999);[46] a Joint Communiqué on Complete Settlement of the Boundary Question (1999);[47] China-Kazakhstani Joint Communiqué (2001);[48] Protocol on the Demarcation of the State Line between China and Kazakhstan (May 10, 2002);[49] Treaty on Good-Neighborliness, Friendship and Cooperation between the People's Republic of China and the Republic of Kazakhstan (December 23, 2002);[50] Agreement on the Establishment of a China-Kazakhstan Cooperation Council (May 21, 2004);[51] Joint Statement on Establishing and Developing a Strategic Partnership between the People's Republic of China and the Republic of Kazakhstan (July 4, 2005);[52] Cooperation Agreements on Mineral Resources, Water Conservancy, Electricity, Communications, and Transportation (July 4, 2005);[53] Cooperation Strategy Between the People's Republic of China and the Republic of Kazakhstan for the 21st Century (December 20, 2006);[54] Agreement on the Management of the China-Kazakhstan Boundary between the Government of the People's Republic of China and the Government of the Republic of Kazakhstan (December 20, 2006);[55] Joint Communiqué between the People's Republic of China and the Republic of Kazakhstan (August 18, 2007);[56] Agreements on Economic, Trade, and Energy Cooperation (August 18, 2007);[57] Joint Communiqué between the People's Republic of China and the Republic of Kazakhstan (April 9, 2008);[58] Joint Communiqué between the People's Republic of China and the Republic of Kazakhstan (October 31, 2008);[59] Agreements on Customs, Public Health, Agriculture, Banking, Energy, and Science and Technology Cooperation (October 31, 2008);[60] Joint Statement Between the People's Republic of China and the Republic of Kazakhstan (July 17, 2009);[61] Comprehensive Strategic Partnership between the People's Republic of China and the Republic of Kazakhstan (2011);[62] China-Kazakhstan Joint Declaration on Further Deepening the Comprehensive Strategic Partnership (September 7, 2013);[63] Memorandum of Understanding on Cooperation between the National People's Congress of China and the Kazakh Parliament's Lower House (October 16, 2013);[64] Joint Communiqué of the Second Regular Meeting Between Premier of China and Prime Minister of Kazakhstan (December 12, 2014);[65] Cooperation Agreements in Energy, Transportation, Finance, People-to-People and Cultural Engagement, and Local-Level Cooperation (December 12, 2014);[66] Agreements in Economy and Trade, Investment, Finance, and Energy Cooperation (December 14, 2014);[67] Joint Declaration on New Stage of Comprehensive Strategic Partnership Between the People's Republic of China and the Republic of Kazakhstan (August 31, 2015);[68] Cooperation Agreements in Judicature, Production Capacity, Investment, People-to-People and Cultural Engagement, Infrastructure Construction, Mineral Exploitation, Finance, Convention and Exhibition (August 31, 2015);[69] Joint Statement Between the People's Republic of China and the Republic of Kazakhstan (December 14, 2015);[70] and Cooperation Agreements in Production Capacity, Finance, Energy, Customs, Quality Inspection and Tourism (December 14, 2015).[71]

The strategic partnerships of 2005 and 2011 will deepen bilateral political, economic, cultural, and security ties but will not constitute formal alliances between China and Kazakhstan.

China and Kazakhstan have established official representation in each other's respective countries. China has its embassy in Astana and Kazakhstan has its embassy in Beijing. China and Kazakhstan also have consulates. In China, Kazakhstan has a consulate in Hong Kong, a consulate general in Shanghai and China has a consulate in Almaty.

ECONOMIC/TRADE RELATIONS

Sino-Kazakhstani economic relations are robust. China was Kazakhstan's largest trading partner after the European Union and Kazakhstan was China's twenty-eighth largest trading partner in 2013.[72] Kazakhstan is also China's second largest trading partner among the Commonwealth of Independent States.[73] Bilateral trade was: $17.5 billion (2008), $13.9 billion (2009), $20.4 billion (2010), $24.8 billion (2011), $25.6 billion (2012), $28.5 billion (2013), $22.4 billion (2014), and $14.2 billion (2015).[74] Since 2000, bilateral trade increased ninefold. In 2012, foreign direct investment into Kazakhstan from China was $2.99 billion and foreign direct investment stock was $6.25 billion.[75]

In terms of bilateral trade, Table 6.1 shows the top five commodities traded between China and Kazakhstan in 2015. Energy commodities, which include crude petroleum and petroleum gas products, appear to be the most traded community. In terms of trade value, 35 percent is attributed to energy commodities, which includes crude petroleum and petroleum gas products. See Table 6.1. Kazakhstan is also rich in uranium, copper, gold, and nickel.[76]

In previous years, China's energy commodities accounted for the following in terms of trade value: 56 percent (2008), 45 percent (2009), 52 percent (2010), 63 percent (2011), 64 percent (2012), 63 percent (2013), and 47 percent (2014).[77]

Bilateral trade is promoted through several organizations such as the Astana Chamber of Commerce and Industry, the Chamber of Commerce and Industry of Kazakhstan, the Kazakhstani Corporation of Export Development and Promotion, the Kazakhstani Economic Research Institute, the Kazakhstani Ministry of Economy and Trade, the Kazakhstan Trade Information Center, the Asia Cooperation Dialogue, the PRC Ministry of Commerce, the PRC Ministry of Foreign Affairs, the All-China Federation of Industry and Commerce, the China-Kazakhstan Entrepreneurs Committee, the Kazakhstan-China Partnership for Success, the Shanghai Cooperation Organization (SCO), the Business Forum of the Conference on Cooperation and Confidence Building, and the Kazakhstan-China Business Council.[78]

Table 6.1 Top Five Commodities Traded between China and Kazakhstan

Commodity	Importer	Trade Value ($)	Percentage (%)
Mineral fuels, mineral oils, and products of their distillation; bituminous substances; mineral waxes	China	2,038,409,907	35
Inorganic chemicals; organic or inorganic compounds of precious metals, rare-earth metals, radioactive elements, or isotopes	China	1,491,804,825	26
Copper and articles thereof	China	954,097,363	16
Iron and steel	China	467,902,601	8
Ores, slag and ash	China	293,112,923	5
Footwear, gaiters and the like; parts of such articles	Kazakhstan	1,351,925,713	16
Nuclear reactors, boilers, machinery and mechanical appliances; parts thereof	Kazakhstan	1,329,779,295	16
Electrical machinery and equipment and parts thereof; sound recorders and reproducers, television image and sound recorders and reproducers, and parts and accessories of such articles	Kazakhstan	832,540,689	`10
Articles of apparel and clothing accessories, knitted or crocheted	Kazakhstan	557,702,656	7
Articles of apparel and clothing accessories, not knitted or crocheted	Kazakhstan	461,048,359	5

Source: United Nations Commodity Trade Statistics Database.

China and Kazakhstan have inked some important agreements to facilitate trade between their countries. The most notable agreements and notes include: Agreement on Opening Up Border Ports between the Two Countries (1992); Agreement on Mutual Visits by Citizens of Both Countries (1992); Government Agreement on Encouragement and Mutual Protection of Investment (1992); Agreement on the Establishment of the Committee of Cooperation in Economy and Trade and Science and Technology (1992); Agreement on the Opening of Shops by China in Kazakhstan (1992); Agreement on the Provision of Chinese Equipment and Commodity Loans to Kazakhstan (1992); Agreement on Transit Railway Transport (1992); Summary of Talks on the Development of Economic Relations (1992); Agreement on Civil Air Transport (1993); Summary of Talks on the Development of Railway Passenger and Freight Transport between China and Kazakhstan (1994); Agreement on the provision of Chinese Government Loans to Kazakhstan (1994); Agreement on the Utilization of the Lianyungang Port to Handle and Transship the Transit Freights of Kazakhstan (1995); Summary of Talks on Economic and Trade Cooperation (1995); Memorandum on Trade (1995);

Agreement on Cooperation between the People's Bank of China and the Kazakhstan National Bank (1996); Agreement on Cooperation in Quality Control and Mutual Certification of Import and Export Commodities (1996); Declaration on the Mutual Relations between the Member States of the Conference on Interaction and Confidence Measures in Asia (1999); Agreement on Cooperation between the two countries in Anti-Improper Competition and Anti-Monopoly (1999); Agreement on the Consultation of the Transshipment Volume of the 1999 Import, Export, and Transit Freights and the Safeguard Measures (1999); Agreement on the Provision of Chinese Government Loan of 100 million to Kazakhstan (1999); Agreement on Economic and Technological Cooperation (July 2000);[79] Agreement of Economic Cooperation (November 17, 2000);[80] Agreement on the Avoidance of Double Taxation (2001);[81] Cooperative Agreements on Economics, Trade, Energy, and Transportation (May 19, 2004);[82] Program for Economic Cooperation in the Non-Resources Sector between the Government of the People's Republic of China and the Government of the Republic of Kazakhstan (August 18, 2007);[83] Plan for Implementation Measures of the Program for Economic Cooperation in the Non-Resources Sector Between the Government of the People's Republic of China and the Government of the Republic of Kazakhstan (April 9, 2008);[84] Cooperation Agreements between Export-Import Bank of China (EXIM), China Development Bank (CDB), China National Petroleum Corporation (CNPC), China International Trust & Investment Corporation (CITIC), and Datang Group, and Kazakh enterprises (September 7, 2013);[85] and Memorandum of Understanding on strengthening Bilateral Production Capacity and Investment Cooperation (March 27, 2015).[86]

China and Kazakhstan also established two strategic partnerships in 2005 and 2011 to further their economic ties in addition to political ties.

China also has been actively involved in Kazakhstan's economic development. China has invested significantly to build highways, pipelines, railways, and electricity grids not only to further Kazakhstan socioeconomic development, but also to ensure that its regime remains friendly to China.[87] This approach not only applies to Kazakhstan but across Central Asia.[88] At least seven deals involving chemicals, energy, and aluminum metals were concluded since October 2005 totaling $6.2 billion in investment.[89] Some of the largest investments include: Shenzhen Zhongxing Telecom Equipment Corporation (ZTE) and Kazakhtelecom agreed to develop a wireless telecommunications network and install more efficient switching systems (2002);[90] China Nonferrous Metal Mining (Group) Co. Ltd. and Kazakhstan Aluminum Co. Ltd. agreed to build a $300 million aluminum plant (October 2005);[91] CDB provided a $2.7 billion line of credit to Kazakmys PLC to fund the development of the Bozshakol copper mining project (December 2009);[92] China Gezhouba Group Co. and Kazakhstan Natural Gas Technology Co.

agreed to build the Cascade Hydropower Station on the Chilik River for $730 million (February 2010);[93] Jinchuan Group Ltd. and Kazakhmys PLC (KAZ Minerals PLC) form a joint venture where Jinchuan Group Ltd. acquired a 49 percent stake to develop the Aktogay copper mining project for $120 million (April 2010);[94] CDB provided a $1.5 billion line of credit to Kazakmys PLC to fund the development of the Aktogay copper mining project (June 2011);[95] China International Water and Electric Corporation (CWE) was contracted by the Government of Kazakhstan to construct the Moynak Hydroelectric Power Plant on the Charyn River for $360 million, of which $200 million was funded by the CDB (June 2012);[96] and China Nonferrous Metal Mining (Group) Co. Ltd. and Kazakhmys PLC (KAZ Minerals PLC) form a joint venture to develop the Bozshakol copper mining project for $490 million (February 2014).[97]

Between 2005 and 2014, CDB, China Nonferrous Metal Mining (Group) Co. Ltd., China International Water and Electric Corporation, China Gezhouba Group Co., and Jinchuan Group Ltd. loaned, invested, granted, debt-relieved, or participated in Kazakhstan's development. CDB contributed $4.4 billion. Between 1991 and 2010, Chinese investment reached $13.5 billion, with the majority going to the energy sector and energy-related services.[98] China also allocated two credit lines to Kazakhstan's welfare fund Samruk Kazyna and to copper corporation Kazakmys totaling $13 billion in 2010 in the wake of global financial crisis.[99] In terms of banking and finance, the Bank of China and the Industrial and Commercial Bank of China opened branch offices in Almaty, the largest city in Kazakhstan.

Bilateral economic cooperation includes transportation. Chinese corporations like CSR have been working to modernize Kazakhstan's railways, passenger trains, and freight wagons since 2008.[100] CSR has sold Kazakhstan more than 100 trains and has become instrumental in providing essential services, maintenance, and technology to Kazakhstan National Railway Company (KNRC).[101]

China's principal economic interest in Kazakhstan is energy. China became involved in Kazakhstan's oil sector in June 1997 when CNPC purchased 60.3 percent of AktobeMunayGas Corporation for $43 billion followed by an additional 25.12 percent in May 2003.[102] CNPC is Kazakhstan's largest corporate investor with investments amounting to $7 billion to date.[103] Establishing economic ties with Kazakhstan is important not only to Sino-Kazakhstani trade but also to Xinjiang's stability because Xinjiang and Kazakhstan share a common physical border. Part of China's economic strategy in Central Asia is to use states like Kazakhstan to ensure Xinjiang's economic livelihood.[104] This in turn promotes political and economic stability in Xinjiang, especially since more than two-thirds of all Sino-Kazakhstani trade is between Xinjiang and Kazakhstan.[105] Notably, China allowed Xinjiang to trade with Central Asia, including Kazakhstan prior to the collapse of the Soviet Union in late 1991. Xinjiang served as a springboard to strengthen Chinese economic presence in Central Asia before and after the dissolution of the Soviet Union.[106]

MILITARY/SECURITY RELATIONS

Sino-Kazakhstan military-security relations appear to be very good today. Both countries have been developing military-security relations since diplomatic relations were established in 1992. China and Kazakhstan currently engage each other militarily through high-level exchanges and visits, security consultations, and joint military exercises. China also provides military training and carries out intelligence sharing with Kazakhstan as well as other Central Asian Republics.[107] Overall, China and Kazakhstan have engaged each other no less than twenty-eight times since 2002 according to the Ministry of National Defense of the People's Republic of China, *PLA Daily*, *Xinhua*, and *China Military Online*. These engagements include: seven visits to the PRC by Kazakhstani military officials, six visits to Kazakhstan by Chinese military officials, six SCO security consultations, six joint anti-terrorism military exercises, and joint military training (patrols, search and rescue, and International Army Games). China and Kazakhstan have also assigned defense attachés at their respective embassies in Beijing and Astana.[108]

Some of the more recent joint military interactions that are notable include: "Peace Mission" anti-terrorism exercises (2003, 2007, 2010, 2012, and 2014) and bilateral and multilateral security consultations which include members of the SCO and joint border patrols. As a member of the SCO, Kazakhstan is focused on the security of Central Asia from the threats of terrorism, separatism, and extremism.[109] Created on June 15, 2001, the SCO is primarily a multilateral military-security organization made up of China, Russia, Kazakhstan, Kyrgyzstan, Tajikistan, and Uzbekistan, otherwise known as the Shanghai Six. The SCO was formerly known as the Shanghai Five Forum, a multilateral security organization consisting of China, Russia, Kazakhstan, Kyrgyzstan, and Tajikistan. Created on April 26, 1996 with the signing of the *Treaty on Deepening Military Trust in the Border Regions*, the purpose of the Shanghai Five Forum was to facilitate border demarcation, border demilitarization, securing support for China's policies in Xinjiang, and strengthen military trust.[110] Prior to the 9/11 terrorist attacks on the United States, Uzbekistan joined the Shanghai Five and the organization became the SCO. After the 9/11 terrorist attacks, the SCO adopted an anti-terrorist role. In June 2002, SCO signed the *Agreement on Regional Anti-Terrorism Structure* (RATS) for a clear-cut legal framework to deal with terrorism, separatism, and extremism.[111] The SCO's goals are especially important with respect to Xinjiang, a strategic region for China as well all Central Asian oil and gas pipelines linking the eastern part of China to Central Asia.[112] This includes any railway links between Western China and Central Asia. The eruption of violence in Xinjiang could seriously affect Chinese oil imports from Central Asia and threaten China's energy security.[113] China needs to maintain Xinjiang's stability and security cooperation with its Central Asian neighbors since both railroads and oil and gas pipelines are vulnerable to terrorist attacks.[114] Xinjiang's strategic importance to both China and Kazakhstan is underscored by the fact that it is the most northwestern region of China, borders Kazakhstan, Kyrgyzstan, and Tajikistan, and lies between Kazakhstan and the rest of China, making it the political and economic gateway to Kazakhstan. Additionally, the Uyghurs living in Kazakhstan, Kyrgyzstan, and Tajikistan have developed strong ethnic and cultural ties with the Uyghurs of Xinjiang province.[115] The Central Asian Republics play a vital role in maintaining both Xinjiang's security and regional security because they can restrict and prohibit "East Turkestan" forces from conducting subversive activities in their territories and prevent terrorist and extremist forces from sneaking into China from their territories.[116] Any breakdown in Central Asia could undermine the security of Western China in general and Xinjiang in particular.[117] To this extent, Kazakhstan supports China's territorial integrity. Kazakhstan specifically supports China's One-China policy and opposes Taiwan's independence.[118]

In addition to energy security threats, China is concerned about ETIM. As a violent separatist group, ETIM has been responsible for many terrorist attacks in Xinjiang. ETIM seeks to create the state of East Turkestan, independent of China. China also worries about Afghanistan becoming a base for Uyghur separatists in Xinjiang and a repetition of the Arab Spring in Central Asia, which could spill over into Western China.[119]

Economic and cultural cooperation also occur within the SCO network. Economically, all SCO members except China are also members of the Eurasian Economic Community. A framework agreement to enhance economic cooperation was signed by the SCO member states on September 23, 2003. At the same meeting, then Chinese Premier, Wen Jiabao proposed a long-term objective to establish a free trade area using the SCO. Culturally, the cultural ministers of SCO met for the first time in Beijing on April 12, 2002, signing a joint statement for continued cooperation. Their third meeting took place in Tashkent, Uzbekistan, on April 27–28, 2006. Since the founding of the SCO, approximately fourteen summits have occurred between SCO heads of state and thirteen summits between the SCO heads of government.

Aside from multilateral security cooperation in the SCO, China and Kazakhstan have signed agreements for their mutual security. Some the agreements executed include:

Memorandum of Cooperation Between the Ministries of National Defense (1995); Agreement on Confidence Building in the Military Field in Border Areas between the People's Republic of China, the Republic of Kazakhstan, the Kyrgyz Republic, the Russian Federation and the Republic of Tajikistan (1996); and Agreement on Mutual Reduction of Military Forces in the Border Areas between the People's Republic of China, the Republic of Kazakhstan, the Kyrgyz Republic, the Russian Federation and the Republic of Tajikistan (1997).[120]

China does not supply military weapons or equipment to Kazakhstan. Kazakhstan's chief arms vendor has been the Soviet Union during the Cold War and its successor Russia in the Post–Cold War period. Kazakhstan has also established itself as a close ally of Russia and an important member of the Russian-backed Collective Security Treaty Organization (CSTO). The United States has also supplied arms and equipment to Kazakhstan after Kazakhstan succeeded from the Soviet Union in 1991 according to SIPRI. Kazakhstan has engaged in considerable defense cooperation with the United States and Europe under the auspices of the North Atlantic Treaty Organization (NATO) Partnership for Peace (PfP) framework.[121]

CULTURAL RELATIONS

China and Kazakhstan have established cultural ties since diplomatic relations were established in 1992. In this respect, several agreements have been signed to promote cultural ties between the two countries. Those agreements include: Government Agreement on Cultural Cooperation (1992); Government agreement on Official Business Travel by Citizens of the Two Countries (1993); 1993–1994 Program of Cultural Cooperation between the Culture Ministries (1994); Agreement on Science and Technology Cooperation (1994); Agreement on Cooperation in Meteorological Technology (1995); Agreement on Educational Cooperation between the State Education Commission of the People's Republic of China and the Education Ministry of the Republic of Kazakhstan (1996); Agreement on Tourism Cooperation 1998); Agreement on Cooperation in Space Research and Exploitation for Peaceful Purposes (1998); 1998–2000 Program of Cultural Cooperation (1998); Exchange of Letters on the Provision of Free Aid by China to Kazakhstan (2001); Agreement of Cooperation on the Exploitation and Protection of the Trans-Border Rivers (2001); Agreement of Scientific and Technological Cooperation on Seismological Research (2001); Agreement on Cooperation in Public Health and Medicine (2001); and 2001–2002 Cultural Cooperation Plan between the Ministry of Culture of the People's Republic of China and the Ministry of Culture, Information and Social Coordination of the Republic of Kazakhstan (2001).[122]

When China and Kazakhstan established a strategic partnership in 2005, the two countries agreed to expand cultural cooperation and people-to-people ties.

China also engages Kazakhstan culturally through the Confucius Institutes. Currently, there are four Confucius Institutes in Kazakhstan: Confucius Institute at Aktobe State Pedagogical Institute, Confucius Institute at Kazakh National University, Confucius Institute at National Technical University of Karaganda of Kazakhstan, and Confucius Institute at Eurasian University.[123] Confucius Institutes are an important tool for developing cultural and educational ties between countries, which includes Chinese language training and classroom instruction on Chinese culture. China and Kazakhstan will also develop the Khorgos International Border Cooperation Center in the near future to promote people-to-people ties.

Sino-Kazakhstani cultural ties have been in existence before official ties were first established in January 1992. In ancient times, Chinese and Kazakhstani merchants and traders engaged each other along the Silk Road. Economic and cultural ties developed in the aftermath. Xinjiang played an important role in establishing economic and cultural ties with Kazakhstan as it shares a common border with China. China authorized Xinjiang authorities to negotiate with Central Asian leaders in order to implement and develop trade and cultural ties.[124] Ethnic ties also developed between the Uyghurs of Xinjiang and Kazakhstan through mitigation of peoples across their common borders. Today, approximately 180,000 Uyghurs live in Kazakhstan and one million ethnic Kazakhs live in China, especially in Xinjiang.[125]

China and Kazakhstan promote cross-cultural ties between ethnic Uyghurs through various venues such as national and regional cultural weeks to channel cross-border contacts, clarify Beijing's policy toward Xinjiang, and promote trade as well as Kazakh investment in Xinjiang. Both countries have also established a tradition of commemorating the establishment of diplomatic ties, most notably in 2012 on their twentieth anniversary.[126]

With the exception of the Sino-Soviet split (1960–1977), bilateral cultural ties developed smoothly. After the Soviet collapse in December 1991, bilateral cultural ties expanded to include cooperation in the arts, aviation, tourism, space research and exploration, education, literature, music, sports, science and technology, public health and medicine, meteorological technology, and people-to-people contacts.

In terms of aviation cooperation, China and Kazakhstan opened direct flights between Almaty and Beijing in 1994. In terms of art and culture, Kazakhstan participated in the 2010 Shanghai International Expo. It established its own pavilion and attracted thousands of visitors. The pavilion showcased Kazakhstan's history and depicted its multiethnic and multicultural nature. In terms of sports, Kazakhstan supported China's hosting of the 2008 Summer Olympics Games and participated in them. Educational exchanges have also progressed between the two countries. Over 8,000 Kazakh students are studying at China's most prestigious universities in the fields of medicine, petroleum engineering, pharmacy, economics, and technology.[127] It is important to note that bilateral cultural cooperation was officially memorialized through the signing of multiple agreements and implementation of programs since 1992.

ENERGY/PETROLEUM RELATIONS

Energy development and exports dominates Sino-Kazakhstani relations.[128] China considers Central Asia, especially Kazakhstan a crucial element in its energy equation.[129] Central Asian countries like Kazakhstan can play a major role in helping China to diversify its energy suppliers and reduce its reliance on Middle East oil exporters where China gets most of its petroleum.[130] Kazakhstan is attractive to China because it has the second largest oil reserves as well as the second largest oil production among the former Soviet Republics after Russia.[131] Kazakhstan also stands as a major oil producing and exporting country to international markets, which includes China, because of its vast oil and gas reserves and very low public consumption.[132] Also, sharing a common physical border with China through Xinjiang makes it easy for Kazakhstan to transport the needed oil and gas supplies to China via pipeline and rail. Most of Kazakhstan's crude oil is exported to Europe via the Baku-Tbilisi-Ceyhan (BTC) pipeline which runs from Baku, Azerbaijan to Ceyhan, Turkey through Tbilisi, Georgia, and through the Northern Route pipeline from Baku, Azerbaijan to Novorossiysk, Russia, a Black Sea port.[133] In 2013, 76 percent of Kazakhstan's crude oil was exported to Europe.[134] Other major oil export routes include the Caspian Consortium Pipeline from Tengiz, Kazakhstan to Novorossiysk, Russia, and the Uzen-Atyrau-Samara (UAS) pipeline to Russia.[135] Another potential export route is through Iran via oil swaps; however, Western sanctions against Iran have complicated Iranian-Kazakhstani oil swaps and no crude oil has been swapped since 2013.[136]

Kazakhstan is China's largest supplier of crude petroleum in Central Asia. China imported 2 to 4 percent of its crude petroleum from Kazakhstan between 2006 and 2015 inclusive. In terms of total trade value, crude petroleum imports ranged from 32 to 59 percent for the same years. Table 6.2 shows Chinese crude oil imports from Kazakhstan in thousands of barrels per day, oil imports share, world ranking, trade value, total commodity trade value, and percentage from 2006 to 2015. See Table 6.2.

Crude petroleum is exported to China from Kazakhstan via pipeline. The pipeline, which spans 1,384 miles, runs from Atyrau Port in northwestern Kazakhstan to Alashankou in China's northwestern region.[137]

Table 6.2 Chinese Crude Petroleum Imports from Kazakhstan

Year	KBPD	Oil Imports Share (%)	World Ranking	Crude Oil Trade Value ($)	Total Commodity Trade Value ($)	Percentage (%)
2006	54	2	14	1,268,934,765	3,607,272,782	35
2007	120	4	7	2,954,061,957	6,431,909,440	46
2008	114	3	9	4,172,746,210	7,727,827,943	54
2009	121	3	10	2,543,538,629	6,255,599,827	41
2010	202	4	8	5,552,401,247	11,108,591,383	50
2011	225	4	9	8,858,660,120	15,349,865,821	58
2012	215	4	8	8,719,228,570	14,675,446,558	59
2013	241	4	8	9,375,483,702	16,050,838,003	58
2014	114	2	14	4,222,821,654	9,739,792,558	43
2015	100	1	14	1,887,216,826	5,840,303,976	32

Source: United Nations Commodity Trade Statistics Database.

The Kazakhstan-China oil pipeline, a joint venture of CNPC and KazMunayGas (KMG) was built in three sections. The first section, linking Atyrau (north Caspian) to the Aktobe oil fields (western Kazakhstan) was completed in 2003. The second section, linking Atasu (central Kazakhstan) to the border town of Alashankou in Xinjiang, was completed in December 2005. The third section, which connects Kenkiyak with Kumpol, was completed on July 11, 2009. This pipeline makes it possible to pump oil directly from the northern Caspian to the Dushanzi refinery in Xinjiang.[138] The pipeline reduces Kazakhstan's economic dependency on Russia and weakens Russian influence and soft power in the Central Asian region.[139]

China also imports petroleum gas products from Kazakhstan but not liquefied natural gas (LNG). Kazakhstan's largest petroleum fields contain substantial volumes of natural gas, most of which is re-injected into oil wells to improve recovery rates.[140] Table 6.3 illustrates China's petroleum gas imports from Kazakhstan in millions of cubic feet, global imports share, world ranking, trade value, total commodity trade value, and percentage from 2006 to 2015. See Table 6.3. This table reveals that Kazakhstan is a sporadic exporter of petroleum gas products to China. While Kazakhstan does not export natural gas to China, it does export natural gas through two major pipelines; the Central Asia Center pipeline and the Central Asia-China (Turkmenistan-China) pipeline.[141] The Central Asia Center pipeline runs from Dauletabad gas field in Okarem, Turkmenistan to Alexandrov Gay, Russia via Uzbekistan and Kazakhstan while the Central Asia-China pipeline runs from Amu Darya, Turkmenistan to Horgos, Xinjiang, China via Kazakhstan. A third major pipeline, the Bukhara-Tashkent-Bishkek-Almaty pipeline, serves local demand in southern Kazakhstan with imported gas

Table 6.3   Chinese Petroleum Gas Product Imports from Kazakhstan

Year	Volume (MMcf)	Global Share (%)	World Ranking	Petroleum Gas Trade Value ($)	Total Commodity Trade Value ($)	Percentage (%)
2006	0.21	<1	21	1,706,112	3,607,272,782	<1
2008	0.000012	<1	23	300	7,727,827,943	<1
2010	0.10	<1	26	998,043	11,108,591,383	<1
2011	0.34	<1	23	4,672,702	15,349,865,821	<1
2012	0.43	<1	23	5,028,488	14,675,446,558	<1
2013	5.92	<1	16	36,333,371	16,050,838,003	<1
2014	17.37	<1	15	136,817,336	9,739,792,558	1
2015	16.17	<1	15	93,081,650	5,840,303,976	2

Source: United Nations Commodity Trade Statistics Database

from Turkmenistan and Uzbekistan.[142] A fourth natural gas pipeline is currently being constructed pipeline as of February 2014: the Beyneu-Bozoy-Shymkent pipeline.[143] This pipeline is a joint CNPC-KMG project and is being built in two sections (Beyneu-Bozoy and Bozoy-Shymkent).[144] When finished, the pipeline will carry 6 billion cubic meters of natural gas from the Caspian Sea to Xinjiang across Kazakhstan's southern provinces.[145] It is imperative to note that these natural gas pipelines help China to counterbalance Russian soft power in the Central Asia.[146] Petroleum gas product trading did not occur in 2007 and 2009.

China has robust oil and gas acquisitions in Kazakhstan. See Table 6.4.

To facilitate Chinese oil trade and investment including oil and gas pipeline development in Kazakhstan, China and Kazakhstan signed important agreements: Agreement on Cooperation in Petroleum and Natural Gas (September 24, 1997);[147] General Agreement on the projects of oil fields development and pipeline construction between the China National Petroleum and Natural Gas Corporation and the Ministry of Energy and Mineral Resources of the Republic of Kazakhstan (1997);[148] Framework Agreement on Projects for Fields Development and Construction of West Kazakhstan-China Oil Pipeline between CNPC and Ministry of Energy and Natural Resources of Kazakhstan (September 1997);[149] Agreement to conduct a joint study for the West Kazakhstan-China Oil Pipeline between CNPC and KazTransOil (June 1998);[150] Agreement between the Chinese National Oil Development Company (CNODC) and the Kazakh National Oil Transportation Company "Kaztransoil" (KTO) about Mutual Preparation of Technical-Economic Justification of a Western Kazakhstan-China Pipeline (June 13, 1998);[151] Agreement on Cooperation in the Oil and Gas Sector between the Governments of Kazakhstan and China (September 1999);[152] Agreement on Joint Study of the Two-Stage Construction of the Kazakhstan-China Pipeline between KMG and CNPC (June 2003);[153] Program of Collaboration between the Republic

Table 6.4 Chinese Oil and Gas Acquisitions in Kazakhstan

Date	Company	Acquisition
March15	Geo-Jade Petroleum	Acquired 100% of KoZhan Joint Stock Company for $350 million
April14	Sinopec	Plans to purchase 50% stake in OAO Lukoil's Caspian Investment Resources, Ltd. for $1.2 billion
December13	Hainan Zhenghe Industrial Group	Purchased 95% of Kazakh oil production company Maten Petroleum for 500 million
September13	CNPC	Signed an agreement to buy 8.33% of the giant Kashagan oil project (for $5 billion), Kazakhstan's offshore oilfield in the Caspian Sea from ConocoPhillips. Other partners include Shell, Eni, Total, ExxonMobil, KazMunayGas, and INPEX
August10	Sinopec	Acquires 50% of Capital Investment Resources Ltd.
September09	CIC	Purchased 11% stake in KMG for $939 million by purchasing global depository receipts
September09	Xinjiang Guanghui Investment	Purchased Kazakhstan TBM's 49% share for $300 million to jointly develop Zaysan block in eastern Kazakhstan
April09	CNPC and KMG	Purchased MMG in Kazakhstan assets with KMG for $1.7 Billion
2006	CITIC Resources Holdings	Purchased 50% of JSC Karazhanbasmunai for assets in Kazakhstan for $500 million
December05	CNPC/ KazMunayGas	Completed Atasu-Alashankou oil pipeline; completely operational in July 2006
October05	CNOOC and CNPC	Signed an MOU with KazMunaiGas Exploration Production to explore the offshore Darkhan oil field
October05	CNPC	Acquired PetroKazakhstan
January05	CNPC	Acquired a 100% in ADM, which has exploration licenses in Aryss & Blinov blocks.
November04	CNPC and NORINCO	Jointly acquired 50% of Konys & Bektas oil field.
October04	Sinopec	Purchased $153 million worth of Kazakh oil assets from First International Oil Corporation, a small U.S. firm.
February04	CNPC	Conveyed a 50% stake of North Buzachi Inc. to Canadian company Nelson Resources for $90 million.
October03	CNPC	Bought out ChevronTexaco's interests of North Buzachi, Inc.
May03	CNPC	Purchased a 25% interest in AktobeMunaigas Corp. increasing its total interest to 85%
June97	CNPC	Purchased 60% of AktobeMunaiGas Production Association for $43 billion

Source: Julie Jiang and Chen Dang, *Update on Overseas Investments by Chinese National Companies: Achievements and Challenges since 2011*, Organization for Economic Cooperation and Development/ International Energy Agency, June 2014, 35-39.

of Kazakhstan and the People's Republic of China for the Years 2003–2008 (June 2003);[154] Memorandum for Accelerating Construction of the First Stage of Kazakhstan-China Pipeline between CNODC and KMG (August 2003);[155] Agreement on the Main Principles for Construction of the Atasu-Alashankou Pipeline between KMG and CNPC (May 2004);[156] Framework Agreement on Comprehensive Cooperation in Oil and Gas between the Government of the People's Republic of China and the Government of the Republic of Kazakhstan (May 21, 2004);[157] Agreement on Joining KazTransOil's and Atasu-Alashankou Pipeline Systems (May 2005);[158] and Agreement on Operation and Maintenance of the Atasu-Alashankou Pipeline between Kazakhstan-China Pipeline Company and KazTransOil (March 2006).[159]

These agreements provided the foundation for and enhancement of Sino-Kazakhstani petroleum relations. The *Program of Collaboration* document was especially important because it declared the strategic importance of collaboration in the energy sector for both countries.[160]

Sino-Kazakhstani energy cooperation began in June 1997 when CNPC purchased 60.3 percent of AktobeMunaiGas Production Association for $43 billion followed by an additional 25.12 percent in May 2003. CNPC was not the first oil company in Kazakhstan as Western oil companies like Chevron and BP sought to develop Kazakhstan's oil and gas sector, which included energy rights and acquisitions immediately after the collapse of the Soviet Union.[161] CNPC made additional investments in Kazakhstan's oil and gas sector in the twenty-first century along with other Chinese oil companies like CIC, CITIC, CNOOC, Hainan Zhenghe Industrial Group Norinco, Sinopec, and Xinjiang Guanghui Investment. These acquisitions are shown in Table 6.5.

Chinese oil-related projects in Kazakhstan have been backed by loans from the Export-Import Bank of China (EXIM). These loans include: Export-Import Bank of China and Sinopec Engineering loaned $1.13 billion to a Sinopec Engineering-KazMunayGas (KMG) joint venture to modernize an oil refinery in Atyrau (December 2009); and Export-Import Bank of China loaned the Government of Kazakhstan $1.13 billion to build an oil refinery in Atyrau (June 2012).[162]

Energy cooperation also extends to a range of oil field services including geophysical prospecting, well-drilling, logging, and testing. In terms of drilling, CNPC successfully drilled through Kazakhstan's Kenkiyak subsalt reservoir in 2008, a deep buried reservoir which presented one of the most difficult drilling conditions in the world. CNPC was also involved in the construction of the major oil and gas pipelines running through Kazakhstan: the Central Asia-China Gas Pipeline, the Kazakhstan-China Gas Pipeline, and the Kazakhstan-China Oil Pipeline.[163]

Energy cooperation also includes the mining of Kazakhstani uranium. China's joint ventures in uranium mining in Kazakhstan are conducted by

China National Nuclear Corporation and the China Guangdong Nuclear Power Company. These companies have less than 50 percent of the shares in Kazakhstan's mines that produce roughly 1,000 tons of uranium annually. Approximately 20 percent of Kazakhstan's annual uranium exports are destined for China.[164]

Other forms of energy cooperation include hydroelectric power and solar power. In 2010, China and Kazakhstan agreed to invest $3 million each to build a new hydroelectric plant, the Jorgos River Hydropower Plant in Almaty, Kazakhstan.[165] China International Water and Electric Corporation (CWE) was contracted by the Government of Kazakhstan to construct the Moynak Hydroelectric Power Plant on the Charyn River for $360 million in June 2012.[166] Kazakhstan has also agreed to provide 40 million kilowatts per hour on an annual basis to China by virtue of the 2005 Sino-Kazakhstani strategic partnership.[167]

In terms of wind power, CDB signed a Memorandum of Understanding with Kazakhstan to develop a 50 MW wind power plant in Pavlodar. On September 1, 2015, Sam Rook energy company, Kazakhstan Development Bank, and the CDB agreed on the financing for Chilik Corridor wind power plant project Corridor 60 megawatts (coming up to 300 megawatts). CDB will provide $120 million USD for the project, while Kazakhstan Development Bank will provide $35 million.[168]

SUMMARY

Sino-Kazakhstani relations date back to the ancient Silk Road; however, bilateral ties are strategic today. Both are engaged diplomatically, economically, militarily, and culturally. Xinjiang province is the centerpiece of Sino-Kazakhstani overall relations because Xinjiang's political and economic stability is the key to the stability of both the countries as well as Central Asia. Kazakhstan is also China's largest crude petroleum supplier in Central Asia; however, Kazakhstan is only a sporadic petroleum gas supplier. Nevertheless, Kazakhstan helps China to diversify its oil suppliers and reduce its dependence on crude petroleum suppliers from the Middle East. China helps Kazakhstan through foreign capital investment and by developing its energy sector.

In terms of energy cooperation, China has invested heavily in Kazakhstan's oil and gas industry. National oil companies like CNPC and Sinopec have acquired oil and gas assets sharing ownership with Kazakhstan's KMG and AtkobeMunaiGas. China has also helped construct major oil and gas pipelines in Kazakhstan especially the Kazakhstan-China oil pipeline which leads into Western China. Chinese investments in oil and gas industry helped

Kazakhstan to be less politically and economically dependent on Russia in the wake of the breakup of the Soviet Union. Essentially, China acts as a hedge against Russian influence over its former Soviet states in Central Asia and as a weight to counterbalance Russian soft power. China and Kazakhstan also cooperate in the nuclear and hydroelectric power sectors. China mines and exports Kazakhstani uranium and agreed to construct the Moynak Hydroelectric Power Plant. Kazakhstan agreed to provide 40 million kilowatts per hour on an annual basis to China based on the Sino-Kazakhstani strategic partnership.

NOTES

1. "China and Kazakhstan," *CCTV*, (n.d.), accessed March 7, 2015, http://www.cctv.com/lm/1039/20/3.html.
2. Ibid.
3. John C. K. Daly, "Kazakhstan Nervously Contemplates Possible Impact of Sanctions Against Russia," *Eurasia Daily Monitor* (Jamestown Foundation), Volume XI, Issue 95, May 21, 2014.
4. Indra Overland, Stina Torjesen, and Heidi Kjaernet, "Introduction: China and Russia: Partners or Firewalls for the Caspian Petro-States?" in Indra Overland, Stina Torjesen, and Heidi Kjaernet, eds., *Caspian Energy Politics: Azerbaijan, Kazakhstan, and Turkmenistan* (New York, NY: Routledge), 2011, 98.
5. Bates McGill and Matthew Oresman, *China's New Journey to the West: China's Emergence in Central Asia and Implications for U.S. Interests* (Washington, DC: Center for Strategic and International Studies), August 2003, 3.
6. Ibid.
7. Ibid., 4.
8. Ibid.
9. Ablat Khodzhaev, "The Central Asian Policy of the People's Republic of China," *China and Eurasia Forum Quarterly* (Central Asia-Caucasus Institute & Silk Road Studies Program), Volume 7, Issue 1, February 2009, 10.
10. Ibid.
11. McGill and Oresman, ibid., 4.
12. Ibid.
13. Ibid.
14. International Crisis Group, *China's Central Asia Problem*, Crisis Group Asia Report No. 244, February 27, 2013, 8, accessed February 28, 2015, http://www.crisisgroup.org/~/media/files/asia/north-east-asia/244-chinas-central-asia-problem.pdf.
15. Ibid.
16. McGill and Oresman, ibid., 16.
17. Marc Lanteigne, "China's Central Asian Energy Diplomacy," in Indra Overland, Stina Torjesen, and Heidi Kjaernet, eds., *Caspian Energy Politics: Azerbaijan, Kazakhstan, and Turkmenistan* (New York, NY: Routledge), 2011, 101–102.

18. Lauren Dickey, "China Takes Steps Toward Realizing Silk Road Ambitions," *China Brief* (Jamestown Foundation), Volume XIV, Issue 11, June 14, 2014, 3.
19. Ibid.
20. International Crisis Group, ibid.
21. Naseer Ahmed Kalis, "Chinese Energy Investment in Kazakhstan: Challenges and Future Prospects," *International Journal of Scientific Research and Education*, Volume 2, Issue 1, January 2014, 264–274.
22. Ibid.
23. Ibid.
24. Ibid., 265–266.
25. Thrassy N. Marketos, *China's Energy Geopolitics: The Shanghai Cooperation Organization and Central Asia* (New York, NY: Routledge), 2009, 19.
26. Sebastien Peyrouse, "Chinese Economic Presence in Kazakhstan: China's Resolve and Central Asia's Apprehension," *China Perspectives* (France: French Centre for Research on Contemporary China), March 2008, 35.
27. Kalis, ibid., 267.
28. Ibid.
29. Sergei Guriev and Andrei Rachinsky, *The Evolution of Personal Wealth in the Former Soviet Union and Central and Eastern Europe* (Helsinki, Finland: UNU World Institute for Development Economics Research), Research Paper No. 2006/120, October 2006, 10, footnote 14.
30. Ibid.
31. International Crisis Group, ibid.
32. "China and Kazakhstan," ibid.
33. Ministry of Foreign Affairs of People's Republic of China, "China–Kazakhstan: Activities," (n.d.), accessed August 9, 2016, http://www.fmprc.gov.cn/mfa_eng/wjb_663304/zzjg_663340/dozys_664276/gjlb_664280/3180_664322/3182_664326/default.shtml.
34. Ibid.
35. "China and Kazakhstan," ibid.
36. Ibid.
37. Ibid.
38. Zhanibek Saurbek, "Kazakh-Chinese Energy Relations: Economic Pragmatism or Political Cooperation?" *China and Eurasia Forum Quarterly* (Central Asia-Caucasus Institute & Silk Road Studies Program), Volume 6, Issue 1, February 2008, 87.
39. "China and Kazakhstan," ibid.
40. Ministry of Foreign Affairs of People's Republic of China, "List of Agreements on Mutual Visa Exemption Between the People's Republic of China and Foreign Countries" November 28, 2004, accessed February 27, 2015, http://cs.mfa.gov.cn/wgrlh/bgzl/P020140328398504621618.pdf.
41. "China and Kazakhstan," ibid.
42. Ibid.
43. Ibid.
44. Ibid.

45. Ibid.
46. Saurbek, ibid., 88.
47. "China and Kazakhstan," ibid.
48. Ibid.
49. Ramakant Dwivedi, "China's Central Asia Policy in Recent Times," *China and Eurasia Forum Quarterly* (Central Asia-Caucasus Institute & Silk Road Studies Program), Volume 4, Issue 4, November 2006, 146.
50. Ministry of Foreign Affairs of People's Republic of China, "Joint Statement Between the People's Republic of China and the Republic of Kazakhstan," April 17, 2009, accessed February 27, 2015, http://www.fmprc.gov.cn/mfa_eng/wjb_663304/zzjg_663340/dozys_664276/gjlb_664280/3180_664322/3181_664324/t559688.shtml.
51. Ministry of Foreign Affairs of People's Republic of China, "President Hu Jintao Holds Talks with His Kazakh Counterpart," May 21, 2004, accessed August 21, 2016, http://www.fmprc.gov.cn/mfa_eng/wjb_663304/zzjg_663340/dozys_664276/gjlb_664280/3180_664322/3182_664326/t115553.shtml.
52. Ministry of Foreign Affairs of People's Republic of China, "Joint Statement Between the People's Republic of China and the Republic of Kazakhstan," ibid.
53. Ministry of Foreign Affairs of People's Republic of China, "Hu Jintao Holds Talks with Nazarbayev and Announces the Establishment of Strategic Partnership between China and Kazakhstan," July 4, 2005, accessed August 21, 2016, http://www.fmprc.gov.cn/mfa_eng/wjb_663304/zzjg_663340/dozys_664276/gjlb_664280/3180_664322/3182_664326/t202534.shtml.
54. Ministry of Foreign Affairs of People's Republic of China, "Joint Statement Between the People's Republic of China and the Republic of Kazakhstan," ibid.
55. Ministry of Foreign Affairs of People's Republic of China, "Hu Jintao Holds Talks with His Kazakh Counterpart Nazarbayev," December 20, 2006, accessed August 21, 2016, http://www.fmprc.gov.cn/mfa_eng/wjb_663304/zzjg_663340/dozys_664276/gjlb_664280/3180_664322/3182_664326/t285010.shtml.
56. Ministry of Foreign Affairs of People's Republic of China, "Hu Jintao Holds Talks with His Kazakh Counterpart Nazarbayev," August 18, 2007, accessed August 21, 2016, http://www.fmprc.gov.cn/mfa_eng/wjb_663304/zzjg_663340/dozys_664276/gjlb_664280/3180_664322/3182_664326/t353591.shtml.
57. Ibid.
58. Ministry of Foreign Affairs of People's Republic of China, "Premier Wen Jiabao Holds Talks with Kazakh Prime Minister Masimov," April 9, 2008, accessed August 21, 2016, http://www.fmprc.gov.cn/mfa_eng/wjb_663304/zzjg_663340/dozys_664276/gjlb_664280/3180_664322/3182_664326/t423831.shtml.
59. Ministry of Foreign Affairs of People's Republic of China, "Wen Jiabao Holds Talks with His Kazakh Counterpart Masimov in Astana," October 31, 2008, accessed August 21, 2016, http://www.fmprc.gov.cn/mfa_eng/wjb_663304/zzjg_663340/dozys_664276/gjlb_664280/3180_664322/3182_664326/t520789.shtml.
60. Ibid.
61. Ministry of Foreign Affairs of People's Republic of China, "Joint Statement Between the People's Republic of China and the Republic of Kazakhstan," ibid.

62. Zhongping Feng and Jing Huang, "China's Strategic Partnership Diplomacy: Engaging with a Changing World" (Fride and ESPO), Working Paper No. 8, June 2014, accessed August 17, 2014, http://www.fride.org/descarga/WP8_China_strategic_partnership_diplomacy.pdf.

63. Ministry of Foreign Affairs of People's Republic of China, "Xi Jinping Holds Talks with President Nursultan Nazarbayev of Kazakhstan Promote Good-Neighbourly Friendship, Mutual Benefit and Win-win Outcomes to Deepen China-Kazakhstan Comprehensive Strategic Partnership," September 7, 2013, accessed August 21, 2016, http://www.fmprc.gov.cn/mfa_eng/wjb_663304/zzjg_663340/dozys_664276/gjlb_664280/3180_664322/3182_664326/t1075414.shtml.

64. Ministry of Foreign Affairs of People's Republic of China, "Zhang Dejiang Holds Talks with Nurlan Nigmatulin, Speaker of the Kazakh Parliament's Lower House," October 16, 2013, accessed August 21, 2016, http://www.fmprc.gov.cn/mfa_eng/wjb_663304/zzjg_663340/dozys_664276/gjlb_664280/3180_664322/3182_664326/t1090479.shtml.

65. Ministry of Foreign Affairs of People's Republic of China, "Ministry of Foreign Affairs Holds Briefing for Chinese and Foreign Media on Premier Li Keqiang's Visit to Kazakhstan and Holding of Second Regular Meeting with Prime Minister of Kazakhstan, Attendance at 13th Meeting of the Council of Heads of Government of the SCO Member States, Attendance at Third Meeting of Heads of Government of China and CEEC and Visit to Serbia, and Attendance at Fifth Summit of the Greater Mekong Subregion Economic Cooperation Program," December 12, 2014, accessed August 21, 2016, http://www.fmprc.gov.cn/mfa_eng/wjb_663304/zzjg_663340/dozys_664276/gjlb_664280/3180_664322/3182_664326/t1219578.shtml.

66. Ibid.

67. Ministry of Foreign Affairs of People's Republic of China, "Li Keqiang Arrives in Astana to Pay an Official Visit to Kazakhstan and Attend the Prime Ministers' Meeting of the Shanghai Cooperation Organization," December 14, 2014, accessed August 21, 2016, http://www.fmprc.gov.cn/mfa_eng/wjb_663304/zzjg_663340/dozys_664276/gjlb_664280/3180_664322/3182_664326/t1219581.shtml.

68. Ministry of Foreign Affairs of People's Republic of China, "Joint Declaration on New Stage of Comprehensive Strategic Partnership Between the People's Republic of China and the Republic of Kazakhstan," August 31, 2015, accessed August 21, 2016, http://www.fmprc.gov.cn/mfa_eng/wjb_663304/zzjg_663340/dozys_664276/gjlb_664280/3180_664322/3182_664326/t1293114.shtml.

69. Ministry of Foreign Affairs of People's Republic of China, "President Xi Jinping Hold Talks with President Nursultan Nazarbayev of Kazakhstan and Decide in Unanimity to Promote China-Kazakhstan Relations to Higher Level and Wider Space," August 31, 2015, accessed August 21, 2016, http://www.fmprc.gov.cn/mfa_eng/wjb_663304/zzjg_663340/dozys_664276/gjlb_664280/3180_664322/3182_664326/t1293118.shtml.

70. Ministry of Foreign Affairs of People's Republic of China, "Li Keqiang and Prime Minister Karim Massimov of Kazakhstan Hold Talks, Stressing to Deeply Promote China-Kazakhstan Production Capacity Cooperation in Order to Better Realize

Mutual Benefits and Win-win Results," December 14, 2015, accessed August 21, 2016, http://www.fmprc.gov.cn/mfa_eng/wjb_663304/zzjg_663340/dozys_664276/gjlb_664280/3180_664322/3182_664326/t1324827.shtml.

71. Ibid.

72. United Nations, United Nations Commodity Trade Statistics Database, accessed May 3, 2015, http://comtrade.un.org/db/default.aspx; and European Commission Directorate-General for Trade, Kazakhstan: EU Bilateral Trade and Trade with the World," April 10, 2015, accessed May 3, 2015, http://trade.ec.europa.eu/doclib/docs/2006/september/tradoc_113406.pdf.

73. Kalis, ibid., 269.

74. United Nations, United Nations Commodity Trade Statistics Database, accessed July 22, 2016, http://comtrade.un.org/db/default.aspx.

75. United Nations, Conference on Trade and Development (UNCTAD FDI/TNC) Database, *Bilateral FDI Statistics 2014*, accessed June 29, 2014, http://unctad.org/Sections/dite_fdistat/docs/webdiaeia2014d3_CHN.pdf.

76. Kalis, ibid., 272.

77. United Nations, United Nations Commodity Trade Statistics Database, accessed July 22, 2016, http://comtrade.un.org/db/default.aspx.

78. International Trade Centre, Directory of Trade Promotion Organizations, and Other Trade Support Institutions, accessed January 5, 2015, http://www.intracen.org/itc/trade-support/tsi-directory; and Muhamad S. Olimat, *China and Central Asia in the Post-Soviet Era* (Lanham, MD: Lexington Books), 2015, 118.

79. "China and Kazakhstan," ibid.

80. Ministry of Foreign Affairs of People's Republic of China, "Vice-President Hu Jintao Met with Kazakh Prime Minister," November 17, 2000, accessed August 21, 2016, http://www.fmprc.gov.cn/mfa_eng/wjb_663304/zzjg_663340/dozys_664276/gjlb_664280/3180_664322/3182_664326/t16664.shtml.

81. "China and Kazakhstan," ibid.

82. Ministry of Foreign Affairs of People's Republic of China, "Wu Bangguo and Wen Jiabao Meets Respectively with Kazakh President Nursultan Nazarbayev," May 19, 2004, accessed August 21, 2016, http://www.fmprc.gov.cn/mfa_eng/wjb_663304/zzjg_663340/dozys_664276/gjlb_664280/3180_664322/3182_664326/t115558.shtml.

83. Ministry of Foreign Affairs of People's Republic of China, "Joint Statement Between the People's Republic of China and the Republic of Kazakhstan," ibid.

84. Ibid.

85. Ministry of Foreign Affairs of People's Republic of China, "Xi Jinping and Nursultan Nazarbayev Jointly Attend Founding Ceremony of China-Kazakhstan Entrepreneurs Committee, Wishing China-Kazakhstan Cooperation Makes Further Progress," September 7, 2013, accessed August 21, 2016, http://www.fmprc.gov.cn/mfa_eng/wjb_663304/zzjg_663340/dozys_664276/gjlb_664280/3180_664322/3182_664326/t1075970.shtml.

86. Ministry of Foreign Affairs of People's Republic of China, "Li Keqiang Holds Talks with Prime Minister Karim Massimov of Kazakhstan Deciding to Comprehensively Carry Out Cooperation in Production Capacity and Push for Important

Results," March 27, 2015, accessed August 21, 2016, http://www.fmprc.gov.cn/mfa_eng/wjb_663304/zzjg_663340/dozys_664276/gjlb_664280/3180_664322/3182_664326/t1250472.shtml.
 87. International Crisis Group, ibid.
 88. Ibid.
 89. The Heritage Foundation and American Enterprise Institute, *China Global Investment Tracker Database*, accessed December 21, 2014, http://www.heritage.org/research/projects/china-global-investment-tracker-interactive-map.
 90. Peyrouse, ibid., 39.
 91. The Heritage Foundation and American Enterprise Institute, ibid.
 92. Richard Orange, "Kazakhmys gets $1.5bn loan from China," *The Telegraph*, June 14, 2011, accessed December 21, 2014, http://www.telegraph.co.uk/finance/newsbysector/industry/mining/8573834/Kazakhmys-gets-1.5bn-loan-from-China.html.
 93. The Heritage Foundation and American Enterprise Institute, ibid.
 94. Ibid.
 95. Orange, ibid.
 96. Peyrouse, ibid.; and the Heritage Foundation and American Enterprise Institute, ibid.
 97. The Heritage Foundation and American Enterprise Institute, ibid.
 98. Kalis, ibid., 269.
 99. Alexander Kim, "China and Kazakhstan: Inevitability of Beijing's Growing Influence," *Eurasia Daily Monitor* (Jamestown Foundation), Volume X, Issue 153, August 16, 2013.
 100. Olimat, ibid., 117.
 101. Ibid., 118.
 102. Noriko Yodogawa and Alexander M. Peterson, "An Opportunity for Progress: China, Central Asia, and the Energy Charter Treaty," *Texas Journal of Oil, Gas, and Energy Law* (Austin, TX: University of Texas), Volume 8, Issue 1, March 12, 2013, 122.
 103. Kalis, ibid., 269.
 104. International Crisis Group, ibid.
 105. Peyrouse, ibid., 39.
 106. Khodzhaev, ibid., 14.
 107. McGill and Oresman, ibid., 20.
 108. United States Department of Defense, Defense Intelligence Agency, *Directory of PRC Military Personalities* (Washington, DC), 2014, 17.
 109. International Crisis Group, ibid.
 110. Linda Jakobson, Paul Holtom, Dean Knox, and Jingchao Peng, *China's Energy and Security Relations with Russia: Hopes, Frustrations and Uncertainties* (Stockholm, Sweden: SIPRI), Policy Paper No. 29, October 2011, 5, accessed February 28, 2015, http://books.sipri.org/files/PP/SIPRIPP29.pdf; and International Crisis Group, ibid.
 111. Dwivedi, ibid., 151.

112. Richard Rousseau, "Kazakhstan: Continuous Improvement or Stalemate in its Relations with China?" *Strategic Analysis* (Routledge), Volume 37, Issue 1, January–February 2013, 46.
113. Ibid.
114. Marketos, ibid., 61–62.
115. Dwivedi, ibid., 141.
116. Marketos, ibid., 12.
117. International Crisis Group, ibid., 2.
118. Ministry of Foreign Affairs of People's Republic of China, "Joint Statement Between the People's Republic of China and the Republic of Kazakhstan," ibid.
119. International Crisis Group, ibid.
120. "China and Kazakhstan," ibid.
121. Overland, Torjesen, and Kjaernet, ibid., 98.
122. "China and Kazakhstan," ibid.
123. Confucius Institute Online, Worldwide Confucius Institutes, "Kazakhstan," accessed August 1, 2014, http://www.chinesecio.com/m/cio_wci.
124. Khodzhaev, ibid., 9.
125. Olimat, ibid., 118.
126. Ibid.
127. Ibid., 119–120.
128. Rousseau, ibid., 42.
129. Ibid.
130. Ibid., 43.
131. Kalis, ibid., 265.
132. Saurbek, ibid., 82.
133. U.S. Energy Information Administration, U.S. Department of Energy, "Country Analysis Briefs: Kazakhstan," January 15, 2015, accessed March 7, 2015, http://www.eia.gov/countries/analysisbriefs/Kazakhstan/kazakhstan.pdf.
134. Ibid.
135. Ibid.
136. Ibid.
137. Ibid.
138. Rousseau, ibid., 44.
139. Saurbek, ibid., 90–91.
140. U.S. Energy Information Administration, U.S. Department of Energy, ibid.
141. Ibid.
142. Ibid.
143. George Voloshin, "China Strengthens Its Hand in Kazakhstan After Xi Jinping's Visit," *Eurasia Daily Monitor* (Jamestown Foundation), Volume X, Issue 164, September 17, 2013.
144. Olimat, ibid., 111.
145. Voloshin, ibid.
146. Yodogawa and Peterson, ibid., 112.
147. "China and Kazakhstan," ibid.
148. Ibid.

149. Olimat, ibid., 110; and Klara Rakhmetova, "Kazakhstan-China Oil Pipeline Project," *KazMunaiGas*, (n.d.), accessed August 21, 2016, http://www.energycharter.org/fileadmin/DocumentsMedia/Presentations/CBP-KZ-CN.pdf.
150. Rakhmetova, ibid.
151. Saurbek, ibid., 89.
152. Rakhmetova, ibid.
153. Ibid.
154. Saurbek, ibid., 88.
155. Rakhmetova, ibid.
156. Ibid.
157. Ministry of Foreign Affairs of People's Republic of China, "President Hu Jintao Holds Talks with His Kazakh Counterpart," ibid.
158. Rakhmetova, ibid.
159. Ibid.
160. Saurbek, ibid., 88.
161. Ibid., Yodogawa and Peterson, ibid., 120, 122.
162. Austin M. Strange, et al., "Tracking Underreported Financial Flows: China's Development Finance and the Aid–Conflict Nexus Revisited," *Journal of Conflict Resolution*, Volume 61, Issue 5 (2017): 935–963.
163. China National Petroleum Company, "CNPC in Kazakhstan, Oilfield Services, Engineering and Construction," accessed February 21, 2015, http://www.cnpc.com.cn/en/Kazakhstan/country_index.shtml.
164. Matthew Stein, *The Wariness in Kazakhstan of Chinese Economic Investments and Interests* (Fort Leavenworth, KS: U.S. Army, Foreign Military Studies Office), February 2013, 3, http://fmso.leavenworth.army.mil/documents/Kazakhstan's-Wariness-of-China.pdf.
165. Strange, et al., ibid.
166. The Heritage Foundation and American Enterprise Institute, ibid.
167. Peyrouse, ibid., 48.
168. Strange, et al., ibid.

Chapter 7

China and Kuwait
Political/Diplomatic Relations

China and Kuwait established diplomatic relations on March 22, 1971 making Kuwait the Gulf Cooperation Council country with the longest diplomatic relationship.[1,2] Kuwait was a British protectorate until 1961, when it gained independence from the United Kingdom. Their relationship has been characterized by bilateral, high-level official visits and bilateral cooperation in trade, energy, finance, and infrastructure development.[3] Both are committed to supporting each other's national sovereignty and territorial integrity. In this respect, China publicly supported Kuwait's national sovereignty, independence, and territorial integrity openly condemning Iraq's invasion of Kuwait during the First Gulf War while Kuwait firmly adheres to the One-China policy, opposes any attempt to forge "two Chinas" or "one China, one Taiwan" and supports any Chinese effort in safeguarding its national sovereignty and territorial integrity.[4] This is especially important for Kuwait, as its independence and territorial integrity has been in question due to continued Iraqi territorial claims over Kuwait since 1961.[5]

Iraq under Qasim questioned Kuwait's independence more than any Arab country. Such an assertion by Iraq created an international crisis in 1961 and the deployment of British troops to Kuwait on June 30, 1961 to safeguard Kuwait's independence and territorial integrity.[6] The Arab League replaced British troops as of October 19, 1961 by deploying an Arab Security Force composed of troops from Egypt, Syria, Jordan, Morocco, and Saudi Arabia. Iraq eventually recognized Kuwait's independence on October 2, 1963 but not before Qasim was overthrown and executed by the Ba'athist-Nationalist Party on February 9, 1963. Iraq tabled its territorial claims but briefly annexed Kuwait in 1990 during the Gulf War until it was ousted by the United States.

Kuwait received its eagerly sought-after diplomatic recognition by June 1962. Seventy-one countries recognized Kuwait which allowed it to become active member of the Arab League, the United Nations, and OPEC.[7]

Formal diplomatic relations between China and Iraq were delayed ten years because of the uncompromising demands China made with respect to its One-China policy and the level of economic cooperation between Kuwait and Taiwan. China was also embroiled in the Omani Civil War, supported the Popular Front for the Liberation of the Occupied Arabian Gulf (PFLOAG) and other communist forces in South Yemen, was destabilizing Jordan and other governments, and supported national, Maoist, and communist forces in the region.[8] These actions did make China diplomatically attractive.

Kuwait tabled its reservations, severed its relations with Taiwan on March 22, 1971, and recognized China, acting purely on national interest, because China's admission in the United Nations was imminent. In doing so, Kuwait became the first Gulf country to recognize China and assume a major role in promoting China in the international scene. With diplomatic ties formalized, China withdrew its support for opposition movements which threatened the status quo. This helped to improve relations with other countries in the region.

China's admission to the United Nations motivated many other countries in the Near East and other regions of the world to recognize it and abide by the One-China policy. As a permanent member of the UN's Security Council, the world would realize the enormity of China's weight and role especially as a counterweight to Western support of Israel in the Arab-Israeli conflict. It is important to also note that U.S.-Sino rapprochement and the subsequent improvement of U.S.-Sino and Sino-Western relations also helped improve relations between China and the Arab world.[9]

China seized on its newfound opportunity as a permanent member of the UN's Security Council to gain access into in the Gulf region. It used Kuwait as a staging point from which to secure diplomatic recognition from Saudi Arabia, the new independent states of the UAE, Qatar and Bahrain, and mend its relations with Oman.[10]

China and Kuwait cooperated on a number of international issues affecting the region between 1980 and 2010: anti-Soviet resistance in Afghanistan, the Iranian Revolution, Iraq's invasion of Kuwait in 1990, and the Arab Spring. China condemned Iraq's invasion of Kuwait, promoted the restoration of Kuwait's sovereignty, and assisted in Kuwait's reconstruction after the United States evicted Iraq with a coalition of forty-two countries in 1991. Consequently, Kuwait became China's major oil supplier. Both China and Kuwait opposed the Arab Spring but for different reasons. Kuwait opposed the revolutionary spirit of the Arab Spring, resisting calls for change and reform in favor of a parliamentary system, while China was fearful that the contagious spirit of the Arab Spring might spread into Tibet and the Xinxiang

Province.[11] Both countries essentially viewed the Arab Spring as destabilizing to their respective regions.

China and Kuwait agree on a number of issues confronting the region today. Both agree on Bahrain's stability and both support the P5+1 negotiation with Iran over its nuclear program; however, China and Kuwait disagree on the nature of the Syrian civil war and the future of the Syrian regime. While China supports the Syrian regime, Kuwait supports President Assad's removal. Syria is one of China's closest allies in the Middle East.[12]

Since 2000 China and Kuwait have engaged each other no less than thirty-two times.[13] Some of the most important exchanges include: President Hu Jintao Meets with Prime Minister Sabah Al-Ahmad Al-Jaber Al-Sabah (July 2004), President Hu Jintao and Emir Al-Sabah (September 2009), and President Hu Jintao and Prime Minister Jaber Al-Mubarak Al-Hamad Al-Sabah (June 2014).[14] Over the course of their diplomatic ties, China and Kuwait have also inked numerous agreements and memorandums of understanding. These include: Joint Communiqué on the Establishment of Diplomatic Relations (March 22, 1971);[15] and an agreement on mutual visa exemption for holders of diplomatic, service and special passports (2014).[16]

China and Kuwait have also established official diplomatic representation respectively in Kuwait and Beijing. Kuwait also has established Consulates-General in Hong Kong and Guangzhou, China.[17]

ECONOMIC/TRADE RELATIONS

Sino-Kuwaiti economic relations predate their diplomatic relations. Trading began in 1955, approximately sixteen years before diplomatic relations were established, but appears robust today. Trade was important to both countries because they used it to advance their political and diplomatic relations. Investment and aid were also used to bolster Kuwait's political legitimacy both regionally and internationally. Kuwait created the Arab Fund for Economic and Social Development in 1962 to bolster its legitimacy as well as to support independence and causes in the region. China also sought to use Kuwait's trade relations model to provide the groundwork for building successful diplomatic ties with the region. China was successful in building diplomatic relations with many countries in the Middle East but not with Saudi Arabia until the end of the 1980s.[18]

In 2013, China was Kuwait's largest trading partner after South Korea, India, Japan, the United States and the European Union.[19] In the same year, Kuwait was China's forty-second largest trading partner.[20] Bilateral trade was: $6.7 billion (2008), $5 billion (2009), $8.5 billion (2010), $11.2 billion (2011), $12.5 billion (2012), $12.2 billion (2013), $13.4 billion (2014),

Table 7.1 Top Five Commodities Traded between China and Kuwait

Commodity	Importer	Trade Value ($)	Percentage (%)
Mineral fuels, mineral oils and products of their distillation; bituminous substances; mineral waxes	China	6,112,300,877	82
Organic chemicals	China	966,114,459	13
Plastics and articles thereof	China	346,410,407	5
Salt; sulfur; earths and stone; plastering materials, lime and cement	China	32,118,625	0.429
Copper and articles thereof	China	14,245,105	0.190
Nuclear reactors, boilers, machinery and mechanical appliances; parts thereof	Kuwait	586,128,875	16
Electrical machinery and equipment and parts thereof; sound recorders and reproducers, television image and sound recorders and reproducers, and parts and accessories of such articles	Kuwait	564,571,841	15
Articles of iron or steel	Kuwait	358,715,853	10
Furniture; bedding, mattresses, mattress supports, cushions and similar stuffed furnishings; lamps and lighting fittings, not elsewhere specified or included; illuminated signs, illuminated name-plates and the like; prefabricated buildings	Kuwait	258,049,283	7
Articles of apparel and clothing accessories, knitted or crocheted	Kuwait	248,961,980	7

Source: United Nations Commodity Trade Statistics Database.

and $11.2 billion (2015).[21] Bilateral trade increased almost twofold in seven years. Since 2000, bilateral trade increased eighteen-fold. In 2012, foreign direct investment into Kuwait from China was -$12 million and foreign direct investment stock was $83 million.[22]

In terms of bilateral trade, Table 7.1 shows the top five commodities traded between China and Kuwait in 2015. Energy commodities, which include crude petroleum and petroleum gas products, appear to be the most traded commodity. In terms of trade value, 82 percent is attributed to energy commodities, which includes crude petroleum and petroleum gas products. See Table 7.1.

In previous years, China's energy commodities accounted for the following in terms of trade value: 93 percent (2008), 86 percent (2009), 84 percent (2010), 85 percent (2011), 85 percent (2012), 81 percent (2013), and 83 percent (2014).[23]

Bilateral trade is promoted through several organizations such as the PRC Ministry of Commerce, the PRC Ministry of Foreign Affairs, All-China

Federation of Commerce and Industry, China-Kuwait Economic Cooperation Forum (CKEC), the Asian Cooperation Dialogue (ACD), the Kuwait Investment Authority (KIA), and Kuwait Fund for Arab Economic Development (KFAED). KFAED provided loans for thirty-four developmental and infrastructural projects in China totaling $880 million.[24]

China and Kuwait has penned some important agreements to facilitate trade between their countries. The most notable agreements and memorandums of understanding include: Agreement on Economic and Technical Cooperation (December 26, 1977);[25] Civil Air Transport Agreement Between the Government of the People's Republic of China and the Government of the State of Kuwait (January 20, 1980);[26] Trade Agreement (October 6, 1980);[27] Loan Agreement between the Kuwaiti Fund for Arab Economic Development and China on a loan of $50 million to help finance the Ningguo Cement Factory in Anhui Province (July 5, 1982);[28] Loan Agreement between the Kuwaiti Fund for Arab Economic Development and China on a loan of $20.5 million to help finance the Xiamen (Amoy) International Airport Project (December 2, 1982);[29] Loan agreement of $45.8 million to help finance an Urumqi fertilizer plant in Xinjiang Province (May 4, 1983);[30] Loan Agreement of $30 million to build a hydroelectric power plant in Fujian Province (January 5, 1985);[31] Loan Agreement of $13.2 million to finance the construction of a mini vehicle plant in Tianjin (July 6, 1985);[32] Agreement between the Government of the People's Republic of China and the Government of the State of Kuwait for the Promotion and Protection of Investments (November 25, 1985);[33] Agreement on Establishing Joint Economic and Trade Committee (1986);[34] Loan Agreement between the Chinese State Administration for Building Materials Industry and the Kuwaiti Arab Foundation for Economic Development (November 15, 1986);[35] Loan Agreement of $240 million to finance the construction for a polypropylene plant in Luoyang in Henan Providence (March 19, 1987);[36] Loan Agreement of $58 million between Arab Chemical Fertilizers Comp. Ltd. and the Bank of China (February 6, 1988);[37] a Revised Agreement on Economic and Technical Cooperation (1989);[38] Loan Agreement of $21 million between China and the Kuwaiti Fund for Arab Economic Development to help finance a ductile cast iron pipe plant in Liaoning Province (September 21, 1989);[39] Agreement Between the Government of the People's Republic of China and the Government of the State of Kuwait for the Avoidance of Double Taxation and the Prevention of Fiscal Evasion with respect to Taxes on Income and Capital (December 25, 1989);[40] Agreement on Economic and Technical Cooperation (December 25, 1989);[41] Agreement on Economic and Technological Cooperation (July 2004);[42] Framework Agreement on Economic, Trade, Investment, and Technological Cooperation between China and the GCC States (2004);[43] a Memorandum of Understanding on cooperation in the field of infrastructure for highways and water channels (2009);[44] Bilateral

Cooperation Agreements in the fields of economy and trade, finance, energy, and aviation (June 2014);[45] an infrastructure investment agreement (2014);[46] a Memorandum of Understanding in the field of cooperation in investment in Africa (2014);[47] a Bilateral Communications Agreement between Kuwait's leading Telecommunications Company, Zain, and China's telecom solutions provider, Huawei (2014);[48] and a Memorandum of Understanding on bilateral cooperation regarding the Silk Road Economic Belt and the Silk City (2014).[49]

In addition to penning agreements to foster bilateral trade, China and Kuwait have been actively involved in each other's economic development in terms of infrastructure, investments, and loans. These include: the Establishment of Sino-Arab Chemical Fertilizer Company Ltd. (1985);[50] the Incorporation of the Kuwait China Investment Company (KCIC) (December 2005);[51] the Kuwait Investment Authority (KIA) acquired stakes worth $270 million in the Industrial and Commercial Bank of China (February 2006);[52] a $410 million construction contract awarded to the China State Construction Engineering Corporation to build the Central Bank of Kuwait Headquarters (March 2007);[53] a $410 million contract to China Communications Construction Company, Ltd. for port entrance construction (Phase 1) of the Barbieri Port Project (June 2007);[54] a $570 million contract between China Metallurgical Group Corporation and MAK Group to construct the Jaber Al-Ahmad City N2 (October 2010);[55] a $390 million contract awarded to Sinohydro to build the Kuwaiti University campus (March 2012);[56] the Boubyan Bridge Construction Contract in Kuwait by China;[57] the Kuwaiti Fund for Arab Economic Development providing $23 million in soft loans to fund Lake Bosten River Basin Environment Protection and Development Project in the Xinjiang Autonomous Region;[58] a $460 million construction contract to the China State Construction Engineering Corporation to build academic support facilities at Kuwait City (April 2016);[59] a $580 million construction contract to the China State Construction Engineering Corporation to build the administrative buildings (Sabah Al Salem University City) of Kuwait University (June 2016).[60]

In terms of China's economic development, Kuwait is notable. It was the first Arab country to directly invest in China.[61] It was also the first Gulf state to offer soft loans to China.[62]

In summary, Chinese companies have invested $3.2 billion in non-energy projects, which includes joint ventures.[63] These investments represent 61 percent of China's total investments.

MILITARY/SECURITY RELATIONS

Sino-Kuwaiti military relations are developing. China and Kuwait have reciprocal military attaché representation in each other's capitals and have conducted

Table 7.2 Chinese Conventional Weapons Transfers to Kuwait

Year(s) of Delivery	No. of Deliveries	Weapon Designation	Weapon Description
2000–2001	27	PCZ-45 (S)	Ammunition Logistics Vehicle
2000–2001	27	PLZ-45 155mm (S)	Self-Propelled Gun
2000	1	W-653/Type-653 (S)	Armored Recovery Vehicle
2000–2001	4	YW-531H/Type-85 (S)	Armored Personnel Carrier
2002–2003	24	PCZ-45 (S)	Ammunition Logistics Vehicle
2002–2003	24	PLZ-45 155mm (S)	Self-Propelled Gun
2002–2003	4	YW-531H/Type-85 (S)	Armored Personnel Carrier
2003	1	W-653/Type-653 (S)	Armored Recovery Vehicle

Source: SIPRI Arms Transfers Database.

high-level military-to-military talks on future defense cooperation.[64] China and Kuwait have also engaged each other no less than five times since 2002 according to the Ministry of National Defense of the People's Republic of China, *PLA Daily*, *Xinhua*, and *China Military Online*. These engagements include: two visits to the PRC by Kuwaiti military officials, two visits to Kuwait by Chinese military officials including a port visit by PLAN ships, and joint military training (Tank Biathlon). China and Kuwait previously signed the Memorandum of Understanding on Military Cooperation in 1995.[65]

China has also been a modest arms supplier to Kuwait but only at the beginning of the twenty-first century. Table 7.2 summarizes the arms transfers from China to Kuwait according to SIPRI. See Table 7.2. China's total arms sales to Kuwait are $158.6 million based on the 2016 CPI index. In 2000, total arms sales to Kuwait were $55.28 million; the difference being $103.32 million over a sixteen-year period. Kuwait's main suppliers include the United States, the United Kingdom, France, and other Western countries.[66]

While China is a very modest arms supplier to Kuwait, both countries support efforts to combat international terrorism. Kuwait has been the subject of terrorist attacks and China needs Kuwaiti support and Gulf Cooperation Council (GCC) support, and Arab and Muslim country support to deal with the growing threat of East Turkestan movements seeking Xinxiang Province's independence.[67]

CULTURAL RELATIONS

Sino-Kuwaiti cultural relations have been developing. Since diplomatic relations were established in 1971, bilateral cultural exchanges have occurred in the fields of sports, health, tourism, and education. China used cultural exchanges, sports, and tourism, in addition to trade ties to secure diplomatic recognition and to abate the anxiety countries in the Near East felt about establishing contacts with a Maoist-revolutionary country like China. These instruments of China's foreign policy were limited in the first two decades since 1949. China was also involved in a fierce competition with two superpowers (United States and Soviet Union) and two major international alliances (NATO and Warsaw Pact).[68]

Sports became an important medium for China to enter the international scene. Kuwait secured China's admission to the Asian Games in 1974.[69] This provided the foundation for further cultural exchanges and improvement of diplomatic relations.

Bilateral cultural relations grew steadily in the wake of diplomatic ties. Kuwaiti options for tourist visits, shopping, or doing business aimed at China increased. Student exchange programs and scholarships are now available for Chinese students particularly interested in studying Arabic in Kuwaiti universities, or Kuwaiti students interested in studying science, technology, and engineering in China.[70]

China and Kuwait have inked agreements to foster cultural cooperation and exchanges. These include: an Agreement on Cultural Cooperation (February 15, 1982);[71] Agreement between the Xinhua News Agency and Kuwait News Agency (September 15, 1985);[72] Agreement for Sports Cooperation (1992);[73] Agreement on Cultural, Media, and Educational Cooperation (December 2003);[74] a Cooperation Agreement in the Field of Higher Education (2009);[75] the Executive Program on Sports Cooperation (2009);[76] a Literary Translation Agreement (2014);[77] and an Air Service Agreement (June 2014).[78]

ENERGY/PETROLEUM RELATIONS

Crude petroleum and petroleum gas trading forms the basis for China and Kuwait's trade relationship even though Kuwait is not a major supplier of oil to China. In this respect, China imported 2 to 4 percent of its crude petroleum from Kuwait between 2006 and 2015 inclusive. In terms of total trade value, crude petroleum imports ranged from 64 to 85 percent for the same years. Table 7.3 shows Chinese crude oil imports from Kuwait in thousands of barrels per day, oil imports share, world ranking, trade value, total commodity trade value and percentage from 2006 to 2015. See Table 7.3.

China also imports petroleum gas products from Kuwait but not liquefied natural gas (LNG). Table 7.4 illustrates China's petroleum gas imports from Kuwait in millions of cubic feet, global imports share, world ranking, trade value, total commodity trade value and percentage from 2006 to 2015. See Table 7.4.

Table 7.3 Chinese Crude Petroleum Imports from Kuwait

Year	KBPD	Oil Imports Share (%)	World Ranking	Crude Oil Trade Value ($)	Total Commodity Trade Value ($)	Percentage (%)
2006	56	2	13	1,234,138,246	1,923,999,896	64.1
2007	73	2	11	1,700,147,433	2,290,622,896	74.2
2008	118	3	8	4,279,021,078	5,038,814,695	84.9
2009	142	3	8	2,862,249,909	3,500,920,762	81.8
2010	197	4	9	5,471,636,575	6,708,788,039	81.6
2011	192	4	10	7,343,680,799	9,175,204,536	80.0
2012	211	4	9	8,415,007,582	10,467,164,717	80.4
2013	188	3	10	7,277,315,570	9,586,638,189	75.9
2014	213	3	9	7,598,348,696	10,004,827,071	75.9
2015	290	4	8	5,706,704,967	7,483,125,047	76.3

Source: United Nations Commodity Trade Statistics Database.

Table 7.4 Chinese Petroleum Gas Product Imports from Kuwait

Year	Volume (MMcf)	Global Share (%)	World Ranking	Petroleum Gas Trade Value ($)	Total Commodity Trade Value ($)	Percentage (%)
2006	28.1	11	5	370,899,596	1,923,999,896	19
2007	24.9	9	4	362,059,989	2,290,622,896	16
2008	20.9	9	3	411,470,602	5,038,814,695	8
2009	10.7	3	9	139,810,012	3,500,920,762	4
2010	8.6	1	11	145,156,188	6,708,788,039	2
2011	21.8	2	10	465,874,533	9,175,204,536	5
2012	19.0	1	9	439,875,248	10,467,164,717	4
2013	22.0	1	11	501,945,166	9,586,638,189	5
2014	25.3	1	13	529,139,899	10,004,827,071	5
2015	32.1	1	12	393,986,321	7,483,125,047	5

Source: United Nations Commodity Trade Statistics Database.

In terms of energy investments, Sinopec Corp. and the Kuwait Oil Company signed a $350 million agreement in 2009 whereby Sinopec Corp. would construct and operate five oil and gas rigs over five years in Kuwait.[79] Kuwait Petroleum International (KPI), a subsidiary of KPC, signed a memorandum of understanding with Sinopec Corp. to jointly construct an $8-$9 billion oil refinery and a petrochemical complex in China.[80] The planned facility would include a refinery that could process 15 million tons of Kuwaiti crude oil a year (300,000 barrels per day) and an ethylene cracker unit with an annual production capacity of one million tons.[81] The project was expected to be complete in late 2014 and operational in mid-2015. China and Kuwait also inked an oil cooperation deal in June 2014.[82] In October 2015, Sinopec Engineering

Group Co. Ltd. formed a consortium with Spanish Tecnicas Reunidas, S.A. and Korean Hanwha Engineering & Construction Corp. and entered a $1.7 billion engineering, procurement, and construction (EPC) contract with Kuwait National Petroleum Company (KNPC) for its Al-Zour refinery project near the border of Saudi Arabia for a 40 percent share.[83] In January 2016, China's land drilling rig manufacturer Honghua Group Ltd. entered into an ultra-deep drilling rig sales agreement (the Sales Agreement) with Kuwait Drilling Company K.S.C. (KDC), with a total value of approximately $25 million (HKD 194 million).[84] Pursuant to the sales agreement, Honghua would provide and deliver one set of ultra-deep drilling rigs to KDC in 2016.[85] Finally, China has opened its domestic market with the Kuwaiti Foreign Petroleum Exploration Company (KUFPEC) to explore for oil and natural gas in southern China.[86]

SUMMARY

Sino-Kuwaiti relations are strong. China and Kuwait are engaged politically, economically, militarily, and culturally. China and Kuwait have signed agreements and memorandums of understanding to promote trade, investment, culture, sports, tourism, and education. China has also supplied Kuwait with conventional military weapons and equipment. Kuwait has also invested into China providing it with infrastructure aid and development. Both are committed to preserving each other's sovereignty and territorial integrity and supported each other in this aspect throughout their history.

In terms of petroleum trading, which includes crude petroleum and petroleum gas products, China imports annually approximately 3.5 percent and 1 percent, respectively. Both have oil and gas projects in each other's countries. In this respect, China is constructing five oil and gas rigs in Kuwait and Kuwait is building an oil refinery and petrochemical complex in China. It is expected that Sino-Kuwaiti petroleum ties will grow further over time.

NOTES

1. Embassy of the People's Republic of China in the State of Kuwait, "China and Kuwait," (n.d.), accessed October 8, 2013, http://kw.china-embassy.org/eng/sbgx/t580302.htm.

2. Embassy of the People's Republic of China in the State of Kuwait, "China and Kuwait," (n.d.), accessed September 21, 2014, http://kw.chineseembassy.org/eng/sbgx/t580302.htm.

3. Ministry of Foreign Affairs of People's Republic of China, "China and Kuwait," accessed May 9, 2014, http://www.fmprc.gov.cn/mfa_eng/wjb_663304/zzjg_663340/xybfs_663590/gjlb_663594/2838_663666/.

4. Khizar Niazi, "Kuwait Looks Towards the East: Relations with China," *Inter-Disciplinary Journal of Asian and Middle Eastern Studies*, Vol. 26, September 2009, accessed September 21, 2014, http://idjames.org/2012/06/kuwait-looks-towards-the-east-relations-with-china/.

5. Muhamad S. Olimat, *China and the Middle East Since World War II* (Lanham, MD: Lexington Books), 2014, 121.

6. Ibid.

7. Ibid., 122.

8. Ibid., 123.

9. Ibid., 123–124.

10. Ibid., 124–125.

11. Ibid., 126.

12. Ibid., 127, 234.

13. Ministry of Foreign Affairs of People's Republic of China, "China–Kuwait: Activities," (n.d.), accessed August 22, 2015, http://www.fmprc.gov.cn/mfa_eng/wjb_663304/zzjg_663340/xybfs_663590/gjlb_663594/2838_663666/2840_663670/.

14. Ibid.

15. Wolfgang Bartke, *The Agreements of the People's Republic of China with Foreign Countries 1949–1990* (Munchen, Germany: K.G. Saur), 1992, 107.

16. Habib Toumi, "Kuwait, China Sign 10 Cooperation Accords," *Gulf News*, June 4, 2014, accessed September 21, 2014, http://gulfnews.com/news/gulf/kuwait/kuwait-china-sign-10-cooperation-accords-1.1342938.

17. Javaid Ahmed, "45 Years of China-Kuwait Diplomatic Relations," *Kuwait Times*, March 16, 2016, accessed August 13, 2016, http://news.kuwaittimes.net/website/45-years-china-kuwait-diplomatic-relations/.

18. Olimat, ibid., 127, 128.

19. European Commission Directorate-General for Trade, "Kuwait: EU Bilateral Trade and Trade with the World," April 10, 2014, accessed May 3, 2015, http://trade.ec.europa.eu/doclib/docs/2006/september/tradoc_113408.pdf.

20. United Nations, United Nations Commodity Trade Statistics Database, accessed August 21, 2015, http://comtrade.un.org/db/default.aspx.

21. Ibid., accessed July 22, 2016.

22. United Nations Conference on Trade and Development (UNCTAD FDI/TNC) Database, *Bilateral FDI Statistics 2014*, accessed September 12, 2014, http://unctad.org/Sections/dite_fdistat/docs/webdiaeia2014d3_CHN.pdf.

23. United Nations, United Nations Commodity Trade Statistics Database, ibid.

24. Olimat, ibid., 129, 130.

25. Niazi, ibid., September 2009.

26. Ministry of Foreign Affairs of People's Republic of China, "Civil Air Transport Agreement Between the Government of the People's Republic of China and the Government of the State of Kuwait," January 20, 1985, accessed September 21, 2014, http://www.fmprc.gov.cn/mfa_eng/wjb_663304/zzjg_663340/xybfs_663590/gjlb_663594/2838_663666/2839_663668/t16371.shtml.

27. Embassy of the People's Republic of China in the State of Kuwait, "China and Kuwait," (n.d.), accessed September 21, 2014, http://kw.chineseembassy.org/eng/sbgx/t580302.htm.

28. Bartke, ibid., 107.
29. Ibid.
30. Ibid.
31. Ibid., 108.
32. Ibid.
33. Ministry of Foreign Affairs of People's Republic of China, "Agreement Between the Government of the People's Republic of China and the Government of the State of Kuwait for the Promotion and Protection of Investments," November 23, 1985, accessed September 21, 2014, http://www.fmprc.gov.cn/mfa_eng/wjb_663304/zzjg_663340/xybfs_663590/gjlb_663594/2838_663666/2839_663668/t16369.shtml.
34. Embassy of the People's Republic of China in the State of Kuwait, "China and Kuwait," (n.d.), accessed September 21, 2014, http://kw.chineseembassy.org/eng/sbgx/t580302.htm.
35. Bartke, ibid., 108.
36. Ibid.
37. Ibid.
38. Niazi, ibid.
39. Bartke, ibid.
40. Ministry of Foreign Affairs of People's Republic of China, "Agreement Between the Government of the People's Republic of China and the Government of the State of Kuwait for the Avoidance of Double Taxation and the Prevention of Fiscal Evasion with Respect to Taxes on Income and Capital," December 5, 1989, accessed September 21, 2014, http://www.fmprc.gov.cn/mfa_eng/wjb_663304/zzjg_663340/xybfs_663590/gjlb_663594/2838_663666/2839_663668/t16370.shtml.
41. Bartke, ibid.
42. Ministry of Foreign Affairs of People's Republic of China, "Premier Wen Jiabao Meets with the Joint Delegation of The Cooperation Council for the Arab States of the Gulf (GCC)," July 6, 2004, accessed August 13, 2016, http://www.fmprc.cn/mfa_eng/wjb_663304/zzjg_663340/xybfs_663590/gjlb_663594/2838_663666/2840_663670/t142366.shtml.
43. Niazi, ibid.
44. Ibid.
45. Ministry of Foreign Affairs of People's Republic of China, "Li Keqiang Holds Talks with Prime Minister Sheikh Jaber Al-Mubarak Al-Hamad Al-Sabah of Kuwait, Stressing to Deepen China-Kuwait Friendly Relationship and Mutually Beneficial Cooperation and to Promote China's Relations with the Gulf Cooperation Council (GCC) and with the Arab Countries," June 3, 2014, accessed August 13, 2016, http://www.fmprc.gov.cn/mfa_eng/wjb_663304/zzjg_663340/xybfs_663590/gjlb_663594/2838_663666/2840_663670/t1162411.shtml.
46. Toumi, ibid.
47. "Kuwait, China Ink Deals," *Arab Times*, June 3, 2014, accessed September 21, 2014, http://www.arabtimesonline.com/NewsDetails/tabid/96/smid/414/ArticleID/206579/reftab/96/t/Kuwait-China-ink-deals/Default.aspx.
48. Ibid.
49. Toumi, ibid.
50. Niazi, ibid.

51. Ibid.
52. Ibid.
53. The Heritage Foundation and American Enterprise Institute, *China Global Investment Tracker Database*, accessed December 28, 2014, http://www.heritage.org/research/projects/china-global-investment-tracker-interactive-map.
54. Ibid.
55. Ibid.
56. Ibid.
57. Niazi, ibid.
58. Ibid.
59. The Heritage Foundation and American Enterprise Institute, ibid.
60. Ibid.
61. Niazi, ibid.
62. Ibid.
63. The Heritage Foundation and American Enterprise Institute, ibid.
64. United States Department of Defense, Defense Intelligence Agency, *Directory of PRC Military Personalities* (Washington, DC), 2014, 17.
65. Niazi, ibid.
66. Stockholm International Peace Research Institute, SIPRI Arms Transfers Database, http://www.sipri.org/databases/armstransfers; and Olimat, ibid., 132.
67. Ibid., 132–133.
68. Ibid., 133.
69. Ibid.
70. Ibid., 134.
71. Bartke, ibid., 107.
72. Ibid., 108.
73. Olimat, ibid., 134.
74. "Kuwait, China sign Cooperation Agreement," *Bahrain News Agency*, December 8, 2003, accessed August 13, 2016, http://bna.bh/portal/en/news/364544?date=2011-04-7.
75. Niazi, ibid.
76. Niazi, ibid.
77. Toumi, ibid.
78. Wendy Dang, "China, Kuwait Sign New Air Service Agreement," *China Aviation Daily*, June 5, 2014, accessed August 13, 2016, http://www.chinaaviationdaily.com/news/35/35186.html.
79. Niazi, ibid.
80. Ibid.
81. Ibid.
82. Toumi, ibid.
83. The Heritage Foundation and American Enterprise Institute, ibid.
84. "China's Honghua Secures $25M Rig Supply Contract from Kuwait Drilling Co.," *Rigzone*, January 6, 2016, accessed August 13, 2016, http://www.rigzone.com/news/oil_gas/a/142342/Chinas_Honghua_Secures_25M_Rig_Supply_Contract_from_Kuwait_Drilling_Co.
85. Ibid.
86. Olimat, ibid., 132.

Chapter 8

China and Oman
Political/Diplomatic Relations

Although Sino-Omani ties date back to ancient times, China and Oman established diplomatic relations on May 25, 1978.[1] Prior to Sultan Qaboo's assumption of power in 1970, Oman had limited contact with the outside world, including neighboring Arab states.[2] India and the United Kingdom were the only countries which had diplomatic representation in Oman.[3]

Oman expanded its diplomatic ties dramatically since 1970.[4] Oman purposely avoided diplomatic relations with communist countries like China and Russia because of communist support for the insurgency in Dhofar.[5] Chinese support of the Dhofar Liberation Front (DLF) in Oman's civil war made it a formidable opponent.[6] The DLF expanded its revolutionary activities beyond Oman to the Gulf region to become the Popular Front for the Liberation of the Occupied Arabian Gulf (PFLOAG).[7] China's fear of Russia, following the latter's invasion of Afghanistan, had prompted it to strengthen diplomatic ties with the countries of the Arabian Gulf like Oman.[8] China also saw the strategic value of Oman to not only counter Russia politically but also economically in terms of Oman's abundant energy resources. China's need to secure long-term energy supplies caused it to revise its foreign policy in the Gulf region.[9] In this respect, China struggled and actively sought to gain diplomatic recognition from Iran, Kuwait, and Saudi Arabia. China's support for the PFLOAG was a major hindrance to its recognition in the region, a goal paramount to China's foreign policy and national security.[10] Consequently, China ended its ties with the DLF communist insurgency in Oman in 1971, thereby cutting aid to the DLF; diplomatic relations were established in 1978, and Oman became the first Arab state to export crude petroleum and petroleum gas products to China.[11] Besides establishing diplomatic relations with Oman in 1978, securing Iran's diplomatic recognition in wake of China's cessation of support for communist liberation movements in the region opened up endless opportunities for China and motivated other countries to recognize it and support its admission to the United Nations in the same year.[12]

Oman Sultan Gaboo consolidated his power in 1975 and pursued a low-profile foreign policy concentrating his energies on domestic politics and the modernization of Oman. Oman refrained from active engagement in international relations contrary to many countries in the region. Oman's low-profile foreign policy and quiet diplomacy were fruitful as it prevented Oman from having catastrophic clashes with its neighbors and regional and international powers. This approach was very beneficial to Iran and the United States and contributed to the stability of the Gulf region because Oman served as an intermediary between the two countries. To this end, Oman is credited with bringing the American and Iranian delegations closer to agreements on the nuclear stalemate between the two countries as well as between Iran and the West.[13]

China and Oman agreed on many international issues affecting the region between 1980 and 2010: the Iran-Iraq War, the restoration of Kuwait's sovereignty in 1991, and the Arab Spring. Both opposed the Iran-Iraq War even though China armed both sides. Oman joined the international coalition to evict Iraq from Kuwait in 1991 even when China did not, and both resented the spirit of revolutionary change brought by the Arab Spring. The Arab Spring marginally affected Oman with only a few demonstrations that demanded political reform, employment, and a degree of political freedom. China was fearful that the contagious spirit of the Arab Spring might spread into Tibet and the Xinxiang Province.[14] Thus, both countries viewed the Arab Spring as destabilizing to their respective regions.

China and Oman have engaged each other no less than twenty-eight times since 2000.[15] Over the course of their diplomatic ties, China and Oman have also inked numerous agreements. Most notably this includes: Joint Communiqué on the Establishment of Diplomatic Relations Between the People's Republic of China and the Sultanate of Oman (1978);[16] and Agreement on Mutual Visa Exemption including diplomatic and service/special passports (April 16, 2010).[17]

China and Oman have also established official diplomatic representation, respectively, in Muscat and Beijing. Oman also has a consulate in Hong Kong.

China and Oman have also conducted strategic consultations annually since 2005 to discuss international and regional security issues.[18] Strategic consultations are essential to securing China's energy security given Oman's strategic location in the Gulf region. Oman is geographically located just outside the Strait of Hormuz making it directly accessible to the Indian Ocean and unencumbered in its ability to export crude petroleum and petroleum gas products, which includes liquefied natural gas (LNG) to China. Energy cooperation in security matters appears to be foundation for their bilateral relationship.

While energy cooperation provides the foundation of their bilateral relationship, bilateral cooperation has expanded to include project contracting, telecommunications, and power plant construction and irrigation facilities.[19] Construction contracts, encompassing a power plant, roads, port, water management, and shipbuilding have occurred since diplomatic relations were established in May 1978.[20]

ECONOMIC/TRADE RELATIONS

Sino-Omani economic relations were established in 1983 when China started to import oil from Oman.[21] Trade ties followed after diplomatic relations were established in 1978 and appeared strong. In 2013, China was Oman's largest trading partner.[22] In the same year, Oman was China's thirty-second largest trading partner.[23] Bilateral trade was: $12.4 billion (2008), $6.1 billion (2009), $10.7 billion (2010), $15.8 billion (2011), $18.7 billion (2012), $22.9 billion (2013), $25.8 billion (2014), and $17.1 billion (2015).[24] Bilateral trade increased one and one half-fold in seven years. Since 2000, bilateral trade increased fivefold. In 2012, foreign direct investment into Oman from China was $3 million and foreign direct investment stock was $33 million.[25]

In terms of bilateral trade, Table 8.1 shows the top five commodities traded between China and Oman in 2015. Energy commodities, which include crude petroleum and petroleum gas products, appear to be the most traded commodity. In terms of trade value, 93 percent is attributed to energy commodities, which includes crude petroleum and petroleum gas products. See Table 8.1.

In previous years, China's energy commodities accounted for the following in terms of trade value: 96.7 percent (2008), 92.5 percent (2009), 93.1 percent (2010), 93.2 percent (2011), 93.5 percent (2012), 94.9 percent (2013), and 95.75 percent (2014).[26]

Bilateral trade is promoted through several organizations such as the Omani Chamber of Commerce and Industry, the Omani Ministry of Commerce and Industry, the Omani-Chinese Joint Committee, the Oman Investment Fund, the China Foreign Trade Center, the Gulf Cooperation Council, the China-GCC Forum, the GCC-Asian Business Forum, the Asian Cooperation Dialogue, the China-Arab States Expo, the China Council for the Promotion of International Trade, the China-Arab Cooperation Forum, the PRC Ministry of Commerce, the PRC Ministry of Foreign Affairs, and All-China Federation of Commerce and Industry.[27]

China and Oman has inked some important agreements to facilitate trade between their countries. The most notable agreements and notes include:

Table 8.1 Top Five Commodities Traded between China and Oman

Commodity	Importer	Trade Value ($)	Percentage (%)
Mineral fuels, mineral oils and products of their distillation; bituminous substances; mineral waxes	China	14,060,520,396	93
Organic chemicals	China	635,045,238	4.0
Ores, slag and ash	China	214,731,453	1.43
Iron and steel	China	52,417,324	0.35
Aluminum and articles thereof	China	37,539,205	0.25
Nuclear reactors, boilers, machinery and mechanical appliances; parts thereof	Oman	481,993,207	23
Articles of iron or steel	Oman	231,711,930	11
Iron and steel	Oman	177,863,654	8
Electrical machinery and equipment and parts thereof; sound recorders and reproducers, television image and sound recorders and reproducers, and parts and accessories of such articles	Oman	161,761,717	8
Furniture; bedding, mattresses, mattress supports, cushions and similar stuffed furnishings; lamps and lighting fittings, not elsewhere specified or included; illuminated signs, illuminated nameplates and the like; prefabricated buildings	Oman	158,546,955	7

Source: United Nations Commodity Trade Statistics Database.

Agreement on Trade between China and Oman (October 14, 1980);[28] Agreement on Civil Air Transport between China and Oman (1983);[29] Agreement between the Government of China and the Government of Oman on Investment Promotion and Protection (1995);[30] Agreement between China and Oman on the Avoidance of Double Taxation (2002);[31] Cooperation Agreement of International Trade Promotion between the Oman Chamber of Commerce and Industry (OCCI) and the China Center (2004);[32] Agreement between the Bank of China and BankMuscat to establish the "Bank of China-BankMuscat China Desk" (March 27, 2010);[33] and Agreement on Two-Way Investment (November 6, 2011).[34]

In addition to inking agreements to foster bilateral trade, China has been actively involved in Oman's economic development. In this respect, China and Oman concluded the following deals to develop Oman's infrastructure: a $150 million Agriculture Contract between Sinohydro and Oman Wastewater Services for irrigation projects (February 2005); a $160 million Construction Contract between Oman Cement Company and China National Building Materials for real estate development (March 2008); and a $1 billion engineering-procurement-construction (EPC) contract awarded to Shandong Electric Power Construction Company to build the Salalah independent water and power plant (November 2009).[35]

The Sino-Omani trade portfolio includes a variety of sectors including: oil and gas, construction, power plant construction, irrigation systems, highways and road construction, housing unit buildings, airports, port development, fishing, shipbuilding, telecommunications, information technology, and consumer goods and services.[36]

Bilateral ties have strengthened in the financial sector.[37] In 2008, the Industrial and Commercial Bank of China (ICBC) opened a branch in Oman.[38] Its main regional branch in Dubai made significant profits and contributed to regional development.[39] The ICBC provides financial services and credits to businesses in the region, especially those involved in bilateral projects including Chinese businesses located in Dubai's Dragon Mart.[40] In 2010, the Bank of China and BankMuscat signed an agreement to create the "Bank of China-BankMuscat China Desk." The services provided by BankMuscat and Bank of China include advisories on local industry and legal framework; account services; wealth management; loans and other types of financing; trade settlement (Letter of Guarantee, Letter of Credit etc.); fund transfer (domestic and cross-border); and cash management.[41]

Omani merchants are regional customers at the Canton Fair in China, which services as the main instrument for prompting China's international trade. This event provides Omani traders to invest into the following Chinese sectors: machinery, electronics, construction, textiles, import-export, distribution, wholesales, and manufacturing. The event typically boasts over 25,000 exhibitors and 200,000 buyers from around the world.[42]

Sino-Omani trade relations also operate through GCC-China trade frameworks. The GCC member states and China signed the Framework Agreement on Economic, Trade, Investment and Technological Cooperation in 2004. Some of its aspects are still unfolding especially in oil and gas, minerals, refinery building and construction. Both countries have continued their negotiations and are working to conclude a Free Trade Agreement (FTA).[43]

Using the GCC network, China and Oman have also cooperated in civil aviation transport. Oman and other Gulf states are attempting to reach major Chinese cities via air, bringing Chinese to tourist destinations in the Gulf region. This network will help boost Oman's tourism sector.[44]

China and Oman are also involved in foreign direct investment in each other's markets. China's main sector is oil and gas and Oman is investing in joint ventures to build oil storage facilities in China to store Omani crude petroleum. Oman called on Chinese investors to develop Oman's most ambitious project to date—the Duqm Port Project. This project includes industrial, trade, and energy sub-projects. Within this project, development includes construction of a new oil storage facility, a refinery, an airport, the largest ship-repair facility of its kind in the region. It is located on the Sea of Oman which makes it very attractive to international corporations seeking to avoid the political tensions occurring the Gulf region and exports through the Hormuz Strait.[45] As of May 23, 2016, government officials from China and Oman signed a $10 billion agreement for Chinese companies to build an industrial park at Oman's southern port of Duqm.[46] The deal is expected to develop the area into a major business zone as part of an effort to diversify Oman's economy beyond oil.[47]

MILITARY/SECURITY RELATIONS

Sino-Omani military relations are developing. Their military-security relationship is evidenced by high-level, official visits and exchanges, port visits in Oman by PLAN ships, and observer participation in the joint military exercise AMAN sponsored by Pakistan in 2007, 2009, 2011, and 2013. China and Oman also signed an agreement in November 2010 to provide personnel training to the Omani military; however, only China posted a defense attaché to its embassy in Oman and Oman has yet to reciprocate.[48]

China and Oman have also engaged each other no less than fifteen times since 2002 according to the Ministry of National Defense of the People's Republic of China, *PLA Daily*, *Xinhua*, and *China Military Online*. These engagements include: one visit to the PRC by the Omani Minister of National Defense, one visit to Oman by China's Minister of National Defense, nine port visits to Oman by PLAN ships, and four joint military exercises (observer at AMAN). China also supported DLF rebels during the Omani civil war (1955–1975). It was the first political movement China supported on the Arabian Peninsula.[49]

China has been a minor arms supplier to Oman. Military equipment and arms transfers include six Type-90 12mm self-propelled mobile rocket launchers (2002) and fifty WZ-551 armored personnel carriers (2003) according to SIPRI Arms Transfer Database. China's total arms sales to Oman are $33.2 million based on the 2016 CPI index. Oman is predominantly armed by the United States and the United Kingdom.[50]

China has also used the Omani Port of Salalah to rest and replenish PLAN ships.[51] This port has served as a base to launch and conduct PLAN counter-piracy patrols in the Gulf of Aden. Given its strategic position at the nexus between the Gulf of Aden and the Arabian Sea—less than a hundred miles from key shipping lanes—Salalah is a useful port for PLAN forces operating in or transiting the Indian Ocean.[52]

China and Oman support efforts in combating international terrorism. Oman operates with a low-profile foreign policy and quiet diplomacy which helps it to evade criticism from extremist organizations and rogue countries. Oman's diplomatic expertise potentially figures into China's domestic policy to ending the insurgency in Xinxiang and incorporate Chinese Muslims into its developmental model.[53]

CULTURAL RELATIONS

China used cultural contacts to establish diplomatic relations especially during the Cold War. In Oman's case, diplomatic relations preceded cultural contacts because of China's involvement in Oman Civil War; however, cultural contacts go back 2,000 years when Omani merchants and their Chinese counterparts made contacts along the Silk Road. Thus, there were no people-to-people contacts other than political cadres which provided support for revolutionary forces operating in Oman. After China terminated its support of communist insurgents in 1975, bilateral cultural contacts were channeled mostly through government organizations like ministries and cultural missions. In 2001, the China-Arab Friendship Association was established to promote bilateral friendship and Arab culture in China. In 2010, the Omani-Chinese Friendship Association was established in Muscat with ambitious cultural and non-cultural goals with the aim of strengthening bilateral ties.[54]

Since the establishment of diplomatic relations, bilateral cooperation has occurred in aviation, health, education, culture, sports, tourism, and people-to-people exchanges.[55] China and Oman have also inked agreements, protocols, and memorandums of understanding to foster cultural cooperation and exchanges. These include: Agreement between the Government of China and the Government of Oman on Cultural, Public Health, and Press Cooperation (1981);[56] Cultural Exchange Plan for a Chinese Culture and Arts Exhibition in Muscat and a Chinese Youth and Young Artists Delegation to visit Oman (May 1, 1983);[57] Summary of Talks on Sports Exchange (January 24, 1985);[58] Protocol between the Ministries of China and Oman on Health and Medical Cooperation (1992);[59] Agreement on Aviation Service between Hong Kong Special Administrative Region of China and the Sultanate of Oman (1998);[60] Agreement to establish a chair of Arabic Studies at China's Peking University (2007);[61] and Memorandum of Understanding on the building of a memorial site for Zheng He in Salalah, Oman (2010).[62]

Cultural and non-governmental exchanges between the two countries have also occurred, which includes the fields of education, information, sports, health, youths, religion, and archeology. These include: Oman's "friendship"

ship Suhar sailed to China along the ancient navigation route (July 1981); the monument of the ancient ship Suhar funded by Oman was built in Guangzhou, South China's Guangdong Province (December 1995); Omani Sultan Kabbus presented to Chinese president Jiang Zemin a model of the ancient ship "Suhar," in celebration of the fifty-second National Day of China as well as in commemoration of the twentieth anniversary of the model ship's visit to China (September 2001); Omani Sultan Kabbus donated US$200,000 to help the Quanzhou Museum of Overseas History build the Islamic Arab Exhibition Room (December 2001); and a successful Omani pavilion at the 2010 Shanghai Expo in China, receiving more than three million visitors (2010).[63]

Chinese universities of science and technology have been destinations for Omani students. Omani colleges and universities have hosted Chinese students desiring to study the Arabic language and literature.[64] Confucius Institutes have been established globally but it is only a matter of time before one is in Oman.

ENERGY/PETROLEUM RELATIONS

Crude petroleum and petroleum gas trading forms the basis for China and Oman's trade relationship. Oman is a major oil supplier to China and China is Oman's top oil importer.[65] In this respect, China imported 6 to 10 percent of its crude petroleum from Oman between 2006 and 2015 inclusive and it is China's largest supplier of crude petroleum after Saudi Arabia. It is one China's top five oil suppliers. 59.4 percent of Oman's total oil production in 2013 was for China.[66] In terms of total trade value, crude petroleum imports ranged from 92 to 99 percent for the same years. Table 8.2 shows Chinese

Table 8.2   Chinese Crude Petroleum Imports from Oman

Year	KBPD	Oil Imports Share (%)	World Ranking	Crude Oil Trade Value ($)	Total Commodity Trade Value ($)	Percentage (%)
2006	265	9	5	6,086,420,586	6,129,474,240	99
2007	275	8	5	6,564,834,861	6,722,948,583	98
2008	293	8	4	11,245,313,217	11,626,847,464	97
2009	236	6	6	4,989,907,163	5,409,904,082	92
2010	319	7	4	9,097,160,559	9,779,203,580	93
2011	365	7	5	13,818,483,656	14,876,687,929	93
2012	393	7	5	15,818,658,133	16,974,956,957	93
2013	511	9	3	19,932,095,656	21,040,612,892	95
2014	597	10	4	22,677,034,611	23,792,679,063	95
2015	644	10	5	13,964,605,897	15,061,979,058	93

Source: United Nations Commodity Trade Statistics Database.

crude oil imports from Oman in thousands of barrels per day, oil imports share, world ranking, trade value, total commodity trade value, and percentage from 2006 to 2015. See Table 8.2.

China has imported petroleum gas products from Oman but on a limited basis. China imports less than 1 percent of its total imports in 2007, 2009, 2012, 2013, 2014, and 2015.[67]

China also imported less than between 1 and 2 percent of its LNG from Oman in 2007, 2009, 2012, 2013, 2014, and 2015.[68]

China also has some oil and gas acquisitions in Oman. In this respect, China finalized the following transactions: CNPC/PetroChina acquired 50 percent of Block 5—Daleel and Mezoon with Oman Oil Company SAOC (OOC) (April 2002); and CNPC signed a Memorandum of Understanding on the investment and cooperation in oil and gas development and downstream operation with Oman Oil Company (June 2005).[69]

Omani's geographic location outside the Straits of Hormuz makes it particularly attractive to crude petroleum shippers. This aspect makes Oman more exceptionally attractive to Chinese energy security. It will make it even more so when China builds the UAE's oil storage capacity at the Port of Fujairah in the Sea of Oman.[70]

CNPC has been very active in Oman's oil and gas production. In addition to owning stakes in two oil fields, CNPC also "provides a wide range of oil field services, including geophysical prospecting, well-drilling, logging, perforation and formation testing," which are essential services for developing Oman's oil and gas sector.[71] Sinopec also has been active and built a 1.88 million cubic-meter commercial crude oil storage facility in Maoming, China to store mainly Omani crude petroleum and Saudi light crude petroleum.[72] China and Oman signed an agreement on June 12, 2005 for Oman to supply oil to China during the same year.[73] On May 22, 2007, China Gas Holdings Limited signed a joint venture agreement with Oman Oil Company S..A.O.C. to import energy products from the Middle East.[74] The move will allow the China Gas Holdings Limited to develop a secure supply of energy for import into China.[75]

SUMMARY

Sino-Omani relations are strong. China and Oman are engaged politically, economically, militarily, and culturally. China and Oman have signed agreements and memorandums of understanding to promote trade, infrastructure, aviation, health, education, culture, sports and people-to-people exchanges. China has also supplied Oman with conventional military weapons and equipment. China and Oman have also participated in joint military exercises in 2007, 2009, 2011, and 2013 sponsored by Pakistan.

In terms of petroleum trading, Oman is a major supplier of crude petroleum, petroleum gas products, and LNG. China imported approximately 9 percent of its annual crude petroleum, less than 1 percent of its petroleum gas products, and less than 1 percent of LNG from Oman.

The strategic position of Oman's Port of Salalah between the Arabian Gulf and the Gulf of Aden facilitates energy trade between China and Oman. It also serves as a rest and replenishment station for PLAN ships. In addition, the port serves as a strategic base for Chinese warships conducting counter-piracy patrols in the Gulf of Aden, or operating in or transiting the Indian Ocean.

NOTES

1. Ministry of Commerce of People's Republic of China, "China–Oman Bilateral Relations," November 28, 2004, accessed October 3, 2014, http://om2.mofcom.gov.cn/article/bilateralcooperation/inbrief/200411/20041100004112.shtml; and Muhammad Zulfikar Rakhmat, "Exploring the China and Oman Relationship," *The Diplomat*, May 10, 2014, accessed October 7, 2014, http://thediplomat.com/2014/05/exploring-the-china-and-oman-relationship/.

2. United States Army, Army Logistics University, ALU International Military Student Office, Country Notes-CENTCOM, *Oman*, (n.d.), accessed October 4, 2014, http://www.alu.army.mil/ALU_INTERNAT/CountryNotes/CENTCOM/OMAN.pdf.

3. Ibid.
4. Ibid.
5. Ibid.
6. Muhamad S. Olimat, *China and the Middle East Since World War II* (Lanham, MD: Lexington Books), 2014, 158.
7. Ibid.
8. Rakhmat, ibid.
9. Ibid.
10. Olimat, ibid., 159.
11. Rakhmat, ibid.
12. Olimat, ibid., 159.
13. Ibid., 160, 161.
14. Ibid., 126, 160–161.
15. Ministry of Foreign Affairs of People's Republic of China, "China–Oman: Activities," (n.d.), accessed August 9, 2016, http://www.fmprc.gov.cn/mfa_eng/wjb_663304/zzjg_663340/xybfs_663590/gjlb_663594/2863_663716/2865_663720/.

16. Ministry of Foreign Affairs of People's Republic of China, "Joint Communiqué on the Establishment of Diplomatic Relations Between the People's Republic of China and the Sultanate of Oman," May 25, 1978, accessed October 3, 2014, http://www.fmprc.gov.cn/mfa_eng/wjb_663304/zzjg_663340/xybfs_663590/gjlb_663594/2863_663716/2864_663718/t16402.shtml.

17. Ministry of Foreign Affairs of People's Republic of China, "List of Agreements on Mutual Visa Exemption Between the People's Republic of China and Foreign Countries" November 28, 2004, accessed October 3, 2014, http://cs.mfa.gov.cn/wgrlh/bgzl/P020140328398504621618.pdf.

18. Rakhmat, ibid.

19. Ministry of Foreign Affairs of People's Republic of China, "China and Oman," (n.d.), accessed October 3, 2014, http://www.fmprc.gov.cn/mfa_eng/wjb_663304/zzjg_663340/xybfs_663590/gjlb_663594/2863_663716/.

20. Rakhmat, ibid.

21. Olimat, ibid., 162.

22. European Commission Directorate-General for Trade, "Oman: EU Bilateral Trade and Trade with the World," April 10, 2015, accessed May 3, 2015, http://trade.ec.europa.eu/doclib/docs/2006/september/tradoc_113430.pdf.

23. United Nations, United Nations Commodity Trade Statistics Database, accessed August 22, 2015, http://comtrade.un.org/db/default.aspx.

24. Ibid.

25. United Nations Conference on Trade and Development (UNCTAD FDI/TNC) Database, *Bilateral FDI Statistics 2014*, accessed October 5, 2014, http://unctad.org/Sections/dite_fdistat/docs/webdiaeia2014d3_CHN.pdf.

26. United Nations, United Nations Commodity Trade Statistics Database, Ibid.

27. Olimat, ibid., 164–165.

28. Ministry of Commerce of People's Republic of China, "China–Oman Bilateral Relations," ibid.

29. Ibid.

30. Ibid.

31. Ibid.

32. Jamal Bin Ramadan Al Maimani, "Economic Relations Between the Sultanate of Oman and China and India," *International Economy*, August/September 2005, No. 154, 14.

33. Mohammed Almasri, "Oman: BankMuscat, Bank of China join Hands to Tap Bilateral Trade & Investments," *Global Arab Network*, March 27, 2010, accessed August 14, 2016, http://www.english.globalarabnetwork.com/201003275296/Economics/oman-bankmuscat-bank-of-china-join-hands-to-tap-bilateral-trade-a-investments.html.

34. "China, Oman to sign MOUs to boost Cooperation," *Xinhua*, November 6, 2011, accessed August 14, 2016, http://www.chinadaily.com.cn/china/2010-11/06/content_11510675.htm.

35. The Heritage Foundation and American Enterprise Institute, *China Global Investment Tracker Database*, accessed October 5, 2014, http://www.heritage.org/research/projects/china-global-investment-tracker-interactive-map.

36. Olimat, ibid., 162.

37. Ibid.

38. Ibid.

39. Ibid.

40. Ibid.

41. Almasri, ibid.
42. Olimat, ibid., 162.
43. Ibid., 163.
44. Ibid., 164.
45. Ibid.
46. "Chinese Investors to build Industrial Park at Oman's Duqm Port," *Reuters*, May 23, 2016, accessed August 16, 2016, http://www.reuters.com/article/oman-china-industry-idUSL5N18K32D.
47. Ibid.
48. "China, Oman to sign MOUs to boost Cooperation," *Xinhua*, Ibid., and United States Department of Defense, Defense Intelligence Agency, *Directory of PRC Military Personalities* (Washington, DC), 2014, 19.
49. Olimat, ibid., 169.
50. Stockholm International Peace Research Institute, SIPRI Arms Transfers Database, http://www.sipri.org/databases/armstransfers; and Olimat, ibid., 170.
51. Daniel J. Kostecka, "Places and Bases: The Chinese Navy's Emerging Support Network in the Indian Ocean," *Naval War College Review*, Winter 2011, Volume 64, Issue 1, 65.
52. Kostecka, ibid., 67.
53. Olimat, ibid., 170.
54. Ibid., 167.
55. Ministry of Foreign Affairs of People's Republic of China, "China and Oman," Ibid.; and Ministry of Commerce of People's Republic of China, "China–Oman Bilateral Relations," ibid.
56. Ministry of Commerce of People's Republic of China, "China–Oman Bilateral Relations," ibid.
57. Wolfgang Bartke, *The Agreements of the People's Republic of China with Foreign Countries 1949–1990* (Munchen, Germany: K.G. Saur), 1992, 137.
58. Ibid.
59. Ministry of Commerce of People's Republic of China, "China–Oman Bilateral Relations," ibid.
60. Ibid.
61. Rakhmat, ibid.
62. Ministry of Foreign Affairs of People's Republic of China, "China and Oman," Ibid.
63. Ministry of Commerce of People's Republic of China, "China–Oman Bilateral Relations," ibid.; and Rakhmat, ibid.
64. Olimat, ibid., 168.
65. Ibid.
66. Ibid., 165.
67. United Nations, United Nations Commodity Trade Statistics Database, ibid.
68. Ibid.
69. Julie Jiang and Chen Dang, *Update on Overseas Investments by Chinese National Companies: Achievements and Challenges Since 2011* (Paris, France: Organization for Economic Cooperation and Development/International Energy Agency), June 2014, 35–39.

70. Olimat, ibid., 165.
71. Ibid., 166–167.
72. Ibid., 168.
73. "Oman, China sign Oil Supply Agreement," *Kuwait News Agency*, June 12, 2005, accessed August 15, 2016, http://www.kuna.net.kw/ArticlePrintPage.aspx?id=1568404&language=en.
74. "China Gas and Oman Oil Form Joint Venture-Set to become Major Energy Importer in China," *China Gas*, May 22, 2007, accessed August 15, 2016, http://www.chinagasholdings.com.hk/uploadfiles/20120514094849411.pdf.
75. Ibid.

Chapter 9

China and Russia
Political/Diplomatic Relations

Sino-Russian diplomatic relations were established on October 3, 1949. To establish diplomatic ties, China and Russian issued the Communiqué on the Establishment of Diplomatic Relations (October 3, 1949).[1]

Sino-Russian diplomatic relations are generally very good but have had a long and often troubled history.[2] Since 1990 their relationship could be considered successful if our observations are confined to top-level political relations and recognize how China and Russia eventually resolved their political disputes, settled border issues, minimized the risk of armed conflict, and eventually formed a strategic partnership relationship in 1996.[3]

Although China and Russia have a strategic partnership today, Russia has been historically anxious and suspicious of China. There is an undercurrent of Russian mistrust of China, even though the Sino-Russian relationship is currently pragmatic. This mistrust is attributed to the Mongol invasion of Russia in the thirteenth century and subsequent rule in the following three centuries. Russian fears about a Chinese demographic tide engulfing the Russian Far East (RFE) is born out of this "Mongol Complex" even though the ancient Mongols and today's Chinese have little connection to the Mongol invasion of Russia in the thirteenth century and subsequent rule during the fourteenth, fifteenth, and sixteenth centuries.[4]

The Mongol invasion was the first of many inevitable violent encounters between the East and Russia. The Russian Empire and the Manchu dynasty clashed in between the seventeenth and nineteenth centuries when the former expanded eastward. The clash of these empires resulted in a territorial, political, and civilizational fault line, where there had been previously nomadic tribes and lots of empty space.[5]

The Treaty of Nerchinsk (1689) brought peace between the two empires that settled not only the boundary between the Qing dynasty and Russian

Empire, but began diplomatic relations on an equal footing. The treaty regularized relations between the two countries and began the period exchange of diplomatic missions. By the mid-1800s, however, China's economy and military was weak when compared to the colonial powers, forcing it to sign unequal treaties with Western countries, such as Russia.

The Treaty of Nerchinsk was reversed with the signing of the Aigun (1858) and Peking (1860) treaties. Tensions exacerbated between the two empires when the Qing dynasty ceded most of the modern-day RFE to the Russian Empire under these treaties. The Russian Empire annexed approximately 1.5 million square kilometers of Chinese territory under these unequal treaties. Further, the Russian Empire expanded into Manchuria in the latter part of the nineteenth century. The fact that the lands ceded to the Russian Empire were made under duress, makes modern-day Russia permanently suspicious of Chinese irredentist ambitions.[6]

Russia acquired even more Chinese territory in the twentieth century. In some cases, armed conflicts ensued. In 1900, Russia participated in the collective intervention in Peking (Beijing) during the Boxer Rebellion and fought the Boxers and Chinese Imperial troops, built a naval base at Port Arthur (Lushun), a commercial port at Dalny on the Yellow Sea in 1898, and founded the city of Harbin in Manchuria. Russian expansion ended only after the Japanese defeated it in the Sino-Japanese War (1904–1905). Consequently, Russia was dislodged from Manchuria.[7] The removal of Russia from Manchuria led to the failed uprising of the Russian Tsar Nicholas Romanov in 1905—the precursor to the 1917 October Revolution that led to the creation of the Soviet Union.[8]

Sino-Soviet relations were factious between 1917 and 1949. The Soviet Russia invaded Xinjiang in 1934 and 1937, which resulted in a ceasefire and Xinjiang being divided into two in the former case and pro-Soviet control of the entire province in the latter case. Soviet Russia was also involved in the Chinese Civil War (1945–1949) and alternated its support of the combatants at the different stages of the conflict by supplying arms and equipment to both the Nationalist Party under Chiang Kai-shek and the Communist Party of China (CPC) under Mao Zedong. Soviet Russia eventually aligned itself firmly with the CPC and established diplomatic relations in October 1949 after the CPC emerged victorious against the Nationalists in same year. The Nationalists retreated to the island of Taiwan and established the Republic of China. The Soviet Union also formed a political alliance and supplied the newly formed People's Republic of China (PRC) (hereinafter China) with massive financial aid and military and technological assistance while treating China as a junior partner. Soviet financial, military, and technological assistance continued until 1960, when ideological differences began to emerge between the two countries after Joseph Stalin's death in 1953.[9]

Although China and the Soviet Union were politically aligned, relations were uncomfortable between Joseph Stalin and Mao Zedong. Stalin disliked Mao's ideological and political independence, while Mao resented Soviet patronizing behavior. While China regarded itself as Soviet Russia's "younger brother," it did not imply satisfaction with its subordinate status.[10]

Tensions between the two countries exacerbated under Stalin's successor Nikita Khrushchev. Ideological disputes such as different interpretations of Marxism-Leninism and the possibility of peaceful coexistence with the West, personality clashes between Khrushchev and Mao (two leaders of vast egos), disagreements over a common border and China's international role such as the leadership of world communism all contributed to a dramatic deterioration in bilateral relations. By 1960, the "unbreakable relationship" collapsed completely.[11]

Tensions between China and the Soviet Union remained unsolved despite Khrushchev's removal from power in 1964. In fact, the political-ideological conflict escalated into military confrontation and small-scale warfare under Khrushchev's successor Leonid Brezhnev. Chinese Red Guards attacked the Soviet Embassy in Beijing in January 1967 during the Cultural Revolution (1966–1976). In 1969 a series of border clashes along the Ussuri River between Chinese and Soviet troops resulted in several thousand casualties, mainly on the Chinese side, with the most serious skirmish occurring on Damansky Island. This was one of the most serious flashpoints of the Cold War era and could have degenerated in a conflict of very serious proportions.[12]

Bilateral relations slightly improved in the 1970s. The United States pursued a foreign policy of *détente,* mainly directed at the Soviet Union to avoid the collision of nuclear risks. The United States also sought to normalize relations with China, beginning with Henry Kissinger's secret trip to Beijing in July 1971 and ending with the Joint Communique on the Establishment of Diplomatic Relations on July 1, 1979.

The strategic triangle of the United States, Soviet Union, and China and the world balance of power became the focal point of in the analysis of Sino-Soviet relations in the 1970s. China began to radically align its foreign policy to obtain world recognition as a great power and obtain Western technological, diplomatic, and financial support to counter the powerful threat it perceived from the Soviet Union. Consequently, it began a rapprochement with the United States as a counterweight. The *détente* initiated by President Richard Nixon had the effect of reducing Sino-Soviet tensions to manageable levels as Soviet president Brezhnev worked to ensure the Soviet Union would not become strategically isolated by enemies in its east and west. China and the Soviet Union still played out their tensions on the international diplomatic stage. In the late 1970s increased Soviet military buildup in East Asia and Soviet treaties with Vietnam and Afghanistan heighted China's awareness of the threat of Soviet encirclement.[13] China realized those fears with the 1979 Soviet invasion of Afghanistan.

Soviet leadership changes between 1982 and 1985 provided openings for renewed diplomacy with China with the deaths of Leonid Brezhnev, Yuri Andropov, and Konstantin Chernenko. Sino-Soviet relations gradually improved in the many areas including trade and technology exchanges. Border pointed and delegates exchanged with no movement on the territorial issue.[14]

Sino-Soviet relations improved remarkably under Soviet president Mikhail Gorbachev. His July 1986 speech at Vladivostok was directed at China such as the announcement of partial troop withdrawals from Afghanistan and Mongolia, the renewal of a concession pertaining to the border dispute, and proposals for agreements on a border railroad, space cooperation, and joint hydropower development. Despite the improvement in bilateral relations, it wasn't until June 1989 when diplomatic relations were reestablished between the two countries that the territorial issue can back onto the negotiating table. Gorbachev's proposals were modest leaving his successors Boris Yeltsin, Dmitri Medvedev, and Vladimir Putin to translate Gorbachev's cooperative sentiments into real policy shifts.[15]

In June 1989, Gorbachev traveled to Beijing and normalized relations with China. Both countries signed a communiqué and agreed to build their relations based on the five principles of coexistence. Both wanted to focus on economic development and avoid the possibility of conflict, especially the Soviet Union because it was wary of a two-front conflict.[16]

Bilateral relations improved dramatically after the dissolution of the Soviet Union especially in the political, economic, and cultural spheres. In the 1990s significant progress was made in resolving some key major issues between the two countries: a common border, Chinese illegal immigration in the RFE, and growing convergence on international issues. With respect to the border issue, China and Russia signed eight agreements between 1991 and 2005. In terms of convergence, China and Russia came together in terms of economic and security interests and attached special importance to issues of sovereign independence and resisting "external interference" in domestic affairs. Both countries also came together institutionally by developing a network of bilateral institutions at all levels to create a lasting foundation for future progress. Nevertheless, Russia maintained pro-Western view in terms of seeing Western liberal democracy as paradigm for political and economic reform, and relying on Western aid and investment to help its economy during its first post-Communist government. Russia's early disappointment with the West in the 1990s led to its foreign policy to become more Eurasian-oriented. Russia did not see its Eurasian foreign policy as anti-Western, but more of a balance correction to overly Western orientation.[17]

In twenty-first century, history saw China and Russia deepening their bilateral relationship finding common ground mostly in economic development and energy security. Both countries issued no less than eleven (11) joint statements and communiqués. Both countries also shared similar perspectives on many international issues such as global governance where the United States does not dominate; cybercrime; and international finance reform where China and Russia have more say in Western-dominated international financial institutions like the World Bank and International Monetary Fund (IMF). China and Russia used international organizations composed of emerging national economies like Brazil, Russia, India, China, South Africa (BRICS) to counter the influence of IMF and World Bank.[18] Additionally, China created the Asian Infrastructure Investment Bank (AIIB) in January 2016 modeled after the IMF and World Bank to support the building of infrastructure in the Asia-Pacific region as well as a hedge against these Western financial institutions.

China and Russia have given great importance to multilateral forums. This includes but is not limited to the Shanghai Cooperation Organization (SCO), the United Nations Security Council, BRICS, and the Asia-Pacific Economic Cooperation (APEC). While participation is meant to strengthen bilateral relations between the two countries in terms of economics and security, they also serve as a soft balancing measure against the United States and its allies.[19]

In terms of sovereignty, China and Russia respect each other's territorial claims. For China, this means supporting Russia's military campaign in Chechnya; for Russia, this means supporting China's One-China policy with respect to Taiwan.[20]

China and Russia diverge on India and Pakistan. Both expressed concern regarding the India-Pakistan nuclear tests of 1998 but China supported Pakistan and Russia supported India. Russia has historically been close to India in the past while China has been close to Pakistan. In fact, Russia has been one of India's closest defense and strategic partners while China and Pakistan have enjoyed an all-weather relationship. Nevertheless, Russia serves an important balance between China and India. China and Russia also share similar views on Afghanistan and wish to include in the SCO.[21]

Since 2000, the levels of political dialogue, consultations and agreements, and diplomacy have risen to new heights due to numerous high-level official visits. In this respect, China and Russia have interacted through official telephonic conversations, high-level visits and exchanges no less than 708 times. The most important bilateral exchanges include: President Jiang Zemin and President Vladimir Putin (July 2000, September 2000, June 2001, July 2001, October 2001, and June 2002), President Hu Jintao and President Dimitri Medvedev (June 2009, September 2009, November 2009, April 2010, May 2010, June 2010, August 2010, September 2010, November 2010, April 2011, June 2011, November 2011, and April 2012), President Hu Jintao and

President Vladimir Putin (June 2012 and September 2012), President Xi Jinping and President Vladimir Putin (April 2013, June 2013, September 2013, October 2013, February 2014, March 2014, May 2014, July 2014, September 2014, November 2014, April 2015, July 2015, September 2015, November 2015, December 2015, and June 2016).[22]

China and Russia also signed numerous agreements to promote political-diplomatic cooperation. These include the following: Agreement on Friendship, Alliance, and Mutual Assistance (February 14, 1950);[23] Consular Agreement (June 23, 1959);[24] Revised Consular Treaty (September 10, 1986);[25] Agreement on Mutual Relations and Cooperation between the State Planning Commission of China and the USSR (September 10, 1986);[26] Consultation Accord between the Two Foreign Ministries (April 25, 1990);[27] Agreement on the Eastern Section of the Boundary between China and Russia (May 16, 1991);[28] Constructive Partnership featuring Good Neighborliness and Mutually Beneficial Cooperation (1994);[29] Agreement on the Western Section of the Boundary between China and Russia (September 3, 1994);[30] Agreement on the Final Section of the Border between China and Russia (1995);[31] Partnership of Strategic Coordination based on Equality and Mutual Benefit and oriented toward the Twenty-First Century (1996);[32] Shanghai Five Agreement on Confidence-Building Measures along the Sino-Soviet Border (April 1996);[33] Protocol on Delineation of the Eastern and Western Sections of the Border (1999);[34] Beijing Declaration of the PRC and the Russian Federation (July 18, 2000);[35] Joint Communiqué on the Fifth Regular Meeting between the Heads of Government of the People's Republic of China and the Russian Federation (November 22, 2000);[36] Agreement on Mutual Exemption of Entry Visas between the People's Republic of China and the Government of Russia on Holders of Ordinary Passports/International Travel Documents When Traveling in Tour Groups Organized by Authorized Travel Agencies of Both Countries (December 1, 2000);[37] Agreement on Mutual Exemption on Entry Visas on Holders of Diplomatic Passports, Trainmen onboard an International Train for Public Affairs, Members of Designated Aircrew, Seafarers Traveling with Seafarer's Passports for Public Affairs (May 25, 2001);[38] Treaty of Good-Neighborliness and Friendly Cooperation between the PRC and the Russian Federation (July 24, 2001);[39] Consular Affairs Treaty between the PRC and the Russian Federation (April 26, 2002);[40] Agreement on the Final Demarcation of the Eastern Border (2004);[41] Joint Communiqué of the Thirteenth Regular Meeting Between the Heads of Government of the People's Republic of China and the Russian Federation (October 29, 2008);[42] Comprehensive Strategic Partnership of Coordination (2011);[43] Joint Declaration of the People's Republic of China and the Russian Federation on Further Deepening the China-Russia Comprehensive Strategic Cooperative Partnership Based on Equality and Mutual Trust (June

5, 2012);[44] Cooperation Agreement between the Shanghai Municipal Government and the St. Petersburg Government (September 5, 2013);[45] Joint Communiqué of the 18th Regular Meeting between Chinese and Russian Prime Ministers (October 22, 2013);[46] China-Russia Joint Statement on a New Stage of Comprehensive Strategic Partnership of Coordination (May 20, 2014);[47] Joint Communiqué of the 19th Regular Meeting Between Chinese and Russian Prime Ministers (October 13, 2014);[48] Joint Statement on Cooperation of Connection Between the Silk Road Economic Belt and Eurasian Economic Union (May 13, 2015);[49] Joint Statement of the People's Republic of China and the Russian Federation (June 25, 2016);[50] Joint Statement on Strengthening Global Strategic Stability Between the President of the People's Republic of China and President of the Russian Federation (June 25, 2016);[51] Declaration of the People's Republic of China and the Russian Federation on the Promotion of International Law (June 26, 2016);[52] and Regulation of Council of Cooperation Between the Upper and Middle Reaches of the Yangtze River and the Volga Federal District (July 20, 2016).[53]

In addition to the signing of numerous bilateral agreements of a political nature, both countries have established diplomatic representation through embassies in their respective capitals in Beijing and Moscow in 1949. Additionally, China established consulates in Khabarovsk and St. Petersburg and Russia established consulates general in Guangzhou, Hong Kong, Shenyang, and Shanghai.[54]

ECONOMIC/TRADE RELATIONS

Sino-Russian economic relations are robust. Bilateral trade has increased from $8 billion to $88.1 billion between 2000 and 2012. Russia was China's eighth largest trading partner accounting for 2.1 percent of China's global trade in 2012.[55] China was also Russia's largest trading partner after European Union accounting for 10.4 percent of Russia's global trade in the same year.[56] In 2013, China was also Russia's largest trading partner after the European Union.[57] Russia was China's ninth largest trading partner in the same year.[58] Russia sees China as its most important trading partner and a market for its raw materials and energy especially since it appears to be facing a shrinking market in Europe/West for its energy products.[59]

Bilateral trade was: $56.9 billion (2008), $38.7 billion (2009), $55.5 billion (2010), $79.2 billion (2011), $88.1 billion (2012), $89.2 billion (2013), $95.2 billion (2014), and $68 billion (2015). Since 2000, bilateral trade increased almost eightfold. However, China and Russia hardly traded during the Cold War (1947–1991). Economic relations revolved around the transplantation of the Soviet economic model to China and consisted mainly of Russia supplying China with personnel support, massive financial aid, and some trade. Bilateral trade picked up in the 1990s with the end of the Cold War and was characterized by the influx of cheap Chinese consumer goods into the Far East. Bilateral trade was modest in the 1990s but picked up in the new century.[60]

Foreign direct investment is relatively small between China and Russia. In 2012, China's foreign direct investment into Russia was $450 million and foreign direct investment stock was $2.152 billion.[61] In the same year, Russia's foreign direct investment in China was $63 million and foreign direct investment stock was $234 million.[62] Foreign direct investment between BRIC countries like China and Russia appears to be limited according to the United Nations Conference on Trade and Development (UNCTAD).[63] Despite China's low foreign direct investment, it is the largest Asian investor in Russia.[64]

Table 9.1 shows the top five commodities traded between China and Russia in 2015. Energy commodities, such as crude petroleum and petroleum products, appear to be the most traded commodity between the two countries with a commodity trade value of 61 percent. Russia's top imports from China

Table 9.1 Top Five Commodities Traded between China and Russia

Commodity	Importer	Trade Value ($)	Percentage (%)
Mineral fuels, mineral oils and products of their distillation; bituminous substances; mineral waxes	China	20,222,796,727	60.88
Wood and articles of wood; wood charcoal	China	3,125,939,803	9.41
Nickel and articles thereof	China	2,282,461,839	6.87
Fish and crustaceans, mollusks, and other aquatic invertebrates	China	1,171,794,715	3.53
Ores, slag and ash	China	906,234,123	2.73
Nuclear reactors, boilers, machinery and mechanical appliances; parts thereof	Russia	5,235,103,150	15
Electrical machinery and equipment and parts thereof; sound recorders and reproducers, television image and sound recorders and reproducers, and parts and accessories of such articles	Russia	5,136,276,749	15
Articles of apparel and clothing accessories, not knitted or crocheted	Russia	2,596,777,820	7
Articles of apparel and clothing accessories, knitted or crocheted	Russia	2,162,292,712	6
Fur skins and artificial fur; manufactures thereof	Russia	1,959,885,113	6

Source: United Nations Commodity Trade Statistics Database.

include: electrical machinery and equipment, nuclear reactors, apparel and clothing accessories, and fur skins. See Table 9.1. During the Cold War, Russia (as a Soviet Socialist Republic) exported machinery and equipment, fertilizers, timber, steel, aluminum to China while the latter exported consumer goods and food products to the former.[65]

In previous years, China's energy commodities accounted for the following in terms of trade value: 50.1 percent (2008), 44.1 percent (2009), 49.6 percent (2010), 56.8 percent (2011) and 66.9 percent (2012), 67.8 percent (2013), and 71.5 percent (2014).[66]

Bilateral trade is promoted through several organizations such as the Far East Chamber of Commerce and Industry, International Investment Center, Ministry of Economic Development and Trade, Moscow Chamber of Commerce and Industry, Moscow International Business Association, Moscow Investment and Export Promotion Agency, Russian Agency for Small and Medium Industry Support, Russian Federation Chamber of Commerce and Industry, Saint Petersburg Chamber of Commerce and Industry, Russian National Trade Point, the PRC Ministry of Commerce, the PRC Ministry of Foreign Affairs, and the All-China Federation of Industry and Commerce.[67]

China and Russia has inked some important agreements to promote economic and trade cooperation between their countries. The most notable agreements and notes include: Agreement on the Changchun Railway Line, Port Arthur (February 14, 1950); Exchange of Notes on the Return, with Indemnities, of the ex-Japanese Property in Manchuria to the Government of PRC (February 14, 1950); Agreement on a Soviet Loan of $300 million (February 14, 1950); Agreement on the Foundation of a Joint-Stock Company for Civil Aviation (March 27, 1950); Agreement on the Foundation of a Joint-Stock Company for the Extraction of Non-Ferrous and Rare Metals in Sinkiang (March 27, 1950); Agreement on Soviet Aid for the Construction of 50 Industrial Enterprises in China (March 27, 1950); 1950 Trade Agreement (April 19, 1950); Protocol on 1950 Goods Exchange (April 19, 1950); Protocol on Common Terms for Goods Exchange in 1950 (April 19, 1950); Protocol on the Soviet Supplies to be delivered in 1950 under the Loan Agreement of February 14, 1950 (April 19, 1950); Protocol on the Establishment of Changchun Railway Company (April 25, 1950); Soviet Statement on the Transfer to China of Assets in connection with the Changchun Railway and ex-Japanese Property in Manchuria (January 18, 1951); Exchange of Notes on the Prolongation of the 1950 Trade Agreement until December 31, 1951 (February 3, 1951); Agreement on a Direct Railway Through Traffic on the Changchun-Harbin Line over the Border to the Siberian Railway (March 14, 1951); Protocol on the 1951 Goods Exchange (June 15, 1951); Protocol on the Soviet Deliveries in 1951 under the Loan Agreement of 1950 (June 15, 1951); Agreement on the Foundation of a Joint-Stock Company for Shipbuilding and

Repair in Dairen (July 28, 1952); Protocol on the Common Terms for Goods Exchange (March 29, 1952); Protocol on the 1952 Goods Exchange (April 12, 1952); Protocol on the Soviet Deliveries in 1952 under the Loan Agreement of 1950 (April 12, 1952); Agreement on the Construction the Tsining-Ulan Bator Railway Line (September 15, 1952); Protocol on the Transfer of the Changchun Railway to China (December 31, 1952); Protocol on the 1953 Goods Exchange (March 21, 1953); Protocol on the Soviet Deliveries in 1953 under the 1950 Loan Agreement (March 21, 1953); Protocol on the Soviet Deliveries in 1954 under the 1950 Loan Agreement (January 23, 1954); Protocol on 1954 Goods Exchange (January 23, 1954); Agreement on the Construction of a Railway Line connecting Lanchou, Urumchi, and Alma Ata (October 12, 1954); Agreement on the Sale of Soviet Shares in the Four Mixed Joint-Stock Companies (for petroleum, non-ferrous metals, civil aviation, and shipbuilding) to China (October 12, 1954); Agreement on a Long-Term Soviet Loan of 520 million rubles (October 12, 1954); Protocol on 1955 Goods Exchange (February 11, 1955); Protocol on Soviet Deliveries in 1955 under the Loan Agreement of 1950 (February 11, 1955); Protocol on the Common Terms of Goods Exchange in 1955 (February 12, 1955); Protocol on Common Terms for Goods Exchange (December 27, 1955); Protocol on Soviet Deliveries in 1956 under the Loan Agreement of 1950 (December 27, 1955); Agreement on the Construction the Railway Line from Lanchou via Urumchi with connection to the Turksib Railway Line and the Inauguration of Through Traffic in 1960 (April 7, 1956); Additional Protocol relating to 1956 Goods Exchange (July 25, 1956); Protocol on the Common Terms of Goods Exchange (April 10, 1957); Protocol on 1957 Goods Exchange (April 12, 1957); Agreement on Commercial Shipping on the Border Rivers and Lakes in the Northeastern Part of China and Sinkiang (December 21, 1957); Agreement on the Settlement of Non-Commercial Payments (December 30, 1957); Agreement on Trade and Shipping (April 23, 1958); Protocol on 1958 Goods Exchange (April 23, 1958); Agreement on the Extension of Economic Cooperation as well as Construction of Seventy-Eight Large Industrial Plants with Soviet Assistance from 1959 to 1967 (February 7, 1959); Protocol on 1959 Goods Exchange (February 26, 1959); Agreement on Border Shipping on Amur River (March 12, 1959); Agreement on Border Trade between Sinkiang and Tajikistan Soviet Republic (October 29, 1959); Protocol of 1960 Goods Exchange (March 29, 1960); Agreement between the State Banks relating to the Cash Exchange Rates and the Amounts of Money that may be carried by those crossing the common border (March 20, 1960); Protocol on Goods Exchange (April 7, 1960); Agreement on the Repayment, by Installments, of China's Debts from the Exchange of Goods from 1960 to 1965 (April 7, 1960); Protocol on the Moratorium for the Repayment of the Chinese Debts in 1960, as well as the Supply of 500,000 tons of sugar and 1 million tons of grain (April 8, 1960); Agreement on Economic and Scientific-Technical Cooperation (June 19, 1961); Protocol on Economic and Technical Cooperation (October 6, 1961); Protocol on 1962 Goods Exchange (April 20, 1962); Protocol on Economic and Scientific-Technical Cooperation (May 13, 1962); Border Trade Agreement between the Inner Mongolian Autonomous Region and the Chita Oblast (June 29, 1962); Protocol on the Examination of the Accounts relating to goods supplied during the first months of 1962 (August 28, 1962); Protocol on the Premature Repayment of Chinese Debts (April 17, 1963); Protocol on 1963 Goods Exchange (April 21, 1963); Protocol on 1964 Goods Exchange (May 13, 1964); Protocol on Premature Repayment of Chinese Debts from Trade in 1960 (May 13, 1964); Protocol on 1965 Goods Exchange (April 29, 1965); Protocol on 1965 Additional Goods Exchange (July 20, 1965); Protocol on 1966 Goods Exchange (April 19, 1966); Protocol on 1967 Goods Exchange (July 27, 1967); Agreement on the Exchange of Goods and Payments (November 22, 1970); Agreement on the Exchange on Goods and Payments (August 5, 1971); Agreement on the Exchange of Goods and Payments (June 13, 1972); Agreement on Goods Exchange and Payments in 1973 (August 1, 1973); Agreement on Goods Exchange and Payments in 1974 (May 15, 1974); Agreement on Goods Exchange and Payments in 1975 (July 24, 1975); Agreement on Goods Exchange and Payments in 1976 (May 21, 1976); Agreement on Goods Exchange and Payments (July 2, 1977); Agreement on Goods Exchange and Payments in 1978 (April 17, 1978); Agreement on Goods Exchange and Payments in 1979 (August 6, 1979); Agreement on Goods Exchange and Payments (June 6, 1980); Agreement on Goods Exchange and Payments (June 16, 1981); Trade Agreement for the Transfer of over 400,000,000 Swiss francs (March 15, 1982); Agreement on Goods Exchange and Payments in 1982 (April 16, 1982); Agreement between the Bank of China and the Bank for USSR on Accounting Procedures in the Border Trade between the Two Countries (December 24, 1982); Agreement on Goods Exchange and Payments in 1983 (March 10, 1983); Minutes of the Border Trade Talks between China's Heilongjiang Province and the Far East Region of the USSR (April 10, 1983); Agreement on Commodity Import and Export between China and the USSR (April 10, 1983); Agreement on Border Trade between the Inner Mongolia Autonomous Region and the China Oblast of the USSR (May 13, 1983); Protocol on Boundary through Railway Traffic (August 22,1983); Supplemental Accord to the one between the China National Publications Import and Export Corporation and the International Publications Corporation of the Soviet Union concluded in 1982 (September 12, 1983); Agreement on Goods Exchange and Payments (February 10, 1984); Minutes of Talks on Border Trade (March 24, 1984); Contracts on Goods Exchange between the Trade Corporation of the Nei Mongol Autonomous Region and the Far East

Trade Corporation of the Soviet Union (April 21, 1984); Protocol on Border Railway Traffic (July 24, 1984); Agreement on Goods Exchange and Payments (November 30, 1984); Agreement on Economic and Technical Cooperation (December 28, 1984); Agreement on the Establishment of a Sino-Soviet Committee for Economic, Trade, Scientific, and Technological Cooperation (December 28, 1984); Minutes of Talks on Trade and Transport for 1985 (April 1, 1985); Agreement on Goods Exchange and Payments for 1986–1990 (July 10, 1985); Agreement on Economic and Technological Cooperation in Building and Upgrading Industrial Projects in China (July 10, 1985); Agreement between Heilongjiang Province and Blagoveshchensk City on Opening Ports, Goods Transfer, and Shipping (July 15, 1985); Summary of Talks on 1986–1990 Transport of Foreign Goods (January 1986); Protocol on Goods Exchange and Payments in 1986 (January 23, 1986); Summary of the 1st Meeting of the Joint Committee on Economic, Trade, Scientific, and Technical Cooperation (March 21, 1986); Agreement on Shipping Cooperation (May 28, 1986); Agreement on the Exchange of Economic and Trade Exhibitions (July 28, 1986); Protocol on Border Railway Traffic (July 30, 1986); Trade Contracts (August 29, 1986); Protocol on the 1st Session of the Sino-Soviet Committee on Economic and Technical Cooperation (October 16, 1986); Trade Protocol for 1987 (March 2, 1987); Trade Protocol outlining the 1987 Fiscal Year Plan for Imports and Exports and Cross-Border Railway Transportation (March 9, 1987); Agreement between the China National Machinery Import-Export Corporation and the Soviet Union Ship Import Corporation (June 18, 1987); Agreement on Private Remittances between the Citizens of the PRC and the USSR (October 29, 1987); Protocol of the 2nd Meeting of the Sub-Committee of the Sino-Soviet Committee on Economic, Trade, Scientific, and Technical Cooperation (December 3, 1987); Protocol on Goods Exchange and Payments (December 28, 1987); Protocol on Railway Transportation (September 7, 1988); Barter Agreement that will allow for the laying of railway track from Wusu in the Xinjiang Uighur Autonomous Region of China to the Ala Pass of the Chinese-Soviet Border (December 28, 1988); Protocol on Commodity Exchange and Payment for 1989 (March 3, 1989); Protocol for the Railway Transport of Import, Export, and Transit Goods among Three Countries (March 4, 1989); Summary of Talks from the 1st Session of the Permanent Working Group for Local and Border Trade Cooperation under the Sino-Soviet Committee of Economic, Trade, Scientific, and Technological Cooperation (April 6, 1989); Summary of the 3rd Meeting of the Permanent Working Group under Sino-Soviet Economic, Trade, Scientific, and Technological on Power Cooperation (July 6, 1989); Protocol on Economic Cooperation (July 26, 1989); Summary of the Sino-Soviet Commission on Economic, Trade, Scientific, and Technological Cooperation (January 23, 1990); Agreement on 1990 Goods Exchange and

Payment (March 13, 1990); Long-Term Cooperation and Development Program of Economy, Science, and Technology (April 25, 1990); Credit Agreement of Daily-Use Commodities provided by China (April 25, 1990); Memorandum on a Soviet Government Loan to China (April 25, 1990); Memorandum of the 5th Meeting of the Sino-Soviet Economic, Trade, Scientific, and Technological Cooperation Committee (July 21, 1990); Agreement on Mutually Encouraging and Protecting Investments (July 21, 1990); Agreement on Avoidance of Double Taxation (July 21, 1990); Agreement on Labor Services (August 30, 1990); Trade Agreement (October 2, 1990); Protocol on Ways of Settling Accounts and Payments (October 2, 1990); Market Access Agreement on Russia's Accession to the World Trade Organization between the People's Republic of China and the Russian Federation (October 14, 2004); Cooperation Agreement between China Development Bank (CDB) and Russia's Sberbank (December 6, 2012); and Memorandum of Strategic Cooperation between the Agricultural Bank of China and Russia's Sberbank (December 6, 2012).[68]

China has been actively involved in Russia's economic development which includes financial aid, infrastructure, and investment especially in the twenty-first century. In this respect, some of the largest and most recent infrastructure and development projects are in agricultural, construction, forestry, metals, mining, real estate, transportation, and technology sectors and total no less than $14.82 billion. These projects include: a Chinese consortium consisting of Shanghai Industrial Investment Group Ltd., Jinjiang International Group Ltd., Greenland Group Ltd., Shanghai Industrial Group Ltd., and Shanghai Brilliance Group Ltd. agreed to invest $1.3 billion in the Baltic Pearl real estate development project in St. Petersburg, Russia (April 2006);[69] China Minmetals Development Co. Ltd. and Mechel agreed to invest $300 million to jointly develop a rail and structural steel mill plant "Chelyabinsk Metallurgical Plant" and the construction of a new coal mining complex at the Elgar Deposit (October 2008); Xiyang Group to invest $480 million in Russia's iron sector (July 2009); Norinco agreed to invest $460 million in an automobile assembly plant in Dagestan (January 2010); Tencent agreed to invest $300 million in Digital Sky Technologies for a 10 percent stake (April 2010); Sinoma International Engineering Co., Ltd. and Lafarge Group signed a $140 million contract to design, supply, install, and commission the Ferzikovo cement production plant (May 2010); the Russian Republic of Tatarstan awarded China National Chemical Engineering Corporation a $330 million contract to build the Ammoni fertilizer plant (November 2010); China Chengtong Development Group invested $350 million to develop the Greenwood International Trade Center (May 2011); Fuyao Glass Industry Group Corporation agreed to invest $200 million to build a glass plant in the Kaluzhskaya Oblast region to supply automakers in Russia (June 2011);

Metallurgical Corporation of China Ltd. invested $240 million to construct the Kimkan iron ore plant in Russia (July 2011); Zijin Mining Group Co. Ltd. invested $100 million to build a mining and concentrating complex in Tuva Republic (April 2012); NORINCO and Basic Element agreed to invest $1 billion to build an aluminum plant in Russia (April 2012); China Investment Corporation (CIC) acquired a 5 percent stake in Polyus Gold for $420 million (May 2012); China Non-ferrous Metals Industry Foreign Engineering and Construction Co., Ltd. and East Siberian Metals Corporation acquire a 50 percent stake in joint venture to develop zinc deposits for $750 million (April 2013); CIC and Russia Forest Products acquire a 21 percent stake in Far East Timber Company for $100 million (April 2013); CIC acquired a 13 percent stake in Uralkali for $2.04 billion (September 2013); China State Construction Engineering Corporation agreed to build the Federazija Complex, Tower A, for $710 million (March 2014); Great Wall Motors Company agreed to build a solely owned automobile assembly plant in Russia for $340 million (May 2014); China National Materials Group Corporation signed a $150 million contract to supply Eurocement Group with construction equipment to build a new plant (May 2014); China National Machinery Industry Corporation signed a $180 million contract to supply Eurocement Group with construction material to build a new plant (May 2014); China Railway Construction Corporation, China International Fund Limited, and JSC Mosinzhproekt signed an agreement to build an underground railway, the new South-West Metro Line, for $1.99 billion (May 2014); Sinosteel and CJSC Chek-Su.VK sign a $740 million contract to produce electrolytic manganese metal using ore from the Usinskoye deposit to make special steels (May 2015); Zoje Resources Management signed an $440 million lease agreement for large plot of land in Russia's Transbaikal region for agricultural exploitation (June 2015); China Railway Group Limited won a $380 million contract to build a high-speed railway connecting Moscow with the city of Kazan (June 2015); and Memorandum of Understanding between China and Russia for the construction of a grain hub including a grain terminal and thirty elevators for $1.1 billion (June 2016).[70]

Key Chinese infrastructure projects in Russia were backed by loans from Chinese banks and financial institutions such as the Export-Import Bank of China. To date, China has invested or promised to invest no less than $500 million. These loans include a $500 million loan from the Export-Import Bank of China to fund the construction of the Baltic Pearl real estate development project in St. Petersburg, Russia (March 24, 2006).[71]

China and Russia have also cooperated in banking, securities, and venture capitalism totaling no less than $500 million in Chinese acquisitions and Sino-Russian joint ventures. In this respect, both countries have concluded the following deals: CIC purchased a $100 million stake in Russian bank's

VTB Group (February 2011); CIC acquired a 20 percent stake in the Moscow Stock Exchange for $100 million (February 2013); China Construction Bank acquired a 2 percent stake in VTB Bank for $100 million (May 2013); and Chinese Cybernaut Investment Group and Skoklovo Foundation established a joint venture fund worth $200 million focusing on companies from information technology, robotics, space technology, and telecommunications (April 2015).[73][72]

MILITARY/SECURITY RELATIONS

Sino-Russian/Sino-Soviet military-security relations have been traditionally close since diplomatic relations were established in October 1949 except for the Sino-Soviet split (1960–1989). To this extent, Soviet Union (1922–1991) and Russian Federation (1991–Present) military influence on China has been profound.[74] Soviet and Russian military assistance helped lay the foundation for Chinese military modernization during both periods.[75] During the Cold War, Chinese military modernization was largely driven by the failure of the People's Liberation Army (PLA) to capture Quemoy in 1950 and the huge casualties that it sustained in the Korean War.[76] Advanced weapons were essential if the PLA was to be able to fight modern wars, especially with the United States, a powerful enemy of China for most of the Cold War and currently a global rival and competitor.[77] In the post–Cold War period, a doctrine of peripheral defense emerged which called for the limited but effective military operations in regions bordering China.[78] This called for a modern defense force capable of deterring major aggression and winning local wars under modern conditions as opposed to preparing for a large-scale war of the Cold War.[79] Doctrinal changes stressed the increasing importance of the People's Liberation Army Navy (PLAN) to broaden its traditional mission of coastal defense to include offshore operations across the Taiwan Strait and force projection into the South China Sea and beyond.[80] Similarly, the requirement of the People's Liberation Army Air Force (PLAAF) to provide effective cover and maintain air control over regions of particular Chinese interest also reflected China's changing defense priorities.[81] Essentially, China sought to modernize its air force and navy to match those of potential adversaries in the South China Sea.[82] Hence, there was a large volume of Chinese arms imports from Russia in the 1990s.[83]

Desert Storm (1990–1991), which showcased the superiority of the United States in modern warfare in terms of the synchronization of modern weapons, superior command, control, communications, and intelligence (C^3I), and the air-land battle (ALB) doctrine, convinced the PLA leadership that force modernization was not only necessary but essential, especially in light of new

Chinese military missions as a result of changed defense posture and military equipment deficiencies at the end of the Cold War. Moreover, China's arm industry was not capable of producing the kinds of weapons that its rivals in the region, including Taiwan, were procuring from the West. Consequently, China sought to close not only its doctrinal gap but also its technological one. Russia played a critical role in closing China's technological gap. It supplied China with 90 percent of its major conventional weapons and equipment between 1991 and 2010.[84]

The arms trade was mutually beneficial to both countries in the post-Cold War.[85] Russia helped to modernize China militarily while China saved the Russian arms industry from death.[86] The 1990s was a period when domestic arms orders and former Soviet Union's clients had dried up.[87] When the Soviet Union collapsed, the new Russian government was unable to generate the domestic orders for equipment necessary to sustain its bloated military-industrial complex.[88] Consequently, the Russian arms industry turned increasingly to foreign sales to remain afloat.[89] China also faced an arms embargo from the United States and the European Union after ruthlessly suppressing a popular demonstration in Tiananmen Square in June 1989.[90] China's behavior at Tiananmen imposed significant constraints on its defense modernization and Russia was more than willing to sell weapons and help modernize China's military, especially since Russian weapons were relatively inexpensive and Moscow was willing to accept flexible payment arrangements, including barter trade.[91] Consequently, China turned to Russia for military arms because it no longer had access to modern military technologies from the West as result of the Tiananmen Square massacre, Russian weapons were relatively inexpensive, and its military modernization was in jeopardy.[92]

China and Russia do not have a formal military alliance today but they cooperate widely on defense matters. In this respect, there are three dimensions of bilateral military cooperation: military-political cooperation in the form of high-level meetings between military chiefs of staff and defense ministers; military training cooperation via exchanges of personnel for training, military education, and joint military exchanges; and military-technical cooperation through the transfer of arms, technology, and know-how for the production of military equipment.[93] China and Russia also have converging interests on important international security issues such as missile defense and space weaponization.[94] Agreements and memorandums have been signed in these areas.

In terms of military training cooperation, China and Russia have conducted joint military exercises to strengthen joint operational capabilities, exchange experience, facilitate cooperation in the fight against the "three forces" of terrorism, separatism, and extremism, and enhance mutual combat readiness against emerging threats.[95] The joint military exercises include the Peace

Mission exercises and members of the SCO. Peace Mission exercises were conducted in 2005, 2007, 2009, 2010, 2012, 2013, and 2014. China and Russia also conducted Joint Sea 2012, 2013, 2014, 2015, and 2016. These naval exercises are their largest exercises in the Pacific and provide Russia with an opportunity to showcase their new weapons to China.[96]

China and Russia have engaged each other no less than seventy-one times since 2002 according to the Ministry of National Defense of the People's Republic of China, *PLA Daily*, *Xinhua*, and *China Military Online*. Between December 1991 (when the Soviet Union collapsed) and 2002, China and Russian engaged each other no less than twenty-seven times and signed many agreements on military cooperation. Interactions since 2002 include: thirty visits to the PRC by Russian military officials (Defense Minister, Chief of the General Staff, Deputy Chief of the General Staff, Army Commander), fifteen visits to Russia by Chinese military officials (Minister of National Defense, Navy Commander, and Vice Chairman of the Central Military Commission) including four port visits by PLAN ships, eight security consultations between Chinese and Russian general staffs, fourteen joint military exercises including Joint Sea and Peace Mission, two joint military training sessions (judicial and military translation), and one educational exchange between military attachés.

In terms of military-technical cooperation, the transfer of major conventional weapons, components, and technologies from Russia to China has been a cornerstone of the Sino-Russian relationship. In this respect, Russia has supplied China with military weapons and equipment since diplomatic relations were first established in 1949 between China and the Soviet Union. Tables 9.2 and 9.3 summarize the weapons and equipment transfers from the Soviet Union (1922–1991) and Russia (1991–present) to China according to SIPRI. See Tables 9.2 and 9.3. Russia's total arms sales to China are $60.22 billion based on the 2016 CPI index. During the Cold War (1946–1991), total Soviet arms sales to China was $61.35 billion based on the 2016 CPI index.[97]

Since the collapse of the Soviet Union and establishment of the Russian Federation, China acquired arms and technology from Russia through a variety of measures, including: import of complete weapon systems; licensed production of complete weapon systems; import of components for Chinese-produced weapon systems; acquisition of technologies and know-how by bringing Russian experts to China and sending Chinese technicians to Russia for training, and industrial espionage. As previously noted, acquisition of weapons and technology from Russia through these means has contributed, in no small measure, to China's military modernization.[98]

Chinese arms transfers from Russia steadily increased from 1991 but notably declined between 2007 and 2012 according to SIPRI data. Several factors

Table 9.2 Soviet Conventional Weapons and Equipment Transfers to China

Year(s) of Delivery	No. of Deliveries	Weapon Designation	Weapon Description
1950–1961	3,000	M-30 122mm (L)	Towed Gun
1950–1958	450	Yak-18/Max (L)	Trainer Aircraft
1955	16	B-34 L/56 100mm (L)	Naval Gun
1953–1960	1,250	MiG-17/Fresco (L)	Fighter Aircraft
1954–1960	150	An-2/Colt (L)	Light Transport Aircraft
1955–1960	100	Mi-4A/Hound-A (L)	Helicopter
1956–1960	125	MiG-15UTI/Midget (L)	Trainer Aircraft
1955–1957	20	Project-122/Kronstadt (L)	Patrol Craft
1954–1965	28	Project-254/T-43 (L)	Minesweeper
1958–1959	4	Project-50/Riga (L)	Frigate
1956–1964	21	Project-613/Whiskey (L)	Submarine
1956–1961	3,000	T-54 (L)	Tank
1956–1961	45	Project-183/P-6 (L)	Fast Attack Craft
1958–1964	200	MiG-19/Farmer (L)	Fighter Aircraft
1958–1963	5	S-75 Dvina/SA-2 (L)	Surface-to-Air Missile System
1958–1960	150	Yak-18A/Max (L)	Trainer Aircraft
1966	1	Type-629/Golf (L)	Ballistic Missile Submarine
1950–1955	600	BM-13 132mm (S)	Self-Propelled Mobile Rocket Launcher
1950–1951	150	Il-10/Beast (S)	Ground Attack Aircraft
1950–1951	50	ISU-122 (S)	Self-Propelled Gun
1950–1951	50	ISU-152 (S)	Self-Propelled Gun
1950–1951	200	La-11/Fang (S)	Fighter Aircraft
1950–1951	250	La-9/Fritz (S)	Fighter Aircraft
1950–1952	50	Li-2T/Cab (S)	Transport Aircraft
1950–1952	750	MiG-15/Fagot (S)	Fighter Aircraft
1951–1952	50	MiG-15UTI/Midget (S)	Trainer Aircraft
1950–1954	2,500	T-34/85 (S)	Tank
1950–1951	150	Tu-2S/Bat (S)	Bomber Aircraft
1950	50	Yak-11/Moose (S)	Trainer Aircraft
1951	50	Il-12/Coach (S)	Transport Aircraft
1950–1953	300	IS-2 (S)	Tank
1950	372	MiG-9/Fargo (S)	Fighter Aircraft
1950–1953	300	SU-100 (S)	Self-Propelled Gun
1950–1953	300	SU-85 (S)	Self-Propelled Gun
1950–1951	43	Yak-17/Feather (S)	Fighter Aircraft
1950–1951	10	Yak-17UTI/Magnet (S)	Trainer Aircraft
1952–1954	1,500	MiG-15bis/Fagot (S)	Fighter Aircraft
1952–1953	70	Project-123/P-4 (S)	Fast Assault Craft
1952–1960	500	Il-28/Beagle (S)	Bomber Aircraft
1953–1954	13	Tu-4/Bull (S)	Bomber Aircraft
1953	50	Yak-12/Creek (S)	Light Aircraft
1954–1955	20	Be-6/Madge (S)	Anti-Ship Warfare Aircraft
1954–1956	50	Il-14/Crate (S)	Transport Aircraft
1954–1955	40	Mi-1/Hare (S)	Light Helicopter
1955	6	Artillerist (S)	Patrol Craft
1954–1955	4	Gordy (S)	Destroyer

Year(s) of Delivery	No. of Deliveries	Weapon Designation	Weapon Description
1954	2	M Type (S)	Submarine
1956–1960	250	PT-76 (S)	Light Tank
1954	2	Shchuka (S)	Submarine
1954	2	S Type (S)	Submarine
1955–1959	500	BM-14 140mm (S)	Self-Propelled Mobile Rocket Launcher
1955–1958	200	IS-3 (S)	Tank
1957–1960	100	BTR-152 (S)	Armored Personnel Carrier
1957–1960	100	BTR-40 (S)	Armored Personnel Carrier
1957	2	M-XV Type (S)	Submarine
1957–1958	4	P-12/Spoon Rest (S)	Air Search Radar
1957	2	S Type (S)	Submarine
1959	5	Tu-16/Badger (S)	Bomber Aircraft
1958–1963	120	V-750; SA-2 (S)	Surface-to-Air Missile
1960	10	D-20 152mm (S)	Towed Gun
1959–1960	250	K-5/AA-1 (S)	Short-Range Air-to-Air Missile
1959–1960	100	MiG-17PF/Fresco-D (S)	Fighter Aircraft
1958–1960	250	SET-53 533mm (S)	Anti-Ship Warfare Torpedo
1958	10	SM-4-1B 130mm (S)	Towed Gun
1960	10	MiG-21F-13/Fishbed-C (S)	Fighter Aircraft
1960–1963	100	P-15/SS-N-2A (S)	Anti-Ship Missile
1960	4	Project-633/Romeo (S)	Submarine
1960	25	K-13A/AA-2 (S)	Short-Range Air-to-Air Missile
1960–1961	75	KS-1/AS-1 (S)	Anti-Ship Missile
1960	10	M-46 130mm (S)	Towed Gun
1960	2	SO-1 (S)	Patrol Craft
1960–1961	4	SS-C-2 CDS (S)	Coastal Defense System
1965–1968	7	Project-205/Osa (S)	Fast Assault Craft
1965–1966	40	AI-20 (S)	Turboprop
1965	4	An-12/Cub (S)	Transport Aircraft
1965–1967	4	Project-183/Komar (S)	Fast Assault Craft
1968	5	Il-18/Coot (S)	Transport Aircraft
1990–1991	24	Mi-8MT/Mi-17/Hip-H (S)	Helicopter
1991	125	R-27/AA-10 (S)	Beyond Visual Range Air-to-Air Missile
1991	3	Su-27S/Flanker-B (S)	Fighter/Ground Attack Aircraft
1991	1	Yak-42/Clobber (S)	Transport Aircraft

Source: SIPRI Arms Transfers Database.

can be attributed: the Chinese defense industry developed the capability to the meet the PLA's needs; there were disputes over the prices of the weapons and their timely delivery; Russia faced competition from other suppliers, such as its former Soviet Republics; China wanted deals which would enable joint arms production or licensed manufacture of the best of Russia's arms; China held a grudge against Russia because it felt that Russia was more forthcoming

Table 9.3 Russian Conventional Weapons and Equipment Transfers to China

Year(s) of Delivery	No. of Deliveries	Weapon Designation	Weapon Description
1998–2007	105	Su-27S/Flanker-B (L)	Fighter/Ground Attack Aircraft
2001–2015	985	Kh-31A1/AS-17 (L)	Anti-Ship Missile/Anti-Radiation Missile
1998–2002	1,100	Krasnopol-M (L)	Guided Shell
2001–2015	1,500	9M119 Svir/AT-11 (L)	Anti-Tank missile
2004–2007	4	Fregat/Top Plate (L)	Air Search Radar
2004–2015	103	AK-630 30mm (L)	Naval Gun
2008–2015	20	Mineral/Band Stand (L)	Sea Search Radar
2013–2015	5	Mineral/Band Stand (L)	Sea Search Radar
2013–2015	23	AK-176 76mm (L)	Naval Gun
1992	300	R-73/AA-11 (S)	Short-Range Air-to-Air Missile
1992	21	Su-27S/Flanker-B (S)	Fighter/Ground Attack Aircraft
1993–1997	150	5V55U/SA-10C (S)	Surface-to-Air Missile
1993	1	76N6/Clam Shell (S)	Air Search Radar
1993	10	Il-76M/Candid-B (S)	Transport Aircraft
1993–1997	4	S-300PMU-1/SA-20A (S)	Surface-to-Air Missile System
1993	1	ST-68/Tin Shield (S)	Air Search Radar
1992	2	Su-27S/Flanker-B (S)	Fighter/Ground Attack Aircraft
1995–1999	75	53-65 533mm (S)	Anti-Ship Torpedo
1997–1999	2	Project-636E/Kilo (S)	Submarine
1995	2	Project-877E/Kilo (S)	Submarine
1995–1999	75	TEST-71 (S)	Anti-Ship/Anti-Submarine Warfare Torpedo
1996–1997	60	Mi-8MT/Mi-17/Hip-H (S)	Helicopter
1996–2004	3,000	R-73/AA-11 (S)	Short-Range Air-to-Air Missile
1996–1997	24	Su-27S/Flanker-B (S)	Fighter/Ground Attack Aircraft
1997	2	Ka-27PL/Helix-A (S)	Anti-Submarine Warfare Helicopter
1999	400	9M338/SA-15 (S)	Surface-to-Air Missile
1999	15	Tor-M1/SA-15 (S)	Mobile Surface-to-Air Missile System
2000	500	9M338/SA-15 (S)	Surface-to-Air Missile
1999–2000	150	9M38/SA-11 (S)	Surface-to-Air Missile
1999	5	Ka-27PL/Helix-A (S)	Anti-Submarine Warfare Helicopter
1999	3	Ka-32/Helix-C (S)	Helicopter
2004	2	MGK-335MS/Bull Horn (S)	Anti-Submarine Warfare Sonar
1999–2000	15	Mi-8MT/Mi-17/Hip-H (S)	Helicopter
2000	48	Moskit/SS-N-22 (S)	Anti-Ship Missile
2004	8	MR-90/Front Dome (S)	Fire Control Radar
1999–2000	2	Project-956/Sovremenny (S)	Destroyer
2004	2	SA-N-12 (S)	Naval Surface-to-Air Missile System
2000	20	Tor-M1/SA-15 (S)	Mobile Surface-to-Air Missile System
2001–2002	100	Kh-29/AS-14 Kedge (S)	Air-to-Surface Missile

Year(s) of Delivery	No. of Deliveries	Weapon Designation	Weapon Description
2004–2006	150	Kh-59ME Ovod/AS-18 (S)	Air-to-Surface Missile
2004–2007	6	Mineral/Band Stand (S)	Sea Search Radar
2000–2002	28	Su-27S/Flanker-B (S)	Fighter/Ground Attack Aircraft
2000–2001	38	Su-30MK/Flanker (S)	Fighter/Ground Attack Aircraft
2001–2005	54	AL-31 (S)	Turbofan
2002	1	Il-76M/Candid-B (S)	Transport Aircraft
2002–2009	750	RVV-AE/AA-12 Adder (S)	Beyond Visual Range Air-to-Air Missile
2002	150	48N6/SA-10D Grumble (S)	Surface-to-Air Missile
2004	150	9M317/SA-17 Grizzly (S)	Surface-to-Air Missile
2002–2003	35	Mi-8MT/Mi-17/Hip-H (S)	Helicopter
2003–2004	4	S-300PMU-1/SA-20A (S)	Surface-to-Air Missile System
2002–2003	38	Su-30MK/Flanker (S)	Fighter/Ground Attack Aircraft
2001–2005	100	Zhuk (S)	Combat Aircraft Radar
2005–2009	150	3M-54 Klub/SS-N-27 (S)	Anti-Ship Missile/Surface-to-Surface Missile
2006–2007	150	48N6/SA-10D Grumble (S)	Surface-to-Air Missile
2005–2006	150	53-65 533mm (S)	Anti-Ship Torpedo
2005–2006	200	9M311/SA-19 (S)	Surface-to-Air Missile
2005–2006	150	9M38/SA-11 (S)	Surface-to-Air Missile
2003–2004	25	Mi-8MT/Mi-17/Hip-H (S)	Helicopter
2005–2006	30	Moskit/SS-N-22 (S)	Anti-Ship Missile
2004–2007	100	PMK-2 (S)	Naval Mine/Torpedo
2004–2006	8	Project-636E/Kilo (S)	Submarine
2005–2006	2	Project-956/Sovremenny (S)	Destroyer
2006–2007	2	S-300FM/SA-N-20 (S)	Naval Surface-to-Air Missile System
2005–2006	150	TEST-71 (S)	Anti-Ship/Anti-Submarine Warfare Torpedo
2003	1	Zmei/Sea Dragon (S)	Multi-Purpose Aircraft Radar
2004	24	Su-30MK/Flanker (S)	Fighter/Ground Attack Aircraft
2007–2008	297	48N6E2/SA-10E (S)	Surface-to-Air Missile
2008–2015	20	AK-176 76mm (S)	Naval Gun
2008–2015	21	Fregat/Top Plate (S)	Air Search Radar
2008–2015	200	Kh-59MK/AS-18MK (S)	Anti-Ship Missile
2008–2015	80	MR-90/Front Dome (S)	Fire Control Radar
2007–2008	8	S-300PMU-2/SA-20B (S)	Surface-to-Air Missile System
2007–2012	3	AK-176 76mm (S)	Naval Gun
2006–2009	100	AL-31 (S)	Turbofan
2007–2012	54	Mi-8MT/Mi-17/Hip-H (S)	Helicopter
2008–2009	750	48N6E2/SA-10E (S)	Surface-to-Air Missile
2009–2010	9	Ka-27PL/Helix-A (S)	Anti-Submarine Warfare Helicopter
2010–2011	9	Ka-31/Helix (S)	Airborne Early Warning Helicopter
2006–2007	24	Mi-8MT/Mi-17/Hip-H (S)	Helicopter
2008–2009	8	S-300PMU-2/SA-20B (S)	Surface-to-Air Missile System

(Continued)

Table 9.3   Russian Conventional Weapons and Equipment Transfers to China (Continued)

Year(s) of Delivery	No. of Deliveries	Weapon Designation	Weapon Description
2010–2012	122	AL-31 (S)	Turbofan
2009–2012	55	D-30 (S)	Turbofan
2010–2011	32	Mi-8MT/Mi-17/Hip-H (S)	Helicopter
2013–2014	2	MR-123/Bass Tilt (S)	Fire Control Radar
2012–2014	123	AL-31 (S)	Turbofan
2012–2015	60	AL-31 (S)	Turbofan
2012–2015	144	D-30 (S)	Turbofan
2013	5	Il-76M/Candid-B (S)	Transport Aircraft
2013–2014	52	Mi-8MT/Mi-17/Hip-H (S)	Helicopter
2015	7	Il-76M/Candid-B (S)	Transport Aircraft
TBD	TBD	S-400/SA-21	Surface-to-Air Missile System
TBD	TBD	Su-35	Fighter/Ground Attack Aircraft

Source: SIPRI Arms Transfers Database.

toward India on the sale of such arms as well as licensing agreements to permit the production of advanced Russian weapons; and there were fears on the Russian side that China would use reverse technology to copy Russian arms.[99]

According to Russian sources, the trend turned around. Russian sources claim that China and Russia have reinvigorated their military cooperation in the commercial sense. In this respect, Russia has now become mainly a supplier of certain high-tech components or systems, rather than complete weapons systems. This was evident in 2013 and 2014. In January 2013, China and Russia to the sale of Su-35 long-range fighter aircraft and in 2014 Russia agreed to sell the S-400 Surface-to-Air Missile to China. In both instances, Russia appeared to be selling more powerful weapons systems to China than it has sold to India. Russian officials have cautioned that arms sales to China may have driven by a profit motive as Russia sought to compensate for the loss of its market to India, which was diversifying its basket of arms imports from the United States, Europe, and Israel.[100]

Russia has not sold China long-range ballistic missiles, strategic bombers, or air or missile defense systems—weapons that could be used against Russia. Moreover, it has not sold advanced land warfare weapons or tactical air support aircraft which could help China in a ground war against Russia. Rather, Russia has sold China weapons for air defense and naval warfare.[101] This is evidenced by sale of naval guns, anti-submarine warfare helicopters, anti-ship missiles, and anti-ship/anti-submarine warfare torpedoes.

China and Russia have signed numerous agreements to promote military and security cooperation. These include the following: Exchange of Notes on the Extension of the Term of the Joint Use of the Naval Base of Port Arthur (September 15, 1952); Joint Communiqué relating the Withdrawal of Soviet Troops from the Jointly Used Naval Base of Port Arthur and Transfer of the Base to Full Jurisdiction of the PRC (October 12, 1954); Protocol on the Withdrawal of the Jointly Used Naval Base of Port Arthur and the Transfer of the installation to China (May 24, 1955); Agreement on the Mutual Reduction of Military Forces on Border Areas and the Guidance of Enhancing Military Trust in the Military Field (April 25, 1990); Agreement of Military Technology Cooperation (June 1990); Memorandum on the Principles of Military and Technical Cooperation between China and Russia (December 1992); Agreement on the Exchange of Defense Experts (1993); Agreement on the Prevention of Dangerous Military Activity (June 11, 1994); Memorandum of Military-Technical Cooperation (1996); Deal for Aircraft Spare Parts and Follow-Up Maintenance for recently purchased advanced Russian Su-27 Fighter Jets (August 24, 1997); Cooperation Agreement on the Training of Military Personnel (June 1999); Memorandum of Understanding on further strengthening Military Cooperation (January 2000); Joint Statement of the President of the People's Republic of China and the President of the Russian Federation on the Issue of Anti-Ballistic Missiles (July 18, 2000); and Agreement on the Supply of Spare Parts for Air Defense Systems, Aircraft and Naval Systems (November 2010).[102]

CULTURAL RELATIONS

Sino-Russian cultural relations are not strong today. Cultural ties were strong up until the Sino-Soviet split. Cultural relations consisted Russian technological assistance to China and Chinese students studying at Russian universities.[103]

China and Russia mended their political and ideological differences after Soviet leader Mikhail Gorbachev's state visit to Beijing in June 1989. Since Gorbachev's visit, both countries have been trying to promote cultural relations through exchanges.[104]

In the twenty-first century, exchanges have been seen in the arts including dance and music. In 2000, China sent a fifty-five-member group of the China Opera and Dance Drama Theater on a performance tour of Russia. Russia sent the following art groups on performance tours of China: an 85-member troupe of the Moscow Stanislavski and Nemirovich-Danchenko Music Theatre in January 2000; the 85-member Moiseyev Dance Troupe in January 2000; a 300-member troupe of the Mariinsky Theatre in April; the 82-member Red Army Song and Dance Ensemble in May 2000; the 80-member Kemerovo Symphony Orchestra in October 2000; and the 80-member Moscow

National Symphony Orchestra in December 2000. In July 2001, the Chinese People's Association for Friendship with Foreign Countries presented two big song and dance soirees entitled "China-Russian Friendship Night" in Moscow in support of Beijing's bid for the hosting of the 2008 Olympic Games. Other important cultural exchanges in 2001 include: China Song and Dance Ensemble (May), Xinjiang Song and Dance Ensemble (May), China Writers' Delegation (June), Mei Lanfang Beijing Opera Troupe of Beijing (June), China Calligraphy and Paintings Exhibition (July), Cultural Delegation of Jiangsu Province (September), Jiangnan Shaolin Kung Fu Performing Delegation (October), China Military Writers' Delegation (October), Big National Song and Dance Drama "The Border Town" Performing Troupe of Hunan Song and Dance Theater (October), Russian Bolshoi Dance Troupe (January), Kremlin Ballet (April), the Red Army Song and Dance Ensemble of the Ministry of Internal Affairs (May), the Opera and Ballet Theatre of Norobrisk (June), Moscow Classic Ballet (September), the Exhibition of 300 Years of Russian Paintings (September), St. Petersburg Symphony Orchestra (November).[105]

In terms of writers' exchanges, the vice president of the Chinese Writers Association Zhang Qie led a writers' delegation on a Russian visit in August 2000.[106]

In terms of educational exchanges, the delegation of the Russian university presidents headed by Academician Sadovnichii, president of Moscow University, paid a visit to China in October 2000. Education minister Chen Zhili met with the delegation and the two sides exchanged views on educational cooperation between the two countries. In May 2001, the Exhibition on Russian Higher Education and China-Russian Higher Learning Institution Cooperation and Exchanges Conference were held in Beijing University. Moreover, at the end of 2001, there were 484 government-sponsored Chinese students in Russia and 122 government-sponsored Russian students in China.[107]

Sino-Russian educational exchanges are weak apart from the establishment of Confucius Institutes.[108] To encourage educational exchanges and promote Chinese language and culture, China established Confucius Institutes in Russia.[109] To date, China has established seventeen Confucius Institutes at the following Russian universities: Far Eastern Federal University, Russian State University for the Humanities, Lomonosov Moscow State University, Saint Petersburg State University, Irkutsk State University, Novosibirsk State University of Technology, Kazan State University, Blagoveshchensk National Pedagogical University, Kalmyk State University, Tomsk State University, Buryat State University, Ural State University, Moscow State Linguistic University, Ryazan State University, Nizhny Novgorod State Linguistic University, Volgograd State Pedagogical University, and Amur State University of Humanities and Pedagogy.[110] Russia established a Russian Information Center in Beijing to promote knowledge of the country.[111]

In terms of the arts, the vice president of the China Federation of Literary and Art Circles Zhao Zhihong led an art group to participate in the first Art Contest in Russia in December 2000. In August 2001, the Russian Contemporary Classic Oils Exhibition was inaugurated in China National Gallery.[112]

In terms of photography, a photo exhibition entitled "The Splendid China" co-sponsored by the Chinese People's Association for Friendship with Foreign Countries and the Russian side was inaugurated in the Museum of the Ostrovsky Humanities and Arts Center in Moscow in September 2001.[113] The exhibition lasted two weeks and was visited by 3000 spectators.[114]

China and Russia participated in large-scale cultural exchanges. Two such events include the celebration of the "Year of Russia" in China in 2006 and "Year of China" in Russia in 2007, which involved some 200 cultural, trade-related, and athletic events.[115] While the emphasis was on culture, these initiatives provided the framework for stimulating economic cooperation between the provisional administrations in both countries as well as business cooperation between companies and establishment of a broader base of cooperation.[116] The 2010 Shanghai World Expo featured the national pavilion of Russia and attracted over 7.5 million visitors and won second prize from the Bureau International des Expositions for theme development.[117] The year 2012–2013 was touted as China-Russian tourism year; over 400 activities occurred including film festivals in each country.[118] Since then tourism between the two countries increased.[119] Moreover, the presidents of China and Russia agreed to make 2014 and 2015 the China-Russia youth friendship and exchange years.[120]

Numerous agreements, protocols, and plans were finalized between China and Russia since diplomatic relations were established in 1949. These include the following: Agreement on Post and Telecommunications (February 7, 1950); Agreement on Soviet Specialists working in China (March 27, 1950); Agreement on the Working Conditions and Payments of the Soviet Specialists in China (October 25, 1950); Agreement on Navigation and Construction of Border Rivers of Amur, Ussuri, Argue, Sungach, and Lake Khanka (January 2, 1951); Agreement on Chinese Students studying in the Soviet Union (August 9, 1952); Agreement on Soviet Technical Assistance relating to the Construction of New and Extension of Existing Electric Power Stations (March 21, 1953); Agreement on the Soviet Economic and Technical Assistance relating to the Construction of 91 Industrial Plants (May 15, 1953); Agreement on Broadcasting Cooperation (August 21, 1954); Agreement on Scientific and Technical Cooperation October 12, 1954); Protocol on Scientific and Technical Cooperation (December 28, 1954); Agreement on Scheduled Air Traffic between China and the Soviet Union (December 30, 1954);

Protocol on Scientific and Technical Cooperation June 30, 1955); Agreement on the Cooperation in the Protection of Agricultural Crops from Disease and Pests (August 16, 1955); Contract on the Mutual Acquisition of Copyrights to Films (November 29, 1955); Agreement on Technical Cooperation in the Field of Civil Air Transport (January 4, 1956); Protocol on Scientific and Technical Cooperation (January 4, 1956); Agreement on Soviet Assistance relating to the Construction of 55 further Industrial Plants, including Technical Equipment at a total value of 2.5 billion rubles (April 7, 1956); Protocol on Scientific and Technical Cooperation (June 23, 1956); Agreement on Cultural Cooperation (July 5, 1956); 1956 Executive Plan on Cultural Cooperation (July 13, 1956); Protocol on Transfer of the Manchurian Archives to China (September 18, 1956); Protocol on Scientific and Technical Cooperation (December 24, 1956); 1957 Executive Plan on Cultural Cooperation (January 18, 1957); Additional Protocol on Post and Telecommunications (February 15, 1957); Protocol on the Further Development of Telecommunications and Scientific and Technical Cooperation in the Fields of Post and Telecommunications (February 15, 1957); Protocol on Scientific and Technical Cooperation (July 17, 1957); 1958 Executive Plan on Cultural Cooperation (November 21, 1957); Protocol on Scientific Cooperation for 1958–1962 (December 11, 1957); 1958 Executive Plan on Scientific Cooperation (December 11, 1957); Protocol on the Joint Implementation of, and Soviet Assistance in, Important Research Projects in the Field of Science and Technology for 1958–1962 (January 18, 1958); Agreement between the Ministries of Higher Education on Cooperation in Scientific and Technical Research (January 18, 1958); Agreement between the Academies of Agro Science on Cooperation in Scientific and Technical Research (January 18, 1958); Protocol on Scientific and Technical Cooperation (July 4, 1958); Agreement on Soviet Technical Assistance in the Construction of 47 Industrial Plants (August 8, 1958); Protocol on Scientific and Technical Cooperation (January 19, 1959); 1959 Executive Plan on Cultural Cooperation (March 18, 1959); 1959 Executive Plan on Scientific Cooperation (June 1, 1959); Protocol on Scientific and Technical Cooperation (July 7, 1959); Agreement on Scientific and Technical Cooperation (October 12, 1959); Agreement on Cultural Cooperation (November 2, 1959); 1960 Executive Plan on Cultural Cooperation (December 31, 1959); Agreement on Joint Measures for the Protection against Fires in the Forests of the Border Region (January 29, 1960); 1960 Executive Plan on Scientific Cooperation (February 20, 1960); 1960 Executive Plan on Scientific and Technical Cooperation (February 24, 1960); Agreement on Public Health Cooperation (June 10, 1960); Message from the Government of the USSR to the Government of PRC relating to the Recalling of 1,300 Soviet Experts from China (July 16, 1960); 1961 Executive Plan on Cultural Cooperation (February 4, 1961); Agreement on Cooperation in

Broadcasting and Television (May 25, 1962); Agreement on Scientific and Technical Cooperation (June 19, 1961); 1961 Executive Plan on Scientific Cooperation (June 21, 1961); 1962 Executive Plan on Cultural Cooperation (January 23, 1962); Protocol on Mutual Technical Supervision of Ships (May 7, 1962); Protocol on Scientific and Technical Cooperation (June 23, 1962); 1962 Executive Plan on Scientific Cooperation (July 21, 1962); Protocol on Mutual Services in Civil Air Transport (December 1, 1962); 1963 Executive Plan on Cultural Cooperation (February 23, 1963); Protocol on Scientific and Technical Cooperation (June 19, 1963); 1963/1964 Executive Plan on Scientific Cooperation (November 29, 1963); 1964 Executive Plan on Cultural Cooperation (February 29, 1964); 1965 Executive Plan on Cultural Cooperation (May 25, 1965); Protocol on Scientific and Technical Cooperation (June 12, 1965); Agreement on Civil Air Transport (April 4, 1966); 1966 Executive Plan on Cultural Cooperation June 27, 1966); Protocol on Scientific and Technical Cooperation (November 6, 1966); Protocol establishing the 1970–1971 Timetables for the running of Passenger Trains and Through Coaches on the Moscow-Zabaykalsk-Peking, Moscow-Ulan Bator-Peking, and other International Trains (December 17, 1969); Protocol on the Civil Air Agreement of December 30, 1954 relating to the simultaneous regular direct flights on the Moscow-Peking route (July 15, 1973); Protocol on Timetables for Passenger Trains (October 21, 1978); Protocol of the 23rd Meeting of the Sino-Soviet Joint Commission for Boundary River's Navigation (March 9, 1981); Protocol of the Session of the Sino-Soviet Boundary through Railway Traffic Committee (April 28, 1981); Minutes of the 24th Meeting of the Sino-Soviet Joint Commission for Boundary Rivers Navigation (March 15, 1982); Protocol on the Session of the Sino-Soviet Boundary through Railway Traffic Committee (July 28, 1982); Minutes of the 25th Regular Meeting of the Sino-Soviet Joint Committee for Navigation on the Boundary Rivers (March 21, 1983); Agreement on Meteorology to improve the Meteorological Circuit Operations between Beijing and Moscow and between Beijing and Khabarosk (December 6, 1983); Protocol on the 26th Regular Meeting of the Sino-Soviet Joint Commission for Navigation on Boundary Rivers (March 24, 1984); Protocol on Student Exchanges for the 1984–85 School Year (April 16, 1984); Agreement on a New International Train Timetable (November 6, 1984); Agreement on Scientific and Technological Cooperation (December 28, 1984); Protocol on Border Railway Transport (February 12, 1985); Minutes of the 27th Session of the Sino-Soviet Joint Commission for the Navigation on Boundary Rivers (March 22, 1985); Protocol on Educational Cooperation (April 4, 1985); Protocol on the Exchange of short-term visits of Journalists between Xinhua News Agency and the TASS News Agency (June 4, 1985); Protocol on Cultural Cooperation for 1985 (June 16, 1985); Protocol on Sports Exchange for 1986 (January 16, 1986); Protocol on the 28th

Session of the Joint Commission for the Navigation on Boundary Rivers (March 21, 1986); Protocol concerning the Exchange of Engineers and Technicians (March 21, 1986); Agreement on Cultural Cooperation for 1986–1987 (March 26, 1986); Agreement on Cultural Cooperation between the Chinese People's Association for Friendship with Foreign Countries and the Union of Societies for Friendship and Cultural Relations with Foreign Countries of the USSR (June 18, 1986); Agreement on Scientific Cooperation between the Academies of Sciences (June 26, 1986); Implementation Program for Scientific Cooperation in 1987–1988 (June 26, 1986); Agreement to establish a Committee to oversee matters with respect to the Ergune and Heilong Rivers (October 23, 1986); Memorandum on the Exchange of Scientific and Technological Cooperation (October 28, 1986); Agreement on Journalistic Exchange between the Xinhua News Agency and TASS (December 11, 1986); Sports Exchange Protocol (February 23, 1987); Minutes of 29th Session of the Joint Commission for Navigation on the Boundary Rivers (March 13, 1987); Protocol on the First Meeting of the Working Group for the Education of the Soviet-Chinese Commission for Economic, Trade, Scientific, and Technological Cooperation (April 30, 1987); Agreement on Cooperation in Television and Radio (May 21, 1987); Plan of Scientific Ties between the USSR Academy of Sciences and the PRC Academy of Social Sciences for 1987–1989 (May 21, 1987); Protocol on Exchanges between the USSR State Committee for Printing, Publishing, and Book Trade and the PRC Press and Publishing Board for 1988–1989 (May 28, 1987); Agreement of Cooperation between the Chinese Journalists' Association and the Union of Journalists of the USSR for 1987–1992 (July 6, 1987); Agreement to exchange Book Fairs in Each Other's Capital Cities and to Plan Joint Publications (September 14, 1987); Sports Protocol for 1988 (December 24, 1987); Plan for Cultural Cooperation in 1988–1990 (December 24, 1987); Plan for Cultural Cooperation in 1988–1990 (May 4, 1988); Fishing Agreement (October 4, 1988); Agreement on Scientific Cooperation (February 16, 1989); Cooperation Agreement of the Peaceful Use and Studies of Space (April 25, 1990); Cooperation Plan between the Academies of Sciences for 1991–1995 (May 8, 1990); Agreement on Public Health and Medical Scientific Cooperation (May 17, 1990); Agreement on the Short-Term Training of Editors (September 19, 1990); Agreement on the Exchange of Book Fairs with the Soviet State Publishing Committee (September 19, 1990); Protocol for Providing Bilateral Radio Transmitters to Transmit Programs to Other Countries and Regions (November 18, 1990); Agreement on Establishing a Joint Foundation for High Technology (November 18, 1990); Cooperation Plan for Science and Technology Management (November 18, 1990); Agreement on Space Cooperation between the Russian Space Agency and the China National Space Administration (March 1994); and Joint Statement on Promoting the

Development of Information and Cyber Space Between the President of the People's Republic of China and President of the Russian Federation (June 25, 2016).[121]

Sino-Russian cultural relations are extensive and include a wide variety of areas of cooperation including: film, fishery, journalism, sports, education, medicine, meteorology, public health, publishing, radio, science, television, transportation, and space technology based on the agreements, protocols, and plans finalized between the two countries.

ENERGY/PETROLEUM RELATIONS

A major component of Sino-Russian relations is energy trading. The energy sector, which includes petroleum and natural gas supply, is the area with the greatest potential for trade expansion.[122] In this respect, energy trading is very likely to continue between both countries because China seeks to establish a strategic petroleum reserve in its coastal region to meet the increasing demand for crude oil in the future and Russia fits nicely in this plan because of its proximity to China.[123] Second, China seeks to diversify its suppliers and be less reliant on its current major oil suppliers in the Middle East and Africa.[124] China provides Russia with ability to mitigate the negative effects of Western economic sanctions because of the Ukraine crisis and reorient its economy toward Asia especially China.[125] This increases China's access to Russia's natural resources, particularly gas, gains contracts for infrastructure projects and new markets for Chinese technology, and turns Russia into a junior partner in the relationship between the two countries. However, Russia does not want to be solely dependent on China to sustain its oil economy as it desires to sell its crude oil, natural gas, and natural gas projects to other major Asian markets such as Japan and South Korea. Nevertheless, the 2013 Ukraine crisis paved way for a new round of Sino-Russian oil and gas cooperation.[126]

Beyond economic reasons, energy trading has the potential to further strengthen long-term diplomatic ties between China and Russia. In this respect, Transneft completed a forty-mile oil pipeline spur from Skovorodino, Siberia to the Amur River on Russia-China border followed by the China National Petroleum Corporation completing a 616-mile section from Russia-China border to Daqing, China in October 2010. Operations began on January 1, 2011.

Transneft also opened the East Siberian Pacific Ocean (ESPO) oil pipeline on December 25, 2012. The first leg of the oil pipeline runs 1,713 miles from Taishet to Skovorodino (in the Amur Region of RFE) and the second leg of the oil pipeline continues for 1,304 miles from Skovorodino to the Pacific Port of Kozmino on Russia's east coast. This oil pipeline is designed to pump annually 30 million metric tons of Siberian oil to China, Japan, and South Korea.[127]

In terms of future strategic energy cooperation, China's largest oil company, China National Petroleum Corporation (CNPC) and Rosneft, one of three major state-run Russian companies, may jointly explore for oil in three offshore areas of the Arctic Circle in the near future based on their signed agreement of March 2013. Oil exploration in the Arctic Circle would be a major energy coup for both countries, but even more so for Russia because it could elevate its position from the world's second largest oil exporter to the first. This would give China greater oil energy security given the geographic location of the event and its geographic inaccessibility to other major oil regions of the world.

Sino-Russian energy relations are not new. Bilateral cooperation began in early 1950s when the Soviet Union provided China with the technology and skills required to develop a modern oil industry. It wasn't until the mid-1990s that both countries considered building an oil pipeline connecting them. However, real collaboration did not occur until 2004.[128]

Today, Russia is a major supplier of crude petroleum to China. In this respect, China imported on the average, approximately 9 percent of its crude petroleum annually from Russia between 2006 and 2015 according to the United Nations Commodity Trade Statistics Database.[129] In 2015, China imported 13 percent of its crude oil from Russia. The percentage of Russia's total commodity trade value of all exports to China was 60 percent for the same year. Thus, crude oil is the principal commodity traded between the two countries.

Russia is typically also China's largest supplier of crude oil after Saudi Arabia and Angola. Russia supplies crude oil China via pipeline, ship, and rail, primarily from Russia's fields in East Siberia. Some Russian oil is delivered from West Siberia to China via Kazakhstan. To meet its obligations, Russia holds a swap agreement with Kazakhstan and exports crude oil through links to the currently underutilized Kazakhstan-to-China oil pipeline.[130]

In terms of total trade value, crude oil petroleum imports ranged from 31 to 60 percent for the same years. Table 9.4 illustrates China's crude petroleum imports from Russia in thousands of barrels per day, oil imports share, world ranking, trade value, total commodity trade value, and percentage from 2006 to 2015. See Table 9.4.

China has imported petroleum gas products from Russia but on a limited basis. Table 9.5 illustrates China's petroleum gas imports from Russia in millions of cubic feet, global imports share, world ranking, trade value, total commodity trade value, and percentage from 2009 to 2015. See Table 9.5. Petroleum gas product trading did not occur in 2006, 2007, 2008, and 2013.

Moreover, Table 9.6 illustrates China's liquefied natural gas (LNG) imports from Russia in millions of cubic feet, global imports share, world ranking, trade value, total commodity trade value, and percentage from 2009

Table 9.4 Chinese Crude Petroleum Imports from Russia

Year	KBPD	Oil Imports Share (%)	World Ranking	Crude Oil Trade Value ($)	Total Commodity Trade Value ($)	Percentage (%)
2006	321	11	4	7,503,770,409	17,554,327,123	42.7
2007	292	9	4	7,219,545,520	19,688,578,673	36.7
2008	234	7	5	8,586,621,443	23,832,761,729	36.0
2009	307	8	4	6,613,853,066	21,282,952,148	31.1
2010	306	6	5	8,882,171,741	25,913,993,644	34.3
2011	396	8	4	16,322,977,122	40,362,599,801	40.4
2012	489	9	3	20,485,270,871	44,138,278,872	46.4
2013	489	9	4	19,742,628,301	39,667,828,205	49.8
2014	665	11	3	24,982,370,394	41,619,136,486	60.0
2015	852	13	2	17,249,272,862	33,216,611,631	51.9

Source: United Nations Commodity Trade Statistics Database

Table 9.5 Chinese Petroleum Gas Product Imports from Russia

Year	Volume (MMcf)	Global Share (%)	World Ranking	Petroleum Gas Trade Value ($)	Total Commodity Trade Value ($)	Percentage (%)
2009	7.8	2	10	44,622,194	21,282,952,148	<1
2010	15.65	3	9	196,027,296	25,913,993,644	1
2011	10.4	1	13	195,877,087	40,362,599,801	<1
2012	15.60	1	11	349,331,947	44,138,278,872	1
2014	5.4	<1	22	87,101,632	41,619,136,486	0.21
2015	8.2	<1	18	111,692,087	33,216,611,631	0.34

Source: United Nations Commodity Trade Statistics Database

to 2015. See Table 9.6. LNG trading did not occur in 2006, 2007, 2008, and 2013.

Table 9.7 illustrates China's oil and gas deals with Russia. China's oil and gas deals appear to be very robust and date back to 2003. See Table 9.7.

China and Russia have signed agreements to promote energy cooperation including petroleum prospecting and extraction. These include the following: Agreement of a Joint-Stock Company for Petroleum Extraction in Sinkiang (March 27, 1950); Agreement on the Energy Cooperation between the People's Republic of China and the Russian Federation (April 1996);

Framework Agreement for the Memorandum of Understanding on Oil Cooperation (2009); Memorandum of Understanding of the China-Russia East Route Gas Cooperation Project (May 2014); Memorandum of Understanding of the China and Russia Purchase and Sales Contract on East Route Gas Project between PetroChina and Gazprom (May 2014); Memorandum

Table 9.6   Chinese Liquefied Natural Gas (LNG) Imports from Russia

Year	Volume (MMcf)	Global Share (%)	World Ranking	Liquefied Natural Gas (LNG) Trade Value ($)	Total Commodity Trade Value ($)	Percentage (%)
2009	8	3	5	44,622,194	21,282,952,148	0.21
2010	16	4	6	196,027,296	25,913,993,644	0.76
2011	10	2	8	195,877,087	40,362,599,801	0.49
2012	16	3	6	349,331,947	44,138,278,872	0.79
2014	5	0.65	11	86,174,124	41,619,136,486	0.21
2015	7.9	0.97	10	107,885,728	33,216,611,631	0.32

Source: United Nations Commodity Trade Statistics Database.

Table 9.7   Chinese Oil and Gas Deals with Russia

Date	Company	Acquisition
December15	Sinopec and SIBUR	Sinopec acquires 10 percent of SIBUR, Russia's largest gas processing and petrochemicals company, for $1.34 billion
November14	CNPC and Gazprom	CNPC signed a framework agreement on gas imports from Russia via the Western route with Gazprom, and a cooperation framework agreement on the Vankor Oilfield project with Rosneft, respectively. Gazprom promised to supply 30 billion cubic meters of gas annually to China over thirty years from Russia's Western Siberian gas fields
October14	CNPC and Gazprom	CNPC signed a technical agreement on the construction and operation of the eastern route of Russia-China Gas Pipeline with Gazprom, and an agreement for furthering strategic cooperation with Rosneft, respectively
May14	CNPC and Gazprom	Power of Siberia Contract: CNPC and Gazprom sign an agreement whereby Gazprom would supply CNPC 3.8 billion cubic meters of gas annually for thirty years for $400 billion
2014	CNPC and Novatek	CNPC and Novatek sign a contract for Novatek to supply three million tons of LNG annually for twenty years
October13	CNPC/ PetroChina and Rosneft	A document on major terms of commissioning schedule and oil supply for Tianjin Refinery was signed with Rosneft. CNPC holds a 51 percent stake and Rosneft holds a 49 percent stake in the Tianjin Refinery project
October13	CNPC	CNPC and Rosneft signed a Memorandum of Understanding to form a joint venture to explore several fields in Siberia for oil and gas, with CNPC taking 49 percent and Rosneft taking 51 percent

Date	Company	Acquisition
October13	Sinopec	Sinopec and Rosneft signed an agreement whereby Rosneft would supply Sinopec with 10 million metric tons of crude oil over ten years for $85 billion
September13	CNPC and Rosneft	CNPC and Rosneft signed a framework agreement on natural gas supply from Russia to China via the eastern route was signed with Gazprom
June13	CNPC and Rosneft	CNPC and Rosneft signed an agreement to jointly explore for oil in three offshore Arctic areas and Rosneft would supply CNPC with 365 million tons of oil for twenty five years' worth $270 billion. CNPC would make a pre-payment of $60-70 billion to Rosneft
June13	CNPC and Novatek	A framework agreement was signed with Novatek to purchase a 20 percent stake in the Yamal LNG Project. A stock purchase agreement was signed between the two sides on September 5, 2013
September10	CNPC	The Russia-China Crude Pipeline became operational from Skovorodino in Russia to Mohe at the Sino-Russian border. Additionally, CNPC inked a general agreement with Transneft over the operation of the Russia-China Crude Pipeline that stretches from Russia's Skovorodino station to China's Mohe station, a framework agreement with Gazprom to import natural gas to China, an agreement with Rosneft on extending oil supply to the Russia-China Crude Pipeline, and an agreement with Lukoil on expanding strategic cooperation
2010	Hudian	Hudian invested $650 million in Russian gas company Sintez, acquiring a 51 percent stake
October09	CIC	Purchased 45 percent share in Nobel Oil Group for $300 million to fund Russian expansion plans
October09	CNPC and Gazprom	CNPC and Gazprom signed a framework agreement on the terms and conditions of gas supply from Russia to China whereby Gazprom would supply CNPC 70 billion cubic meters of gas annually
February09	CNPC, Rosneft, and Transneft	CNPC signs an agreement to design, construct, and operate a pipeline from Skovorodino in Russia to China's border area with Transneft, and two agreements on a long-term crude oil trading deal with Rosneft and Transneft, respectively, laying the foundation for the construction of a Russia-China Crude Pipeline
October08	CNPC and Transneft	An agreement in principle is signed with Transneft on the construction and operation of a crude pipeline from Skovorodino in Russia to Mohe at the Sino-Russian border

(Continued)

Table 9.7 Chinese Oil and Gas Deals with Russia (Continued)

Date	Company	Acquisition
November06	Sinopec and Rosneft	Sinopec and Rosneft form a joint venture Taihu Ltd. where Sinopec has a 49 percent stake and Rosneft has a 51 percent stake.
October06	CNPC and Rosneft	Jointly established as Vostok Energy Ltd., in which CNPC has a 49 percent stake. In August 2007, Vostok Energy Ltd. won an auction for licenses to explore for oil and gas in two Siberian blocks in Irkutsk Province of Russia—Verkhneichersky and West Chonsky.
September06	CNPC and Lukoil	CNPC and Lukoil signed a strategic cooperation agreement.
May06	CNPC and Government of Russia	CNPC and the Government of Russia sign a Memorandum of Understanding on supplying natural gas to China; an Agreement on the Basic Principles for the Establishment of Joint Ventures in China and Russia for Strengthening Oil Cooperation and a Minute on CNPC-Transneft Meeting with Gazprom, Rosneft, and Transneft.
2006	Sinopec	Purchased 97 percent of Udmurtneft for assets in Russia for $1.7 billion.
July 05	CNPC and Rosneft	CNPC and Rosneft signed a long-term cooperation agreement.
December 03	CNPC and Sakhalin Energy	CNPC and Sakhalin Energy signed a framework agreement on exploration and development in Russia's Sakhalin oil field.

Source: CNPC, ansd Julie Jiang and Chen Dang, *Update on Overseas Investments by Chinese National Companies: Achievements and Challenges Since 2011*, Organization for Economic Cooperation and Development/International Energy Agency, June 2014, 35–39.

of Understanding on the Russian Federation's Gas Supply to the People's Republic of China through the West Route Natural Gas Pipeline (November 2014); Framework Agreement between China National Petroleum Corporation and Gazprom on Gas Supply from the Russian Federation to the People's Republic of China through the West Route Natural Gas Pipeline (November 2014); Memorandum of Understanding between China National Petroleum Corporation and Gazprom in the field of Underground Gas Storage and Gas-Fired Power Generation (June 27, 2016); and Framework Agreement between Sinopec and Russia's OJSC Rosneft to jointly develop a grassroots natural gas processing and petrochemical complex in East Siberia (June 27, 2016).[131]

Key Chinese oil-related projects in Russia were backed by loans from China Development Bank (CDB). To date, CDB has invested or promised to invest no less than $31 billion. These loans include: a $6 million loan to

Rosneft in return for 48.4 million tons of crude oil over five years (2005); a $10 billion loan to Rosneft in return for ten years of crude oil deliveries at 180,000 barrels per day via a spur of the ESPO (2009); and a $15 billion loan to Transneft in return for ten years of crude oil deliveries at 120,000 barrels per day via a spur of the ESPO (2009).[132]

Chinese energy-related activities extend beyond oil and gas operations. CNPC provided engineering and oil field service, including geophysical prospecting and pipeline construction to Russia. In 2006, CNPC provided 3D seismic data acquisition services for Rosneft's company TNK-BP. In 2007, in the construction of Russian's Far-East Crude Pipeline project, CNPC installed the 106-mile long trunk pipeline in the eastern section from Aldan to Tynda, with the application of various welding techniques. The welding of the main part of the pipeline has been completed in June 2008. In 2010, CNPC signed a sales and technical service contract of MCI5570 micro-resistivity scanning instrument with Russia's TNG Group. Additionally, CNPC subsidiary Baoji Petroleum Steel Pipe Company Limited won a contract to supply pipes to the ESPO oil pipeline.[133]

China and Russia energy cooperation extends beyond the hydrocarbon sector. In terms of nuclear energy cooperation, Chinese and Russian companies collaborated to build the Tianwan nuclear power plant in Jiangsu province using two Russian-designed reactors. Tianwan nuclear power plant became operational in 2007.[134] Additional agreements have been signed to build more nuclear reactors at same facility.

China and Russian have also been engaged in trading electricity, acquiring interests in electrical companies or forming joint ventures to transfer electricity. In this respect, Russia has exported electricity since 2004 from 0.3 billion kilowatts to 1.3 billion kilowatts in 2012 and 3.375 billion kilowatts in 2014. In 2010, China's largest hydropower corporation, Three Gorges Dam, invested $2.29 billion, and later $190 million, in December 2010, in the Russian power generation company EuroSibEnergo, thus acquiring a 50 percent stake in the company. In February 2011, China Yangtze International and EuroSibEnergo PLC announced a joint venture with YES Energo Ltd. to develop hydro and thermal power projects in Russian Siberia and the Far East. The electricity generated by the hydro and thermal power plants would be transmitted to China.[135]

China and Russia have also inked agreements in energy cooperation not related to petroleum operations. These include the following: Agreement on the Construction of an Atomic Energy Research Center and the Supply of Technical Data (April 27, 1955); Agreement on the Development and Exploitation of the Natural Resources in the Amur Basin (August 18, 1956); Memorandum on the Construction of a Nuclear Power Plant in China (April 25, 1990); $3.2 billion Joint Construction Contract (Phase I) between Jiangsu

Nuclear Power Corporation and Atomstroyexport to build the Tianwan Nuclear Power Plant (September 1997); Russian Unified Energy Systems Inc. and China State Grid Corporation signed a framework agreement on Russian electricity exports to China (2005); CIAE, CNEIC, and Atomstroyexport signed an agreement to start pre-project and design works for a commercial nuclear power plant with two BN-800 fast neutron reactors (October 2009); a $6 billion "coal for loans" agreement to aid Russian infrastructure and equipment in Eastern Siberia and the RFE in return for 15 million tons of coal annually for five years and 20 million tons annually for twenty years (September 2010); Joint Construction Contract (Phase II) between Jiangsu Nuclear Power Corporation and Atomstroyexport to build the Tianwan nuclear power plant (November 2010); Memorandums of Understanding on energy market assessment, a roadmap of cooperation in the coal sector, and an Agreement on Electricity Supply (December 2012); Agreement between China and Russia for the early repayment of a $2.5 billion loan to China for the Russian construction of the Tianwan Nuclear Power Plant (June 27, 2016); Shareholder's Agreement between Rosseti and State Grid Corporation of China (SGCC) to set up a joint venture to build a new power grid infrastructure and refurbish an existing one in Russia and other countries (June 27, 2016).[136]

SUMMARY

Early Sino-Russian relations date back to the seventeenth century. In the modern sense, diplomatic ties were established in October 1949, after the founding of the People's Republic of China, following the Chinese Civil War (1945–1949). Initial relations were generally good as the Soviet Union provided China with massive financial aid and military and technological assistance while treating it as a junior partner. Soviet financial, military, and technological assistance continued until 1960, when ideological differences began to emerge between the two countries in after Joseph Stalin's death in 1953.[137]

Diplomatic relations broke down after 1960 fueling sporadic military confrontations and a bitter and acrimonious political struggle lasting almost thirty years. Ideological disputes such as different interpretations of Marxism-Leninism and the possibility of peaceful coexistence with the West, personality clashes between Khrushchev and Mao, disagreements over a common border, and China's international role such as the leadership of world communism all contributed to a dramatic deterioration in bilateral relations. It was not until June 1989 that ties were normalized when President Mikhail Gorbachev made an official visit to Beijing.

Bilateral ties improved dramatically after the dissolution of the Soviet Union in December 1991. From the ashes, the Russian Federation or Russia emerged. Relations improved in the political, economic, and cultural spheres. China and Russia saw convergence on many issues including global governance, international finance, cybercrime, sovereignty, participation in multilateral forums, economic development, and energy security. While relations are close and cordial there is an undercurrent of mistrust mostly from the Russian side. Nevertheless, since diplomatic relations were established in 1949, no less than twenty-one agreements, treaties, communiqués, consultations, declarations have been finalized and no less than 679 high-level diplomatic exchanges have occurred since 2000.

Economic relations are robust. Since diplomatic ties were established in 1949, no less than 130 agreements, contracts, and protocols were finalized to promote trade. Bilateral trade is strong and has increased almost twelvefold (from $8 billion to $95.2 billion) between 2000 and 2014 with crude oil being the most traded commodity between the two countries. Russia is a major supplier of crude oil where China imports approximately 8 percent annually. China also imports natural gas products and LNG from Russia but in limited quantities. With a new round of oil and gas cooperation in the wake of Ukraine crisis, China is expected to import more Russian gas projects and LNG through pipelines connecting the two countries.

China has also invested heavily into Russia's economy which includes infrastructure development and financial aid in the agricultural, construction, forestry, metals, mining, real estate, transportation, and technology sectors at total no less than $13.82 billion. Key Chinese infrastructure projects in Russia were backed by loans from Chinese banks and financial institutions such as China EXIM Bank at no less than $500 million. Key Chinese oil-related projects in Russia were also backed by loans from CDB at no less than $31 billion in return for 48.4 million tons of crude oil over five years, ten years of crude oil deliveries at 180,000 barrels per day, and ten years of crude oil deliveries at 120,000 barrels per day.

Sino-Russian military/security relations have been close since 1949 except for the Sino-Soviet split (1960–1989). Russia has had a profound effect on China's military modernization during the Cold War and after the fall of the Soviet Union. Russia helped China close the technological gap vis-à-vis with the United States and supplied it with modern military weapons and equipment especially in the period after the Cold War. China saved Russia's arms industry from certain death after foreign military sales dried up in the wake of the collapse of the Soviet Union and the end of the Cold War. Russia has traditionally been China's chief arms supplier since 1949.

China and Russia do not have a formal military alliance but cooperate widely in defense matters. Both conduct joint exercises on land and at sea, joint training, high-level exchanges between senior officers, military-technical cooperation, and educational exchanges. Both are members of the SCO to combat extremism, separatism, and terrorism and have signed numerous agreements to promote military and security cooperation.

Sino-Russian cultural relations are weak today. Nevertheless, both countries have finalized no less than 113 agreements, plans, protocols, and memorandums to promote cooperation in film, fishery, journalism, sports, education, medicine, meteorology, public health, publishing, radio, science, television, transportation, and space technology. To realize cooperation, both countries promoted cultural exchanges in the same areas after diplomatic relations were established in 1949.

China and Russia cooperate on energy matters both in the hydrocarbon and non-hydrocarbon sectors. In terms of hydrocarbons, Russia is China's largest supplier of crude petroleum after Saudi Arabia and Angola. Russia completed the construction of the ESPO oil pipeline on December 25, 2012, not only to export crude oil to China but also open its markets to the Asian market. China also completed a 616-mile offshoot pipeline from the Russia-China border to Daqing, China in October 2010.

To facilitate crude oil and gas trade, China and Russia finalized no less than twenty-three agreements and contracts involving CNPC, Sinopec, CIC, Hudian, Gazprom, Rosneft, Transneft, Lukoil, and Sakhalin Energy to: form joint ventures to explore for and extract crude oil and gas in Siberia, Sakhalin Island and the Arctic; acquire public shares in Russian companies; acquire oil and gas from Russia; construct oil and gas pipelines; and build an oil refinery. China and Russia also signed no less than seven agreements and MoUs since 1949 to promote oil and gas cooperation. Beyond these formal transactions, China's CNPC provided engineering and oil field service, including geophysical prospecting and pipeline construction to Russia.

Sino-Russian energy cooperation extends beyond hydrocarbon sector. Since 1955, no less than nine agreements, contracts, and MoUs have been finalized in support of energy cooperation in the nuclear, coal, and thermoelectric and hydroelectric sectors. In realization of these agreements, contracts, and MoUs, Chinese and Russian companies collaborated to build the Tianwan nuclear power plant in Jiangsu province using two Russian-designed reactors and plan to install at least six more reactors in the near future.

Agreements, contracts, and MoUs were also realized in Russia's thermoelectric and hydroelectric sectors. In this respect, China and Russia collaborated in construction and development projects in the latter country. In this respect, China's Three Gorges Dam invested $2.48 billion in, and acquired 50 percent of Russia's EuroSibEnergo. China Yangtze International and EuroSibEnergo PLC formed a joint venture with YES Energo Ltd. to develop hydro and thermal power projects in Russian Siberia and the Far East to transmit electricity back to China. Russia has been exporting electricity to China since 2004: from 0.3 billion kilowatts to 3.375 billion kilowatts in 2014.

NOTES

1. Wolfgang Bartke, *The Agreements of the People's Republic of China with Foreign Countries 1949–1990* (Munchen, Germany: K.G. Saur), 1992, 163.
2. Robert G. Sutter, *Chinese Foreign Relations: Power and Policy Since the Cold War* (Landam, MD: Rowman & Littlefield Publishers), 2008, 327.
3. Matti Nojonen, "Introduction: Adjusting to the Great Power Transition," in Arkady Moshes and Matti Nojonen, eds., *Russia–China Relations: Current State, Alternative Futures, and Implications for the West* (Helsinki, Finland: The Finnish Institute of Foreign Affairs), 2011, 14.
4. Bobo Lo and Andy Rothman, *Asian Geopolitics* (Hong Kong, China: CLSA), May 2006, 5, 6.
5. Ibid., 6.
6. Ibid., 7.
7. Ibid.
8. Nandan Unnikrishnan and Uma Purushothaman, *Trends in Russia–China Relations: Implications for India* (New Delhi, India: Observer Research Foundation), 2015, 5.
9. Ibid., 6.
10. Lo and Rothman, ibid., 7.
11. Ibid.
12. Robert L. Worden, Andrea Matles Savada and Ronald E. Dolan, eds., *China: A Country Study* (Washington, DC: GPO for the Library of Congress), 1987; and Lo and Rothman, ibid., 7.
13. Jing-Yun Hsu and Jenn-Jaw Soong, "Development of China–Russia Relations (1949–2011): Limits, Opportunities, and Economic Ties," *The Chinese Economy* (New York, NY: M.E. Sharpe, Inc.), Volume 47, Issue 3, May–June 2014, 73; Worden, Savada and Dolan, eds. ibid.; and Lo and Rothman, ibid.
14. Lo and Rothman, ibid., 7; and Worden, Savada and Dolan, eds. ibid.
15. Lo and Rothman, ibid., 8; and Worden, Savada and Dolan, eds. ibid.
16. Unnikrishnan and Purushothaman, Ibid., 6.
17. Lo and Rothman, ibid., 8, 11, 12; and Hsu and Soong, ibid., 74.
18. Unnikrishnan and Purushothaman, Ibid., 9–12; and Ministry of Foreign Affairs of People's Republic of China, "China–Russia: Documents," (n.d.), accessed January 10, 2016, http://www.fmprc.gov.cn/mfa_eng/wjb_663304/zzjg_663340/dozys_664276/gjlb_664280/3220_664352/3221_664354/.
19. Unnikrishnan and Purushothaman, ibid., 13–19; and Lo and Rothman, ibid., 13.
20. Lo and Rothman, ibid., 4, 10; and Hsu and Soong, ibid., 77.
21. Unnikrishnan and Purushothaman, Ibid., 3, 59–60; and Hsu and Soong, ibid.
22. Ministry of Foreign Affairs of People's Republic of China, "China–Russia: Activities," (n.d.), accessed August 9, 2016, http://www.fmprc.gov.cn/mfa_eng/

wjb_663304/zzjg_663340/dozys_664276/gjlb_664280/3220_664352/3222_664356/; and "China and Russia," *CCTV*, (n.d.), accessed January 18, 2015, http://www.cctv.com/lm/1039/20/1.html.

23. Bartke, ibid., 163.
24. Ibid., 165.
25. Ibid., 169.
26. Ibid.
27. Ibid., 171.
28. "China and Russia," *CCTV*, (n.d.), accessed January 18, 2015, ibid.
29. Zhongping Feng and Jing Huang, "China's Strategic Partnership Diplomacy: Engaging with a Changing World" (Fride and ESPO), Working Paper No. 8, June 2014, accessed August 17, 2014, http://www.fride.org/descarga/WP8_China_strategic_partnership_diplomacy.pdf.
30. "China and Russia," *CCTV*, (n.d.), accessed January 18, 2015, ibid.
31. Lo and Rothman, ibid., 11.
32. Feng and Huang, ibid.
33. Lo and Rothman, ibid., 11.
34. Ibid.
35. "China and Russia," *CCTV*, (n.d.), accessed January 18, 2015, ibid.
36. Ministry of Foreign Affairs of People's Republic of China, "China–Russia: Documents," (n.d.), accessed January 10, 2016, ibid.
37. Ministry of Foreign Affairs of People's Republic of China, "List of Agreements on Mutual Visa Exemption Between the People's Republic of China and Foreign Countries" March 29, 2014, accessed March 5, 2016, http://cs.mfa.gov.cn/wgrlh/bgzl/P020140328398504621618.pdf.
38. Ibid.
39. Ministry of Foreign Affairs of People's Republic of China, "China–Russia: Documents," (n.d.), accessed January 10, 2016, ibid.
40. "China and Russia," *CCTV*, (n.d.), accessed January 18, 2015, ibid.
41. Lo and Rothman, ibid., 11.
42. Ministry of Foreign Affairs of People's Republic of China, "China–Russia: Documents," (n.d.), accessed January 10, 2016, ibid.
43. Feng and Huang, ibid.
44. Ministry of Foreign Affairs of the People's Republic of China, "Hu Jintao Holds Talks with Russian President Putin," June 5, 2012, accessed August 20, 2016, http://www.fmprc.gov.cn/mfa_eng/wjb_663304/zzjg_663340/dozys_664276/gjlb_664280/3220_664352/3222_664356/t939577.shtml.
45. Ministry of Foreign Affairs of People's Republic of China, "Xi Jinping Meets with Russian President Vladimir Putin," September 5, 2013, accessed August 20, 2016, http://www.fmprc.gov.cn/mfa_eng/wjb_663304/zzjg_663340/dozys_664276/gjlb_664280/3220_664352/3222_664356/t1074364.shtml.
46. Ministry of Foreign Affairs of People's Republic of China, "Premier Li Keqiang Co-Chairs with Dmitry Anatolyevich Medvedev the 18th Regular Meeting between Chinese and Russian Prime Ministers, Jointly Deciding to Fully Deepen China–Russia Cooperation in All Fields and Push forward Bilateral Comprehensive Strategic Cooperative Partnership to a New High," October 22, 2013, accessed

August 20, 2016, http://www.fmprc.gov.cn/mfa_eng/wjb_663304/zzjg_663340/dozys_664276/gjlb_664280/3220_664352/3222_664356/t1092653.shtml.

47. Ministry of Foreign Affairs of People's Republic of China, "Xi Jinping Holds Talks with President Vladimir Putin of Russia, Stressing to Expand and Deepen Practical Cooperation, Promoting China–Russia Comprehensive Strategic Partnership of Coordination to Higher Level," May 20, 2014, accessed August 20, 2016, http://www.fmprc.gov.cn/mfa_eng/wjb_663304/zzjg_663340/dozys_664276/gjlb_664280/3220_664352/3222_664356/t1158516.shtml.

48. Ministry of Foreign Affairs of People's Republic of China, "Li Keqiang and Prime Minister Dmitry Medvedev of Russia Co–chair 19th Regular Meeting Between Chinese and Russian Prime Ministers," October 13, 2014, accessed August 20, 2016, http://www.fmprc.gov.cn/mfa_eng/wjb_663304/zzjg_663340/dozys_664276/gjlb_664280/3220_664352/3222_664356/t1200657.shtml.

49. Ministry of Foreign Affairs of People's Republic of China, "Commemorating Great Victory of World War II and Composing New Chapter of Silk Road Cooperation Foreign Minister Wang Yi's Remarks on President Xi Jinping's Attendance at Celebrations Marking 70th Anniversary of Victory of Great Patriotic War in Russia and His Visits to Russia, Kazakhstan and Belarus," May 13, 2015, accessed August 21, 2016, http://www.fmprc.gov.cn/mfa_eng/wjb_663304/zzjg_663340/dozys_664276/gjlb_664280/3180_664322/3182_664326/t1263828.shtml.

50. Ministry of Foreign Affairs of People's Republic of China, "Xi Jinping Holds Talks with President Vladimir Putin of Russia Both Heads of State Stress Unswerving Commitment to Deepening China–Russia Comprehensive Strategic Partnership of Coordination," June 25, 2016, accessed August 20, 2016, http://www.fmprc.gov.cn/mfa_eng/wjb_663304/zzjg_663340/dozys_664276/gjlb_664280/3220_664352/3222_664356/t1375791.shtml.

51. Ibid.

52. Ministry of Foreign Affairs of People's Republic of China, "Declaration of the People's Republic of China and the Russian Federation on the Promotion of International Law," June 26, 2016, accessed August 20, 2016, http://www.fmprc.gov.cn/mfa_eng/wjb_663304/zzjg_663340/dozys_664276/gjlb_664280/3220_664352/3222_664356/t1386141.shtml.

53. Ministry of Foreign Affairs of People's Republic of China, "Yang Jiechi Holds Meeting and Jointly Attends First Meeting of Council of Cooperation Between the Upper and Middle Reaches of the Yangtze River and the Volga Federal District with Plenipotentiary Representative of the Russian President in the Volga Federal District Mikhail Babich," July 20, 2016, accessed August 20, 2016, http://www.fmprc.gov.cn/mfa_eng/wjb_663304/zzjg_663340/dozys_664276/gjlb_664280/3220_664352/3222_664356/t1383610.shtml.

54. Chinese-Embassy.info, "China embassies and consulates in Russia," (n.d.), assessed July 3, 2016, http://www.chinese-embassy.info/europe/rus.htm; and "Russian Consulates around the World," (n.d.), accessed July 3, 2016, http://www.russian-consulates.com/consulate.aspx?ConsulateID=1139.

55. European Commission Directorate-General for Trade, "China: EU Bilateral Trade and Trade with the World," July 5, 2013, accessed October 13, 2013, http://trade.ec.europa.eu/doclib/docs/2006/september/tradoc_113366.pdf.

56. European Commission Directorate-General for Trade, "Russia: EU Bilateral Trade and Trade with the World," April 16, 2014, accessed May 3, 2014, http://trade.ec.europa.eu/doclib/docs/2006/september/tradoc_113440.pdf.

57. European Commission Directorate-General for Trade, "Russia: EU Bilateral Trade and Trade with the World," April 10, 2015, accessed May 3, 2015, http://trade.ec.europa.eu/doclib/docs/2006/september/tradoc_113440.pdf.

58. European Commission Directorate-General for Trade, "China: EU Bilateral Trade and Trade with the World," April 10, 2015, accessed May 3, 2015, http://trade.ec.europa.eu/doclib/docs/2006/september/tradoc_113366.pdf.

59. Unnikrishnan and Purushothaman, ibid., 2.

60. Lo and Rothman, Ibid., 8; Unnikrishnan and Purushothaman, ibid., 21; Hanbing Kong, "The Transplantation and Entrenchment of the Soviet Economic Model in China," in Thomas P. Bernstein and Hua-Yu Li, eds., *China Learns from the Soviet Union, 1949–Present* (Lanham, MD: Lexington Books), 2010, 160; and United Nations, United Nations Commodity Trade Statistics Database, accessed July 22, 2016, http://comtrade.un.org/db/default.aspx.

61. United Nations Conference on Trade and Development (UNCTAD FDI/TNC) Database, *Bilateral FDI Statistics 2014*, accessed February 20, 2016, http://unctad.org/Sections/dite_fdistat/docs/webdiaeia2014d3_RUS.pdf.

62. Ibid.

63. United Nations Conference on Trade and Investment, "The Rise of the BRICS FDI and Africa," March 25, 2013, accessed October 13, 2013, http://unctad.org/en/PublicationsLibrary/webdiaeia2013d6_en.pdf.

64. Unnikrishnan and Purushothaman, ibid., 2.

65. Ibid., 21.

66. United Nations, United Nations Commodity Trade Statistics Database, accessed July 22, 2016, http://comtrade.un.org/db/default.aspx.

67. International Trade Centre, Directory of Trade Promotion Organizations and Other Trade Support Institutions, accessed February 20, 2016, http://www.intracen.org/itc/trade-support/tsi-directory.

68. Ministry of Foreign Affairs of the People's Republic of China, "The 16th Meeting of the Joint Commission for the Regular Meetings of Heads of Government of China and Russia Is Held in Moscow," December 6, 2012, accessed August 20, 2016, http://www.fmprc.gov.cn/mfa_eng/wjb_663304/zzjg_663340/dozys_664276/gjlb_664280/3220_664352/3222_664356/t996119.shtml.; Ministry of Foreign Affairs of People's Republic of China, "China–Russia: Documents," (n.d.), accessed January 10, 2016, ibid.; and Bartke, ibid., 163–172.

69. The Heritage Foundation and American Enterprise Institute, *China Global Investment Tracker Database*, accessed March 11, 2016, http://www.heritage.org/research/projects/china-global-investment-tracker-interactive-map; and "China Announce U.S. $1.3 b Russian Real Estate Project," *ChinaDaily.com.cn,* July 20, 2006, accessed March 11, 2016, http://www.chinadaily.com.cn/china/2006-07/20/content_645771.htm.

70. The Heritage Foundation and American Enterprise Institute, ibid., and "Russia-China Agreement on Grain Hub calls for investing $1.1 billion," *Russia*

Beyond the Headlines, June 24, 2016, accessed August 26, 2016, http://rbth.com/business/2016/06/24/russia-china-agreement-on-grain-hub-calls-for-investing-11-bln_605857.

71. "Construction Begins of 'Baltic Pearl' Project," *PetersburgCity.com,* March 24, 2006, accessed March 23, 2016, http://petersburgcity.com/news/city/2006/03/24/baltic_pearl/.

72. The Heritage Foundation and American Enterprise Institute, ibid.

73. Ibid.

74. You Ji, "The Soviet Model and the Breakdown of the Military Alliance," in Thomas P. Bernstein and Hua-Yu Li, eds., *China Learns from the Soviet Union, 1949–Present* (Lanham, MD: Lexington Books), 2010, 131.

75. Ibid., 132.

76. Ibid.

77. Ibid.

78. Jing-Dong Yuan, "Sino-Russian Defense Ties: The View from Beijing," in James Bellacqua, ed., *The Future of China–Russia Relations.* (Lexington, KY: The University Press of Kentucky), 2010, 205.

79. Ibid., 204–205.

80. Ibid., 205.

81. Ibid.

82. Linda Jakobson, et al., *China's Energy and Security Relations with Russia: Hopes, Frustrations and Uncertainties* (Stockholm, Sweden: SIPRI), October 2011, accessed October 13, 2013, 15–16, http://books.sipri.org/files/PP/SIPRIPP29.pdf.

83. Ibid.

84. Unnikrishnan and Purushothaman, ibid., 49; and Yuan, ibid., 205.

85. Ibid.

86. Ibid.

87. Ibid.

88. Kevin Ryan, "Russo–Chinese Defense Relations: The View from Moscow," in James Bellacqua, ed., *The Future of China–Russia Relations.* (Lexington, KY: The University Press of Kentucky), 2010, 181.

89. Unnikrishnan and Purushothaman, Ibid., 49; and Ryan, ibid.

90. Ryan, ibid., 180.

91. Yuan, ibid., 207–208.

92. Ryan, ibid.

93. Jakobson, et al., ibid.

94. Yuan, ibid., 221.

95. Jakobson, et al., ibid.

96. Unnikrishnan and Purushothaman, ibid., 54.

97. Stockholm International Peace Research Institute, SIPRI Arms Transfers Database, http://www.sipri.org/databases/armstransfers.

98. Unnikrishnan and Purushothaman, ibid., 49.

99. Ibid., 51–52.

100. Ibid., 52, 53.

101. Ibid., 53.

102. Jakobson, et al., ibid., 15; Bartke, ibid., 164, 171; Yuan, ibid., 207, 208, 210, 211; Unnikrishnan and Purushothaman, ibid., 53, 55; and "China and Russia," *CCTV*, (n.d.), accessed January 18, 2015, ibid.
103. Unnikrishnan and Purushothaman, ibid., 57.
104. Ibid.
105. "China and Russia," *CCTV*, (n.d.), accessed March 26, 2016, ibid.
106. Ibid.
107. Ibid.
108. Elizabeth Wishnick, "Why a 'Strategic Partnership?' The View from China," in James Bellacqua, ed., *The Future of China–Russia Relations*. (Lexington, KY: The University Press of Kentucky), 2010, 72.
109. Ibid., 72–73.
110. Confucius Institute Online, Worldwide Confucius Institutes, accessed March 27, 2016, http://english.hanban.org/node_10971.htm.
111. Wishnick, ibid., 73.
112. "China and Russia," *CCTV*, (n.d.), accessed March 26, 2016, ibid.
113. Ibid.
114. Ibid.
115. Wishnick, ibid., 72.
116. Unnikrishnan and Purushothaman, ibid., 57.
117. *Graphisoft*, "ARCHICAD-designed Russian Pavilion at World Expo 2010 in Shanghai Takes the Silver," November 16, 2010, accessed March 27, 2016, http://www.graphisoft.com/info/news/press_releases/russian-pavilion-shanghai.html.
118. Unnikrishnan and Purushothaman, ibid.; and Ministry of Foreign Affairs of People's Republic of China, "China–Russia," (n.d.), accessed March 27, 2016, http://www.fmprc.gov.cn/mfa_eng/wjb_663304/zzjg_663340/dozys_664276/gjlb_664280/3220_664352/.
119. Unnikrishnan and Purushothaman, ibid.
120. Ministry of Foreign Affairs of People's Republic of China, "China–Russia," (n.d.), accessed March 27, 2016, ibid.
121. Bartke, Ibid., 163–172; Yuan, Ibid., 215.; and Ministry of Foreign Affairs of People's Republic of China, "Xi Jinping Holds Talks with President Vladimir Putin of Russia Both Heads of State Stress Unswerving Commitment to Deepening China–Russia Comprehensive Strategic Partnership of Coordination," June 25, 2016, accessed August 20, 2016, http://www.fmprc.gov.cn/mfa_eng/wjb_663304/zzjg_663340/dozys_664276/gjlb_664280/3220_664352/3222_664356/t1375791.shtml.
122. Hsu and Soong, ibid., 81.
123. Ibid.
124. Ibid., 82.
125. Alexander Gabuev, *A "Soft Alliance"? Russia–China Relations After the Ukraine Crisis* (London, UK: European Council on Foreign Relations), May 2015, 1.
126. Keun-Wook Paik, *Sino-Russian Gas and Oil Cooperation: Entering into a New Era of Strategic Partnership?* (Oxford, UK: The Oxford Institute for Energy Studies), OIES Paper WPM 59, April 2015, 1.

127. Mikhail Fomichev, "Transneft to Boost Pacific Oil Pipeline Capacity to 67M tones," *Ria Novosti*, July 31, 2013, accessed October 13, 2013, http://en.rian.ru/business/20130731/182511026.html.

128. Hsu and Soong, ibid., 83.

129. United Nations, United Nations Commodity Trade Statistics Database, accessed July 6, 2016, ibid.

130. U.S. Energy Information Administration, U.S. Department of Energy, "Country Analysis Briefs: China," May 14, 2015, 11, accessed July 6, 2016, https://www.eia.gov/beta/international/analysis_includes/countries_long/China/china.pdf; United Nations Commodity Trade Statistics Database, accessed July 6, 2016, ibid.; and Hsu and Soong, ibid., 84.

131. Ze Shi, *Building Strong China–Russia Energy Strategic Partnership* (Beijing, China: China Institute of International Studies), December 2, 2015, accessed July 7, 2016, http://www.ciis.org.cn/english/2015-12/02/content_8422032.htm; Bartke, Ibid., 164; and Alexander Korablinov, "Russia, China sign 30 Cooperation Agreements," *Russia Beyond the Headlines*, June 27, 2016, accessed August 26, 2016, http://rbth.com/international/2016/06/27/russia-china-sign-30-cooperation-agreements_606505.

132. Erica Downs, *Inside China, Inc: China Development Bank's Cross-Border Energy Deals* (Washington, DC: The Brooking Institution Press), March 2011, 39–40.

133. China National Petroleum Company, "CNPC in Russia, Oilfield Services, Engineering and Construction," accessed July 6, 2016, http://www.cnpc.com.cn/en/Russia/country_index.shtml.

134. Unnikrishnan and Purushothaman, ibid., 45.

135. Unnikrishnan and Purushothaman, ibid., 46; and Shi, ibid.

136. Korablinov, ibid.; Unnikrishnan and Purushothaman, ibid., 42, 45, 47; and Bartke, ibid., 164, 165, 172.

137. Unnikrishnan and Purushothaman, ibid., 6.

Chapter 10

China and Saudi Arabia
Political/Diplomatic Relations

Official Sino-Saudi diplomatic relations were established on July 21, 1990.[1] While diplomatic relations have developed since 1990, oil and gas trading and investment have formed the crux of the Sino-Saudi relationship.[2] China and Saudi Arabia have built a strategic relationship based in energy cooperation.

The earliest encounters of China and Saudi Arabia date back to seventh century when Chinese and Saudi merchants developed trade ties along the Silk Road.[3] Muslim merchants were spotted in Xian as early as 630 during the life of the Prophet Muhammad. Chinese-Hui Muslims like Admiral Zheng He make voyages to Saudi Arabia between 1407 and 1433 to forge trade ties.

Bilateral relations date back to 1939 when Saudi Arabia was the first Arab country to normalize its political ties with Republican China.[4] Diplomatic relations continued until the Chinese Communist Party (CCP) seized power in 1949, when diplomatic relations broke off.[5] Saudi Arabia recognized Taiwan in the same year and became the main source of energy for the Republic of China (Taiwan).[6] In 1971, Saudi Arabia also voted against admitting China into the United Nations and expelling Taiwan from the United Nations. Despite this, unofficial ties developed (religiously, economically, and militarily) in the wake of China's opening up to the outside world in 1979 (such as establishing trade representative offices in 1989) and culminated with the normalization of diplomatic relations in 1990.[7]

Ideological reasons and religious reasons such as the harsh treatment of Muslims of China prevented establishment of official Sino-Saudi diplomatic relations between 1949 and 1990 despite China's futile attempts to change Saudi perceptions. Ideologically, Islam was incompatible with communism or socialism. Saudi Arabia, and in particular, many Islamic scholars, viewed that Islam and communism as antitheses, especially since Saudi Arabia was the self-proclaimed protector of Islam since the 1950s. This did not mean

Saudi foreign policy was solely conducted on the basis of ideology because Saudi Arabia and the Soviet Union established trade relations as early as 1927. What made it different were China's systemic restrictions imposed on Chinese Muslims. China forbade Chinese Muslims to worship and make Hajj missions (or pilgrimages) to Mecca from China. Saudi Arabia protested and China eased restrictions on Chinese Muslims by allowing them pilgrimages to Mecca between 1956 and 1966; however, no significant level of freedom of worship was reported.[8] The Hajj missions stopped in 1966 because of the Cultural Revolution, and resumed again in 1979, after China initiated massive economic reforms based to a degree on free-market principles.

Sino-Saudi relations were complicated by other factors which made it impossible for any improvement in bilateral ties. China was heavily involved in supporting left-wing revolutionary movements in the Gulf region, in Yemen, and in Jordan. China was supporting the Dhofar Liberation Front (which renamed itself the Popular Front for the Liberation of Occupied Arabian Gulf [PFLOAG]). DLF was a leftist organization that was trying to liberate Oman, the Trucial States (UAE, Bahrain and Qatar), and Kuwait, in addition to providing support to fellow Arab leftists in the Middle East battling Western colonialism, imperialism, and neo-imperialism.[9] China and Saudi Arabia were on opposite sides with respect to the civil war in Yemen as well as any left-wing revolutionary liberation movements in the region.

Sino-Saudi relations started to improve in the wake of a rift between China and Soviet Union. This became apparent when Soviet Union decided to invade Afghanistan in 1979. China and Saudi Arabia viewed the invasion consistent with Soviet expansionism as well as Soviet attempts to extend its influence and outreach to the Gulf region. Both countries were particularly alarmed by the Soviet Union's increasing influence in South Yemen. Accordingly, China, Saudi Arabia, and the United States formed a Tripartite Containment Network to the Soviets in Afghanistan. Consequently, the Soviet Union withdrew in 1988 and collapsed in 1991.[10]

Sino-Saudi relations were influenced by developments which occurred on a regional and national level. Internationally, China was admitted into the United Nations in October 1971, an event where many Arab countries including Palestine suddenly found China as a powerful ally on the United National Security Council. Regionally, China ended its support for leftist organizations in the region, thereby contributing to the process of ending the Omani civil war, and strengthening the stability of the Gulf region. The U.S.-Sino rapprochement of 1971 had the greatest impact on defusing tensions between China and Saudi Arabia as well as the end the Cultural Revolution in 1976 and its impact on leadership change in China.[11]

Sino-Saudi relations improved in the late 1980s in the wake of end of the Iran-Iraq war in 1988. China sold Saudi Arabia fifty medium-range missiles in 1988, trade offices were established later that year with representatives assuming offices in 1989, and bilateral ties were upgraded to full diplomatic recognition in 1990.[12]

Since the establishment of diplomatic relations, rapid development and cooperation in political, economic, cultural, and religious matters have occurred.[13] Official documents were also finalized between China and Saudi Arabia on matters of mutual political interest. These include: a Communiqué on the Establishment of Diplomatic Relations Between the People's Republic of China and the Kingdom of Saudi Arabia (July 21, 1990);[14] the Agreement on Water Conservancy Cooperation between the Government of the People's Republic of China and the Government of Saudi Arabia (October 2002);[15] a Nuclear Cooperation Pact (January 15, 2012);[16] and Joint Statement on the Establishment of a bilateral Comprehensive Strategic Partnership (January 18, 2016).[17]

China and Saudi Arabia also established an embassy and consulates in Riyadh (Chinese Embassy), Beijing (Saudi Embassy), and Jeddah (Chinese Consulate) to strengthen diplomatic ties. High-level bilateral visits and exchanges rapidly followed. No less than eighty-nine high-level bilateral visits and exchanges have been conducted since 2003, which has deepened mutual political trust between the two countries. Some of the most important exchanges include: President Hu Jintao and King Abdullah Ibn Abdul-Aziz (January 2006, April 2006, and September 2009) and President Xi Jinping and Crown Prince Salman Bin Abdulaziz Al Saud (March 2014, January 2016). In 2010, both countries celebrated twenty years of diplomatic ties.[18]

At the highest political levels, diplomatic ties were strengthened. Chinese president Hu Jintao and Saudi Arabian king Abdullah conducted high-level exchange visits to each other's countries in early 2006 in which President Hu laid a four-point proposal for enhancing Sino-Saudi relations. One point called for the mutual safeguard of each other's national sovereignty and territorial integrity and the continued support and cooperation on international and regional affairs. The collective security aspect of this proposal became very apparent in the aftermath of the September 11, 2001 terrorist attacks on the United States. U.S.-Saudi relations were broken because most of the 9/11 terrorists came from Saudi Arabia and the United States blamed Saudi Arabia. Consequently, Saudi Arabia turned to China for security support because Saudi Arabia was never as vulnerable in its modern history as it was in post-September 11, 2001.[19]

Saudi Arabia was also strategically vulnerable from the civil war that ensued in neighboring Iraq in the wake of U.S. presence and the Arab Spring. The Arab Spring threatened Saudi Arabia's national security because of the political and social instability the uprising generated across the Arab world. China viewed the Arab Spring as potentially destabilizing in the sense that it could motivate a similar movement in Xinjiang and Tibet, or possibly in an urban uprising in one of its major cities. Both countries agreed about the potential dangers posed by the Arab Spring except Syria. While Saudi Arabia welcomed change in Syria in the backdrop of a protracted civil war, China opposed it and supported the Assad regime.[20]

Despite their differences over a possible regime change in Syria, China and Saudi Arabia have forged a strategic relationship based in energy cooperation. This relationship has been extended to the economic-trade, military-security, and cultural aspects of their relationship.[21]

ECONOMIC/TRADE RELATIONS

Sino-Saudi economic relations are robust. China initiated a strategic partnership with Saudi Arabia in 1999.[22] Saudi Arabia is China's largest trading partner in West Asia and Africa.[23] In 2013, China was Saudi Arabia's largest trading partner after the European Union.[24] Saudi Arabia was China's tenth largest trading partner in the same year.[25] Bilateral trade was: $41.8 billion (2008), $32.6 billion (2009), $43.2 billion (2010), $64.3 billion (2011), $73.3 billion (2012), $72.1 billion (2013), $69 billion (2014), and $51.8 billion (2015).[26] Bilateral trade increased about $10 billion in seven years. Since 2000, bilateral trade increased sixteen-fold. In 2012, foreign direct investment into Saudi Arabia from China was $154 million and foreign direct investment stock was $1.206 billion.[27]

Table 10.1 shows the top five commodities traded between China and Saudi Arabia in 2015. Energy commodities, such as crude petroleum and petroleum products, appear to be most traded commodity between the two countries at 71 percent. See Table 10.1.

China's energy commodities accounted for the following in terms of trade value in previous years: 85 percent (2008), 82 percent (2009), 79 percent (2010), 80 percent (2011), 82 percent (2012), 81 percent (2013), and 78 percent (2014).[28]

Bilateral trade is promoted through several organizations such as the Sino-Saudi Joint Commission on Economic, Trade, and Technological Cooperation, the Office of Chinese Cooperation in Saudi Arabia, the China-Arab States Cooperation Forum, the Asia Cooperation Dialogue, China-GCC Forum on Economic and Trade Cooperation, the Saudi Chamber of Commerce, the PRC Ministry of Commerce, the PRC Ministry of Foreign Affairs, and the All-China Federation of Industry and Commerce.[29]

Bilateral trade has grown significantly since diplomatic relations were established in 1990. Saudi Arabia has become a major investor in China because of an increase in bilateral trade. Saudi Arabia has invested $750

Table 10.1 Top Five Commodities Traded between China and Saudi Arabia

Commodity	Importer	Trade Value ($)	Percentage (%)
Mineral fuels, mineral oils and products of their distillation; bituminous substances; mineral waxes	China	21,253,248,947	70.5
Organic chemicals	China	4,913,589,337	16
Plastics and articles thereof	China	3,295,910,726	11
Salt; sulfur; earths and stone; plastering materials, lime and cement	China	405,413,774	1
Copper and articles thereof	China	81,668,187	0.3
Nuclear reactors, boilers, machinery and mechanical appliances; parts thereof	Saudi Arabia	3,149,758,209	15
Electrical machinery and equipment and parts thereof; sound recorders and reproducers, television image and sound recorders and reproducers, and parts and accessories of such articles	Saudi Arabia	2,386,964,104	11
Furniture; bedding, mattresses, mattress supports, cushions and similar stuffed furnishings; lamps and lighting fittings, not elsewhere specified or included; illuminated signs, illuminated name-plates and the like; prefabricated buildings	Saudi Arabia	2,065,957,901	10
Articles of apparel and clothing accessories, not knitted or crocheted	Saudi Arabia	1,185,861,805	6
Vehicles other than railway or tramway rolling-stock, and parts and accessories thereof	Saudi Arabia	1,162,695,090	5

Source: United Nations Commodity Trade Statistics Database.

million of the $3 billion needed to construct a petrochemical complex in southeastern Fujian Province that will process 8 million tons of Saudi crude oil. Saudi Arabia along with several members of the Organization of the Petroleum Exporting Countries (OPEC) also agreed to finance and build a new oil refinery in Guangzhou at a cost of $8 billion. In 2014, China has also invited Saudi Arabia to join the Silk Road Economic Belt, a Chinese-led initiative aimed at rejuvenating the Silk Road trade route. China also aims to develop Xinjiang Providence and has encouraged its Middle Eastern and Central Asian partners to invest in the development of Western China. To date, China has invested at least $120 billion into infrastructure projects with the goal of stabilizing the region.[30]

Chinese investment (apart from infrastructure investment) in Saudi Arabia is limited in comparison to Saudi investment in China. Chinese National Oil Companies' (NOCs) activities in Saudi Arabia are very much limited to engineering services, such as pipeline and well repair, seismic data collection, and natural gas projects. Although Saudi Arabia does not allow foreign companies (including Chinese companies) to invest in its upstream (exploration and production) oil sector, it has allowed them to invest in the upstream gas sector and refinery sector.[31] Despite these restrictions, bilateral investment is likely to grow between China and Saudi Arabia.

Some of the important agreements and memorandums of understanding that have been ratified to develop and enhance trade between the two countries include: the Agreement on Economic, Trade, Investment, and Technological Cooperation between China and Saudi Arabia (November 1992);[32] the Exchange of Notes on Mutual Rendering of the Most Favored Nation Treatment between China and Saudi Arabia (December 1993);[33] the Agreement on Mutual Promotion and Protection of Investment between China and Saudi Arabia (February 1996);[34] the Memorandum of Economic and Trade Cooperation between China and Saudi Arabia (October 1998);[35] an Economic, Trade, and Technical Cooperation Agreement (2002);[36] Summary of the 3rd Meeting of the Mixed Committee on Economic, Trade, Investment, and Technological Cooperation between China and Saudi Arabia (January 23, 2006);[37] Investment Cooperation Agreement (March 14, 2014);[38] and Memorandum of Understanding Between the Government of the People's Republic of China and the Government of the Kingdom of Saudi Arabia on Jointly Promoting the Silk Road Economic Belt and the 21st-Century Maritime Silk Road (January 20, 2016).[39]

China has been actively involved in Saudi Arabia's economic development, which includes stakes in Saudi companies and infrastructure development. Currently, 140 Chinese companies operate in Saudi Arabia, the bulk of which are in the construction, infrastructure, and petrochemicals industries.[40] Approximately twenty-three deals involving real estate, chemicals, energy, metals, transportation, agriculture, and utilities, port construction, housing construction, railroads, highways, airports, and seawater desalination were concluded since March 2005. Some of the largest deals include: Sinoma International Engineering Co. Ltd. and Riyadh Cement Company agreed to construct a turnkey cement factory for $170 million (March 2005); Sinoma International Engineering Co. Ltd. and Saudi Cement Company agreed to build two cement production lines for $580 million (December 2005); China Non-ferrous Metal Industry's Foreign Engineering and Construction Co Ltd., China National Machinery Industry Corporation (SINOMACH), and Saudi company Western Way for Industrial Development Co (WWIDC) agreed to develop an alumina and aluminum complex in Jazan Economic City for $3.39 billion (April 2007); Chinalco acquired a 40 percent stake in an aluminum smelter for $1.2 billion with the Saudi Bin Laden Group and Malaysia Mining Corporation (November 2007); Guizhou Hongfu

Industry and Commerce Development Co. Ltd. of China won $350 million contract for construction of a beneficiation plant (December 2007); China Communications Construction Company has won a contract worth US$ 230 million (AED 840 million) for the construction of the container terminal at Jeddah Port (December 2007); Guangdong Overseas Construction Group Co., Ltd. won a $350 million contract to construct King Khalid University Project Phase One (July 2008); China Railway Construction Corporation awarded a $390 million contract to construct the Mecca Light Rail (February 2009); Shandong Electric Power Construction Corporation (SEPCO) and Saudi Electricity Company awarded a $1.8 billion contract to extend the Rabigh Power Plant (July 2009); SEPCO and Al-Arrab Contracting Company awarded a $1.72 billion contract to build the Ras Al Khair Power Plant (May 2010); a Joint Venture consisting of Al-Toukhi Company for Industry, Trading, and Contracting, Shanghai Electric Co. (33 percent share), and Samsung Engineering Co. awarded a $2.99 billion contract to construct to a 2,700-megawatt water desalinization plant in Yanbu (November 2012); China National Chemical Engineering Corporation awarded a $400 million contract to build a shipping terminal at King Fahd Industrial Port (November 2012); China Communications Construction Company awarded a $500 million utility contract (July 2013); China Communications Construction Company awarded a $390 million transportation contract (September 2013); and China Communications Construction Company awarded a $500 million contract by Aramco to construct a water intake and outlet, water intake pumping station, and a water intake ditch (May 2014).[41]

In summary, Chinese companies have invested no less than $18.5 billion in non-energy projects since March 2005. These investments represent 97 percent of China's total investments.[42]

MILITARY/SECURITY RELATIONS

Sino-Saudi military relations appear to be expanding in the wake of robust energy ties. China and Saudi Arabia engaged each other militarily through high-level exchanges and visits and educational exchanges including three visits to Saudi Arabia by China's Minister of National Defense and four visits to the PRC by Saudi military officials. In January 2008, the PRC Minister of Defense visited Saudi Arabia.[43] From September 2011 to January 2012, pilots from the Royal Saudi Arabian Air Force participated in PLAFF sponsored course on tactics, combat methods, and simulated training.[44] China also maintains a permanent defense attaché in the capital city of Riyadh and has conducted official, high-level talks with Saudi defense ministers while Saudi Arabia also assigns a permanent defense attaché in Beijing.[45] No less than eight military interactions have occurred since 2002 according to Ministry of National Defense of People's Republic of China, *PLA Daily*, *Xinhua*, and *China Military Online*.

China's total arms sales to Saudi Arabia are $966.37 million based on the 2016 CPI index. In 2000, total arms sales to Saudi Arabia were $829.26 million; the difference being $137.11 million over a sixteen-year period. Bilateral arms sales appear to be shrouded in extreme secrecy apart from the Saudi purchase of fifty CSS-2 missiles, fifty-four PLZ-45 self-propelled howitzers, and two CH-4 unmanned aerial vehicles.[46]

China and Saudi Arabia concluded their first arms sales transaction in 1988 with the Kingdom's purchase of fifty CSS-2 intermediate-range ballistic missiles "which are capable of carrying a nuclear payload." The sale came as a shock to the United States because the arms deal was unexpected. The United States perceived Sino-Saudi relations were unfriendly and that Saudis were reliant on them for arms. In reality, the arms purchase was a response to the growing objection of the Israel lobby in the U.S. Congress that providing Saudi Arabia with medium-range or long-range missiles constituted a threat to Israel's national security.[47]

Saudi Arabia has expressed an interest in China's J-17 jet fighter given Chinese military technological advancements. The J-17 is a joint venture fighter jet which was produced by China and Pakistan, both with close ties to the Kingdom. At this time, the Saudi's are reviewing the JF-17 program and considering becoming a partner in its development and production.[48]

Sino-Saudi military-security cooperation appears to have grown remarkably in the twenty-first century. China has provided security guarantees to Saudi Arabia at two important junctures since 2001. China has also assured Saudi Arabia of regime survival in the wake of the September 11, 2001 terrorist attacks against the United States. Regime survival is vital to Saudi Arabia considering the destabilizing effects of the Arab Spring and U.S. pressure against the Saudi system. In the event of a U.S. pivot out of the region, Saudi Arabia wants to ensure Chinese security support. Should the U.S. pivot out, China would pivot in, and a potential scenario would be one where Saudi Arabia may be willing to host Chinese military bases and strengthen its security cooperation similarly to the United States at the peak of the U.S.-Saudi strategic partnership.[49] It not entirely certain at this juncture.

Sino-Saudi security cooperation has occurred with respect to China's War on Terror. Saudi Arabia has condemned attacks orchestrated by the East Turkestan Islamic Movement (ETIM) against Chinese citizens and called on Muslims in China to engage in efforts of development and peaceful coexistence. To this extent, China has provided $120 billion in project development assistance to balance its enhanced security efforts to combat the ETIM and crackdown on separatists. China also has solicited support from Saudi Arabia, Kuwait, the

UAE, and Turkey to conduct development projects in China's predominantly western regions and northwestern China.⁵⁰ In summary, Sino-Saudi military-security ties have developed rapidly and strengthened in the wake of regional and international developments and the establishment of diplomatic ties.

CULTURAL RELATIONS

Sino-Saudi cultural relations date back to the fifteenth century when Chinese explorer Zhang He attempted to forge cultural ties to the region between 1407 and 1433. China attempted to establish cultural ties in 1955; however, the Saudi religious reestablishment, the media community, and the academic community opposed any contacts with China and resisted any improvement in Sino-Saudi ties on ideological, religious, and cultural grounds. China was considered a "godless" country by many Saudis while Chinese viewed Saudi Arabia as a "reactionary kingdom" serving as a cradle for Western imperialism in the Middle East. China was also harsh on Chinese Muslims but eventually eased some restrictions placed on them, such as freedom of worship and the Hajj delegations to Mecca. In fact, 13,000 Chinese Muslims made pilgrimages to Saudi Arabia in 2010. China also encouraged its Muslim communities to strengthen their economic ties with Saudi Arabia, Turkey, and other Muslim countries. While China faced fierce opposition from Saudi Arabia due to the "Islamic Factor," it was China's treatment of its Muslim communities that determined Saudi ties with China for three decades. Once China removed these obstacles, it established bilateral cultural and strategic ties.⁵¹

China gained significant political and cultural capital in 2011 from the construction of the Mecca Light Metro. Constructed between 2009 and 2011 by the China Railway Construction Corporation (CRCC) at a loss of 4.1 billion Yuan ($644.11 million), it allowed millions of pilgrims to travel to, in, and around the holy city of Mecca with greater ease especially during the Hajj season. By easing the congestion of pilgrims in the holy city of Mecca, China scored high marks across the Muslim world.⁵²

Saudi Arabia participated actively in the Shanghai World Expo and spent $150 million in on its pavilion. The Saudi Pavilion was one of the most popular pavilions in China during the Expo and received over 4 million Chinese visitors. It included a 1,600 square-meter screen to show short films about the Kingdom. The pavilion remains open today and serves as a permanent cultural institution.⁵³

In 2011, the Saudi-Chinese Youth Forum was established to strengthen joint youth and exchange programs in both China and Saudi Arabia. Joint activities were organized to develop a better understanding of the younger generation in each country.⁵⁴

Saudi Arabia has also started to send students to Chinese universities to study science, technology, and petroleum engineering. China has also been sending students to Saudi Arabia to study the Arab language and religious studies. The danger of communist indoctrination is no longer a concern for many Saudi parents unlike before 1990.[55]

Finally, at least 140 Chinese corporations now operate in the Kingdom manned by a growing community of at least 10,000 Chinese nationals. The Chinese community in Saudi Arabia is well received and highly regarded, especially in terms of their contributions to the Kingdom's development.[56]

Since diplomatic relations were established in 1990, a number of agreements have been inked. Some of the important agreements signed between China and Saudi Arabia with respect to the promotion of culture include: a Joint Cooperation Agreement Between the Saudi Press Agency and the Chinese Xinhua News Agency (1999);[57] the Agreement on Radio and Television Cooperation between China's Radio and Television Bureau and Saudi Arabia's Ministry of Information (October 1999);[58] the Agreement on Educational Cooperation (October 1999);[59] the Agreement on Cultural and Educational Cooperation between China and Saudi Arabia (December 2002);[60] Agreement on Vocational Training Cooperation between China and Saudi Arabia (January 23, 2006);[61] Agreement of Quality Inspection between China and Saudi Arabia (March 14, 2014);[62] Agreement of Space Science and Technology Cooperation between China and Saudi Arabia (March 14, 2014);[63] Agreement of Communications Cooperation (January 20, 2016);[64] Agreement of Environmental Cooperation (January 20, 2016);[65] Agreement of Cultural Cooperation (January 20, 2016);[66] Agreement of Aerospace Cooperation (January 20, 2016);[67] and Agreement of Science and Technology Cooperation (January 20, 2016).[68]

ENERGY/PETROLEUM RELATIONS

The major component of the Sino-Saudi relationship is energy trading. Economic ties centering on energy resources is the primary driver of their relationship.[69] In fact, Saudi Arabia is China's largest supplier of crude oil in the world, followed by Angola and Iran.[70] China's oil imports from Saudi Arabia averaged about 18 percent per year from 2006 to 2015. Table 10.2 illustrates China's crude petroleum imports from Saudi Arabia in thousands of barrels per day, oil imports share, world ranking, trade value, total commodity trade value, and percentage from 2006 to 2015. See Table 10.2.

China also imports petroleum gas products from Saudi Arabia but not liquefied natural gas (LNG). Table 10.3 illustrates China's petroleum gas imports from Saudi Arabia in millions of cubic feet, global imports share,

Table 10.2 Chinese Crude Petroleum Imports from Saudi Arabia

Year	KBPD	Oil Imports Share (%)	World Ranking	Crude Oil Trade Value ($)	Total Commodity Trade Value ($)	Percentage (%)
2006	479	16	1	11,033,638,243	15,084,532,094	73
2007	529	16	1	13,112,732,864	17,560,475,696	75
2008	730	20	1	25,815,459,076	31,022,697,923	83
2009	841	21	1	18,922,893,211	23,620,243,562	80
2010	897	19	1	25,538,596,067	32,829,047,702	78
2011	1,010	20	1	39,015,427,640	49,467,519,877	79
2012	1,083	20	1	44,165,045,207	54,861,126,276	81
2013	1,082	19	1	42,368,087,201	53,450,710,541	79
2014	997	16	1	36,940,644,812	48,508,025,980	76
2015	1,015	15	1	20,775,949,646	30,150,710,600	69

Source: United Nations Commodity Trade Statistics Database.

Table 10.3 Chinese Petroleum Gas Product Imports from Saudi Arabia

Year	Volume (MMcf)	Global Share (%)	World Ranking	Petroleum Gas Trade Value ($)	Total Commodity Trade Value ($)	Percentage (%)
2006	39.2	16	3	518,542,437	15,084,532,094	3
2007	25.6	9	3	372,752,377	17,560,475,696	2
2008	19.6	8	4	341,407,154	31,022,697,923	1
2009	18.9	5	7	237,565,401	23,620,243,562	1
2010	15.4	2	10	270,318,860	32,829,047,702	1
2011	12.8	1	12	273,571,551	49,467,519,877	1
2012	24.8	2	7	535,751,723	54,861,126,276	1
2013	22.2	1	10	471,147,864	53,450,710,541	1
2014	14.7	0.71	16	314,171,866	48,508,025,980	1
2015	28.3	1	13	366,050,399	30,150,710,600	1

Source: United Nations Commodity Trade Statistics Database.

world ranking, trade value, total commodity trade value, and percentage from 2006 to 2015. See Table 10.3.

China is Saudi Arabia's most important "market for its 'distressed' medium-grade oil-a viscous, acidic, often sulfurous product that Saudi Arabia has in abundance but that has few takers on the international market." Thus, "Saudi Arabia has been working to develop China's capacity to develop and use Saudi heavy crude, investing in two refineries along China's coast": the upgrading of the Quanzhou refinery in Fujian Province and the development of the Qingdao refinery in Shandong province. With respect to developing the Qingdao refinery, Saudi Arabia is assisting China to increase its oil reserve capacity from thirty days to ninety days, especially since the United States has an oil storage capacity of 150 days to offset any unpredictable shifts in oil supplies. Therefore, Saudi Arabia is assisting China in building three additional strategic oil reserves all of which are located near Chinese navy bases for their protection and for use during wartime: Dalian, Ningbo, and Zhoushan. The fact that Saudi Arabia is assisting China in the construction of its oil reserve capacity indicates that Sino-Saudi energy cooperation extends beyond crude petroleum and petroleum gas product trading.[71]

China and Saudi Arabia also agreed in 2006 to jointly construct an oil storage facility on China's Hainan Island and Saudi Arabia invited Chinese firms to participate in infrastructure development worth $624 billion.[72]

China does not have oil and gas assets in Saudi Arabia other than Sinopec's Red Sea Refining Company joint venture to build the Yanbu Aramco with Saudi Aramco. Sinopec will have a 38 percent stake worth $3.3 billion. The Yanbu Sinopec refinery (YASREF) was expected to be fully operational by the end of 2014 but was not realized until January 2016 coinciding with President Xi Jinping's state visit to Saudi Arabia. In October 2015, China's SEPCO, a contract from Saudi Aramco to expand the capacity of the main gas pipeline across Saudi Arabia. Under the terms of the $700 million contract, SEPCO would build a gas compressor station to boost the capacity from 8.4 billion cubic feet per day to 9.6 billion cubic feet per day.[73]

Some of the important agreements signed with respect to establishing petroleum cooperation include: a Memorandum of Understanding On Petroleum Cooperation between the Government of the People's Republic of China and the Government of the Kingdom of Saudi Arabia (October 31, 1999);[74] Protocol on Cooperation in the areas of Petroleum, Natural Gas, and Mineral Resources between the Government of the People's Republic of China and the Government of the Kingdom of Saudi Arabia (January 23, 2006);[75] Memorandum of Understanding for implementing Industrial Production Capacity Cooperation (January 20, 2016);[76] and Framework Agreement between Saudi Arabian Oil Co. (Saudi Aramco) and China Petroleum & Chemical Corp. (Sinopec) for cooperation in activities related to oil and other energy (January 21, 2016).[77]

In addition to hydrocarbon energy cooperation, Sino-Saudi energy cooperation extends to the nuclear realm. In January 2012, a bilateral agreement was signed "to enhance cooperation between the two countries in the development of atomic energy for peaceful purposes." Apparently, atomic energy development "is essential to meet to the Kingdom's growing requirements for energy to generate electricity, produce desalinated water, and to reduce reliance on depleting hydrocarbon resources." Already, Saudi Arabia has announced its intention to construct sixteen reactors by 2030, and has large plans to produce 100 gigawatts by 2021, mainly through fossil fuels. It is important to note that independent experts have stated that Saudi Arabia's drive for civil nuclear power is seen by some as a "security hedge" against Iran and that if Iran was not on a path of nuclear weapons capability, there would be no need to rush to develop civil nuclear power.[78]

SUMMARY

Sino-Saudi relations appear to be strategic; however, bilateral ties were virtually non-existent until 1990 when official ties were established. Between 1949 and 1990, China and Saudi Arabia were polarized over political, ideological, and religious issues. Today, China and Saudi Arabia engage each other on all levels: politics, economics, military, culture, and petroleum. Moreover, in terms of annual trade value for 2013, 81 percent is attributable to energy commodities which include crude petroleum from Saudi Arabia. Thus, energy ties, which largely include oil, play the most important role in the Sino-Saudi relationship even though Chinese investment in Saudi Arabia's oil and gas industry is restricted to engineering services, such as pipeline and well repair, seismic data collection, and natural gas projects.[79] After energy, trade relations factor the most in the Sino-Saudi relationship; however, cultural and military-security ties have grown exponentially since 2001. Sino-Saudi energy cooperation is strategic in the hydrocarbon realm but it extends to nuclear energy cooperation as well.

NOTES

1. Ministry of Foreign Affairs of People's Republic of China, "China–Saudi Arabia," 08/22/2011, accessed October 8, 2013, http://www.fmprc.gov.cn/eng/wjb/zzjg/xybfs/gjlb/2878/.
2. Jon B. Alterman and John W. Garver, The Vital Triangle: China, The United States and the Middle East (Washington, DC: CSIS Press), 2008, 33.
3. Muhamad S. Olimat, *China and the Middle East Since World War II* (Lanham, MD: Lexington Books), 2014, 213.
4. Naser Al-Tamimi, *China–Saudi Arabia Relations: Economic Partnership or Strategic Alliance?* (Durham, UK: Al Sabah), Number 2, June 2012, accessed August 31, 2014, https://www.dur.ac.uk/resources/alsabah/China-SaudiArabiaRelations.pdf.
5. Ibid.
6. Olimat, ibid., 213.
7. A-Tamimi, ibid.
8. Olimat., 214–215.
9. Ibid., 214–215.
10. Ibid., 214, 215–216.
11. Ibid., 216.

12. Ibid.

13. A-Tamimi, ibid.

14. Ministry of Foreign Affairs of People's Republic of China, "Communiqué Concerning the Establishment of Diplomatic Relations Between the People's Republic of China and the Kingdom of Saudi Arabia," 11/15/2000, accessed May 26, 2014, http://www.fmprc.gov.cn/mfa_eng/wjb_663304/zzjg_663340/xybfs_663590/gjlb_663594/2878_663746/2879_663748/t16422.shtml.

15. Ministry of Foreign Affairs of People's Republic of China, "China and Saudi Arabia," November 26, 2004, accessed August 29, 2014, http://jeddah.china-consulate.org/eng/zsgx/t172060.htm.

16. Summer Said. "Saudi Arabia, China Sign Nuclear Cooperation Pact," *The Wall Street Journal*, January 16, 2012. Web, April 20, 2012, accessed May 26, 2014, http://online.wsj.com/article/SB10001424052970204468004577164742025285500.html.

17. Ministry of Foreign Affairs of People's Republic of China, "Foreign Ministry Holds Briefing for Chinese and Foreign Media on President Xi Jinping's State Visits to Saudi Arabia, Egypt and Iran," January 18, 2016, accessed August 19, 2016, http://www.fmprc.gov.cn/mfa_eng/wjb_663304/zzjg_663340/xybfs_663590/gjlb_663594/2878_663746/2880_663750/t1333116.shtml.

18. Ministry of Foreign Affairs of People's Republic of China, "China–Saudi Arabia," Ibid; and Ministry of Foreign Affairs of People's Republic of China, "China–Saudi Arabia-Activities," accessed August 9, 2016, http://www.fmprc.gov.cn/mfa_eng/wjb_663304/zzjg_663340/xybfs _663590/gjlb_663594/2878_663746/2880_663750/default_1.shtml.

19. Alterman and Garver, ibid., 35; and Olimat, ibid., 217.

20. Ibid.

21. Ibid., 200, 217, 218.

22. Dawn Murphy, "China and the Middle East," testimony, June 6, 2013, before U.S.–China Economic and Security Review Commission.

23. Ministry of Foreign Affairs of People's Republic of China, "China–Saudi Arabia," ibid.

24. European Commission Directorate-General for Trade, "Saudi Arabia: EU Bilateral Trade and Trade with the World," April 10, 2015, accessed May 3, 2015, http://trade.ec.europa.eu/doclib/docs/2006/september/tradoc_113442.pdf.

25. United Nations, United Nations Commodity Trade Statistics Database, accessed August 22, 2015, http://comtrade.un.org/db/default.aspx.

26. Ibid.

27. United Nations Conference on Trade and Development (UNCTAD FDI/TNC) Database, *Bilateral FDI Statistics 2014*, accessed August 1, 2014, http://unctad.org/Sections/dite_fdistat/docs/webdiaeia2014d3_CHN.pdf.

28. United Nations, United Nations Commodity Trade Statistics Database, accessed July 22, 2016, ibid.

29. Olimat, ibid., 221.

30. Geoffrey Kemp, *The East Moves West: India, China, and Asia's Growing Presence in the Middle East* (Washington, DC: Brookings Institution Press), 2010, 81; and Olimat, ibid., 220–221.

31. Naser Al-Tamimi, "China–Saudi Relations: Booming Trade," *Al Arabiya News*, February 22, 2013, accessed October 8, 2013, http://english.alarabiya.net/views/2013/02/22/267670.html.
32. Ministry of Foreign Affairs of People's Republic of China, "China and Saudi Arabia," ibid.
33. Ibid.
34. Ibid.
35. Ibid.
36. Olimat, ibid., 220.
37. Ministry of Foreign Affairs of People's Republic of China, "Hu Jintao Holds Talks with Saudi Arabian King Abdullah," January 23, 2006, accessed August 19, 2016, http://www.fmprc.gov.cn/mfa_eng/wjb_663304/zzjg_663340/xybfs_663590/gjlb_663594/2878_663746/2880_663750/t232890.shtml.
38. Ministry of Foreign Affairs of People's Republic of China, "Li Yunshan Holds Talks with Crown Prince Salman Bin Abdul-Aziz Al Saud, the First Deputy Prime Minister and Defense Minister of Saudi Arabia," March 14, 2014, accessed August 19, 2016, http://www.fmprc.gov.cn/mfa_eng/wjb_663304/zzjg_663340/xybfs_663590/gjlb_663594/2878_663746/2880_663750/t1138412.shtml.
39. Ministry of Foreign Affairs of People's Republic of China, "Xi Jinping Holds Talks with King Salman bin Abdulaziz Al Saud of Saudi Arabia Two Heads of State Jointly Announce Establishment of China–Saudi Arabia Comprehensive Strategic Partnership," January 20, 2016, accessed August 19, 2016, http://www.fmprc.gov.cn/mfa_eng/wjb_663304/zzjg_663340/xybfs_663590/gjlb_663594/2878_663746/2880_663750/t1333527.shtml.
40. Olimat, ibid., 220.
41. The Heritage Foundation and American Enterprise Institute, *China Global Investment Tracker Database*, accessed October 17, 2014, http://www.heritage.org/research/projects/china-global-investment-tracker-interactive-map.
42. Ibid.
43. Kenneth Allen, "Trends in PLA International Initiatives Under Hu Jintao," Paper presented at The National Bureau of Asian Research and Strategic Studies Institute of the U.S. Army War College Conference "Assessing the People's Liberation Army in the Hu Jintao Era," October 19–21, 2012.
44. Heidi Holz and Kenneth Allen, "Military Exchanges with Chinese Characteristics: The PLA Experience with Military Relations," Paper presented at The National Bureau of Asian Research, Strategic Studies Institute of the U.S. Army War College, and Texas A&M University's Bush School Conference "The PLA at Home and Abroad," (Carlisle Barracks, PA), September 25–27, 2009.
45. United States Department of Defense, Defense Intelligence Agency, *Directory of PRC Military Personalities* (Washington, DC), 2014, 20.
46. Stockholm International Peace Research Institute, SIPRI Arms Transfers Database, http://www.sipri.org/databases/armstransfers; and Olimat, ibid., 224
47. Olimat, ibid., 223–224.
48. Ibid., 225.
49. Ibid.

50. Ibid.
51. Olimat, ibid., 221–222; and Ministry of Foreign Affairs of People's Republic of China, "China–Saudi Arabia," ibid.
52. Ibid.
53. Ministry of Foreign Affairs of People's Republic of China, "China–Saudi Arabia," Ibid.; and Olimat, ibid., 223.
54. Ibid.
55. Ibid.
56. Ibid.
57. Ministry of Foreign Affairs of People's Republic of China, "A Joint Cooperation Agreement Between the Saudi Press Agency and the Chinese Xinhua News Agency," 06/05/2012, accessed May 26, 2014, http://www.fmprc.gov.cn/mfa_eng/wjb_663304/zzjg_663340/xybfs_663590/gjlb_663594/2878_663746/2879_663748/t16424.shtml.
58. Ministry of Foreign Affairs of People's Republic of China, "China and Saudi Arabia," ibid.
59. Ibid.
60. Ibid.
61. Ministry of Foreign Affairs of People's Republic of China, "Hu Jintao Holds Talks with Saudi Arabian King Abdullah," ibid.
62. Ministry of Foreign Affairs of People's Republic of China, "Li Yuanchao Holds Talks with Crown Prince Salman Bin Abdulaziz Al Saud, the First Deputy Prime Minister and Defence Minister of Saudi Arabia," March 14, 2014, accessed August 19, 2016, http://www.fmprc.gov.cn/mfa_eng/wjb_663304/zzjg_663340/xybfs_663590/gjlb_663594/2878_663746/2880_663750/t1138412.shtml.
63. Ibid.
64. Ministry of Foreign Affairs of People's Republic of China, "Xi Jinping Holds Talks with King Salman bin Abdulaziz Al Saud of Saudi Arabia Two Heads of State Jointly Announce Establishment of China–Saudi Arabia Comprehensive Strategic Partnership," ibid.
65. Ibid.
66. Ibid.
67. Ibid.
68. Ibid.
69. Kemp, ibid., 80.
70. Al-Tamimi, "China-Saudi Relations: Booming Trade."
71. Alterman and Garver, ibid., 58., 59; Olimat, ibid., 218; and Kemp, ibid., 82.
72. Jon B. Alterman, "China's Soft Power in the Middle East," in Carola McGiffert, ed., *Chinese Soft Power and Its Implications for the United States* (Washington, DC: CSIS Press), March 2009, 65.
73. "China's SEPCO set to win gas booster contract from Saudi Aramco," *Reuters*, September 14, 2015, accessed August 26, 2016, http://www.reuters.com/article/sepco-saudi-aramco-gas-idUSL5N10Y0NR20150914; the Heritage Foundation and American Enterprise Institute, ibid; Olimat, ibid., 218; and Ministry of Foreign Affairs of People's Republic of China, "Xi Jinping and King Salman bin Abdulaziz

Al Saud of Saudi Arabia Together Attend the Launch Ceremony of the Yasref Oil Refinery," January 21, 2016, accessed August 20, 2016, http://www.fmprc.gov.cn/mfa_eng/wjb_663304/zzjg_663340/xybfs_663590/gjlb_663594/2878_663746/2880_663750/t1333960.shtml.

74. Ministry of Foreign Affairs of People's Republic of China, "Memorandum of Understanding On Petroleum Cooperation between the Government of the People's Republic of China and the Government of the Kingdom of Saudi Arabia," 06/05/2012, accessed May 26, 2014, http://www.fmprc.gov.cn/mfa_eng/wjb_663304/zzjg_663340/xybfs_663590/gjlb_663594/2878_663746/2879_663748/t16423.shtml.

75. Ministry of Foreign Affairs of People's Republic of China, "Hu Jintao Holds Talks with Saudi Arabian King Abdullah," ibid.

76. "China, Saudi Arabia Elevate Bilateral ties, Eye More Industrial Capacity Cooperation," *Xinhua*, January 20, 2016, accessed May 12, 2017, http://news.xinhuanet.com/english/2016-01/20/c_135025406_2.htm.

77. "Aramco, Sinopec move to expand Cooperation," *Oil and Gas Journal*, January 21, 2016, accessed August 19, 2016, http://www.ogj.com/articles/2016/01/aramco-sinopec-move-to-expand-cooperation.html.

78. Olimat, ibid., 219.

79. Al-Tamimi, "China–Saudi Relations: Booming Trade."

Chapter 11

China and South Sudan
Political/Diplomatic Relations

Sino-South Sudan diplomatic relations were established when South Sudan achieved independence from Sudan on July 9, 2011.[1] Since South Sudan achieved its independence, both countries have interacted through official, high-level visits and exchanges no less than forty-three times.[2] Some of the most important exchanges include President Hu Jintao and President Salva Kiir Mayardit (April 2012).[3] South Sudan's succession from Sudan was made possible by the signing of the 2005 Comprehensive Peace Agreement (CPA). The Comprehensive Peace Agreement ended the thirty-eight-year civil war (1983–2005) between northern Sudan and southern Sudan; however, the CPA granted greater autonomy to a regional government in the South and contained a self-determination referendum at the end of the CPA period in 2011.[4] The CPA's six-year period began in July 2005 during which the CPA provisions would be jointly implemented through a "one-country, two-systems" structure.[5] When the referendum was organized in January 2011, 98 percent of South Sudanese voters voted for independence.[6] Consequently, the Republic of South Sudan (RSS) was created. To establish and further diplomatic relations, China and South issued: Joint Communiqué on the Establishment of Diplomatic Relations (July 9, 2011);[7] and Agreement on Mutual Visa Exemption including diplomatic and service passports (July 9, 2011).[8]

South Sudan's political relations with China are recent compared to Sudan's political relations with China; however, diplomatic ties are very good.[9] China first encountered southern Sudan during the two cycles of the Sudanese civil war, during which China stood by Sudan. The first cycle was from 1956 to 1972 and the second round lasted from 1985 to 2005. During these times, China supported Sudan with military arms and support. Strong ties have been present since diplomatic relations were established in 1959. Prior to 1959, delegates of China and Sudan met at the Bandung Conference in 1955 where China was admired by Sudan's role in furthering the process of national liberation across the African continent. China also admired Sudan's stability as well as its progressive and modern outlook. China was also a strong supporter of Sudan defending it against the Soviet threat in the 1970s and a communist military coup which sought to destabilize Sudan in 1972.[10]

During the 1970s, Sudan received some aid from China but was advised to approach Washington. Sino-Sudanese ties strengthened in the 1990s and Sudan received $8 billion to develop its oil sector. China also supported the peace process and encouraged government in Khartoum and the southern rebels to conclude the 2005 CPA. In the interim, China worked with both sides to develop Sudan's oil sector and infrastructure projects.[11]

China also developed ties with South Sudan in preparation for its independence. China established strong ties with two of South Sudan's most influential leaders: Salva Kiir Mayardit (South Sudan's first president) and John Garang. China opened a consulate in Juba in 2008 (and South Sudan reciprocated with the establishment of an embassy in Beijing in 2011), dispatched diplomats to establish political ties, sent peacekeepers, and deployed a support mission to observe the 2011 referendum on independence. China became one of first countries to recognize South Sudan's independence and pledged political and economic support from the beginning. China also provided South Sudan with a $8 billion preferential credit line in the wake of President Kiir's first state visit to China in April 2012. China also pledged to develop South Sudan's infrastructure through various projects including a network of highways, roads, and bridges over the Nile Rivers; schools and housing projects; water systems and power plants; and convention centers, sports facilities, and a modern airport.[12]

Since mid-December 2013, all development projects have been placed on hold because of the ongoing conflict in South Sudan. U.S. sanctions also have been imposed on military generals fighting on both sides of the conflict; oil workers and personnel have been evacuated; and some donors and countries have threatened the leaders of the warring factions with stringent sanctions.[13]

South Sudan has been embroiled in two major wars since 2011: with the Sudan and its own civil war. With respect to the war with Sudan, South Sudan was accused of supporting separatists in Kordofan to destabilize the government of Sudanese president Omar al-Bashir. Sudan also accused South Sudan of invading and annexing some of Sudan's territory. Consequently, Sudan denied access to its ports for South Sudan's oil exports, declared war against South Sudan, and allowed its forces to penetrate deep beyond the border region and into South Sudan's territory. China was exerted pressure on both sides to end the conflict.[14]

China dispatched a special representative to mediate the conflict especially since it had a compelling political and economic interest to ensure its oil imports from Sudan and South Sudan. Other political entities like the United

States, the United Nations, the African Union, and the European Union were also involved in conflict resolution.[15]

During President Salva Kiir Mayardit's state visit to China in April 2012, the main issue was the peace process between Sudan and South Sudan. Both Sudan and South Sudan resigned themselves to the fact that China was the solution to their problems.[16]

The conflict between Sudan and South Sudan centered mainly around border issues and the absence of an agreement on how the oil wealth would be shared prior to the succession of South Sudan. While Chinese corporations developed Sudan's oil sector between 2000 and 2010, there were no agreements on oil wealth, division of the national debt, the status of citizen's in each territory, and other important issues. Thus, the conflict was imminent and unavoidable but peaceful and well-tempered.[17]

China opposed the war and joined the international community to end it. In addition to help mediating the conflict, it deployed peacekeepers consisting of soldiers, policemen, security guards, engineers, and medical personnel. It also called for peace through United Nation's resolutions and supported the African Union's peace mission in both Sudan and South Sudan.[18]

Not long after the conflict between Sudan and South Sudan ended, a civil war broke out between the government forces led by President Salva Kiir Mayardit and rebel forces led by Vice President Reik Machar on December 15, 2013. The South Sudanese Civil War's (December 15, 2013–Present) origins are linked to the pre-independence period. It began as a political conflict between the two principals (Mayardit and Machar) but it is deeply rooted in the ethnic conflict between the Dinka and the Nouer, South Sudan's two major ethnic groups.[19]

China and the international community have been involved in resolving the conflict but to no avail. A cease fire agreement was signed in January 2014 but has been frequently violated despite their best diplomatic efforts. The civil war and human rights violations associated with it (murder, ethnic cleaning, and genocide) not only undermines South Sudan's stability and continued viability as a state, but also threatens the stability of the entire region. The civil war also undermines South Sudan's political, economic, and social development as all infrastructure projects are now on hold. Essentially, the conflict between Salva Kiir Mayarit and Reik Machar has undermined South Sudan's future making South Sudan another failed African state.[20]

ECONOMIC/TRADE RELATIONS

Sino-South Sudanese economic relations have been developing since South Sudan became an independent country in 2011.[21] Sino-South Sudanese trade appears strong but is negligible when compared to China's overall trade with Africa; however, it is growing in South Sudan's strategic sector of mineral fuels. In 2014, South Sudan was China's seventy-third largest trading partner.[22] According to the United Nations Commodity Trade Statistics database and the 2013 China Statistical Yearbook, bilateral trade was: $133 million (2011), $533.7 million (2012), $2.5 billion (2013), and $4.3 billion (2014). Bilateral trade increased $4 billion in five years. Since 2011, bilateral trade increased almost thirty-three-fold. South Sudan's economic growth rate has been remarkable since becoming independent in 2011 but the South Sudanese Civil War halted not only its growth rate but the country's unity and territorial integrity.[23]

South Sudan's oil sector is its most lucrative sector given that 75 percent of the former Sudan's oil production is in South Sudan. South Sudan's mining sector is rich in gold, silver, copper, aluminum, and limestone; however, the ongoing civil war has effectively ceased any efforts to exploit these natural resources. South Sudan also has vast arable land for farming but agriculture remains underdeveloped today.[24]

In terms of bilateral trade, Table 11.1 shows the top five commodities traded between China and South Sudan in 2014. Energy commodities, which include crude petroleum, appear to be most traded commodity. In terms of trade value, almost 100 percent is attributed to energy commodities, which includes crude petroleum. See Table 11.1.

Table 11.1 Top Five Commodities Traded between China and South Sudan

Commodity	Importer	Trade Value ($)	Percentage (%)
Mineral fuels, mineral oils and products of their distillation; bituminous substances; mineral waxes	China	4,329,174,256	99.99
Wood and articles of wood; wood charcoal	China	67,846	0.0016
Vehicles other than railway or tramway rolling-stock, and parts and accessories thereof	South Sudan	16,684,725	25
Nuclear reactors, boilers, machinery and mechanical appliances; parts thereof	South Sudan	14,022,934	21
Electrical machinery and equipment and parts thereof; sound recorders and reproducers, television image and sound recorders and reproducers, and parts and accessories of such articles	South Sudan	8,895,220	13
Plastics and articles thereof	South Sudan	3,744,997	6
Other made up textile articles; sets; worn clothing and worn textile articles; rags	South Sudan	3,714,702	6

Source: United Nations Commodity Trade Statistics Database.

In 2012, 2013, and 2014, China's energy commodities accounted for almost 100 percent in terms of trade value.[25] Energy commodities, namely crude oil, represent 98 percent of South Sudan's total government revenues, which is important to its economic and social stability given it is a landlocked country.[26]

Bilateral trade is promoted through several organizations such as the Forum on China-Africa Cooperation, the China-Arab States Expo, the China-Arab States Cooperation Forum, the China-Africa Development Fund, the China Business Network, the PRC Ministry of Commerce, the PRC Ministry of Foreign Affairs, and the All-China Federation of Industry and Commerce.[27]

China and South Sudan has inked some important agreements and memorandums of understanding to facilitate trade between their countries. The most notable includes: Memorandum of Understanding between the Southern Sudanese Ministry of Water Resources and Irrigation and China Construction and Machinery Company for Future Investment (2006);[28] Trade, Economic and Technical Agreement (November 22, 2011);[29] and Agreement on Economic and Technical Cooperation (April 24, 2012).[30]

China and Sudan also established a bilateral joint economic and trade committee on November 22, 2011.[31]

China has also been actively involved in South Sudan's economic development. At least 60 Chinese-funded enterprises have registered in South Sudan, related mainly to petroleum, construction, road and bridge, and communications as of October 2012. As of December 2014, approximately 140 Chinese companies are currently registered in South Sudan mostly doing business in South Sudan's non-oil sectors. Chinese companies first operated in South Sudan in 1996 (when the North and South were united) and have been involved in ambitious projects. China and South Sudan concluded deals to develop South Sudan's infrastructure in the sectors of agriculture, emergency response, education, government and civil society, construction, social infrastructure, storage, transportation, mining, health, energy generation and supply, water supply, and communications. These deals include: a $760,000 grant to build the Bentiu China Hospital (2011); a $30.9 million grant to fund multisector development projects in Agriculture, Education, Health, and Water Supply (2011); a $158 million preferential loan from the Export-Import Bank of China for China Harbour Engineering Company to develop South Sudan's Juba International Airport (2011); a $200 million loan from the Export-Import Bank of China to South Sudan's Commerce Ministry (2012); a $1.42 billion loan from the Bank of China for China Gezhouba Group to build the Biden Hydropower Station (2012); an agreement for a borehole drilling project (2012); Donation of Desktop Computers and Laser Printers to South Sudan's ruling party, Sudan People's Liberation Movement

(2012); a $1–2 billion loan to fund infrastructure projects, the mining industry, and agricultural projects in South Sudan (2013); a $150 million grant to upgrade Juba International Airport (2013); a Memorandum of Understanding between ZTE and the South Sudan's Ministry of Information and Broadcasting to transform the state-owned SSTV from analogue to digital (2013); a $27 million loan from the Export-Import Bank of China to a build 5-megawatt hydroelectric dam on the Kineti River (2013); Sinosteel Equipment and Engineering Co. Ltd. signed a $380 million contract with Sudar Oil Company to provide services including engineering design, equipment procurement, civil construction, and debugging for a 100-megawatt heavy oil power station, an affiliated power transformer line, and five transformer stations (October 2015); and China Communications Construction Company signed a $400 million contract with South Sudan's Ministry of Transport, Roads and Bridges to build a Nile water transport network (January 2016).[32]

Investments total over $1.76 billion since 2008 and represent almost all of China's total investments in South Sudan. During President Salva Kiir Mayardit's state visit to China in April 2012, China pledged $8 billion in preferential loans from the Bank of China and Export-Import Bank of China to support South Sudan's infrastructure and construction projects. Export-Import Bank of China allegedly signed a memorandum of understanding to finance approximately $1 billion of South Sudan's non-energy-related projects in return for future oil reserves. The Export-Import Bank of China also offered a $2 billion preferential loan to build a 1,500-mile highway connecting Juba with Port Sudan on the Red Sea, along with reconstructing Juba's International Airport, building bridges over the Nile River housing, schools, power plants, a gymnasium, and a convention center. China also pledged assistance in the areas of economic development, social development, and political stability. China also promised to encourage extensive involvement of Chinese corporations in development projects, and South Sudan pledged to create a favorable business environment conducive for investment and to protect Chinese corporations and nationals operating within its borders. China also called upon South Sudan to properly handle its oil cooperation with China and guarantee the stability and continuity of the cooperation considering South Sudan's assumption of 75 percent of the former Sudan's oil assets after the partition in July 2011. The infrastructures to exploit South Sudan's oil resources were in the North: pipelines, refineries, and export terminals.[33]

In terms on infrastructure projects, Chinese construction companies have built or contracted to build or upgrade the Juba International Airport, the Biden Hydropower Station, and Bentiu China Hospital.[34] Chinese companies planned to build a network of roads and highways to connect South Sudan's natural wealth, minerals, and products to the world market, but the ongoing civil war in South Sudan has restricted its global access.[35]

In summary, Sino-South Sudanese cooperation includes trade in commodities and services, agriculture, energy, communications, training, construction, investments, infrastructure, minerals, emergency response, government and civil society, construction, social infrastructure, storage, transportation, mining, health, energy generation and supply, and water supply. While many development projects are ambitious in nature, the ongoing South Sudanese Civil War has placed everything on hold.

MILITARY/SECURITY RELATIONS

Sino-South Sudanese military relations are not developed even though South Sudan has an attaché assigned to its embassy in Beijing. China and South Sudan do not have any bilateral military agreements, defense cooperation or military exchanges like China and Sudan other than providing de-mining equipment to South Sudanese officers in 2008, a de-mining course in 2008, consignment of weapons from China North Industries Group (NORINCO) and supplying a peacekeeping force of over 1,500 personnel since 2011.[36] However, South Sudanese president Salva Kiir Mayardit visited China in April 2012 and discussed a wide range of bilateral cooperation programs, including arms sales and security cooperation.[37] Defense-security cooperation does not figure prominently in China's courting of South Sudan unless Chinese officials decide it is in their national interest.[38] Given South Sudan's existing military-security relationship with the United States, the shape of any potential military-security cooperation between China and South Sudan will largely depend on how the U.S.-South Sudanese military-security relationship develops.[39] The United States declared that South Sudan was eligible to receive defense articles and services on a pro forma basis but has no intention of providing South Sudan with any lethal weapons especially in light of ongoing tension between the North and the South and the South Sudan Civil War.

The fact that the United States did not provide arms to South Sudan has forced South Sudan to look elsewhere, including China and any other country which will impose few conditions to arms transfers. U.S. reluctance to supply weapons to South Sudan provides China with new opportunities to supply South Sudan with military arms and equipment as the Sudan People's Liberation Army (SPLA) has traditionally field Eastern bloc weapons. In this respect, NORINCO delivered its first arms consignment of a $38 million weapons deal to South Sudan in June 2014 but halted any further orders after the international community openly questioned China's conflict resolution efforts in South Sudan's Civil War. Any additional Chinese arms sales have been shrouded in secrecy but observers noticed the presence of Chinese weapons in South Sudanese Civil War and confrontation between South

Sudan and Sudan in 2012. Although secret, China has supplied weapons to South Sudan since its independence. China exported 1,200 Red Arrow-73D anti-tank missiles in 2014 to date. The dearth of military transfers indicates China is a modest supplier of military arms and equipment. China's total arms sales to South Sudan are $22.13 million based on the 2016 CPI index.[40]

South Sudan's main arms vendors have been Russia, South Africa, and Ukraine. Russia supplied nine military helicopters (Mi-8, Mi-17, and Hip-H) in 2009 while South Africa provided ten Mamba Armed Personnel Carriers (APCs) in 2012 and Ukraine provided eleven self-propelled BM-21 122mm Mobile Rocket Launchers (MRL) between 2007 and 2009 and seventy-seven T-72M1 Tanks between 2007 and 2008.[41]

Military-security cooperation figures in South Sudan's desires for China to reorient its relationship with Sudan. As North-South Sudan tensions continued to escalate in November 2011, the vice chairman of the Central Military Commission pledged expanded bilateral military cooperation during a visit by Sudan's defense minister. This visit signaled China's intention to maintain strong relations with Sudan but the timing of the visit caused some in South Sudan to complain that China hedging by maintaining relations with both North Sudan and South Sudan. On the one hand, Chinese companies desire a stable investment environment but continue to sell arms which are destabilizing the borders and driving conflict in Southern Kordofan, the Blue Nile, Darfur, and Abyei.[42] However, China seeks to balance its relations between the North and South.

Although China does not have formal military-security ties with South Sudan, it is engaged in international security cooperation in South Sudan and elsewhere. China dispatched 2,181 peacekeepers worldwide since 2000 in support of United Nations peacekeeping operations in Sudan (Darfur), South Sudan, Cote d'Ivoire, Cyprus, the Democratic Republic of Congo, Liberia, and Western Sahara. China also has participated in the UN Mission in South Sudan (UNMISS) since 2011. China has deployed fifteen police personnel, three mission experts, and 331 contingency troops. In September 2014, China decided to send a battalion of 700 soldiers to UNMISS, the first ever Chinese battalion to a peacekeeping operation. This will be in addition to the 359 Chinese peacekeepers already in country, mainly consisting of engineering units, medical staff, and liaison officers, which have been helpful in providing medical assistance to both local refugees and other peacekeepers, as well as lending logistical support to international humanitarian organizations. The 700-member combat force will be responsible for protecting civilian populations at oil installations. China's significant stake in South Sudan, particularly its oil sector, motivates its participation in the peacekeeping mission there to an unprecedented level compared to other peacekeeping missions.[43]

China could arrange the deployment of combat troops as peacekeepers via United Nations Resolution 2155, which reprioritized the mandate of

UNMISS toward the protection of civilians. China could garner support to charge the beefed-up peacekeeping mission with responsibility for protecting civilians living in the proximity of major oil installations. China's effort to secure the arrangement in UN Resolution 2155 confirms the link between its overseas assets and its participation in UN peacekeeping missions. Moreover, China's deployment of combat troops as peacekeepers confirms its willingness to fully explore all available means under the UN umbrella to protect its overseas interests.[44]

Some South Sudanese officials suggested that China troops will be deployed to protect "vital installations" in the oil-rich Unity and Upper Nile States, which reinforces the mercantilist interpretation of China's proactive engagement with UNMISS. However, there is scant empirical evidence to suggest Chinese peacekeepers are being dispatched to protect South Sudan's oil infrastructure. A closer look at a UN deployment map for South Sudan reveals that Chinese forces are concentrated in oil-rich states, but in Wau of Western Bahr el Gazal state. Their presence brings tangible benefits for the protection of Chinese nationals such as enhancing prevention measures and crisis-response planning.[45]

China has taken a more active role in mediating an end to the South Sudanese Civil War. China's diplomatic presence in South Sudan is characterized by an active and constant presence in the ongoing Intergovernmental Authority on Development (IGAD)-led medication process. China's hands-on approach emerged shortly after the outbreak of the conflict; however, it does not wish to get sucked into Africa's ongoing cycles of wars and conflicts. By adopting a proactive role, China is succumbing to pressure from several sides (Chinese businesses and oil corporations, the UN, Western countries, the African Union and its member states), all of whom regard China as important broker of peace. Despite China's active involvement as a peace broker, caution is warranted against the overly optimistic estimate over the depth and width of its involvement in the conflict resolution. China is only playing a secondary role to IGAD and Troika countries behind the mediation process. China's decision to primarily rely on regional organizations, such as IGAD, to lead peace talks between the warring parties, despite important Chinese interests at stake, highlights the continuity in China's approach to solving disputes far beyond its border.[46]

CULTURAL RELATIONS

Sino-South Sudanese cultural relations were conducted though Sudan from 1956 to 2011; however, China has been contributing to South Sudan's social development since 1971 when China sent medical teams to offer medical treatment. China stopped sending medical teams in 1985 when a civil war erupted between North Sudan and South Sudan but resumed in 2012 after both signed a memorandum of understanding. China has sent two medical teams in 2012 and 2014. China also sent agricultural experts to Juba, Wau, and Malakal to teach rice cultivation technology to farmers.[47]

China supported South Sudan's independence and was active in South Sudan's economic and social development by building hospitals and schools, digging wells, providing medical equipment, musical instruments, antimalarial drugs and other emergency humanitarian supplies, as well as human resources training.[48]

Bilateral cultural cooperation extends to the celebration of national days. In 2012, China's embassy in Juba organized South Sudan's National Day celebration. Senior officials from both countries attended. Similarly, on July 2012, South Sudan's embassy in Beijing celebrated its first anniversary as the RSS and pledged an ambitious agenda of cooperation between China and South Sudan.[49]

Political party cooperation is also an aspect of Sino-South Sudanese cultural cooperation. Sudan People's Liberation Movement (SPLM) officials have met with their Chinese counterparts during official visits to strengthen ties with the Communist Party of China (CPC), as well as party-to-party and people-to-people relations. South Sudanese officials have benefited from workshops and seminars organized by Chinese entities in the areas administrative and bureaucratic development. Since 2009, over 500 South Sudanese government officials and technical personnel received training in China to improve their public service capacity and management skills. South Sudanese students received government scholarships to study in China. As of October 2012, twenty-three students won scholarships; many are studying at various Chinese colleges and universities.[50]

President Salva Kiir Mayardit received wide support for his country's social development projects during his official visit to China in 2012. These projects include: building schools, hospitals, housing projects, training for civil service employees, and student scholarships. In terms of education, over 200 students are studying in China's finest universities. However, there is a need to foster more people-to-people ties between China and South Sudan as there is a gap because of the lack of information. In response, China established a radio station in Juba to disseminate information about bilateral culture, music, relations, and other areas of mutual interest. China-Central TV is also an important outlet on the African continent to foster and strengthen not only Sino-South Sudanese relations but also Sino-African relations.[51]

Although bilateral cultural cooperation occurred in the fields of the arts, culture, education, media, public health, and public administration, China and South Sudan have not signed any cultural agreements since South Sudan became independent in July 2011. Nevertheless, in terms of financial assistance and aid for social and development projects and programs, China and South Sudan concluded the following deals which include agreements and memorandums of understanding: a $700 million Juba University Education and Award Fund established by the China National Petroleum Corporation (2008); the Juba University Computer Center funded by the China National Petroleum Corporation (2008); Donation of Musical Instruments (2009); an agreement between China and South Sudan to donate radio stations to South Sudan (2011); Memorandum of Understanding to send Medical Teams to South Sudan to provide medical assistance (January 2012); Agreement on Water and Health Cooperation (January 2012); Memorandum of Understanding on Agricultural Cooperation and Rice Planting (2012); $1.05 million in Emergency Food Relief to South Sudan (2013); $50K for flood relief in South Sudan (2013); Construction of a Disarmament Training Center (2013); a Memorandum of Understanding to provide anti-malarial drugs (2013); a Memorandum of Understanding to provide training to medical personnel to run Rumbek hospital (2013); Diplomacy Workshop for twenty-five South Sudanese diplomats (2013); material aid worth $24 million to conflict-torn South Sudan (2014); humanitarian aid materials worth $3 million to conflict-torn Sudan (2014); and a $1.6 million grant to build shelters for displaced South Sudanese (2014).[52]

ENERGY/PETROLEUM RELATIONS

Crude petroleum trading forms the basis for China and South Sudan's trade relationship even though South Sudan is modest supplier of crude oil to China. In this respect, China imported approximately 1 percent of its crude petroleum from South Sudan in 2012 and 2014 inclusive. Sudan/South Sudan previously accounted for 5 percent of all Chinese oil imports in 2011; but this figure dropped to less than 1 percent in 2012.[53] In terms of total trade value, crude petroleum imports was almost 100 percent for the same years. Table 11.2 shows Chinese crude oil imports from South Sudan in thousands of barrels per day, oil imports share, world ranking, trade value, total commodity trade value, and percentage in 2012, 2013, and 2014. See Table 11.2.

China does not import petroleum gas products including liquefied natural gas (LNG) from South Sudan. On the other hand, China has oil acquisitions in the country. In this respect, CNPC finalized and/or acquired the following: the development rights of Block 6 (September 1995); a 40 percent stake in the Greater Nile Petroleum Operation Company consortium to explore and develop the Heglig & Unity fields (March 1997); the tender for Block 1/2/4 and jointly established GNPOC together with Petronas, SPC, and Sudapet (June

Table 11.2 Chinese Crude Petroleum Imports from South Sudan

Year	KBPD	Oil Imports Share (%)	World Ranking	Crude Oil Trade Value ($)	Total Commodity Trade Value ($)	Percentage (%)
2012	14	<1	30	499,465,121	499,465,321	100.000
2013	70	1	14	2,468,313,737	2,468,344,369	99.999
2014	129	2	13	4,329,172,366	4,329,242,102	99.998

Source: United Nations Commodity Trade Statistics Database

1997); the tender for Block 3/7 owning a 41 percent stake (November 2000); and agreed to produce 300,000 b/d at the Adar/Yale oil fields (June 2004).[54]

Sino-South Sudanese energy relations predates South Sudan's 2011 independence. China invested over $8 billion in Sudan's oil sector between 1995 and 2011, making it the third largest producer of crude oil in Sub-Saharan Africa. After the partition of Sudan, South Sudan acquired 80 percent of the oil fields and sovereignty over the oil facilities. The new republic was created with an established strategic relationship with China centered on energy. Chinese corporations worked with the new authorities in Juba but not without difficulties such as kidnappings of Chinese oil workers in 2008 and 2012 and a fourteen-month suspension of oil imports over a transit-fee dispute between Sudan and South Sudan from 2011 to 2012. Consequently, South Sudan shutdown all its oil production in January 2012 and restarted it in April 2013.[55]

Bilateral energy cooperation includes CNPC training programs to help train South Sudanese techniques relevant to the petroleum industry and training assistance.[56] It appeared to be promising in 2013 until South Sudan entered a civil war.[57] CNPC's investments were profitable and China was importing 1.9 million tons of oil (with 1.4 million tons from South Sudan); however, the civil war forced China to evacuate some Chinese oil workers and cease production in some oil fields. Oil production dropped by a third to about 160,000 barrels per day by January 2014 and CNPC became the most affected oil corporation.[58] To remedy the decrease in oil production during 2014, CNPC and South Sudan signed an agreement in December 2014 to boost oil production at least three oil blocks.[59]

South Sudan explored the possibility of constructing an oil pipeline from its oil fields through Ethiopia to Kenya's Lamu Port. If built, the cost is estimated to be $4 billion and will be constructed by the Toyota corporation. The pipeline will boost Ethiopia's economic development and bring valuable returns for Kenya by pulling South Sudan away from Sudan toward other countries in Africa. "The overall port structure and pipeline costs are estimated at $16 billion." To memorialize the possibility of a joint venture between South Sudan, Ethiopia, and Kenya, a memorandum of understanding was signed in 2013. China will naturally object to Japan's entry into South Sudan's oil sector; however, several oil corporations have submitted bids for another alternative oil pipeline that runs from South Sudan, through Ethiopia to Djibouti Port, with an estimated cost of $4 billion. As CNPC already has stakes in South Sudan's oil sector, it is a major contender and is expected to win the bid.[60]

Oil is the primary source of Sudan's instability, civil wars, the South's separation, and the current civil war in South Sudan. Sudan lost 80 percent of its oil fields but South Sudan's gains have brought no peace, development, or stability. Rather, it has brought civil wars, ethnic cleansing, and genocide. Development has ceased and oil revenues have plummeted. Consequently, state revenues are devoted to the war effort. The civil war also has disrupted China's efforts to build two refineries in South Sudan, explore for oil and natural gas, and invest in solar energy and wind energy. Additionally, China's increasing reliance from Africa and Middle East has forced it to embrace rogue regimes such as Sudan and Iran as well as intervene in African conflicts such as those in Sudan and South Sudan.[61]

SUMMARY

Sino-South Sudanese relations were established on July 9, 2011 after South Sudan succeeded from Sudan. Prior to South Sudan's independence, China has been involved in South Sudan's economic and social development and pledged billions to develop South Sudan's infrastructure. A strategic partnership also formed based on energy cooperation with CNPC and the Export-Import Bank of China being at the center.

South Sudan's economic and social development initially appeared promising but fell into despair after a war emerged between Sudan and South Sudan after South Sudan became an independent country. While this conflict ended in September 2012, a civil war broke out in mid-December 2013 which placed South Sudan's future in jeopardy. All infrastructure projects have been placed on hold and South Sudan has suffered. Despite all diplomatic efforts, China and the international community have yet to resolve the conflict which has resulted in the murder, genocide, and ethnic cleansing of thousands of South Sudanese.

NOTES

1. David H. Shinn and Joshua Eisenman, *China and Africa: A Century of Engagement* (Philadelphia, PA: University of Pennsylvania Press), 2012, 379.
2. Ministry of Foreign Affairs of People's Republic of China, "China–South Sudan: Activities," (n.d.), accessed August 9, 2016, http://www.fmprc.gov.cn/mfa_eng/wjb_663304/zzjg_663340/xybfs_663590/gjlb_663594/sousu_663756/ssaa_663760/.

3. Ministry of Foreign Affairs of People's Republic of China, "China–South Sudan: Activities," (n.d.), accessed February 8, 2015, Ibid.

4. International Crisis Group, *China's New Courtship in South Sudan*, Crisis Group Africa Report No. 186, April 2012, 3, accessed February 8, 2015, http://www.crisisgroup.org/~/media/Files/africa/horn-of-africa/sudan/186-chinas-new-courtship-in-south-sudan.pdf.

5. Ibid.

6. Muhamad S. Olimat, *China and North Africa Since World War II* (Lanham, MD: Lexington Books), 2014, 141.

7. Embassy of the People's Republic of China in South Sudan, "Sino–South Sudan Political Exchanges," November 23, 2012, accessed February 5, 2015, http://ss.chineseembassy.org/eng/sbgx/zjjw/.

8. Ministry of Foreign Affairs of People's Republic of China, "List of Agreements on Mutual Visa Exemption Between the People's Republic of China and Foreign Countries" November 28, 2004, accessed February 13, 2015, http://cs.mfa.gov.cn/wgrlh/bgzl/P020140328398504621618.pdf.

9. Daniel Large and Luke Patey, "Sudan Looks East," in Daniel Large and Luke Patey, eds., *Sudan Looks East: China, India and The Politics of Asian Alternatives* (Rochester, NY: James Currey Ltd.), 2011, 27.

10. Olimat, Ibid., 141-142.

11. Ibid., 142.

12. Ibid.

13. Ibid., 142–143.

14. Ibid.

15. Ibid, 142, 143.

16. Ibid.

17. Ibid., 142, 143, 144.

18. Ibid., 144.

19. Ibid., 144, 145.

20. Ibid., 145, 146.

21. Embassy of the People's Republic of China in South Sudan, "Sino–South Sudan Economic & Trade Cooperation," November 23, 2012, accessed February 5, 2015, http://ss.chineseembassy.org/eng/sbgx/jmwl/.

22. United Nations, United Nations Commodity Trade Statistics Database, accessed August 7, 2016, http://comtrade.un.org/db/default.aspx.

23. Olimat, ibid., 147.

24. Ibid., 147, 148.

25. United Nations, United Nations Commodity Trade Statistics Database, accessed July 22, 2016, ibid.

26. U.S. Energy Information Administration, U.S. Department of Energy, "Country Analysis Briefs: Sudan and South Sudan," September 3, 2014, 1–2, accessed February 14, 2015.

27. International Trade Centre, Directory of Trade Promotion Organizations and Other Trade Support Institutions, accessed January 25, 2015, http://www.intracen.org/itc/trade-support/tsi-directory.

28. Austin M. Strange, et al., "Tracking Underreported Financial Flows: China's Development Finance and the Aid–Conflict Nexus Revisited," *Journal of Conflict Resolution*, Volume 61, Issue 5 (2017): 935–963.

29. Embassy of the People's Republic of China in South Sudan website, "Sino-South Sudan Economic and Trade Cooperation," ibid.

30. Ministry of Foreign Affairs of People's Republic of China, "Hu Jintao Holds Talks with South Sudanese President Silva Kari Mayardit" April 24, 2012, accessed August 13, 2016, http://www.fmprc.gov.cn/mfa_eng/wjb_663304/zzjg_663340/xybfs_663590/gjlb_663594/sousu_663756/ssaa_663760/t926468.shtml.

31. Embassy of the People's Republic of China in South Sudan website, "Sino-South Sudan Economic & Trade Cooperation," ibid.

32. Embassy of the People's Republic of China in South Sudan website, "Sino-South Sudan Economic & Trade Cooperation," ibid.; Hang Zhou, "Testing the Limits: China's Expanding Role in the South Sudanese Civil War," *China Brief* (Jamestown Foundation), Volume XIV, Issue 19, October 10, 2014, 4; Strange, et al., ibid., and The Heritage Foundation and American Enterprise Institute, *China Global Investment Tracker Database*, accessed August 13, 2016, http://www.heritage.org/research/projects/china-global-investment-tracker-interactive-map.

33. International Crisis Group, ibid., 11, 26; and Olimat, ibid., 147.

34. Strange, et al., ibid.

35. Olimat, ibid., 147.

36. Zhou, ibid.; and Strange, et al., ibid.

37. Olimat, ibid., 151.

38. International Crisis Group, Strange, et al., ibid., 14.

39. Ibid.

40. Olimat, ibid., 152; Zhou, ibid.; International Crisis Group, ibid., 14; and Stockholm International Peace Research Institute, SIPRI Arms Transfers Base, http://www.sipri.org/databases/transfers

41. Ibid.

42. International Crisis Group, ibid., 15.

43. Zhou, ibid., 5; Olimat, ibid., 153; and United Nations Peacekeeping Website, *UN's Missions Detailed by Country*, December 31, 2014, accessed January 6, 2015.

44. Ibid.

45. Ibid.

46. Zhou, ibid., 6; and Olimat, ibid., 152.

47. Embassy of the People's Republic of China in South Sudan, "Sino-South Sudan Economic and Trade Cooperation," ibid.; and Strange, et al., ibid.

48. Olimat, ibid.

49. Ibid., 150–151.

50. Embassy of the People's Republic of China in South Sudan, "Sino-South Sudan Cultural and Educational Exchanges," November 23, 2012, accessed February 7, 2015, http://ss.chineseembassy.org/eng/sbgx/whjw/; and Olimat, ibid., 151.

51. Olimat, ibid.

52. Hang Zhou, "China and South Sudan: Economic Engagement continues amid Conflict," *African Arguments*, September 12, 2014, accessed August 13, 2016, http://

africanarguments.org/2014/09/12/china-and-south-sudan-economic-engagement-continues-amid-conflict-by-zhou-hang/; Strange, et al., ibid., and International Crisis Group, ibid., 7.

53. Olimat, ibid., 149.

54. Julie Jiang and Chen Dang, *Update on Overseas Investments by Chinese National Companies: Achievements and Challenges Since 2011* (Paris, France: Organization for Economic Cooperation and Development/International Energy Agency), June 2014, 35–39.

55. U.S. Energy Information Administration, U.S. Department of Energy, "Country Analysis Briefs: Sudan and South Sudan," ibid., 10; and Olimat, ibid., 148.

56. Strange, et al., ibid.

57. Olimat, ibid., 148.

58. U.S. Energy Information Administration, U.S. Department of Energy, "Country Analysis Briefs: Sudan and South Sudan," ibid., 7; and Olimat, *China and North Africa Since World War II*, 149.

59. Nicholas Bariyo, "South Sudan Signs Agreement With China's CNPC to Boost Oil Production," *The Wall Street Journal*, December 22, 2014, accessed February 7, 2015, http://www.wsj.com/articles/south-sudan-signs-agreement-with-chinas-cnpc-to-boost-oil-production-1419242796.

60. Olimat, ibid., 149.

61. Ibid., 149, 150.

Chapter 12

China and Sudan
Political/Diplomatic Relations

Sino-Sudanese diplomatic relations were established February 4, 1959.[1] To establish and further diplomatic ties, China and Sudan issued the following: Joint Communiqué on the Establishment of Diplomatic Relations (1958);[2] Agreement on Mutual Visa Exemption including diplomatic and service/special official passports (October 26, 1995);[3] and Joint Statement Between the People's Republic of China and the Republic of the Sudan on the Establishment of Strategic Partnership (September 1, 2015).[4]

In February 1983, both China and Sudan also concluded the *Protocol between the CCP and the Sudanese Socialist Union* to develop their relations based on independence, total equality, mutual respect, and non-interference in each other's internal affairs.[5]

Prior to its independence from the United Kingdom and Egypt on January 1, 1956, Sudan was ruled either by the Ottoman or British Empire. The Ottoman Empire ruled Sudan from 1821 to 1899 and United Kingdom ruled Sudan (Anglo-Egyptian Sudan) from 1899 to 1956. Sudan was a condominium of the United Kingdom and Egypt, but in practice the structure of the condominium ensured full British rule over Sudan. British rule over Sudan was established in 1899 after the British fought a series of military campaigns against the Mahdist forces between 1896 and 1898. After achieving independence in 1956, Sudan sought to international recognition as a sovereign state.

Sudan became the fourth African country (after Egypt, Yemen, and Syria) to establish official relations with China; however, no significant ties emerged until the mid-1990s when China started pursuing external energy resources.[6] Becoming a net importer of crude oil in 1993, China was in critical need of energy resources to sustain its economy, especially hydrocarbon-based products. Sudan's oil sector was fledging and its economy was in crisis as its war with southern Sudan loomed (1983–2005) and needed a non-Western energy partner to develop it, especially since the United States and Western countries withdrew their political and economic support and the exodus of major Western oil companies like Chevron from Sudan in 1992 in the wake of National Party Congress' (then the National Islamic Front) assumption of power in 1989, political ideology, and ties to terrorism. China was an ideal non-Western energy partner especially since in principle it practiced a non-interference policy based on the five principles of peaceful coexistence and had the financial and technical resources to develop Sudan's oil industry.

China not only developed Sudan's oil sector but revolutionized its economy, which was almost entirely based on oil revenues. China also became Sudan's largest foreign investor and contributed greatly to its infrastructure development. In this respect, China's investment in Sudan's oil industry in the 1990s completely changed the nature of the Sino-Sudanese relationship, converting Sudan's fledging oil industry into the driving force behind its economic growth and turning Sudan into a net exporter.[7] China also played a leading role in the reorientation of Sudan's economic relations toward Asia.[8] When South Sudan broke away from Sudan and became independent in 2011, Sudan lost the majority of its oil production, revenues, and investment. Specifically, Sudan lost 80 percent of its oil production, 55 percent of its revenues, and 90 percent of its investment to South Sudan because South Sudan now had legal jurisdiction.[9] The volume of oil exported from Sudan to China decreased significantly from 261,000 barrels per day in 2011 to 37,000 barrels per day in 2012 and China's oil imports dropped from 5 percent to 1 percent in the same year.[10] Disputes between Sudan and South Sudan between January 2012 and April 2013 over oil transportation fees via Sudanese pipelines and the South Sudanese Civil War (December 2013–present) also contributed to the decrease in oil exports, if not the cessation of oil exports to China from both Sudan and South Sudan.[11] Despite these setbacks, an energy partnership was formed between China and South Sudan given the new political and economic realities.

Sudan lost territory in addition to a loss of oil revenues and production. Sudan was the largest country in Africa and the Arab world until 2011. With the succession of South Sudan, Sudan became the third largest country in Africa after Algeria and the Democratic Republic of the Congo and the third largest country in the Arab world after Algeria and Saudi Arabia.

China and Sudan had their earliest recorded contacts when the Han Dynasty was in power from 206 BC to 24 CE, despite the vast geographic distances that separate their two countries. Most of their early contacts were centered on trade, especially on Sudanese goods and commodities like gold, ivory, rhinoceros' horns, and tortoise shells.[12]

China and Sudan met at the Bandung Conference in Indonesia in 1955; however, Sino-Sudanese relations were conducted in the shadow of

Sino-Egyptian relations, based on similarities between Egypt and Sudan in terms of the "Nile-Unity Framework" and its impact on their foreign and domestic politics. What Egypt and Sudan had in common was that the focus of their foreign policies was directed toward the Middle East, and to a lesser extent, in Africa, despite both countries being geographically located in Africa.[13]

Egypt and Sudan also had a shared history in their resistance to colonialism and foreign rule, of which they received high marks from China. Egypt resisted foreign rule and influenced under monarchical rule while Sudan resisted British colonialism, of which it had a long history of domination by the United Kingdom. China and Sudan also had a symbolic link, which has lasted for successive generations given their shared history and events involving British General Charles "Chinese" Gordon. It is important to note that the nature of resistance to colonialism, especially European colonialism, became a scale on how China judged countries, especially during the first two decades of China's history under communism (1949–1969).[14]

Although China developed a scale to judge countries according to their nature of their resistance to colonialism, China was not enthusiastic about Gamal Abdel Nasser, or the Free Officers 1952 military coup and the subsequent coup in Sudan in 1958, both of which were major setbacks to the process of the national independence of Egypt, and by default, Sudan, since the latter followed in Egypt's footsteps. In this respect, both Egypt and Sudan had relatively stable governments until their respective coups in 1952 and 1958. Afterwards, both countries were under mostly military dictatorships, with some civilian governance in between, which was seen by some as burdensome and counterproductive to state development. Despite Egypt and Sudan's military dictatorial rule throughout most of its post-colonial history, China praised Egypt's abrogation of the Anglo-Egyptian Treaty of 1936 and Sudan's abrogation of the Anglo-Sudan Agreement of 1898.[15]

The military governance model of Sudan, inspired by the Free Officers Movement in Egypt, dominated the political scene in most Middle Eastern and African countries. In the case of Sudan, General Ibrahim Abboud overthrew the short-lived democratic government of Ismail al-Azahari (1955–1958) and remained in office until he was forced out in 1964. Between 1964 and 1969, an unstable civil government administered Sudan. In 1969, General Gaafar Numeiri launched a successful military coup in Sudan, only to be removed by a bloodless military coup in 1985 by Lieutenant General Abdul Rahman Suwar al-Dahab, followed by an elected civilian government led by Sadiq al-Mahdi, which was overthrown by another military coup in 1989 led by General Omar- al-Bashir, the current president of Sudan. The government of Sadiq al-Mahdi was deposed because Sadiq al-Mahdi was unable to control the country or carry out political or economic reforms.

General Omar al-Bashir's coup was carried out in coordination with the Islamists (the National Salvation Front), which made Sudan the target of consistent Western criticism and destabilization efforts. China also became the target of Western criticism because of the Tiananmen Square massacre that occurred in the same year. This caused a cooling in U.S-Sino relations during the 1990s. This condition also brought China, Africa, and Third World countries closer together including Sudan because Sudan needed a new non-Western partner in the wake of Western criticism and destabilization efforts. Consequently, Sudan reproached China and a strategic partnership was established—one that has grown since 1989.[16]

It is important to note that Sino-Sudanese relations improved significantly under President Gaafar Nimeiri's rule (1969–1985), especially since Sudan enjoyed good relations with the United States in the fluctuating context of the Cold War. Gaafar Nimieri was determined to improve bilateral relations with China. Nimieri visited China in March 1970 and met with Chairman Mao and other high-ranking officials to secure Chinese expertise in oil exploration, economic development, and military assistance. However, China was not able to provide the technical expertise or substantial economic aid that Sudan needed.[17]

Prior Gaafar Nimeiri's rule as president, Sino-Sudanese relations remained at a low level until the early 1970s. However, China supported the northern Sudan government during the first North-South Civil War between 1955 and 1972. China also held Sudan's resistance to Soviet intervention in the Middle East in very high regard, especially its resistance to the Soviet-backed Sudanese Communist Party's military coup on July 19, 1971, against Nimieri. China even recommended that Sudan seek U.S. aid to prevent it from falling to Soviet-style communism. The United States provided aid to Sudan helping it reduce its reliance on the Soviet Union. China also endorsed the U.S.-Sudanese rapprochement and worked closely with Sudan to reduce the Soviet threat and infiltration.[18]

Sino-Sudanese political relations are multi-tiered. In addition to elite political ties at the executive level, China and Sudan established party-to-party relations especially after 1989. In this respect, political party cooperation occurred between Sudan's ruling Islamic party, the National Congress Party (NCP) and the Communist Party of China (CPC). This was significant given the power and role of both ruling parties. China's state-owned companies also conducted bilateral relations because corporate-state interaction was particularly important in China's energy diplomacy, especially when China was dependent on foreign hydrocarbons to sustain its economy.[19]

Since 1989, several developments occurred in Sudan. These include the Sino-Sudanese strategic partnership, the escalation of a civil war in southern Sudan, the discovery of oil, the Darfur genocide, the creation of the Republic of South Sudan (RSS) in 2011, and the current political turbulence and near economic collapse of both countries, Sudan and South Sudan.[20] During this time, China faithfully stood by Sudan, denouncing the imposition of economic sanctions especially at the United Nations, supporting the peace conferences and dialogue related to the South and Darfur, and even sending peacekeeping forces to support the United Nations Mission in Sudan and South Sudan.[21] Conversely, Sudan supported China during the Tiananmen Square crackdown in the face of Western criticism. Both countries essentially supported each other on conversational issues that came before international forums or attracted foreign press attention.[22]

Since 2000, China and Sudan have interacted through official, high-level visits and exchanges no less than seventy-nine times. Some of the most important exchanges include: President Jiang Zemin and President Omar al-Bashir (November 2000) and President Hu Jintao and President Omar al-Bashir (April 2005, November 2006, June 2011, and September 2015).[23] Both countries have also established diplomatic representation through embassies in their respective capitals in Beijing and Khartoum.

In summary, China and Sudan have enjoyed a traditional friendship since the Bandung Conference and the establishment of diplomatic ties.[24] Sino-Sudanese political relations are considered close and firmly bilateral today.[25] Their ties extend to forms of cooperative interaction in regional organizations like FOCAC or the China-Arab Cooperation Forum and international organizations like the UN or the G77.[26]

ECONOMIC/TRADE RELATIONS

Sino-Sudanese economic relations have been generally good since South Sudan's independence in 2011, but prior to independence, economic ties were robust. China was Sudan's largest trading partner through 2011; however, the United Arab Emirates replaced China as Sudan's top trading partner in 2012 because of the partition of Sudan into two parts: the north and the south. South Sudan's independence stripped away 75 percent of Sudan's oil production, devastating Sudan's economy after 2011. It also resulted in the loss of 55 percent of Sudan's revenues and about two-thirds of its foreign exchange earnings, according to the International Monetary Fund (IMF). Sudan's crude oil export revenues fell from almost $11 billion in 2010 to just under $1.8 billion in 2012. Despite the loss of government revenues, crude oil still plays a part in Sudan's economy but to a lesser extent. Oil revenues accounted for 27 percent of Sudan's government revenues and grants in 2012, down from nearly 60 percent from the year before, according to the IMF.[27]

While China was Sudan's major trading partner before 2012, Sudan has never been a China's major trading partner except for energy commodities. In this respect, China was Sudan's major export partner before 2012. In 2012, China was not even one of Sudan's top ten trading partners and Sudan became China's seventy-first largest trading partner in the same year.[28] Nevertheless, crude oil development and trading transformed Sudan's economy. China's investment into Sudan's oil industry transformed Sudan's economy as well as their overall bilateral relationship, turning Sudan into a net oil exporter. China was also Sudan's main buyer of Sudanese crude oil, accounting approximately for 80 percent of Sudan's exports.[29] However, most of Sudan's oil exports ended after 2011 and were replaced by China's new energy partnership with South Sudan, which opened prospects for cooperation in agriculture, mining, and minerals.[30]

Bilateral trade increased markedly in the latter part of 1999 after oil exports began, and it has grown substantially since then.[31] Sudan's booming oil-based economy also resulted in increased demand for Chinese manufactured goods in Sudan.[32] The volume of bilateral trade was robust in the twenty-first century but dropped between 2011 and 2012 in terms of trade value. Bilateral trade was: $8.2 billion (2008), $6.3 billion (2009), $8.6 billion (2010), $11.5 billion (2011), $3.7 billion (2012), $4.4 billion (2013), and $3.4 billion (2014), and $5.6 billion (2015).[33] Since 2000, bilateral trade increased almost sixfold. In 2012, foreign direct investment into Sudan from China was -$2 million and foreign direct investment stock was $1.23 billion.[34] In the prior year (2011), foreign direct investment was $912 million and foreign direct investment stock was $1.52 billion.[35] It is imperative to note that Chinese foreign direct investment flows to Sudan in the 1990s was largely driven by a desire to secure a source of energy and raw materials for the unprecedented growth in China's economy.[36] Oil transformed Sudan's economy. China was a less significant economic partner to Sudan prior to China's entry into Sudan's oil sector.[37] Afterwards, China transformed Sudan's economy making it a net oil exporter.

Table 12.1 shows the top five commodities traded between China and Sudan in 2015. Energy commodities, which include crude petroleum, appear to be most traded commodity. In terms of trade value, almost 94.3 percent is attributed to energy commodities, which includes crude petroleum. See Table 12.1.

China's energy commodities accounted for the following in terms of trade value in previous years: 99.4 percent (2008), 99.1 percent (2009), 98.4 percent (2010), 98.7 percent (2011), 96.3 percent (2012), 90.5 percent (2013), and 88.7 percent (2014).[38]

Bilateral trade is promoted through several organizations such as the Forum on China-Africa Cooperation, the China-Arab Trade Forum, the

Table 12.1 Top Five Commodities Traded between China and Sudan

Commodity	Importer	Trade Value ($)	Percentage (%)
Mineral fuels, mineral oils and products of their distillation; bituminous substances; mineral waxes	China	2,881,242,551	94.29
Oil seeds and oleaginous fruits; miscellaneous grains, seeds and fruit; industrial or medicinal plants; straw and fodder	China	146,944,255	4.81
Cotton	China	12,301,199	0.40
Ores, slag and ash	China	7,582,832	0.25
Plastics and articles thereof	China	3,978,770	0.13
Electrical machinery and equipment and parts thereof; sound recorders and reproducers, television image and sound recorders and reproducers, and parts and accessories of such articles	Sudan	299,814,384	12
Nuclear reactors, boilers, machinery and mechanical appliances; parts thereof	Sudan	277,671,478	11
Vehicles other than railway or tramway rolling-stock, and parts and accessories thereof	Sudan	213,301,830	8
Footwear, gaiters and the like; parts of such articles	Sudan	196,072,054	8
Articles of iron or steel	Sudan	176,256,180	7

Source: United Nations Commodity Trade Statistics Database.

China-Arab States Cooperation Forum, the China-Africa Development Fund, the China-Arab States Financial Corporation, the Arab Bank for Economic Development in Africa, the Sudanese Ministry of Foreign Trade, the Sudan Trade Point, the Sudanese Businessmen and Employers Foundation, the Sudanese Chambers of Industries Association, the Union of Sudanese Chambers of Commerce, the PRC Ministry of Commerce, the PRC Ministry of Foreign Affairs, and the All-China Federation of Industry and Commerce.[39]

China and Sudan has inked some important agreements, protocols, exchanges of notes, and memorandums of understanding to facilitate trade between their countries. The most notable agreements include: Trade Agreement (May 1962); Exchange of Notes on the Trade Agreement (April 1964); Trade Protocols for 1967, 1968, 1969, 1970, 1971, 1972, 1973, 1974, 1975, 1976, 1977, 1978–1979, 1979–1980, 1980–1981, 1981–1982, 1982–1983, and 1983–1984; Agreement on a Chinese Loan of $35 million (August 1970); Protocol on China's Financing and Implementing the Medani-Gedarif Road Project under the Economic Cooperation Agreement (June 1971); Agreement on Economic and Technical Cooperation (1970, December 1971 and

June 1977); Protocol on Economic and Technical Cooperation (October 1975); Loan Agreement (December 1979, December 1981, December 1984 and December 1987); General Agreement on Construction Cooperation between the United Arab Emirates, Sudan Investment Company Ltd., and the China Construction Engineering Company (April 1980); Trade Protocol (1984, 1986, 1988, and 1989); Protocol on the Chinese Grant to supply 2,000 tons of Maize (December 1984); Agreement on the Establishment of Mixed Committee for Economic and Trade Cooperation (January 1986); Protocol on the Implementation of Economic and Technical Cooperation (January 1986); Protocol on the building of a Modernized Granary and to Renovate the Equipment of the Al Hasaheisa Textile Mill (October 1986); Agreement on Economic and Technical Cooperation (1990); Trade Protocol to promote a trade volume of $100 million (April 1990); Agreement on Economic, Trade, and Technical Cooperation (1992); Grant for the Construction of a Bridge on the White Nile (1996); Agreement to Establish an Oil Information Center (1997); Agreement to obtain a Commercial Loan equal to $5 million to purchase equipment for the White Nile State through SOGEC Company (1998); Agreement to build a Thermal Electricity Station at Rahad in Southern Kordofan (1998); Agreement for a Commercial Loan of $106 million to purchase cables for the National Electricity Corporation through CAMC (1998); Agreement with the Sudanese Ministry of Finance and National Economy (MFNE) to import electricity generators for a number of cities (2000); Agreement to rehabilitate and improve the capacity of Sudan Airways through loans equal to $180 million (2001); Commercial Loan Agreement of $149.5 million for the establishment of the Gari Power Station (2001); Grant of $1.2 million for the manufacture of solar cells (2001); Interest-Free Loan of $3.7 million (2001); Agreement to write-off a debt equivalent to $66.4 million (2001); Memorandum of Understanding between the China Construction and Machinery Company (CCM) and the Sudanese Ministry of Water Resources for future investment (2006); Agreement between Ball and the Sudanese Ministry of Energy and Minerals to mine iron ore in the Red Sea Province (2007); China and Sudan sign a Zero-Tariff Agreement for forty-four commodities exported to China (2007); Air Transport Agreement between China and Sudan (2009); Agreement of Technical Cooperation between China and Sudan for $15.4 million (2011); and Memorandum of Understanding between the Ministry of Land Resources of the People's Republic of China and the Ministry of Minerals of the Republic of the Sudan on Cooperation in the Mining Industry (2012).[40]

In addition to inking agreements, protocols, and exchanges of notes and establishing a bilateral mixed committee for economic and trade cooperation in January 1986, China has been actively involved in Sudan's economic development. To this extent, China has played a leading role in the reorientation of

Sudan's economic relations toward Asia, otherwise known as the "Look East" policy, a term which is used as a general category encompassing the main players, China, India, Malaysia, Japan, and South Korea.[41] United States and Western companies like Chevron were active in Sudan beginning in the 1980s but left in 1992 for security reasons.[42] Other companies like Occidental Petroleum Corporation were in Sudan but were barred by the United States Congress from dealing with Sudan for supporting international terrorism.[43] This created an opportunity to fulfill an economic vacuum left vacant by the west.

Chinese companies first operated in 1996 (when the North and South were united) and were initially involved in Sudan's oil sector such as CNPC paying $441 million to buy a 40 percent majority share of the Greater Nile Petroleum Operating Company (GNPOC), a recently created consortium;[44] however, Chinese corporate concentration changed as its business engagement diversified into a broader spectrum of activities.[45] It is important to note that CNPC played a central role in the development of Sudan's oil sector.[46]

As a result of China's development of Sudan's oil security sector, direct investment by Chinese government-owned companies and private Chinese entrepreneurs has grown substantially in diverse activities such as mining, building, and construction of roads and bridges and electricity and water sectors.[47] China and Sudan also concluded deals to develop Sudan's infrastructure in the sectors of agriculture, actions related to debt, emergency response, education, government and civil society, construction, social infrastructure, forestry, fishing, storage, transportation, health, energy generation and supply, sanitation, trade, tourism, and communications.[48]

China and Sudan have also cooperated in aviation. Both signed a civil aviation agreement in 2009 and Hainan Airlines now operates direct flights between Beijing and Khartoum.[49]

China has been involved in Sudan's infrastructure development since diplomatic relations were established in February 1959. Compared to China's infrastructure development and aid in the twenty-first century, Chinese development assistance was small and concentrated into roads, bridges, and public buildings construction;[50] however, economic ties deepened when China helped developed Sudan's oil sector.[51] Between 1970 and 1979, Sudan received three interests from China, which were used for the following projects: Medani-Gadarif Road, Friendship Hall in Khartoum, Fisheries in Wadi-Halfa, Rice Development in Awei (Southern Sudan), and Textile and Weaving Factory in Hassa-Heissa.[52] Between 1981 and 1987, China provided Sudan three interest-free loans for the following: Singa Town Bridge, Ready Made Cloth Factory, Friendship Hospital, a Vocational Training Center, and Rice Cultivation Development.[53] Between 1990 and 1992, economic and technical cooperation surged and a number of interest-free loans were provided to Sudan to fund the following projects: University Laboratory

Equipment, Hospital Equipment, Renovation of Friendship Hall, Irrigation Equipment, and Means of Production to support income generation for Needy Families.[54]

Between 1992 and 2001, several agreements were executed between China and Sudan and relate to the latter's economic development. Between 2002 and 2006, China supplied Sudan with approximately $1.1 billion in loans and grants, which represented 37 percent of all loans and grants contracted by Sudan from various sources. These loans and grants were used to finance investment in the following projects: 2002: Khartoum state electricity ($12 million), equipment, and spare parts; 2003: Water Project equipment valued at $10 million from the Boshan Company; 2004: Soft Loan ($3.6 million) and Water Equipment ($11.2 million); 2005: Electric Generators (CNEEN Co.); Rehabilitation of the Cotton Ginning Factories (Boshan), Khartoum North Thermal Electricity Generation (CAMC Co.), Gedarif Water Project, (Elfashir Water Project (CAMC Co.), Drilling of 150 Wells (Tiangin Co.), Irrigation Equipment (Boshan Co.), Engineering Equipment (CAMCO Co.), Drilling of 50 Wells in North Kordofan State (Tiangin), Port Sudan Water Project (CMIC Co.), and Rabbak Grain Silo; 2006: North Kordofan Solar Energy (US$ 4.6 million), Importation of water pipes (US$ 17.2), grant for the National Capital Power Project (US$19.5 million), Mek-Nimer Bridge (US$14.4 million), and Water Projects in towns in different states (US$ 119 million).[55]

Many infrastructure development deals were finalized between China and Sudan between 1997 and 2013 according to China AidData. Most of the projects associated with these infrastructure deals have been completed and supplement the list previously mentioned for the years 2002–2006. These deals include the following: China National Construction & Agricultural Machinery Import & Export Corporation (CAMCO) agreed to build the Santos Agricultural Pump Station (1997); China Machinery Engineering Corporation agreed to give the Sudan Railway Corporation $18 million to buy four light and four heavy train cars (2000); China gave Sudan $30,000 in emergency response aid (2000); China agreed to give Sudan $2.5 million in aid to spend on any project (2000); China agreed to give Sudan $3 million in aid (2001); China agreed to grant Sudan $1.2 million (2001); China agreed to fund the construction of the Friendship Hall for $3.6 million (2002); China agreed to rehabilitate the Radiotherapy Hospital for $2.5 million (2002); China agreed to finance $3.6 million in economic cooperation projects (2002); Harbin Electricity Company agreed to build Phase One of the Garri (Qarre) Combined Cycle Power Plant for $149 million funded by the China Central Bank (2002); the Export-Import Bank of China agreed to finance the upgrade of Khartoum's electrical power system for $150 million (2002); an unknown Chinese company agreed to construct a 261-kilometer electricity power line at a cost of $26 million (2003); the Export-Import Bank of China agreed to loan $519 million to purchase the hydro-mechanical components of the 1,250-kilowatt Merowe hydroelectric dam (2003); the People's Bank of China financed the purchase of water pumps and water equipment for $10 million (2003); the Export-Import Bank of China financed the construction of power transmission and transformation lines for the Merowe hydroelectric dam project for $337.4 million (2003); Harbin Electricity Company agreed to build Phase Two of the Garri (Qarre) Combined Cycle Power Plant for $94 million, which is funded by the Export-Import Bank of China (2004); CAMC Engineering Company agreed to complete the Dali Mazmoom Water Supply Project (2004); China agreed to give Sudan $604,098 in emergency response aid (2004); China agreed to give Sudan $7.2 million in aid (2004); Shandong Electric Power Capital Construction Corporation agreed to build a coal-fired power plant in Port Sudan and a gas-fired in Rabak for $512 million, which is financed by the Export-Import Bank of China (2004); China CAMC Engineering, Co. Ltd. agreed to construct a water supply system for Al-Fashir in North Darfur, Sudan for $32.5 million, which is financed by the Export-Import Bank of China (2005); China CAMC Engineering, Co. Ltd. agreed to construct a water supply system for Gedarif, Sudan for $67.1 million, which is financed by the Export-Import Bank of China (2005); China agreed to provide $1.2 million to rehabilitate Darfur (2005); the Export-Import Bank of China agreed to loan Sudan Telecom $200 million to purchase communication equipment from Zhongxing Technologies (ZTE) (2005); China Poly Group Corporation agreed to finance and build the Ruffa Bridge for $22.74 million (2006); China National Construction & Agricultural Machinery Import & Export Corporation (CAMCO) agrees to construct the Wad Medani 100,000-Ton Water Treatment Plant for $29 million, which is financed by the Export-Import Bank of China (2006); Shandong Electric Power Capital Construction Corporation agreed to build a 300-MV gas-fired power plant in Al-Fulah for $518 million, which is financed by the Export-Import Bank of China (2007); China Railway Engineering Group Co. Ltd. signed a contract to construct a 762-kilometer railway from Khartoum to Port Sudan for $1.154 billion, which is financed by the Chinese Government (2007); China forgives a $99.7 million debt (2007); North China Geological Exploration Bureau agreed to explore for gold for $3.9 million (2007); China agreed to extend a loan for $11.8 million (2007); China provided Darfur with $7.8 million in humanitarian aid (2007); China agreed to loan $13.1 million to build the presidential palace in Khartoum (2007); China supplied $8.6 million to support the voluntary repatriation of displaced Sudanese (2008); China supplied $2.8 million to Sudan to support north-south unity (2008); the China Urban Construction Design and Research Institute agreed to build a hospital in the Blue Nile State (2008); China granted financial assistance to the Sudanese Government (2008); China provided an interest-free loan to Sudan (2008); CGC Overseas Construction Co., Ltd. (CGCOC) agreed to construct the Zalingei-El Geneinah Road for $120 million, which is financed by the Export-Import Bank of China (2008); China CAMC Engineering Co., Ltd., agreed to implement the Dali Water Supply Project for $24 million, which is financed by the Export-Import Bank of China (2009); China Poly Group Corporation agreed to construct the El Fashir-Um Kaddada Road for $96 million, which is financed by the Export-Import Bank of China (2009); China Chongqing International Construction Corporation (CICO) agreed to construct the El Nahood-Um Kaddada Road for $122 million, which is financed by the Export-Import Bank of China (2009); China Chongqing International Construction Corporation (CICO) agreed to construct the Eldibeibat-El Fula Road for $100 million, which is financed by the Export-Import Bank of China (2009); Zhongxing Technologies (ZTE) agreed to establish a fodder factory (2009); China pledged $3 million to support an election (2009); China provided $11.7 million to finance unidentified projects (2009); China agreed to supply $2.9 million in emergency response aid (2009); China Poly Technology Company obtained a license to explore and mine for gold (2009); China provided $45.7 million to finance unidentified projects (2009); Sinohydro agreed to construct the Renk-Malakal Road for $220 million, which is funded by the Export-Import Bank of China (2009); China Machinery Engineering Corporation (CMEC) agreed to construct a 630-kilometer South Kordofan power transmission line, which is funded by the Export-Import Bank of China (2009); China Three Gorges Corporation (CTG) and the China Overseas Engineering Group Co., Ltd., agreed to implement the Upper Atbara Dams Complex Project in eastern Sudan (2010); China forgave $5.9 million in debt (2010); China National Construction & Agricultural Machinery Import & Export Corporation (CAMCO) provided a $30 million loan for the electrification, compilation, and rehabilitation of the Blue Nile Agricultural Projects in the Sinnar State (2010); the Nantong Company agreed to build the Africa Technological City for $90 million, which is financed by the Export-Import Bank of China (2011); China provided a $20.4 million loan to construct bridges in eastern Sudan (2011); China provided a $200 million loan to Sudan to launch key development projects (2012); China donated fifty Saloon cars to the Sudanese President's Office (2012); China agreed to finance the construction of a 100-kilometer highway connecting Sudan and Ethiopia at a cost of $27 million (2012); the Sudan Railway Corporation and Chinese HEPO agreed to establish a factory to produce concrete sleepers at a cost of $5 million (2012); and China Harbour Engineering Company (CHEC) agreed to construct Khartoum International Airport for $1.38 billion, which is financed by the Export-Import Bank of China (2013).[56]

China National Petroleum Corporation (CNPC) has been also been involved in Sudan's infrastructure development. In addition to financing the construction of schools, hospitals, refugee camps, donating medical equipment, providing disaster relief, humanitarian aid, medical and sanitary services, poverty relief, and offering academic scholarships, and funding sports events, CNPC and its subsidiaries have funded the following infrastructure deals: a $10 million grant to construct the Merowe Bridge across the Nile River toward the Aswan Dam (2004); a $10 million loan for railroad development (2004); a $3 million for infrastructure improvement (2008); and Construction of a 400-kilometer gravel-based road to the Heglig Oil Field (2009). Investments total over $8 billion since 1997. At least $6.7 billion has been invested in non-energy sector infrastructure projects. Since 2012, Chinese companies have invested more than $20 billion in Sudan.[57]

The Export-Import Bank of China was instrumental in financing many infrastructure projects, which includes providing government grants and loans, including loans to Chinese private companies directly or on behalf of the Chinese Government.[58] Other banks like the People's Bank of China and the China Central Bank also funded infrastructure projects. In addition, the Export-Import Bank of China, the China Development Bank, the Bank of China, the China Construction Bank, the Agricultural Bank, the Shanghai Pudong Development Bank, and the Industrial and Commercial Bank of China and other financial institutions are actively providing investment loans and financial services to develop Sudan's agricultural sector.[59]

Although Sudan has benefited from Chinese infrastructure investment, it has felt the competitive impacts from the importation of Chinese manufactured goods. Cheap manufactured goods from China have replaced goods produced by local producers: footwear, furniture, cloth, and textiles. Sudanese craftsmen in industries like furniture and cloth have been affected and their jobs have been threatened as cheap Chinese products displaced their production. Small repair shops of electrical appliances have even complained from the slackened demand for their services in the presence of cheap spare parts and substitutes. There has been a loss of jobs in uncompetitive firms and the Sudanese Government potentially gains revenue from indirect taxes and import duties on these goods as Sudanese businesses close and production is lost.[60]

MILITARY/SECURITY RELATIONS

Sino-Sudanese military cooperation historically has been as close as their bilateral energy cooperation. Bilateral military-security cooperation strengthened after 2002 in the wake of a program of military-security cooperation after the Sudanese Armed Forces Chief of Staff visited Beijing in March

2012.⁶¹ Prior to 2002, China offered to help train and equip the Sudanese armed forces in order to cultivate better relations with Sudan in 1971.⁶² Sino-Sudanese military-security cooperation is generally secretive making it difficult at times to determine the extent and the specifics of their military interactions.⁶³

Bilateral security coordination is also essential aspect of their bilateral relations. Sudanese security assistance is necessary to protecting Chinese interests, assets, and personnel who have been targeted on various occasions by various parties: rebels in Omdurman, the SPLA, and Darfur. Both countries also have similar views on international terrorism even though Sudan has been accused of supporting international terrorism by the West.⁶⁴

In addition to coordinating security for Chinese workers in Sudan and sharing similar views on international terrorism, both countries have reciprocal defense attaché offices in their respective capitals.⁶⁵ Both also have conducted high-level military visits and meetings between 2002 and 2014. In addition, China has supplied Sudan with small arms and fighter aircraft between 1997 and 2004, tanks between 2002 and 2003, portable surface-to-air missiles in 2005 and licensed infantry fighting vehicles in 2003.⁶⁶ In 2008, China provided de-mining equipment to South Sudanese officers and a de-mining course.⁶⁷ It is possible that China may have trained Sudanese military jet pilots and provided Sudanese armed forces with training on Chinese-supplied weapons and military equipment.⁶⁸ China did train fifty Sudanese military pilots on helicopter gunships.⁶⁹ Finally, China has been engaged in UN peacekeeping operations (UNAMID) in Darfur. China has contributed 230 contingency troops to the United Nations mission in Sudan to date, mostly from the Chinese Army Engineering Division.⁷⁰

Since 2002, China and Sudan engaged each other militarily and in terms of security through bilateral visits: seven visits to the PRC by Sudanese military officials (Defense Minister, Chief of the General Staff) and five visits to Sudan by Chinese military officials (Vice Chairman of the Central Military Commission, Air Force Commander, Assistant Chief of the General Staff) including one port visit by PLAN ships. China and Sudan have engaged each other no less than twelve times since 2002 according to the Ministry of National Defense of the People's Republic of China, *PLA Daily*, *Xinhua*, and *China Military Online*.

Arms sales are the third aspect of bilateral military-security cooperation. China has been a modest arms supplier to Sudan in during the Cold War when compared to Russia, Ukraine, and Belorussia.⁷¹ The Soviet Union and later Russia supplied Sudan with 75 percent of its weapon systems.⁷² China's total arms sales to Sudan are $1.75 billion based on the 2016 CPI index.⁷³ In 2000, total arms sales to Sudan were $1.04 billion; the difference being $710

Table 12.2 Chinese Conventional Weapons Transfers to Sudan

Year(s) of Delivery	No. of Deliveries	Weapon Designation	Weapon Description
2001–2014	460	Type-63 107mm (L)	Towed Mobile Rocket Launcher
1968–1969	4	MiG-15UTI/Midget (S)	Trainer Aircraft
1970	10	FT-5 (S)	Trainer Aircraft
1970	16	MiG-17PF/Fresco-D (S)	Fighter Aircraft
1971–1973	70	Type-62 (S)	Light Tank
1972	50	Type-59 (S)	Tank
1978	10	Type-63 (S)	Light Tank
1981	14	F-6/Farmer (S)	Fighter Aircraft
1981	20	M-30 122mm (S)	Towed Gun
1981	20	Type-59-1 130mm (S)	Towed Gun
1981	50	YW-531/Type-63 (S)	Armored Personnel Carrier
1987	12	F-7A (S)	Fighter Aircraft
1989	10	Type-59-1 130mm (S)	Towed Gun
1992	18	D-30 122mm (S)	Towed Gun
1991	2	Y-8 (S)	Transport Aircraft
1997	6	F-7A (S)	Fighter Aircraft
2002–2006	25	Type-85-IIM (S)	Tank
2003	12	A-5C/Fantan (S)	Fighter-Ground Attack Aircraft
2006–2015	50	WZ-551/Type-92 (S)	Infantry Fighting Vehicle
2005	9	BT-6 (S)	Trainer Aircraft
2005–2008	12	K-8 Karakorum-8 (S)	Trainer/Combat Aircraft
2006	50	FN-6 (S)	Portable Surface-to-Air Missile
2009–2012	450	Red Arrow-8 (S)	Anti-Tank Missile
2010–2015	50	Type-59D (S)	Tank
2014	6	WS-1 302mm (S)	Self-Propelled Rocket Launcher

Source: SIPRI Arms Transfers Database.

million over a sixteen-year period.[74] It is imperative to note that Sudan's oil wealth helped fuel Sudan's war economy with respect to the Sudanese Civil War and facilitate its arms purchases from China.[75] Table 12.2 summarizes the arms transfers from China and Sudan according to SIPRI. See Table 12.2. Sudan has used Chinese arms in its internal wars with the southern secessionist guerillas (1983–2005) and with Darfur (2003 to present).[76] China sold about 90 percent of Sudan's small arms purchases from 2004 to 2006.

China has also helped Sudan develop its own arms-manufacturing capacity now known as the Military Industrial Corporation. Beginning in 1991, China built factories in Sudan for the local production of weapons, ammunition, vehicles, communications equipment, and rockets. The main weapons factories that China built are Khartoum's Giad Industrial Complex and other facilities in Kalakla, Chojeri, and Bageer. Thus, Sudan is the African's continent third most important manufacturer of military equipment after Egypt and South Africa.[77]

Chapter 12

CULTURAL RELATIONS

Sino-Sudanese cultural relations have early beginnings in educational exchanges between the two countries. Educational exchanges included cultural weeks on reciprocal campuses where students celebrated their culture, folklore, music, and popular culture. In conjunction with these cultural weeks, China and Sudan increased the number of scholarships for students interesting in studying in their respective countries. Beginning in the 1960s, Sudanese students began studying in China but with the rapid improvement of bilateral relations, more Sudanese students were studying science, technology, engineering, medicine, language, and related fields. Conversely, Chinese students came to Sudan to learn Arabic, culture and history, and provide expertise to Chinese corporations operating in region.[78]

Cultural and educational exchanges are sponsored through the Confucius Institute at Khartoum in partnership with China's Northwest Normal University. A memorandum of understanding was signed on October 25, 2007 to establish the Confucius Institute at Khartoum and the formal partnership was established on October 7, 2008. By September 2010, the Confucius Institute of the University of Khartoum had held more than twenty short-term Chinese language courses for over 150 students from the Sudanese government and the Ministry of Minerals. In the same year, China received 580 Sudanese students on scholarships.[79]

Sino-Sudanese cooperation also extends to health sector. Since the 1960s, China has been sending health missions to Sudan. Approximately 29 missions comprising 768 health officials have been sent to date.[80] All the missions sent to Sudan were officiated through agreements and protocols issued by China and Sudan.

China also established malaria control centers and medical care facilities in Sudan. China has also built hospitals in Sudan to meet its growing health-care needs. Chinese NGOs like the China Foundation for Poverty Alleviation have funded the construction of China-Sudan Friendship Hospital for Maternity and Child Care in Abu Ushar in the Central Gezira region of Sudan. China has also built Omdurman's Sino-Sudanese Hospital, at a cost of $15 million.[81]

CNPC also have been actively involved in Sudan's cultural development in terms of the arts, education, and health. CNPC has offered academic scholarships for thirty-five Sudanese students to study in Beijing; constructed the KRC Friendship School and a primary school; provided funds for Sudanese students to study acrobatics; donated funds to build the Academic Report Hall at Khartoum University; donated medical equipment, including ambulances and surgical operation rooms to the Malual Hospital; established the Geophysics Research and Development Center; provided medical facilities for the Al Zariba Hospital and Melovue Hospital; funded the construction of the Fula Friendship Hospital, the Heglig Hospital, the Palogue Friendship Hospital, and the KRC Friendship Hospital; provided disaster relief funds and humanitarian aid including to Darfur; donated gifts to the Sudanese My Goma Orphanage; provided $1 million to improve the living and medical facilities of orphanages, senior citizens' homes and public medical institutions in Khartoum State; donated $30,000 to launch a one-month campaign in the remote areas and provide medical and sanitary services to local residents in Block 6; provided funds for disaster relief; donated funds to support the twentieth Sudan National High School Sports Games; constructed a refugee camp in Darfur; donated $3 million to charity; and agreed to provide poverty relief funds.[82]

Sudan exhibited an impressive cultural display at its national pavilion at the Shanghai 2010 International Expo. Sudan's national pavilion represented its civilizational depth and diverse cultures and showcased its development, economy, terrain, rivers, and rich wildlife.[83]

Sino-Sudanese cultural relations are promoted through several organizations such as the China-Sudan Friendship Association, the Chinese-African People's Friendship Association, the China-Arab Friendship Association, the Confucius Institute, the Sudan Council for International People's Friendship and the Sudanese World Friendship Association.[84]

China and Sudan concluded the following deals which include agreements, contracts, executive plans, and protocols to foster cultural cooperation: Contract on Films Exchange (March 1963, October 1964); Agreement on Radio-Telegraphic Communication between Shanghai and Khartoum (September 1963); Cultural, Scientific, and Technical Protocol (1970); Protocol on Dispatching a Chinese Medical Team to Sudan (December 1970); Protocol on Expanding Rice Cultivation in Sudan (July 1974); Protocol on Sending a Chinese Medical Team to Sudan (January 1979); Document under which China will provide Sudan with experts for training Sudanese Workers for the Nuba Lake Fishery Scheme (June 1979); Protocol on the Dispatch of a Chinese Medical Team (July 1980); 1982–1983 Executive Plan for Cultural Cooperation (December 1981); Protocol on Designing a Vocational Training Center with Chinese Aid (December 1983); Protocol on Cultural Cooperation for 1984–1985 (June 1984); Protocol on Increased Sports Exchanges (January 1985); Summary of Talks on Cultural and Educational Cooperation (January 1986); 1988–1990 Executive Plan for Cultural Cooperation (December 1987); Agreements of Educational Cooperation between Khartoum University and Gezira University (1996); Agreement to purchase Irrigation Equipment for the Ministry of Irrigation through the Chinese company CAMC (1997); Agreement to send Chinese Agricultural Experts to Sudan (2008); Agreement to build an Agricultural Technology Demonstration Center by the China Shandong International Economic and Technical Cooperation Corporation

(2008); China Harbour Engineering Co. Ltd. finances the graduate education of ten Sudanese students at the Nanjing-based Honai University for $230,060 (2009); Agricultural Investment Agreement between the Sudanese Ministry of Agriculture and Zhongxing Technologies (ZTE) to cultivate oil seeds in the White Nile State (2009); Memorandum of Understanding between the China Machinery Engineering Corporation (CMEC) and Sudan's Gezira State to modernize irrigation and improve seeds (2009); Memorandum of Understanding between the Gezira State, White Nile State, and China for Zhongxing Technologies (ZTE) to remove Mesquite Trees in two provinces (2009); Shenzhen Xing & Ye International Industrial Co. Ltd., implemented the Bio-energy Project in the Tabat area of Sudan (2010); China Foundation of Poverty Alleviation (an NGO) donated $110,000 in medical equipment (2010); China donated ten mobile medical clinics (2010); Agreement to send a Medical Team of thirty-seven Physicians to Sudan (2011); China Foundation of Poverty Alleviation (an NGO) provided $9.2 million to construct a hospital in Abu Ushar in the Gezira State (2011); China donates Musical Instruments (2011); the Export-Import Bank of China agreed to finance the Integrated Information Project for Higher Education for $10 million (2011); Cooperation Agreement between China Central Television (CCTV) and Sudan State Television (May 2012); Memorandum of Understanding to establish an Agricultural Free Trade Zone in Sudan (2012); China Foundation of Poverty Alleviation (an NGO) launched a maternal and infant health-care project at the Abuousher Friendship Hospital at a cost of $16 million (2012); and Agricultural Agreement giving Chinese companies more options to operate in Sudan (2013).[85]

ENERGY/PETROLEUM RELATIONS

Energy cooperation forms the nexus of their bilateral relationship. Until 2012, Sudan exported approximately 6 percent of China's annual oil requirements; however, Sudan now exports approximately less than 1 percent to China. Nevertheless, China still has significant hydrocarbon energy stakes in Sudan in terms of equity shares in oil fields, prospecting and oil pipeline construction but most of it is in South Sudan. Chinese investment in Sudan's oil industry has resulted in 936 miles of oil pipelines, the construction of a crude oil processing plant with a capacity of 18.3 million barrels per year and several gas stations. With Chinese financial and technical assistance, Sudan established its own oil industry, consisting of prospecting, exploiting, refining and transportation facilities and sales networks. China has helped Sudan transform itself from an oil-importing country into an oil-exporting country.[86]

Today, Sudan is a modest supplier of crude oil to China. In this respect, China imported approximately 1 percent of its crude petroleum from Sudan in

2012, 2013, and 2014 but increased to 2 percent according to United Nations Commodity Trade Statistics Database. Previously, Sudan/South Sudan combined accounted for 5 percent of all Chinese oil imports in 2011; but this figure dropped to less than 1 percent in 2012.[87] In terms of total trade value, crude petroleum imports was almost 100 percent for the same years. Table 12.3 shows Chinese crude oil imports from Sudan in thousands of barrels per day, oil imports share, world ranking, trade value, total commodity trade value, and percentage from 2006 to 2015. See Table 12.3.

China does not import petroleum gas products including liquefied natural gas (LNG) from Sudan. On the other hand, China has oil acquisitions in the country. Table 12.4 illustrates China's oil acquisitions in South Sudan. See Table 12.4.

Table 12.3 Chinese Crude Petroleum Imports from Sudan

Year	KBPD	Oil Imports Share (%)	World Ranking	Crude Oil Trade Value ($)	Total Commodity Trade Value ($)	Percentage (%)
2006	97	3	8	1,872,079,062	1,943,481,721	96.3
2007	207	6	6	4,143,191,548	4,171,239,208	99.3
2008	211	6	6	6,290,576,862	6,325,889,462	99.4
2009	245	6	5	4,644,710,638	4,684,821,913	99.1
2010	253	5	6	6,556,198,574	6,671,907,016	98.3
2011	261	5	7	9,417,862,243	9,541,533,519	98.7
2012	37	1	19	1,495,178,413	1,554,266,756	96.2
2013	48	1	19	1,900,058,296	2,100,023,168	90.5
2014	36	<1	19	1,349,814,461	1,521,283,337	88.7
2015	161	2	12	2,881,242,491	3,055,829,717	94.3

Source: United Nations Commodity Trade Statistics Database.

Table 12.4 Chinese Oil Acquisitions in Sudan

Date	Company	Acquisition
June 2007	CNPC	Won 40% stake in Block 13 including a 20-year concession and exploration right along with PT Pertamina Oil Company
September 2005	CNPC	Offshore exploration and production of block 15.
December 2004	Sinopec	Adar-Port Sudan pipeline
June 2000	CNPC	Khartoum refinery, 70,000 b/d
April 1999	CNPC	Heglig-Port Sudan Pipeline (500,000 bpd) – A pipeline from fields to the Red Sea

Source: Julie Jiang and Chen Dang, *Update on Overseas Investments by Chinese National Companies: Achievements and Challenges Since 2011*, Organization for Economic Cooperation and Development/International Energy Agency, June 2014, 35–39.

Sino-Sudanese energy relations predate the partition of Sudan and the independence of South Sudan in 2011. China invested over $8 billion in Sudan's oil sector between 1995 and 2011, making it the third largest producer of crude oil in Sub-Saharan Africa.[88] After the partition of Sudan, South Sudan acquired 80 percent of the oil fields and sovereignty over most of Sudan's oil facilities.[89] Consequently, Sudan maintained 20 percent of the oil fields, the Khartoum refinery, and Adar-Port Sudan and Heglig-Port Sudan pipelines terminating at Port Sudan. Prior to the partition, Sudan controlled Blocks 1, 2, 3, 4, 6, and 7, the Adar and Yale oil fields, and the Heglig and Unity oil fields. It is imperative to note that most of Sudan's oil fields are located along the North-South border.[90]

China's entry into Sudan's oil sector began in 1995 after Chevron relinquished its interest in 1992. China's entry transformed not only Sudan's economy but also deepened Sino-Sudanese economic ties including bilateral energy cooperation. This lasted until the end of 2011. Thus, oil was an important component of Sino-Sudanese relations between 1995 and 2011;[91] however, South Sudan became independent in 2011 and acquired 75 percent of Sudan oil reserves.

The idea of joint oil exploration occurred in 1970 when then Sudanese president Numeiri requested China's assistance to explore for oil. China lacked the necessary expertise then and advised President Numeiri to approach the United States and its oil industry. Several Western oil companies led by Chevron explored for and managed to find oil in commercial quantities by 1985; however, Sudan's internal political developments, civil war, and repeated attacks on oil installations led to the departure of American and Canadian oil corporations by 1992. The United States also put pressure on Chevron to withdraw and ends its operations. Once again, Sudan now under President Omar al-Bashir approached China in 1995 and sought to establish a strategic partnership, which encompassed not only energy, but also politics, economics, and culture.[92]

China was more than willing to develop Sudan's oil sector. China had an increasing demand for oil, was heavily invested in Africa, had African support for China after the Tiananmen Square Massacre, and the U.S. and Canadian oil corporations withdrew from the country. These factors influenced China's involvement in Sudan's oil sector. By 1995, China had made its first investment after finding oil in commercial quantities in the Heglig Field and the Unity Field.[93]

The most important Chinese oil investment was the first: CNPC purchased a 40 percent concession share in Block 6 in South Kordofan in September 1995. In March 1997, CNPC won the tender covering three blocks in the Mughlad Basin: Unity (number 1), Heglig (number 2), and Kaikang (number

4). In conjunction with the establishment of the three blocks, it established the GNPOC with Petronas (30 percent), ONGC (25 percent), Sudapet (5 percent), and Nilepet (5 percent). CNPC's share was 40 percent. In November 2000, CNPC won a 41 percent share of Blocks 3 and 7 in the Malut Basin in the Upper Nile State. It also formed the Petrodar Operating Company (PDOC) with Petronas (40 percent), Nilepet (8 percent), Sinopec (6 percent), Egypt Kuwait Holding (3.5 percent), and other partners (1.4 percent) on October 1, 2001. In September 2005, CNPC took a majority holding of the deepwater Block 15. In June 2007, CNPC won a 40 percent stake in Block 13 and a 20-year concession and exploration right with PT Pertamina Oil Company. CNPC's oil exploration efforts obviously attracted Indian and Malaysian oil companies in joint ventures.[94]

In addition to winning majority stakes in Blocks 1, 2, 3, 4, 6, and 7, CNPC and the Sudanese government's Ministry of Energy & Mining (MEM) formed the Sudan Khartoum Refinery Company (KRC) in 1997 and built the Khartoum Refinery in 2000. Each partner owns 50 percent and the refinery produces 100,000 barrels per day, mostly refining the Nile blends. In 2003, CNPC agreed to build a 450-mile oil pipeline from El Fula oil field from Block 6 in Western Kordofan to the main oil refinery in Khartoum. This oil pipeline was completed in 2005 with a design capacity of 200,000 barrels per day. The GNPOC, which CNPC holds a majority stake, also built a 1,000-mile oil pipeline from the Heglig oil field to Port Sudan Refinery at Bashayer Terminal One on the Red Sea. This pipeline became operational in 1999 and has a design capacity of 450,000 barrels per day. The DPOC, which CNPC also owns a majority share, built an 850-mile oil pipeline from Blocks 3 and 7 to the Port Sudan Refinery at Bashayer Terminal Two on the Red Sea. This pipeline became operational in 2004 and has a design capacity of 500,000 barrels per day.[95]

CNPC also trained Sudanese petroleum specialists. From 2006 to 2009, CNPC trained fifty technical and management personnel for the Sudanese Ministry of Energy and Mining. CNPC also signed an agreement on October 5, 2007 to spend $900,000 to train local oil professionals. On January 6, 2010, CNPC signed a new agreement with the Sudanese Ministry of Energy and Mining to donate $1 million to help Sudan implement a three-year training program for ninety petroleum specialists.[96]

Beyond bilateral energy cooperation in Sudan's oil sector, energy cooperation extends to electricity production by building dams. While costly, China does not hesitate to undertake such projects essentially since it builds goodwill. In this respect, China assisted in the construction of the $1.8 billion, 1,250-megawatt Merowe Dam, a large project which was commissioned in March 2009. The Export-Import Bank of China and Arabian investment banks partly funded the construction, which was built under a joint venture between China Water Resources & and Hydropower and China International Water & Electric Corporation.[97]

Located in Sudan's Nubian region, the Merowe Dam is very controversial because it caused the displacement of over 50,000 people and the disappearance of dozens of Sudanese villages. Nevertheless, Sudan insists that the dam was necessary not only for producing electricity but also for providing systemic water resources for agricultural enterprises located within the vicinity of the dam.[98]

Sino-Sudanese energy cooperation extends to Sudan's nuclear sector. In this respect, China's state-owned China National Nuclear Corporation and Sudan's Ministry of Water Resources and Electricity signed a framework agreement to build Sudan's first nuclear reactor by 2021 and to start commercial operations by 2027. China also plans to export thirty homegrown nuclear units to Sudan by 2030. China is seeking wider acceptance for its atomic technology and expertise amid a global call for cleaner energy.[99]

SUMMARY

Sino-Sudanese diplomatic relations were established on February 4, 1959. Since then, China has been integral to Sudan's political and economic development. Bilateral relations are traditional and close. Given their close ties, China has also supported Sudan's independence, stability, and territorial integrity. China also helped Sudan resisted Soviet infiltration and destabilization policies during the 1970s and defended Sudan against Western criticism and destabilization after General Omar al-Bashir came to power in 1989. China used its power and influence as a permanent member of the United Nations Security Council to deflect international criticism and sanctions against Sudan in the Darfur crisis. It also supported South Sudan's secession and independence.

China has invested over $20 billion into Sudan's oil sector, infrastructure projects, dams, highways, airports, schools, hospitals, and agriculture industry.[100] China also transformed Sudan's oil sector turning Sudan into a net exporter. While most of China's oil investments are now located in South Sudan, China has not abandoned Sudan even though Sudan's oil economy is now weak. South Sudan is a landlocked country and still depends on Sudan's pipelines to transport its oil. Therefore, in the interim, both China and South Sudan will depend on Sudan for the transportation and the refinement of South Sudan's hydrocarbons.

NOTES

1. David H. Shinn and Joshua Eisenman, *China and Africa: A Century of Engagement* (Philadelphia, PA: University of Pennsylvania Press), 2012, 377.
2. Wolfgang Bartke, *The Agreements of the People's Republic of China with Foreign Countries 1949–1990* (Munchen, Germany: K.G. Saur), 1992, 178.
3. Ministry of Foreign Affairs of People's Republic of China, "List of Agreements on Mutual Visa Exemption Between the People's Republic of China and Foreign Countries" November 28, 2004, accessed February 13, 2015, http://cs.mfa.gov.cn/wgrlh/bgzl/P020140328398504621618.pdf.
4. Ministry of Foreign Affairs of the People's Republic of China, "President Xi Jinping Meets with President Omar Hassan Ahmad al-Bashir of Sudan," September 1, 2015, accessed August 20, 2016, http://www.fmprc.gov.cn/mfa_eng/wjb_663304/zzjg_663340/xybfs_663590/gjlb_663594/2883_663766/2885_663770/t1294136.shtml.
5. Bartke, ibid., 178.
6. Yitzhak Shichor, "Sudan: China's Outpost in Africa," *China Brief* (Jamestown Foundation), Volume V, Issue 21, October 13, 2005.
7. Benjamin A. Hale, "Arrighi on Sino-Sudanese Relations: Trade, Investment, and Diplomacy in Twenty-First Century" (Bachelor of Arts Thesis, Edith Cowan University), 2013, 32, http://ro.ecu.edu.au/cgi/viewcontent.cgi?article=1086&context=theses_hons.. Stockholm International Peace Research Institute, SIPRI Arms Transfers Database, http://www.sipri.org/databases/armstransfers.
8. Daniel Large, *Sudan's Foreign Relations with Asia: China and the Politics of "Looking East,"* (Philadelphia, PA: Institute for Security Studies), ISS Paper 158, February 2008, 1, http://dspace.africaportal.org/jspui/bitstream/123456789/30875/1/PAPER158.pdf?1.
9. Muhamad S. Olimat, *China and North Africa Since World War II* (Lanham, MD: Lexington Books), 2014, 161; and U.S. Energy Information Administration, U.S. Department of Energy, "Country Analysis Briefs: Sudan and South Sudan," September 3, 2014, 1, accessed February 14, 2015.
10. United Nations, United Nations Commodity Trade Statistics Database, accessed February 13, 2015, http://comtrade.un.org/db/default.aspx.
11. U.S. Energy Information Administration, U.S. Department of Energy, "Country Analysis Briefs: Sudan and South Sudan," ibid.
12. "The Sudanese Chinese Relations Glorious Past and Bright Future," *Sudan Vision News Daily*, November 3, 2013, accessed February 16, 2015, http://news.sudanvisiondaily.com/details.html?rsnpid=228544.
13. Olimat, ibid., 157.
14. Olimat, ibid., 157; and Large, ibid., 2.
15. Ibid., 157, 158.
16. Ibid., 158, 159.
17. Large, ibid., 2; and Olimat, ibid., 158.
18. Shinn and Eisenman, ibid., 251; and Olimat, ibid., 158.

19. Daniel Large and Luke Patey, *Riding the Sudanese Storm: China, India, Russia, Brazil and Two Sudans* (Johannesburg, South Africa: South African Institute of Foreign Affairs), Occasional Paper No. 197, July 17, 2014.

20. Olimat, ibid., 159.

21. Ibid.

22. Shinn and Eisenman, ibid., 253.

23. Ministry of Foreign Affairs of People's Republic of China, "China–Sudan: Activities," (n.d.), accessed August 9, 2016, http://www.fmprc.gov.cn/mfa_eng/wjb_663304/zzjg_663340/xybfs_663590/gjlb_663594/2883_663766/2885_663770/.

24. He Wenping, "The Darfur Issue: A New Test for China's Africa Policy" in Fantu Cheru and Cyril Obi, eds., *The Rise of China and India in Africa: Challenges, Opportunities and Critical Interventions* (New York, NY: Zed Books), 2010, 159; and Olimat, ibid., 159.

25. Daniel Large and Luke Patey, "Sudan Looks East," in Daniel Large and Luke Patey, eds., *Sudan Looks East: China, India and The Politics of Asian Alternatives* (Rochester, NY: James Currey Ltd.), 2011, 24.

26. Ibid.

27. U.S. Energy Information Administration, U.S. Department of Energy, "Country Analysis Briefs: Sudan and South Sudan," September 3, 2014, accessed February 14, 2015; and European Commission Directorate-General for Trade, "Sudan: EU Bilateral Trade and Trade with the World," April 16, 2014, accessed February 13, 2015, http://trade.ec.europa.eu/doclib/docs/2006/september/tradoc_147395.pdf.

28. United Nations, United Nations Commodity Trade Statistics Database, accessed February 13, 2015, ibid.

29. Large and Patey, "Riding the Sudanese Storm: China, India, Russia, Brazil and Two Sudans," ibid., 10.

30. Olimat, ibid., 163.

31. Large, ibid., 6.

32. Ibid., 15.

33. United Nations, United Nations Commodity Trade Statistics Database, accessed July 22, 2016, ibid.

34. United Nations Conference on Trade and Development (UNCTAD FDI/TNC) Database, *Bilateral FDI Statistics 2014*, accessed February 13, 2015, http://unctad.org/Sections/dite_fdistat/docs/webdiaeia2014d3_CHN.pdf.

35. Ibid.

36. Nour Eldin A. Maglad, *Scoping Study on Chinese Relations with Sudan* (Nairobi, Kenya: African Economic Research Consortium), February 11, 2008, accessed February 14, 2015, http://hdl.handle.net/10419/93162.

37. Large, ibid., 2.

38. United Nations, United Nations Commodity Trade Statistics Database, accessed July 22, 2016, ibid.

39. Olimat, Ibid., 164; and International Trade Centre, Directory of Trade Promotion Organizations and Other Trade Support Institutions, accessed February 13, 2015, 2015, http://www.intracen.org/itc/trade-support/tsi-directory.

40. Austin M. Strange, et al., "Tracking Underreported Financial Flows: China's Development Finance and the Aid–Conflict Nexus Revisited," *Journal of Conflict Resolution,* Volume 61, Issue 5 (2017): 935–963. Bartke, ibid., 178–179; Maglad, ibid., 2, 14, 15; and Ministry of Foreign Affairs of People's Republic of China, "China and Sudan," (n.d.), accessed February 13, 2015, http://www.fmprc.gov.cn/mfa_eng/wjb_663304/zzjg_663340/xybfs_663590/gjlb_663594/2883_663766/.

41. Large, ibid., 1.
42. Shichor, ibid.
43. Ibid.
44. Ibid.
45. Large and Patey, ibid., 13.
46. Rose Bradbury, "Sudan, the Hollow State: What Challenges to Chinese Policy," *Journal of Politics & International Studies* (Leeds, UK), Volume 8, Winter 2012/2013, 371, http://www.polis.leeds.ac.uk/assets/files/students/student-journal/ug-winter-12/130227-win12-rose-bradbury-10.pdf.
47. Maglad, ibid., 3.
48. Strange, et al., ibid.
49. Olimat, ibid., 164.
50. Maglad, ibid., 11.
51. Caroline Francis et al., *China and Sudan–South Sudan Oil Free Impasse: Implications of Chinese Foreign Aid, Diplomacy, and Military Relations* (Ann Arbor, MI: University of Michigan), April 24, 2012, 5, http://sites.fordschool.umich.edu/china-policy/files/2012/09/China-and-the-Sudan_South-Sudan-Oil-Fee-Impasse.pdf.
52. Maglad, ibid., 14.
53. Ibid.
54. Ibid.
55. Maglad, ibid., 14, 15.
56. Strange, et al., ibid.
57. Olimat, ibid., 163.; and Strange, et al., ibid.
58. Maglad, ibid., 16.
59. Olimat, ibid., 164.
60. Maglad, ibid., 10.
61. Large, Ibid., 8–9; and Large and Patey, ibid., 19.
62. Shinn and Eisenman, ibid., 251.
63. Francis et al., ibid., 13.
64. Olimat, ibid., 168.
65. United States Department of Defense, Defense Intelligence Agency, *Directory of PRC Military Personalities* (Washington, DC), 2014, 20.
66. SIPRI Arms Transfers Database, http://www.sipri.org/databases/armstransfers.
67. Strange, et al., ibid.
68. Francis et al., ibid.
69. Shinn and Eisenman, ibid., 252.
70. United Nations Peacekeeping Website, *UN's Missions Detailed by Country,* December 31, 2014, accessed January 6, 2015.

71. Olimat, ibid., 168.
72. Hale, ibid., 34.
73. Stockholm International Peace Research Institute, SIPRI Arms Transfers Database, http://www.sipri.org/databases/armstransfers.
74. Ibid.
75. Francis et al., ibid., 6.
76. Olimat, ibid., 168.
77. Shinn and Eisenman, ibid., 252; and Olimat, ibid., 170.
78. Olimat, ibid., 166–167.
79. Ministry of Foreign Affairs of People's Republic of China, "China and Sudan," (n.d.), accessed February 15, 2015, ibid.
80. Olimat, ibid., 167
81. Ibid.
82. Strange, et al., ibid.
83. Olimat, ibid., 168.
84. Ibid.
85. Strange, et al., ibid., Bartke, ibid., 178, 179; Maglad, ibid., 2, 14; and Embassy of the People's Republic of China in Sudan, "CCTV and Sudan State Television Signed a Cooperation Agreement," June 7, 2012, accessed February 13, 2015, http://sd.china-embassy.org/eng/whjl/t939073.htm.
86. Wenping, ibid.
87. United Nations, United Nations Commodity Trade Statistics Database, accessed February 13, 2015, ibid.
88. Olimat, ibid., 148.
89. Ibid.
90. Francis et al., ibid., 3.
91. Olimat, ibid., 164.
92. Ibid.
93. Ibid., 164–165.
94. Olimat, ibid., 165.; and Large and Patey, "Riding the Sudanese Storm: China, India, Russia, Brazil and Two Sudans," 11.
95. Olimat, Ibid., 165–166.; and U.S. Energy Information Administration, U.S. Department of Energy, "Country Analysis Briefs: Sudan and South Sudan," September 3, 2014, 9, accessed February 14, 2015.
96. Strange, et al., ibid.
97. Olimat, ibid., 166.
98. Ibid.
99. Stephen Stapczynski and Aibing Guo, "China's CNNC Seeking to Build Sudan's First Nuclear Reactor," *Bloomberg*, May 23, 2016, accessed July 23, 2016, http://www.bloomberg.com/news/articles/2016-05-24/china-s-cnnc-seeking-to-build-sudan-s-first-nuclear-reactor.
100. Olimat, ibid., 170.

Chapter 13

China and United Arab Emirates
Political/Diplomatic Relations

Sino-Emirati diplomatic relations were established on November 1, 1984.[1] While diplomatic ties have developed since 1984, the crux of their relationship is trade, investment, and energy cooperation including oil, gas, renewables, and nuclear energy. Prior to the establishment of Sino-Emirati diplomatic relations, the United Arab Emirates (hereafter "UAE") was a British protectorate until it gained independence from the United Kingdom in December 1971; however, thirteen years (1971–1984) lapsed between the time of the UAE's independence and its recognition of China.

Although diplomatic ties were established in 1984, the earliest political encounters of China and the UAE date back to the Sultanate of Oman when trade routes were established between Ancient China and the Middle East. Chinese-Hui Muslim Admiral Zheng passed by the shores of the UAE on his way to holy city of Mecca in 1421.[2]

Chinese political interest in the UAE began in the 1950s, with its support of the Dhofar Liberation Front (DLF) during the Omani Civil War (1955–1975). The DLF expanded its operations to what is now known as the UAE, Bahrain, Qatar, and Oman and transformed itself into a regional organization with the goal of liberating the Arabian Gulf from British occupation under the banner of the Popular Front for the Liberation of the Occupied Arabian Gulf (PFLOAG). PFLOAG was a leftist organization composed of communist, Marxist, and Maoist thought mixed with Arab nationalist tone.[3]

China's support of the DLG/PFLOAG delayed the establishment of diplomatic relations with the UAE despite China's assurances of goodwill. Saudi Arabia also placed considerable pressure on the UAE not to recognize China for political, ideological, and religious reasons. The UAE was also involved in a decade of negotiations with the United Kingdom and neighboring states about the proposed federation with the Trucial States. Qatar, Bahrain, Kuwait, and seven other emirates composing the UAE were exploring the possibility of becoming a single, federalized state; however, this did not materialize because of a complex host of factors at the local, regional, and international levels. Thus, the UAE's foreign policy was still in the early stages of formation. Once China revised its foreign policy and terminated its support for the PFLOAG in mid-1970s, Gulf countries were more eager to establish diplomatic relations with China, because China's policy change eliminated any fear of it intervening in their domestic affairs.[4] It also paved the way for the UAE to recognize China in 1984; however, the UAE did not recognize China even though China started to cease its support to PFLOAG in 1971.

UAE's recognition of China was an "outcome of the process of state formation and growing sense of independence in its foreign policy as it was relatively free of Saudi pressure." China's foreign policy was also drastically altered in favor of economic development in the post-Mao era (1979–Present). This was accomplished by an active policy centered on trade relations, technology transfer, and energy cooperation. China also abandoned its support completely to the PFLOAG and ended its support for liberation movements in the Near East.[5]

Sino-Emirati political ties and bilateral cooperation developed contemporaneously with regional crises in the Near East, which, for the most part, both countries were in agreement with respect to their resolutions, such as peaceful settlements: First Gulf War (1980–1988), Second Gulf War (1990–1991), and Third Gulf War (2003–2011). Both countries also opposed the Arab Spring on national security grounds; however, the UAE supported regime change in Libya and Syria, "while diplomatically participating in resolving the conflict peacefully in Yemen." In contrast, China opposed the entire process of change, seeing it as destabilizing, and as a threat to its homeland, national security, stability, and prosperity. Sino-Emirati political cooperation currently centers on a political solution to the Syrian civil war and supporting the end of violence in Iraq, Libya, and Yemen.[6]

Bilateral cooperation developed through high-level, official exchanges and accords. Bilateral cooperation expanded to include the following sectors: aviation, culture, public health, trade, the economy, energy and finance. Bilateral cooperation also occurred below the national level between Chinese provincial leaders and the UAE's cabinet ministers. Such exchanges improved diplomatic ties and mutual political trust between China and the UAE.[7] As testimony of enhanced political trust, China and the UAE have engaged each other through high-level, official visits and exchanges no less than thirty-five times since 2004.[8] Some of the most important exchanges include: President Hu Jintao Meets and Vice President and Prime Minister Mohammed bin Rashid Al Maktoum (January 2007 and March 2008), President Hu Jintao and Crown Prince Mohammed bin Zayed Al Nahayan (August 2009), Vice

President Xi Jinping and Crown Prince Mohammed bin Zayed Al Nahayan (August 2009), and President Xi Jinping and Crown Prince Sheikh Mohammed bin Zayed Al Nahyan (December 2015).[9]

The establishment of official diplomatic ties and bilateral political cooperation was accomplished through the issuance or inking of: Joint Communiqué on the Establishment of Diplomatic Relations Between the People's Republics of China and the United Arab Emirates (November 1, 1984);[10] Memorandum of Understanding on Strengthening Bilateral Relations between the Foreign Ministries of China and the UAE (April 9, 2007);[11] and Agreement of Mutual Visa Exemptions on Diplomatic Passports between the People's Republics of China and the United Arab Emirates (March 21, 2012).[12]

China and the UAE also established diplomatic ties and promoted bilateral political cooperation through official representation in each other's countries. China established an embassy in Abu Dhabi and the UAE established an embassy in Beijing.

China also initiated a strategic partnership with the UAE in 2012 to further diplomatic ties as well as economic, cultural, energy, and military-security ties.[13]

One incident which caused a temporary chill in diplomatic relations occurred in September 2005. In violation of the UAE's commitment to a One-China policy, it permitted then Taiwanese Ppesident Chen Shui-bian to pass through the country and carry out political activities. Consequently, Chinese officials urged the UAE to end its official contacts with Taiwan.

ECONOMIC/TRADE RELATIONS

Sino-Emirati economic relations are robust. China is considered a major trading partner of the UAE. China's presence is visible in the form of the Dragon Mart, a huge shopping and trading hub covering eighty-two square miles in Dubai.[14] The Dragon Mart serves as a hub to Chinese corporations not only in the Gulf region, but also in the entire Near East, Central Asia, Europe, and Sub-Saharan Africa.[15]

In 2013, China was the UAE's largest trading partner after the European Union and India.[16] In the same year, the UAE was China's twenty-first largest trading partner.[17] Bilateral trade was: $28.2 billion (2008), $21.2 billion (2009), $25.6 billion (2010), $35.1 billion (2011), $40.4 billion (2012), $46.2 billion (2013), $54.7 billion (2014), and $48.6 Billion (2015).[18] Bilateral trade increased by $20 billion in seven years. Since 2000, bilateral trade increased almost twenty-fold. In 2012, foreign direct investment into the UAE from China was $105 million and foreign direct investment stock was $1.33 billion.[19]

Bilateral trade began in the 1980s. Prior to 1980, China traded with the UAE via Kuwait.[20] In terms of bilateral trade, Table 13.1 shows the top five commodities traded between China and the UAE in 2015. Energy commodities, which include crude petroleum and petroleum gas products, appear to be the most traded commodity. In terms of trade value, 74 percent is attributed to energy commodities, which includes crude petroleum and petroleum gas products. See Table 13.1.

In previous years, China's energy commodities accounted for the following in terms of trade value: 87 percent (2008), 79 percent (2009), 79.5 percent (2010), 79.4 percent (2011) and 81 percent (2012), 80 percent (2013), and 82 percent (2014).[21]

Bilateral trade is promoted through several organizations such as the UAE-China Forum, the UAE-China Economic Committee, China-Arab States Cooperation Forum, the Asia Cooperation Dialogue, China-GCC Forum on

Table 13.1 Top Five Commodities Traded between China and the UAE

Commodity	Importer	Trade Value ($)	Percentage (%)
Mineral fuels, mineral oils and products of their distillation; bituminous substances; mineral waxes	China	8,552,788,843	74
Plastics and articles thereof	China	1,680,760,479	15
Organic chemicals	China	344,315,574	3
Commodities not specified according to kind	China	242,258,491	2
Salt; sulfur; earths and stone; plastering materials, lime and cement	China	228,936,826	2
Electrical machinery and equipment and parts thereof; sound recorders and reproducers, television image and sound recorders and reproducers, and parts and accessories of such articles	UAE	7,247,413,817	20
Nuclear reactors, boilers, machinery and mechanical appliances; parts thereof	UAE	5,677,881,459	15
Articles of apparel and clothing accessories, knitted or crocheted	UAE	3,404,919,487	9
Articles of apparel and clothing accessories, not knitted or crocheted	UAE	2,291,271,887	6
Furniture; bedding, mattresses, mattress supports, cushions and similar stuffed furnishings; lamps and lighting fittings, not elsewhere specified or included; illuminated signs, illuminated name-plates and the like; prefabricated buildings	UAE	1,954,989,324	5

Source: United Nations Commodity Trade Statistics Database.

Economic and Trade Cooperation, the China-Arab States Expo, the PRC Ministry of Commerce, the PRC Ministry of Foreign Affairs, and the All-China Federation of Industry and Commerce.[22]

China and the UAE have inked some important agreements to facilitate trade between their countries. The most notable agreements and notes include: Agreement on Economic, Trade, and Technological Cooperation (1985);[23] Trade Protocol (January 6, 1986);[24] Economic, Trade, and Scientific Agreement (1986);[25] Air Cargo Agreement (1993);[26] Agreement on the Protection of Investment (1993);[27] Agreement on Avoidance of Double Taxation (1993);[28] Joint Communiqué establishing a Strategic Partnership in the Areas of Trade, Political Cooperation, Security, Energy, Construction, Culture, and Tourism (2012);[29] and Memorandum of Understanding on Establishing China-UAE Investment Cooperation Fund valued at $10 billion (December 14, 2015).[30]

In addition to inking agreements to foster bilateral trade, China and the UAE also established a Joint Commission of Economic, Trade and Technical Cooperation in November 1985.[31] The Commission has since convened at least four meetings. It serves as a major platform for the promotion of bilateral trade cooperation.[32]

China and the UAE also have been active participants in the China-GCC FTA negotiations since 2009.[33] Several rounds have met with the hope of inking an agreement between China and the Gulf Cooperation Council (GCC).

China has been actively involved in the UAE's economic development. China and the UAE concluded the following deals to develop the UAE's infrastructure, which includes construction, ports development, highways, pipeline construction, agro-technology, renewable energy, information technology, and telecommunications: a $300 million Real Estate Construction Contract between China State Construction Engineering Company and Dubai Properties for the Mirdif Villa and Apartment project (January 2006); a $300 million Real Estate Construction Contract awarded to China State Construction Engineering Company for the Skycourt Apartment Complex project (January 2007); a $140 million Real Estate Construction Contract awarded to Sinohydro for the Novotel and Ibis Hotel project (December 2007); a $260 million Auto Transport Contract awarded to China State Construction Engineering Company for Emirates Road Improvement Project (Phase 2) (December 2008); a $130 million Agriculture Contract awarded to China Harbor Engineering Company (subsidiary of China Communications Construction Company) for the Food Reserve project (January 2010); a $2.95 billion Real Estate Construction Contract between China National Chemical Engineering Company and the Dubai Government for National House Scheme project (May 2012); a $1.35 billion Real Estate Construction Contract between China State Construction Engineering Company and Aabar Company to develop thirty properties in Abu Dhabi (May 2012); a $160 million Aviation Transport Contract awarded to China State Construction Engineering Company (January 2013); a $120 million Real Estate Construction Contract between China State Construction Engineering Company for the Al Amal Psychiatric Hospital project (March 2013); a $240 million Real Estate Construction Contract between State Construction Engineering Company and Skai Company for the Palm Jumeirah Garden Home Project (January 2014); a $110 million Auto Transport Contract awarded to China State Construction Engineering Company (April 2014); a $100 million Aviation Transport Contract awarded to China State Construction Engineering Company (May 2014); a $170 million Real Estate Construction Contract awarded to China State Construction Engineering Company (January 2016); a $100 million Real Estate Construction contract awarded to China State Construction Engineering Company (May 2016); and Cosco Shipping Co. and Abu Dhabi Ports Co. sign a $738 million accord for Cosco Shipping to build and operate a new container terminal in Abu Dhabi (October 2016).[34]

Since January 2006, Chinese companies have invested or finalized contracts no less than $7.48 billion. These investments are non-energy related and represent 97 percent of China's total investments. Conversely, UAE companies are investing in China. Dubai Port International, Abu Dhabi National Oil Company, Emmar, DAMAC, and other corporations are heavily investing in China in the petrochemicals sector, refineries, construction, and technology sectors. China hopes to get UAE companies to invest in its Western and northwestern provinces, especially where the Chinese Muslims live.[35]

China and the UAE have also cooperated in banking and finance.[36] In terms of banking, some of China's major banks have established a presence in Dubai. Industrial and Commercial Bank of China (ICBS), the Bank of China, and China Development Bank (CDB) have opened branches offering an array of services, from project financing to asset management.[37] PetroChina International and the Agricultural Bank of China also have opened branches in Dubai's International Financial Center.[38] Conversely, in 2009, Mashreq Bank, an Abu Dhabi-based major financial institution, agreed to establish a branch in China, a joint venture.[39]

China and the UAE signed a currency swap on January 17, 2012, the second of its kind since 2007. The purpose was to make visible the presence of the yuan in the international financial market to motivate the International Monetary Fund to include it in its international currency basket. In other forms of financial cooperation, the "UAE Central Bank is considering holding some of its currency assets in Chinese Yuan, which would make it the first central bank to do so in a dollar-dominated region."[40]

In terms of banking and finance, China and the UAE held the first China-UAE Conference on Islamic Banking and Finance under the theme "Islamic

Banking and Finance Perspectives, Challenges and Sustainable Impact" on May 30, 2016. Experts in banking and finance gathered to discuss current emerging trends and challenges in the industry today as well as tackle joint collaborative opportunities to globally promote Islamic economics.[41]

MILITARY/SECURITY RELATIONS

Sino-Emirati military relations are good. Their military-security relationship is evidenced by high-level, official visits and exchanges, PLAN ship visits to the UAE, and the UAE's observer participation in the joint military exercise AMAN sponsored by Pakistan in 2007, 2009, 2011, and 2013. China and the UAE have engaged each other no less than twelve times since 2002 according to the Ministry of National Defense of the People's Republic of China, *PLA Daily*, *Xinhua*, and *China Military Online*. China and the UAE have also assigned defense attachés at their respective embassies in Abu Dhabi and Beijing.[42]

China has been a very minor arms supplier to the UAE in early 1990s providing twenty Type-59–1 130mm towed guns according SIPRI Arms Transfers Database. China's total arms sales to the UAE are $25.82 million based on the 2016 CPI index. The United States, the United Kingdom, and France are the UAE's main weapons suppliers.[43]

The UAE has expressed an interest in purchasing military weapons and equipment from China even though most of its vendors are Western. China has been proactive in showcasing its military arms and equipment portfolio to the UAE at international defense exhibitions like the 1993 International Defense Exhibition, 2011 Gulf Defense and Aerospace Expo, and the 2013 Dubai Airshow. Chinese defense manufacturers are expected to attend the 2015 Dubai Airshow to market their training and fighter aircraft brands like the L-15 Falcon, J-10, J-12, and J-17.[44]

China and the UAE signed a defense and cooperation pact in 2008 to strengthen military-security cooperation. Their security partnership provides for services to Chinese warships patrolling the Horn of Africa and the Indian Ocean for the purpose of protecting freighters from Somali pirates.[45]

Territorial integrity and combating international terrorism are two important aspects of their military-security cooperation. The UAE supports China's One-China Principle but needs Chinese support for its sovereignty over the Three Islands, Lesser Tunab, Greater Tunab, and Abu Musa, which have been occupied by Iran since 1971. While public reassurances have been made by China to the UAE as recently as 2012, there was no mention of the Three Islands; however, both China and the UAE agree about combating international terrorism. China needs the UAE's support as well as other

Arab countries with respect to growing security threat of the East Turkestan Islamic Movement. The movement is considered a threat to China's stability, security, and economic development.[46]

CULTURAL RELATIONS

Bilateral cooperation has occurred in aviation, education, culture, public health, sports, tourism, and jurisprudence. China and the UAE have also inked agreements and protocols to foster cultural cooperation and exchanges. These include: Sino-Sharjah Bilateral Aviation Agreement (1980); Sino-UAE Agreement on Cultural Cooperation (1989); Sino-UAE Agreement on Civil Air Transportation (1989); Agreement on Medical and Health Technical Cooperation Between the Ministries of Health of China and the United Arab Emirates (1992); Protocol on China's Sending Doctors to the United Arab Emirates (1992); Protocol on China's Further Sending Nurses to the United Arab Emirates (1992); Sino-UAE Agreement on Information and Cultural Cooperation (2001); Sino-UAE Agreement on Judiciary Extradition (May 2002); Memorandum of Understanding on the Implementation Plan of Chinese Tourist Groups to the UAE (April 9, 2007); Sino-UAE Treaty on Extradition (April 14, 2011); Sino-UAE Treaty on Criminal Judicial Assistance (May 14, 2011); and Sino-UAE Memorandum of Understanding on the Framework for Collaboration in the Studies and Development in Space Science and the Peaceful Exploration of Outer Space (December 2015).[47]

The mainstay of China and the UAE's cultural cooperation are in sports, media, public health, tourism, aviation, space, and higher education.

Bilateral cultural cooperation began in 1975 with the exchange of sports delegations. Cultural ties expanded to include a wide range of areas including the inking of numerous agreements and protocols. The agreements and protocols provided for further cooperation in media and journalism, public health, aviation, tourism, and higher education. In terms of media and journalism cooperation, China established the branch of Xinhua News Agency and offices for People's Daily and Economic Daily in the UAE in 2001. Moreover, Chinese medical personnel have traveled to the UAE in the 1980s and 1990s. Presently, China has more than sixty nurses in the UAE and has established Chinese Medical Centers in Abu Dhabi, Sharjah, Al Ain, and Ajman.[48]

People-to-people exchanges have been fruitful. At least eighty million Chinese have visited the UAE. Both countries are working diligently to attract tourists to their countries. The Abu Dhabi Tourism Authority opened an office in Beijing and an increasing number of Chinese tourists visited the UAE. Conversely, the UAE participated in the 2010 Shanghai World Expo through its national pavilion display, thereby attracting thousands of guests. The national pavilion of the UAE at the Shanghai World Expo was quite popular and received over 1.8 million visitors.[49]

China and the UAE also have opened the doors of their colleges and universities to students interested in higher education. China enticed Emirati students to study science and technology through government scholarships. Conversely, Chinese students were encouraged to study the Arab language and history at the UAE's most prominent universities. China also used the UAE's universities to promote Chinese culture through the Confucius Institutes. China has established Confucius Institutes at the University of Dubai and at Zayed University.[50]

In terms of aviation cooperation, the UAE's two main carriers, Emirates (Dubai) and Etihad (Abu Dhabi), operate regular flights to China's major cities. These airlines serve China's growing business community in the UAE and tourists.[51]

Finally, in terms of space cooperation, the UAE Space Agency and China National Space Agency will represent the two countries in exchanging information, studies and scientific data in the field of space exploration and peaceful exploitation. The data exchange will include scientific and research expertise, as well as training, capacity building, lectures, conferences, and other space-related domains. Bilateral collaboration is expected to occur in research and development of satellites for scientific, testing, remote sensing, and communications purposes. The collaboration will include services such as launching, follow up, control, as well as developing and controlling ground satellite systems.[52]

ENERGY/PETROLEUM RELATIONS

Crude petroleum and petroleum gas product trading establishes the foundation for the Sino-Emirati trade relationship. The UAE is a significant petroleum supplier to China in terms of oil and gas. The UAE is also the world's eighth largest oil producer and fifth largest net oil exporter. Moreover, the UAE ranks seventh worldwide in proven oil and natural gas reserves. For these reasons, the UAE is strategically important.[53]

In terms of crude oil trade volume, China imported 2 to 4 percent of its crude petroleum from the UAE between 2006 and 2015 inclusive according to United Nations Commodity Trade Statistics Database. In terms of total trade value, crude petroleum imports ranged from 53 to 73 percent for the same years. Table 13.2 shows Chinese crude oil imports from the UAE in thousands of barrels per day, oil imports share, world ranking, trade value, total commodity trade value, and percentage from 2006 to 2015. See Table 13.2.

Table 13.2 Chinese Crude Petroleum Imports from the UAE

Year	KBPD	Oil Imports Share (%)	World Ranking	Crude Oil Trade Value ($)	Total Commodity Trade Value ($)	Percentage (%)
2006	61	2	12	1,468,466,850	2,796,745,203	53
2007	73	2	10	1,880,432,006	3,012,026,771	62
2008	92	3	10	3,355,750,233	4,613,250,116	73
2009	66	2	14	1,526,864,974	2,595,229,265	59
2010	106	2	13	3,109,351,110	4,451,552,488	70
2011	135	3	11	5,518,694,070	8,306,605,795	66
2012	176	3	10	7,479,299,061	10,851,923,958	69
2013	206	4	9	8,367,314,981	12,823,525,641	65
2014	234	4	8	9,088,433,658	15,762,862,757	58
2015	252	4	10	5,129,798,576	11,531,800,805	44

Source: United Nations Commodity Trade Statistics Database.

Table 13.3 Chinese Petroleum Gas Product Imports from the UAE

Year	Volume (MMcf)	Global Share (%)	World Ranking	Petroleum Gas Trade Value ($)	Total Commodity Trade Value ($)	Percentage (%)
2006	40.6	16	2	528,444,723	2,796,745,203	19
2007	24.6	9	5	359,974,917	3,012,026,771	12
2008	22.1	9	2	417,750,657	4,613,250,116	9
2009	24.9	6	5	288,608,307	2,595,229,265	11
2010	19.4	3	8	314,343,975	4,451,552,488	7
2011	26.1	2	9	548,855,273	8,306,605,795	7
2012	33.8	2	6	768,838,984	10,851,923,958	7
2013	45.0	3	8	1,006,950,639	12,823,525,641	8
2014	151.2	7	4	3,112,579,260	15,762,862,757	20
2015	212.4	9	4	2,519,453,985	11,531,800,805	22

Source: United Nations Commodity Trade Statistics Database.

China has imported petroleum gas products from the UAE. Table 13.3 illustrates China's petroleum gas imports from the UAE in millions of cubic feet, global imports share, world ranking, trade value, total commodity trade value and percentage from 2006 to 2015. See Table 13.3. The UAE is one of China's top five petroleum gas product suppliers.

China has imported liquefied natural gas (LNG) on a very limited basis. In 2010, it imported 3MMcf or 1 percent of its total LNG imports. The UAE was its eighth largest supplier of LNG in the same year.

China and the UAE have also concluded the following deals to develop the UAE's energy infrastructure: a $3.29 billion Energy Contract between CNPC's China Petroleum Engineering & Construction Corporation and

International Petroleum Investment Company for the Abu Dhabi Crude Oil Pipeline project (December 2008); a $330 million contract between CNPC's China Petroleum Engineering & Construction Corporation and Abu Dhabi for Offshore Oil Operations (ADCO) to develop the Mender oilfield (May 2015); and Hassyan Energy Company awarded a $690 million EPC contract to Harbin Electric International and General Electric (GE) to develop the Hassyan Coal Plant to produce 2,400 megawatts of electricity (April 2016).[54]

China and the UAE cooperate in oil and gas exploration, pipeline construction, building oil rigs, and renewable energy sources in addition to oil trading.[55]

In terms of oil and gas exploration, CNPC and the Abu Dhabi National Oil Company (ADNOC) have a signed a strategic partnership agreement whereby CNPC was granted concessions to explore four undeveloped blocks on the Western Abu Dhabi Emirate. The goal of partnering with CNPC is a 70 percent recovery rate, which is double the average rate in similar oil fields.[56] CNPC has been successful with the project.

In terms of pipeline construction and oil rig construction and supply, Baoji Oil Machinery, a subsidiary of CNPC, won a bid to supply the UAE with oil rigs for onshore drilling in 2009. CNPC also finished the construction of the Abu Dhabi-Fujairah pipeline in 2012. The pipeline is strategic in nature because it bypasses the Hormuz Straits, a chokepoint at the mouth of the Arabian Gulf. The oil pipeline runs approximately 230 miles from Habshan, the UAE's largest oil field to Fujairah, on the Gulf of Oman with a capacity of 1.5 mbpd. The oil pipeline provides the UAE with the needed economic security in the Gulf region considering Iranian security threats.[57]

The success of the Fujairah oil pipeline paved the way for negotiations between PetroChina and the Fujairah Government (one of seven emirates) to construct a 1 million cubic meter oil storage container. This is an ideal location strategically because it frees the region from the tension of exporting oil through the Hormuz Strait, as well as providing for the freedom of ocean bound navigation across the Indian Ocean free of security threats. Additionally, the peaceful nature of the Gulf of Oman makes the Port of Fujairah into one of the most attractive storage ports in the Near East and the Gulf Region.[58]

Bilateral energy cooperation extends to the training of personnel and sharing of exploration technology. CNPC and ADNOC signed an agreement in which both corporations would train each other personnel. CNPC also pledged to share its exploration technology with ADNOC. This includes the most advanced technology globally: Enhanced Oil Recovery Technology (EORT). This technology enabled CNPC to double its recovery of oil in Iran and Iraq.[59]

An area of potential energy cooperation is oil recovery and rehabilitation. CNPC has expertise in this area which the Emirate of Dubai needs. Dubai's oil production had deteriorated from 410 kbpd in 1991 to 70 bpd in 2012, forcing the Emirate of Dubai to import oil from Abu Dhabi rather than exporting it. CNPC has already undertaken an evaluation of seven undeveloped blocks in the west of Abu Dhabi in accordance with the 2013 CNPC-ADNOC Strategic Cooperation Agreement. Abu Dhabi's Supreme Petroleum Council (ADSPC) is seriously considering granting CNPC concessions to develop Abu Dhabi's oil and gas resources and restore Dubai as an oil-producing emirate. CNPC has promise as an oil company as it has gained an unprecedented level of expertise and efficiency in oil upstreaming, downstreaming, refining, and global marketing.[60]

China and the UAE also cooperate on green energy. China is providing the UAE with solar and wind energy technology. To facilitate this technology, the UAE established the Masdar City, a sustainable project where solar energy is utilized to power the city and the Abu Dhabi International Airport. The UAE also hosted the World's Future Energy Summit since 2008, to attract leaders and leading corporations in sustainable and renewable energy sources, especially wind and solar energy.[61]

The UAE is also seeking to use nuclear energy to produce electricity to meet the increasing needs of the country including the city of Abu Dhabi. The UAE's increasing demand for electricity is supported by the desalination plants in its coastal areas. The UAE has consulted and signed contracts with several nuclear corporations from China and other countries with expertise in reactor design, operation, fuel supply and monitoring. The idea is to have a fully functional nuclear reactor operating by 2017.[62]

SUMMARY

Sino-Emirati relations are strategic. Sino-Emirati relations are strong today but ties were established rather late in comparison to other Arab nations. Nevertheless, China and the UAE are engaged diplomatically, economically, militarily, and culturally. China is also considered a major trading partner of the UAE. The UAE is the largest market for Chinese-made products in the GCC as well as China's second-largest trade partner in the GCC.[63] This is evidenced by the astronomical growth in bilateral trade in twenty-first century, and the phenomenal success of the Dragon Mart in Abu Dhabi, which serves as a hub to Chinese corporations not only in the Gulf region, but also the entire Near East, Central Asia, Europe, and Sub-Saharan Africa.[64]

In terms of petroleum relations, the UAE is a significant supplier of crude petroleum and petroleum gas products. The UAE is one of China's top ten suppliers of both commodities making it a valuable trading partner of petroleum products. Sino-Emirati energy cooperation is significant in the hydrocarbon sector but it extends to renewable and nuclear energy cooperation.

NOTES

1. Geoffrey Kemp, *The East Moves West: India, China, and Asia's Growing Presence in the Middle East* (Washington, DC: Brookings Institution Press), 2010, 86.
2. Muhamad S. Olimat, *China and the Middle East Since World War II* (Lanham, MD: Lexington Books), 2014, 245.
3. Ibid.
4. Ibid., 196, 197.
5. Ibid., 246.
6. Ibid., 248.
7. Ministry of Foreign Affairs of People's Republic of China, "China–United Arab Emirates," 08/22/2011, accessed October 8, 2013, http://www.fmprc.gov.cn/eng/wjb/zzjg/xybfs/gjlb/2903/.
8. Ministry of Foreign Affairs of People's Republic of China, "China–United Arab Emirates: Activities," (n.d.), accessed August 9, 2016, http://www.fmprc.gov.cn/mfa_eng/wjb_663304/zzjg_663340/xybfs_663590/gjlb_663594/2903_663806/2905_663810/.
9. Ibid.
10. Ministry of Foreign Affairs of People's Republic of China, "Joint Communiqué on the Establishment of Diplomatic Relations Between the People's Republics of China and the United Arab Emirates," November 1, 1984, accessed October 11, 2014, http://www.fmprc.gov.cn/mfa_eng/wjb_663304/zzjg_663340/xybfs_663590/gjlb_663594/2903_663806/2904_663808/t16458.shtml.
11. Ministry of Foreign Affairs of People's Republic of China, "Li Zhaoxing Holds Talks with UAE Foreign Minister," April 9, 2007, accessed August 16, 2016, http://www.fmprc.gov.cn/mfa_eng/wjb_663304/zzjg_663340/xybfs_663590/gjlb_663594/2903_663806/2905_663810/t310396.shtml.
12. Ministry of Foreign Affairs of People's Republic of China, "List of Agreements on Mutual Visa Exemption Between the People's Republic of China and Foreign Countries" November 28, 2004, accessed November 7, 2014, http://cs.mfa.gov.cn/wgrlh/bgzl/P020140328398504621618.pdf.
13. Dawn Murphy, "China and the Middle East," testimony, June 6, 2013, before U.S.–China Economic and Security Review Commission.
14. Kemp, ibid., 87.
15. Olimat, ibid., 249.
16. European Commission Directorate-General for Trade, "United Arab Emirates: EU Bilateral Trade and Trade with the World," April 10, 2015, accessed May 3, 2015, http://trade.ec.europa.eu/doclib/docs/2006/september/tradoc_113458.pdf.
17. United Nations, United Nations Commodity Trade Statistics Database, accessed August 22, 2015, http://comtrade.un.org/db/default.aspx.

18. Ibid.

19. United Nations Conference on Trade and Development (UNCTAD FDI/TNC) Database, *Bilateral FDI Statistics 2014*, accessed October 11, 2014, http://unctad.org/Sections/dite_fdistat/docs/webdiaeia2014d3_CHN.pdf.

20. Olimat, ibid., 248.

21. United Nations, United Nations Commodity Trade Statistics Database, accessed July 22, 2016, ibid.

22. Olimat, ibid., 251.

23. Embassy of the People's Republic of China in the United Arab Emirates, "China and the United Arab Emirates," (n.d.), accessed October 11, 2014, http://ae.china-embassy.org/eng/sbgx/t150466.htm.

24. Wolfgang Bartke, *The Agreements of the People's Republic of China with Foreign Countries 1949–1990* (Munchen, Germany: K.G. Saur), 1992, 193.

25. Olimat, ibid., 248.

26. Ibid.

27. Embassy of the People's Republic of China in the United Arab Emirates, "China and the United Arab Emirates," ibid.

28. Ibid.

29. Olimat, ibid., 249.

30. Ministry of Foreign Affairs of People's Republic of China, "Xi Jinping Meets with Crown Prince Sheikh Mohammed Bin Zayed Al-Nahyan of Abu Dhabi Emirate of the UAE," December 14, 2015, accessed August 16, 2016, http://www.fmprc.gov.cn/mfa_eng/wjb_663304/zzjg_663340/xybfs_663590/gjlb_663594/2903_663806/2905_663810/t1324821.shtml.

31. Embassy of the People's Republic of China in the United Arab Emirates, "China and the United Arab Emirates," ibid.

32. Olimat, ibid., 248.

33. Ibid.

34. Olimat, ibid., 249; The Heritage Foundation and American Enterprise Institute, *China Global Investment Tracker Database*, accessed October 11, 2014, http://www.heritage.org/research/projects/china-global-investment-tracker-interactive-map; Mahmoud Habboush, "Cosco Shipping Signs $738 Million Deal to Expand U.A.E. Port," *Bloomberg*, September 28, 2016, accessed October 5, 2016, http://www.bloomberg.com/news/articles/2016-09-28/cosco-shipping-signs-738-million-deal-to-expand-u-a-e-port.

35. The Heritage Foundation and American Enterprise Institute, ibid.; and Olimat, ibid., 249, 250.

36. Ibid.

37. Y. Aweti and A. Rodgers, "China—Doing Business with the UAE," *Zawya*, July 31, 2013, accessed October 10, 2014, http://www.zawya.com/story/China__Doing_business_with_the_UAE-ZAWYA20130812055249/.

38. M. Mcilhone, "China—Doing Business with the UAE," *Arabbrains*, August 13, 2013, accessed October 11, 2014, http://arabbrains.com/2013/08/13/china-doing-business-with-the-uae/.

39. Olimat, ibid., 251.

40. Ibid.

41. Hamdan Bin Mohammed Smart University, "First China-UAE Conference on Islamic Banking & Finance concludes with Positive Outlook for Future of Islamic Economy," May 30, 2016, accessed August 16, 2016, https://www.hbmsu.ac.ae/news/first-china-uae-conference-on-islamic-banking-finance-concludes-positive-outlook-for-future-of.

42. United States Department of Defense, Defense Intelligence Agency, *Directory of PRC Military Personalities* (Washington, DC), 2014, 21.

43. Stockholm International Peace Research Institute, SIPRI Arms Transfers Database, http://www.sipri.org/databases/armstransfers; and Olimat, ibid., 257.

44. Ibid., 256, 257.

45. Ibid.

46. Ibid., 256–257, 258.

47. Embassy of the People's Republic of China in the United Arab Emirates, "China and the United Arab Emirates," Ibid.; Ministry of Foreign Affairs of People's Republic of China, "Li Zhaoxing Holds Talks with UAE Foreign Minister," Ibid.; Ministry of Foreign Affairs of People's Republic of China, "Assistant Foreign Minister Liu Zhenmin Meets UAE Ambassador to China and the Two Sides Exchange the Instruments of Ratification of the Treaty between China and UAE on Criminal Judicial Assistance," April 14, 2011, accessed August 16, 2016, http://www.fmprc.gov.cn/mfa_eng/wjb_663304/zzjg_663340/xybfs_663590/gjlb_663594/2903_663806/2905_663810/t816038.shtml; and "UAE signs an MOU with People's Republic of China for Cooperation in Space Science," *Zawya*, December 28, 2015, accessed August 5, 2016, https://www.zawya.com/story/UAE_signs_MoU_with_China_for_cooperation_in_space_science-ZAWYA20151228061816/.

48. Embassy of the People's Republic of China in the United Arab Emirates, "China and the United Arab Emirates," ibid; and Olimat, ibid., 255.

49. Ministry of Foreign Affairs of People's Republic of China, "China and United Arab Emirates," (n.d.), accessed October 7, 2014, http://www.fmprc.gov.cn/mfa_eng/wjb_663304/zzjg_663340/xybfs_663590/gjlb_663594/2903_663806/; and Olimat, ibid., 255–256.

50. Confucius Institute Online, Worldwide Confucius Institutes, "United Arab Emirates," accessed October 7, 2014, http://www.chinesecio.com/m/cio_wci; and Olimat, ibid., 256.

51. Olimat, ibid., 256.

52. "UAE signs an MOU with People's Republic of China for Cooperation in Space Science," ibid.

53. Olimat, ibid., 251, 252.

54. Anthony McAuley, "China State Oil Company win Abu Dhabi Oilfield Contract," *The National Business*, May 18, 2015, accessed August 16, 2016, http://www.thenational.ae/business/energy/china-state-oil-company-wins-abu-dhabi-oilfield-contract; and The Heritage Foundation and American Enterprise Institute, ibid.

55. Olimat, ibid., 252.

56. Ibid.

57. Ibid., 252–253.

58. Ibid.

59. Ibid.
60. Ibid., 254.
61. Ibid.
62. Ibid., 254, 255.
63. "Dubai International Convention Centre Hosts Showcase of Chinese Building Wares," *Arabian Industry*, May 13, 2013, accessed October 11, 2014, http://arabian-industry.com/construction/news/2013/may/13/dubai-international-convention-centre-hosts-showcase-of-chinese-building-wares-4307225/.
64. Olimat, ibid., 249.

Chapter 14

China and Venezuela
Political/Diplomatic Relations

Sino-Venezuelan diplomatic relations were established on June 28, 1974. To establish diplomatic ties, China and Venezuela issued the Joint Communiqué Between the Government of the People's Republic of China and the Government of the Bolivarian Republic of Venezuela on the Establishment of Diplomatic Relations (1974).[1] The Joint Communiqué stipulated that the Venezuela recognized the One-China policy and that Taiwan is an alienable part of China's territory.

From 1949 and 1974, China and Venezuela did not have diplomatic relations because Venezuelan government recognized the Chinese National (*Kuomintang*) government in Taiwan. Contacts were limited to cultural interactions in the form of people-to-people exchanges. To this end, China sent sixteen delegates to Latin America and Venezuela sent twenty-five delegates to China between 1950 and 1959.[2]

Sino-Venezuelan diplomatic relations have developed smoothly since 1974 and were characterized by frequent high-level official visits, a steady expansion of trade and economic cooperation, and increasing exchanges in fields of culture, education, and science and technology. In terms of official high-level visits and exchanges, China and Venezuela interacted no less than five times between 1974 and 2000. The most important bilateral visits include: President Luis Herrera Campins and Paramount Leader Deng Xiaoping (October 1981), President Jaime Lusinchi and Premier Zhao Ziyang (November 1985), President Rafael Caldera and Premier Li Peng (November 1996), President Hugo Chavez and President Jiang Zemin (October 1999) and President Hugo Chavez and Premier Li Ruihuan (May 2000). The results of this bilateral visits paved the way for stronger overall bilateral relations in the twenty-first century, in terms of bilateral cooperation in the fields of diplomacy, trade, culture, agriculture, animal husbandry, fishery, energy, petroleum prospecting, sports, and science and technology. No less than fourteen agreements were signed in these areas.³

Since 2000, the levels of political dialogue, consultations and agreements, and diplomacy have risen to new heights due to numerous high-level official visits.⁴ In this respect, China and Venezuela interacted through official, high-level visits and exchanges no less than fifty-five times.⁵ The most important bilateral exchanges include: President Hugo Chavez and President Jiang Zemin (April 2001 and May 2001), President Hugo Chavez and President Hu Jintao (December 2004, August 2006, September 2008, and April 2009), and President Nicholas Maduro and President Xi Jinping (April 2013, July 2014, and September 2015).⁶

The results of these high-level visits have been extraordinary as evidenced by an unprecedented increase in bilateral trade and cooperation.⁷ Approximately 460 bilateral agreements have been signed to date, of which 98 percent were finalized during Hugo Chavez's presidency.⁸ Included in these agreements are 160 projects in virtually every field of cooperation.⁹ These fields include agriculture, energy, planning, science and technology, telecommunications, mining, industries, manufacturing, infrastructure, aerospace and homebuilding.¹⁰ Given the high level of cooperation between the two countries, their relationship could be characterized as strategic in nature. China and Venezuela enhanced their relationship to one of a "strategic partnership for common development" in 2001.¹¹ China's motivation for enhanced relations with Venezuela is pragmatic and economically driven, but initially seen as a political aim: international support for its One-China policy.¹² Venezuela sees enhanced relations with China as a means to counterweigh the traditional U.S. dominance in Latin America, as well as a bargaining chip for participation in multilateral organizations.¹³

Since Venezuelan president Nicolas Maduro has taken office in April 2013, more than twelve new bilateral agreements have been signed in the fields of energy, construction, science, and technology. In terms of significant bilateral agreements negotiated, China's Sinopec agreed to invest $14 billion in Venezuela's Orinoco Oil Belt to produce oil jointly with Venezuela's state-owned oil company, Petróleos de Venezuela, S.A. (PDVSA). China Development Bank also agreed to provide $5 billion for social reform and $700 million to develop Venezuela's mining sector in return for oil. Lastly, China's Export-Import Bank agreed to finance the development of a port for Pequiven, Petrochemical Company of Venezuela for $391 million.¹⁴

China and Venezuela also signed numerous agreements to promote political-diplomatic cooperation. These include the following: Agreement on Mutual Exemption of Entry Visas between the People's Republic of China and the Government of Venezuela on Holders of Diplomatic and Service

Passports (July 13, 1989);[15] Memorandum of Understanding on Consultative Mechanism between Foreign Ministry of the People's Republic of China and Foreign Ministry of the Republic of Venezuela (October 21, 1991);[16] Agreement on Retention of Venezuelan Consulate General in Hong Kong Special Administrative Region of the People's Republic of China between the Government of the People's Republic of China and the Government of the Republic of Venezuela (November 13, 1996);[17] Exchange of Notes on the Expansion of the Consular District of the Venezuelan Consulate General in Hong Kong to Macao (October 1999);[18] Agreement on providing Convenience in Visa Processing for Government Staff to implement a Plan of Action (January 30, 2005);[19] Agreement between the Government of the People's Republic of China and the Government of the Bolivarian Republic of Venezuela on Mutual Visa Exemption for Holders of Diplomatic, Service Passports and Passports for Public Affairs (September 23, 2013);[20] Agreement on Mutual Exemption of Entry Visas between the People's Republic of China and the Government of Venezuela on Holders of Public Affairs Passports (January 8, 2014);[21] and Joint Statement on Establishing Comprehensive Strategic Partnership between the People's Republic of China and the Bolivarian Republic of Venezuela (July 22, 2014).[22]

Both countries have established diplomatic representation through embassies in their respective capitals in Beijing and Caracas in 1974 in addition to finalizing numerous agreements of political cooperation. Venezuela established a Consulates-General in Shanghai and Hong Kong.[23]

ECONOMIC/TRADE RELATIONS

Sino-Venezuelan economic relations are very robust. Bilateral trade has increased from $350 million to $23 billion between 2000 and 2012.[24] Venezuela was China's twenty-sixth-largest trading partner accounting for less than 1 percent of China's global trade in 2012.[25] Moreover, China was Venezuela's second-largest trading partner accounting for 15 percent of Venezuela's global trade in 2012.[26] In 2014, China was also Venezuela's second-largest trading partner.[27] Venezuela was China's largest trading partner in South America after Brazil and Chile and thirty-seventh in the same year.[28] Bilateral trade was: $9.9 billion (2008), $7.1 billion (2009), $10.3 billion (2010), $18.2 billion (2011), $23.8 billion (2012), $19.1 billion (2013), $16.9 billion (2014), and $12.2 billion (2015).[29] Since 2000, bilateral trade increased almost thirty-five-fold. In 2012, foreign direct investment into Venezuela from China was $1.542 billion and foreign direct investment stock was $2.043 billion.[30] China's foreign direct investment in Venezuela has been $44.5 billion since 2005.[31]

Table 14.1 shows the top five commodities traded between China and Venezuela in 2015. Energy commodities, such as crude petroleum and petroleum products, appear to be the most traded commodity between the two countries with a commodity trade value of 96 percent. The next top two commodities, ores, slag and ash, and iron and steel have commodity trade value of 4 percent and less than 1 percent, respectively. See Table 14.1. While bilateral trading has been strong, Venezuela has initiated nine anti-dumping investigations and eleven anti-dumping measures against China since the 1995.[32]

China's energy commodities accounted for the following in terms of trade value in previous years: 88 percent (2008), 86 percent (2009), 84 percent (2010), 90 percent (2011), 94 percent (2012), 96 percent (2013), and 97 percent (2014).[33]

Bilateral trade is promoted through several organizations such as Venezuelan Association of Exporters, Foreign Trade Bank, Venezuelan Confederation of Industries, CAF Development Bank of Argentina, Venezuelan Federation of Chambers of Commerce and Production, Venezuelan Ministry of Popular Power for Light Industries and Commerce, Venezuelan Bureau of Foreign Affairs and Trade of the State of Sucre, the PRC Ministry of Commerce, the PRC Ministry of Foreign Affairs, and the All-China Federation of Industry and Commerce.[34]

Table 14.1 Top Five Commodities Traded between China and Venezuela

Commodity	Importer	Trade Value ($)	Percentage (%)
Mineral fuels, mineral oils and products of their distillation; bituminous substances; mineral waxes	China	6,585,413,350	96
Ores, slag and ash	China	282,115,782	4
Iron and steel	China	12,579,218	<1
Plastics and articles thereof	China	3,027,703	<1
Raw hides and skins (other than furskins) and leather	China	2,960,701	<1
Nuclear reactors, boilers, machinery and mechanical appliances; parts thereof	Venezuela	1,231,392,142	23
Vehicles other than railway or tramway rolling-stock, and parts and accessories thereof	Venezuela	1,010,011,824	19
Electrical machinery and equipment and parts thereof; sound recorders and reproducers, television image and sound recorders and reproducers, and parts and accessories of such articles	Venezuela	922,011,074	17
Articles of iron or steel	Venezuela	327,833,813	6
Iron and steel	Venezuela	317,359,520	6

Source: United Nations Commodity Trade Statistics Database.

China and Venezuela has inked some important agreements to promote economic and trade cooperation between their countries. The most notable agreements and notes include: Minutes of Trade Talks (November 19, 1972);[35] Trade Agreement between the Government of the People's Republic of China and the Government of the Republic of Venezuela (July 16, 1973);[36] Trade Agreement between the Government of the People's Republic of China and the Government of the Republic of Venezuela (November 12, 1985);[37] Memorandum of Understanding on concluding Mutual Investment Protection (October 1999);[38] Memorandum of Understanding on the provision of $30 million of Credit Loans to Venezuela by the Bank of China (October 1999);[39] Agreement on Economic and Technological Cooperation between the Government of the People's Republic of China and the Government of the Republic of Venezuela (September 23, 2000);[40] Memorandum of Understanding on Establishing Sino-Venezuelan Senior Mixed Committee between China and Venezuela (April 17, 2001);[41] Agreement on Avoiding Double Taxation on Income and Property and Preventing Taxes Evasion between the People's Republic of China and the Republic of Venezuela (April 17, 2001);[42] Framework Agreement on China Providing Preferential Loan to Venezuela (April 17, 2001);[43] Statutes of the Senior Mixed Committee between the Government of the People's Republic of China and the Government of the Republic of Venezuela (May 24, 2001);[44] Minutes on the Third Meeting of the High-Level Joint Committee of the Two Governments recognizing China's Full Market Economy Status (December 23, 2004);[45] Agreement of Economic and Technological Cooperation (December 24, 2004);[46] Agreement on Infrastructure Construction (December 24, 2004);[47] Memorandum of Understanding on further enhancing the Work of China-Venezuela High-Level Committee (January 30, 2005);[48] Letter of Intent on Investment and Cooperation on the Agricultural Special Economic Zone Development in the Cumana Island (January 30, 2005);[49] Memorandum of Understanding on Maritime Shipping Agency Business (January 30, 2005);[50] Letter of Intent on Investment in developing a National Telecommunications Network (January 30, 2005);[51] Memorandum of Understanding on the Economy (January 30, 2005);[52] Long-Term Finance Cooperation Agreement between the China Development Bank, the China National Petroleum Corporation and the Government of Venezuela (2010);[53] Minutes of the 12th High-Level Joint Commission Between the Government of the People's Republic of China and the Government of the Bolivarian Republic of Venezuela (September 23, 2013);[54] Third Protocol of the Amendment of the Agreement between the Government of the People's Republic of China and the Government of the Bolivarian Republic of Venezuela on the Joint Finance Fund (September 23, 2013);[55] and Agreement on Section C of the China-Venezuela Joint Finance Fund (September 23, 2013).[56]

China has been actively involved in Venezuela's economic development which includes financial aid, infrastructure, and investment especially in the twenty-first century. In this respect, some of the largest and most recent infrastructure and development projects include: Sinomach agreed to supply Venezuela with $140 million in agricultural machinery (July 2008);[57] Zhongxing Technologies Energy (ZTE) and Venezuela's Movilnet form a joint venture to build a $19.5 million cell-phone manufacturing factory (February 2009);[58] Huawei and Venezuela agreed to construct a second cell-phone manufacturing factory in Miranda (May 2009);[59] Venezuela awarded China Railway Engineering Corporation a $7.5 billion project to construct a 290-mile railroad linking from the north coast of Venezuela to the mining region in the interior of the country (July 2009);[60] Sinomach agreed to supply Venezuela with $310 million in agricultural machinery (December 2009);[61] China Gezhouba Group Corporation won a $290 million contract for an irrigation project (December 2010);[62] China Construction Corporation was awarded a $161 million contract to dredge the Orinoco River (2011);[63] Metallurgical Corporation of China (MCC) was awarded a $200 million contract to expand the Port of Palua (2011);[64] Chevy Automobile Corporation agreed to build a $200 million automobile factory (May 2011);[65] China Harbor Engineering Company (CHEC) and Bolivarian Ports agreed to construct a $260 million container terminal (October 2011);[66] CHEC and Petroquimica de Venezuela signed an agreed to expand the Moron petrochemical complex for $460 million (November 2011);[67] China Railway Group and C.V.G. Ferromineria Orinoco CA signed a five-year, $414 million iron ore mining contract (June 2012);[68] Power Construction Corporation and Camargo Correa Company implemented a $480 million joint venture to construct 12.4 miles of the Santa Lucia-Kempis highway (February 2014);[69] and China Aluminum International Engineering Corporation Limited (CHALIECO) and aluminum producer C.V.G. Venalum signed a $498 million engineering, procurement, and construction (EPC) contract to to recover the capacities of 720 aluminum cells, remold five values, and four electrolytic series rectifiers (April 2014).[70]

China and Venezuela have also cooperated in banking. Major Chinese banks have established a physical presence in Venezuela in support of major deals between the two countries. These include: ICBC, CDB, and Export-Import Bank of China (EXIM). To date, more than $45 billion has been loaned to Venezuelan government in support of various projects.[71]

MILITARY/SECURITY RELATIONS

Sino-Venezuelan military relations are good. Bilateral military cooperation includes military and defense-related educational exchanges, frequent official visits by senior defense leaders, joint special operations training, and security consultations.

Sino-Venezuelan military ties have existed since diplomatic relations were established in 1974.[72] Between 1981 and 2000, no less than twelve bilateral exchanges were conducted between senior military and defense officials of China and Venezuela.[73] Since 2002, China and Venezuela mainly engaged each other through bilateral visits. China and Venezuela have engaged each other no less than thirteen times according to the Ministry of National Defense of the People's Republic of China, *PLA Daily*, *Xinhua*, and *China Military Online*. These interactions include: two visits to the PRC by Venezuelan military officials, seven visits to Venezuela by Chinese military officials including the Vice Chairman of the Central Military Commission, one security consultation (China-Latin America Defense Forum), two joint military sessions including the International Army Games, and one educational exchange where Chinese Special Forces attended a Venezuelan military training school. Both China and Venezuela have also defense attachés assigned to their respective embassies in Beijing and Caracas.[74]

China has also modestly supplied Venezuela with military weapons and equipment. Table 14.2 summarizes the weapons and equipment transfers from China to Venezuela according to SIPRI. See Table 14.2. The dearth of transfers indicates China is a modest supplier of military arms and equipment. The United States has been Venezuela's top supplier of

Table 14.2 Chinese Conventional Weapons Transfers to Venezuela

Year(s) of Delivery	No. of Deliveries	Weapon Designation	Weapon Description
2006–2007	3	JYL-1 (S)	Air Search Radar
2008–2009	7	JYL-1 (S)	Air Search Radar
2010–2011	3	JY-11 (S)	Air Search Radar
2010	18	K-8 Karakorum-8 (S)	Trainer/Fighter Aircraft
2010	100	PL-5E (S)	Short-Range Air-to-Air Missile
2012–2014	8	Y-8 (S)	Transport Aircraft
TBD	TBD	AS565S Panther (S)	ASW Helicopter
2014–2015	18	SM-4 81mm (S)	Self-Propelled Mortar
2014–2015	18	SR-5 (S)	Self-Propelled Mobile Rocket Launcher
2014–2015	40	Type-07P/VN-1	Infantry Fighting Vehicle
2013–2015	121	VN-4	Armed Personnel Vehicle/Armored Personnel Carrier
2015	25	ZBD-05/VN-18 (S)	Infantry Fighting Vehicle
2015	25	ZTD-05/VN-16 (S)	Light Tank
TBD	TBD	K-8W Karakorum-8 (S)	Trainer/Fighter Aircraft
TBD	TBD	L-15	Trainer/Combat Aircraft

Source: SIPRI Arms Transfers Database.

military arms and equipment since 1950. After the United States, Russia, France, Italy, and the Netherlands are Venezuela's top arms suppliers. China's total arms sales to Venezuela are $1.1 billion based on the 2016 CPI index.[75]

Chinese weapons manufacturers provided equipment training to the Venezuela military given China supplied Venezuela with fighter aircraft, helicopters, and air search radars. In this respect, Venezuela sent eleven pilots and fifty-six technicians to China for aviation training as pilots and maintenance and logistics support staff in the second half of 2009. This is a standard practice when China has supplied aircraft, ships, artillery pieces and other military equipment to other countries. China also spearheaded the introduction of Chinese command and control equipment in Venezuela. China also funded a program at the Venezuelan military institute Universidad Nacional Experimental Politecnica de las Fuerzas Armadas, as well as the construction of a $54 million laboratory at the Venezuelan armed forces technical university.[76]

China and Venezuela signed agreements to cooperation in military and security matters such as student exchanges including the Agreement on Academic Cooperation between the Defense University of China and the Advanced Defense Research Institute of Venezuela (July 2002).[77]

CULTURAL RELATIONS

Bilateral cultural ties developed in tandem with diplomatic relations. Prior to the establishment of formal diplomatic ties in 1974, cultural ties were almost non-existent. Like many other Latin American countries, Cold War tensions precluded the establishment of formal political ties until after China was admitted into the United Nations in October 1971. Nevertheless, Cold War tensions did not prevent China and Venezuela from engaging each other in the fields of culture, journalism, and literature.

Early cultural interactions were manifested in the form of people-to-people exchanges between China and Latin America in the 1950s. Between 1950 and 1959 more than 1,200 Latin Americans from nineteen countries visited China while China successfully sent sixteen delegates of culture, economy, and trade to Latin America.[78] Of those who visited China, approximately twenty-five were Venezuelans.[79]

Since diplomatic relations were established, numerous agreements, memorandums of understanding, and notes were finalized between China and Venezuela. These include the following: Agreement to promote Sports Exchanges (September 29, 1981); Cultural Agreement between the Government of People's Republic of China and the Government of the Republic of

Venezuela to promote cooperation and exchanges in the Fields of Culture, the Arts, Education, Sports, the Press, Broadcasting, Film, and Television (November 1, 1981); Agreement on Science and Technological Cooperation between the Government of the People's Republic of China and the Government of the Republic of Venezuela (November 1, 1981); Implementation Plan of Cultural Exchange for 1985 to 1988 (November 12, 1985); Agreement on Scientific and Technological Cooperation in Geology and Mineral Resources between Ministry of Geology and Mineral Resources of the People's Republic of China and Ministry of Energy and Mining of the Republic of Venezuela (September 30, 1988); Cooperation Pact to expand Technical Cooperation for Geological and Mining Cooperation (September 28, 1990); Agreement on Cooperation in Agriculture, Animal Husbandry and Fishery between the Government of the People's Republic of China and the Government of the Republic of Venezuela (September 29, 1991); Program on Sports Cooperation between State Physical Culture and Sports Commission of the People's Republic of China and State Sports Commission of the Republic of Venezuela (September 9, 1998); Exchange of Notes of Extension of Agreement on Cooperation in Agriculture, Animal Husbandry, and Fishery between the Government of the People's Republic of China and the Government of the Republic of Venezuela (September 8, 1998); Agreement of Cooperation between Foreign Affairs College of China and Venezuelan Academy of Higher Research (October 1999); Framework Agreement on Cooperation between Nanjing University of China and Andes University (October 1999); Executive Plan of the Agreement on Cultural Cooperation between China and Venezuela for 2001–2003 (April 17, 2001); Memorandum of Understanding on Engineering and Technology Cooperation between Chinese Academy of Engineering and Venezuelan Ministry of Planning and Development (April 17, 2001); Agreement on Cooperation in Geology and Mineral Resources between Chinese Geology Survey Administration and Venezuelan National Geology and Mineral Resources Bureau (April 17, 2001); Memorandum of Understanding on Long-term Agricultural Cooperation between the Chinese Ministry of Agriculture and the Venezuelan Ministry of Industry and Trade (May 24, 2001); Letter of Intent on Cooperation in Science, Technology and Creation between Chinese and Venezuelan Ministries of Science and Technology (May 24, 2001); Memorandum of Understanding concerning Cooperation on Water Conservancy (October 2001); Memorandum of Understanding on Technical Cooperation in the Peaceful Utilization of Outer Space (January 30, 2005); Memorandum of Understanding on Social Housing Programs (January 30, 2005); Executive Program to the Cultural Cooperation Agreement for the period from 2014 to 2019 (September 23, 2013); Executive Plan for Educational Exchanges (September 23, 2013); Memorandum of Understanding for the development of Venezuela's Mining

Reserves (September 23, 2013); Framework Agreement to establish a State System of Public Safety and Emergency Management (September 23, 2013); and Agreement of Intent to Promote Agriculture in Venezuela (September 23, 2013).[80]

Based on the agreements, memorandums, and plans finalized between the two countries, Sino-Venezuelan cultural relations are extensive and include a wide variety of areas of cooperation including: the arts, music, film, photography, sports, education, and space technology.

Sino-Venezuelan cultural exchanges have been witnessed in the arts including music, film, dance, and photography. China has sent Beijing opera troupes, acrobatic troupes, martial arts teams and song and dance ensembles to Venezuela to give performances. Film weeks, exhibitions on photography, arts and crafts, traditional Chinese painting and pottery were also held in Venezuela. In return, Venezuela sent its chorus, dance ensembles, quartette group and music conductor to China. Moreover, a Venezuelan harpist came to perform in China on the twenty-fifth anniversary of the establishment of diplomatic relations in June 1999. On a large scale, the Shanghai World Expo featured the national pavilion of Venezuela. In 2013, China successfully held a series of "Happy Spring Festival" events. A Venezuelan delegation performed at the opening concert of the first Latin America Arts Season in China.[81]

In terms of educational exchanges and cooperation, China and Venezuela have mutually sent students to study in each other's country since 1976. To date, Venezuela has sent twenty-seven students to China while China sent four students to Venezuela.[82]

Sport exchanges between China and Venezuela has increased since the 1990s. A Venezuelan sports delegation, basketball team, football team, and table tennis team visited China successively and football coaches were invited to china for teaching. In September 1998, a program for cooperation in sports was signed between the Chinese State Physical Culture and Sports Commission and the Venezuelan State Sports Commission.[83]

China has also established a Confucius Institute in Venezuela at the Universidad Bolivariana de Venezuela.[84] Confucius Institutes promote Chinese culture and foster language training for Venezuelan students.

In terms of space technology, China sold Venezuela two satellite systems: the Venesat-1 telecommunications satellite, which was launched in October 2008, and the Venezuela Remote Sensing Satellite (VRSS), which was launched in September 2012. The Venesat-1 sale included construction of two ground control stations in the country and training of Venezuelan personnel. These sales have been valuable in enabling Chinese space companies, such as Great Wall, to prove their space products and services and expand their presence in Latin America.[85]

ENERGY/PETROLEUM RELATIONS

Venezuela is major supplier of crude petroleum to China. In this respect, China imported less than 4 percent annually of its crude petroleum from Venezuela between 2006 and 2015. In 2015, China imported 5 percent of its crude oil from Venezuela. The percentage of Venezuela's total commodity trade value of all exports to China was 74 percent for the same year. Thus, crude oil is the principal commodity traded between the two countries.

In terms of total trade value, crude oil petroleum imports ranged from 43 to 77 percent for the same years. Table 14.3 illustrates China's crude petroleum imports from Venezuela in thousands of barrels per day, oil imports share, world ranking, trade value, total commodity trade value, and percentage from 2006 to 2015. See Table 14.3.

China does import petroleum gas products or liquefied natural gas from Venezuela. On the other hand, China has oil and gas acquisitions. Table 14.4 illustrates China's oil and gas acquisitions in Venezuela. China's oil and gas acquisitions in Venezuela do not appear to be robust. See Table 14.4.

China and Venezuela can trace their hydrocarbon energy relationship back to 1985 when the two countries signed their first agreement of energy cooperation. Since 1985, China has burgeoning investments in Venezuela's upstream sector including equity in at least two exploration blocks. Venezuela has also agreed to build an oil refinery in Guangzhou to accommodate Venezuela's sour oil.

China is not technologically equipped to refine Venezuela's heavy crude oil. Special refineries are required to refine Venezuela's heavy, sulfur-rich crude petroleum which China does not have.[86] Thus, most of the crude

Table 14.3 Chinese Crude Petroleum Imports from Venezuela

Year	KBPD	Oil Imports Share (%)	World Ranking	Crude Oil Trade Value ($)	Total Commodity Trade Value ($)	Percentage (%)
2006	84	3	10	1,257,502,487	2,637,956,048	48
2007	83	3	9	1,313,744,852	3,052,881,008	43
2008	130	4	7	3,653,812,125	6,567,059,276	56
2009	106	3	11	1,988,188,929	4,340,905,362	46
2010	152	3	11	3,568,906,018	6,698,877,600	53
2011	231	5	8	7,297,437,029	11,731,209,657	62
2012	307	6	7	10,492,472,800	14,539,106,137	72
2013	312	6	7	10,148,889,185	13,120,096,546	77
2014	277	4	7	8,345,368,766	11,320,412,432	74
2015	321	5	7	5,088,827,869	6,888,273,198	74

Source: United Nations Commodity Trade Statistics Database.

Table 14.4 Chinese Oil and Gas Acquisitions in Venezuela

Date	Company	Description
May08	PetroChina and PDVSA	Agreed to build a refinery in Guangzhou, China
January07	CNPC	Signed an agreement with Venezuela's Ministry of Energy and Mines to jointly develop and produce 20 million metric tons of heavy oil annually. On November 6, 2007, CNPC and PDVSA signed a MOU to extend integrated upstream and downstream cooperation in the Orinoco heavy oil belt
December04	CNPC	Signed an agreement with Petroleos de Venezuela (PDVSA) to jointly explore the Zumano Oil fields in Eastern Venezuela
June97	CNPC	Won tenders to develop the Caracoles and Intercampo Oil fields

Source: Julie Jiang and Chen Dang, *Update on Overseas Investments by Chinese National Companies: Achievements and Challenges Since 2011*, Organization for Economic Cooperation and Development/International Energy Agency, June 2014, 35–39.

petroleum that China currently buys from Venezuela is traded in Singapore to third markets.[87]

China and Venezuela have signed agreements to promote energy cooperation with respect to petroleum prospecting and emulsified oil development. These include the following: Agreement on Scientific and Technological Cooperation in Petroleum Prospecting and Development between Ministry of Petroleum Industry of the People's Republic of China and Ministry of Energy and Mining Industry of the Republic of Venezuela (November 12, 1985);[88] Supplementary Agreement on Scientific and Technological Cooperation in Oil Exploration (October 1991);[89] Agreement on Cooperation in the Field of Petroleum between the Government of the People's Republic of China and the Government of the Republic of Venezuela (November 13, 1996);[90] Memorandum of Understanding on Joint Production of Emulsified Oil between China Petroleum and Natural Gas Corporation and Venezuela Petroleum Corporation (November 13, 1996);[91] Agreement on Cooperation in Emulsified Oil (November 13, 1996);[92] Three-Year Contract on Supplying Emulsified Oil (November 13, 1996);[93] Letter of Intent on Long-Term Goods Credit of Emulsified Oil between China Petroleum and Gas Corporation and Venezuelan Petroleum Company (October 1999);[94] Agreement on Cooperation in exploiting Oil Fields and Natural Gas (January 30, 2005);[95] Joint Venture Agreement between CNPC and PDVSA to drill for and upgrade the super-heavy oil at the Junin 4 Oil Block in the Orinoco Oil Belt with a target annual productivity of 20 million tons (May 2008);[96] Agreement between CNPC and PDVSA to build an oil refinery in China (May 2008);[97] Joint

Venture Operation Agreement between CNPC and the Ministry of People's Power for Energy and Petroleum of Venezuela on development of the Junín 4 Project of Orinoco Heavy Oil Belt for an initial payment of $900 million (April 2010);[98] China's Wison Engineering in consortium with Hyundai Engineering Construction Company and Hyundai Engineering Company were awarded a $930 million contract by PDVSA to upgrade the Puerto La Cruz Oil Refinery (June 2012);[99] Memorandum of Understanding to create a Joint Venture to develop a section of the Junin I Oil Block in the Orinoco Oil Belt (September 23, 2013);[100] CNPC and PDVSA signed a new fuel oil trading contract through the Joint Chinese-Venezuelan Fund, under which CNPC will purchase an additional 100,000 barrels per day for three years (July 21, 2014).[101]

Key Chinese oil-related projects in Venezuela were backed by loans from CDB. China has invested or promised to invest no less than $4.5 billion to date. These CDB loans include: $500 million to Venezuela in return for oil-related products (February 2012); and PDVSA $4 billion to PDVSA to increase production at the Sinovensa heavy oil venture in the Orinoco Belt (June 2013).[102]

Chinese energy-related activities extend beyond oil and gas operations. CNPC also provided oil field services ranging from geophysical prospecting, well drilling, logging, as well as engineering and construction. CNPC provided 3-D seismic services and integrated acquisition of gravity, magnetic and electric data as well as directional well downhole services for PDVSA and CVP, and won the bid logging and perforation contracts from PDVSA in Barines and east of Venezuela. Finally, CNPC and PDVSA formed the joint venture company Industria China Venezolana de Taladros (ICVT) in 2009. In 2012, ICVT began assembling oil rigs imported from China in the Gulf of West Paria, Venezuela. A total of 138 rigs were to be purchased and imported.[103]

Sino-Venezuelan energy cooperation extends beyond the hydrocarbon sector. In May 2010, Sinohydro began work on the El Palito Thermoelectric Power Plant based on agreement signed with PDVSA in April 2010.[104] The plant is equipped with four gas-fired generating units with a total capacity of 772 megawatts and a total value of $1.04 billion.[105] In September 2010, Sinomach and Venezuela National Electric Power Company signed a joint agreement to construct a 500-megawatt El Vigia Thermoelectric Power Plant valued at $960 million.[106] The plant went into full operation on January 26, 2015.[107] In July 2012, China State Grid Corporation and Venezuela's National Electric Corporation signed a $1.31 billion power transmission agreement which included the construction of a power transmission facility in Caracas and nearby regions.[108] In August 2014, Dongfang Electric Corporation won a contract to renovate the Guri Hydroelectric Dam at a cost $230 million.[109] In January 2015, China Energy Engineering Corporation and Venezuela

National Power Corporation signed contracts on the Southern Power Grid Project and the Portuguesa Power Grid Project at a cost of $1.6 billion.[110] The former consists of the construction of transformer substation and power transmission lines. The latter consists of the construction of a transformer substation, expansion, and replacement of subsidiary transmission lines.[111]

China and Venezuela have signed agreements related to energy cooperation in Venezuela's non-hydrocarbon energy sectors. These include the following: Memorandum of Understanding on the Establishment of a Mixed Joint Energy Committee (October 1999); and Memorandum of Understanding on Energy Cooperation Decade (2001–2011) between Chinese State Development Planning Commission and Venezuelan Ministry of Energy and Mineral Resources (May 24, 2001).[112]

SUMMARY

Sino-Venezuelan relations were established in mid-1974 but early contacts were confined to cultural representations during the Cold War. Like many other Latin American countries, diplomatic ties were officiated until after China was admitted into United Nations in 1971. China and Venezuela did not have formal diplomatic ties because Venezuela recognized the Chinese National (*Kuomintang*) Government in Taiwan.

Between 1974 and 1990, bilateral relations developed smoothly and were characterized by frequent high-level official visits, a steady expansion of trade and economic cooperation, and increasing exchanges in fields of culture, education, and science and technology.[113] The results of the bilateral visits between 1974 and 2000 paved the way for stronger overall bilateral relations in the twenty-first century, in terms of bilateral cooperation in the fields of diplomacy, trade, culture, agriculture, animal husbandry, fishery, energy, petroleum prospecting, sports, and science and technology.

In the twenty-first century, bilateral relations reached new heights. China and Venezuela conducted no less than fifty-seven official, bilateral exchanges with at least eight presidential visits. The result of these visits was an unprecedented increase in bilateral trade and cooperation. No less than 460 bilateral agreements were signed, of which 98 percent were finalized during Hugo Chavez's administration. Included in these agreements are 160 projects in virtually every field of cooperation. These fields include agriculture, energy, planning, science and technology, telecommunications, mining, industries, manufacturing, infrastructure, aerospace, and homebuilding.[114] Given the high level of cooperation between the two countries, their relationship could be characterized as strategic in nature.

While bilateral relations are strategic, the most important aspect of their relationship is trade. Bilateral trade increased forty-eight-fold between 2000 and 2014 with crude oil being the most traded commodity between China and Venezuela. On a similar vein, Venezuela is a major oil supplier to China. China imports approximately 4 percent of its crude oil from Venezuela annually. Interestingly, most of the oil China purchases from Venezuela are traded in Singapore to third markets because China cannot refine Venezuela's heavy, sulfur-rich petroleum.[115] Nevertheless, this impediment has not prevented China from investing heavily into Venezuela's agricultural, housing, manufacturing, mining, telecommunications, and transportation sectors in terms of construction and development as well as making loans for oil from China's largest banks and financial institutions such as CDB, ICBC, and Export-Import Bank of China (EXIM). To date, Chinese banks and financial institutions have loaned no less than $50 billion to Venezuela to fund various infrastructure projects with at least $4.5 billion for key oil-related projects.

China and Venezuela also cooperate in energy matters related to petroleum prospecting and emulsified oil development. In this respect, no less than fourteen agreements, contracts, and MoUs have been signed since 1985. Beyond formal agreements, contracts, and MoUs for petroleum prospecting and emulsified oil development, China's CNPC provided oil field services ranging from geophysical prospecting, well drilling, logging, as well as engineering and construction.[116] CNPC also formed the joint venture company ICVT with PDVSA to import and assemble oil rigs in Venezuela.[117]

Sino-Venezuelan energy cooperation extends beyond hydrocarbon sector. China has been involved in construction and development projects associated with Venezuela's thermoelectric and hydroelectric sectors. These include agreements to build or expand thermoelectric and hydroelectric power plants, and transmission lines such as: the El Palito Thermoelectric Power Plant, the El Vigia Thermoelectric Power Plant, the Guri Hydroelectric Dam, the Southern Power Grid Project, and the Portuguesa Power Grid Project. In tandem, China and Venezuela signed important MoUs to form a mixed joint energy committee and promote energy cooperation for a decade.

NOTES

1. Wolfgang Bartke, *The Agreements of the People's Republic of China with Foreign Countries 1949–1990* (Munchen, Germany: K.G. Saur), 1992, 204.

2. Bingwen Zheng, Hongbo Sun, and Yunxia Yue, "The Present Situation and Prospects of China–Latin American Relations: A Review of the History Since 1949," in Shuangrong Hu, ed., *China–Latin America Relations Review and Analysis*

(Volume 1) (Reading, UK: Path International Ltd.), 2012, 2, and William Ratliff, *China in Latin America's Future*,(n.d.), 5, Paper presented at CEAS China Brown Bag Series, the Center for Latin American Studies, Stanford University, Spring 2009-2010.

3. Ministry of Foreign Affairs of the People's Republic of China, "China Venezuela Bilateral Relations," (n.d.), accessed April 12, 2015, http://news.xinhuanet.com/english/2007-03/16/content_5857909.htm.

4. "Venezuela, China: 38 years of diplomatic relations," *ChinaDaily.com.cn,* June 28, 2012, accessed October 13, 2013, http://www.chinadaily.com.cn/cndy/2012-06/28/content_15528289.htm.

5. Ministry of Foreign Affairs of People's Republic of China, "China–Venezuela: Activities," (n.d.), accessed August 9, 2016, http://www.fmprc.gov.cn/mfa_eng/wjb_663304/zzjg_663340/ldmzs_664952/gjlb_664956/3538_665158/3540_665162/.

6. Ministry of Foreign Affairs of People's Republic of China, "China–Venezuela: Activities," accessed December 25, 2015, ibid.

7. "Venezuela, China: 38 years of diplomatic relations," *ChinaDaily.com.cn,* Ibid.

8. Ibid.
9. Ibid.
10. Ibid.

11. Zhongping Feng and Jing Huang, "China's Strategic Partnership Diplomacy: Engaging with a Changing World" (Freed and ESPO), Working Paper No. 8, June 2014, accessed August 17, 2014, http://www.fride.org/descarga/WP8_China_strategic_partnership_diplomacy.pdf.

12. Maxime Tania, "China's Energy Security Towards Venezuela: Transnationalization and the Geopolitical Impact of the Sino-Venezuelan Relationship" (Master's Thesis, University of Amsterdam), July 2012, 111.

13. Ibid.

14. Yagmur Ersan, "China and Venezuela strengthen bilateral relations," *Turkish Weekly,* October 2, 2013, accessed October 13, 2013, http://www.turkishweekly.net/news/157211/china-and-venezuela-strengthen-bilateral-relations.html.

15. Ministry of Foreign Affairs of People's Republic of China, "List of Agreements on Mutual Visa Exemption Between the People's Republic of China and Foreign Countries" August 5, 2014, accessed April 24, 2015, http://www.travelchinaguide.com/embassy/pdf/non-visa.pdf.

16. Ministry of Foreign Affairs of the People's Republic of China, "China Venezuela Bilateral Relations," ibid.

17. Ibid.
18. Ibid.

19. Ministry of Foreign Affairs of People's Republic of China, "Great Achievements Obtained in Zeng Qinghong's Visit to Venezuela: 19 Cooperation Documents Signed Between the Two Countries," January 30, 2005, accessed May 26, 2014, http://www.fmprc.gov.cn/mfa_eng/wjb_663304/zzjg_663340/ldmzs_664952/gjlb_664956/3538_665158/3539_665160/t182097.shtml.

20. Ministry of Foreign Affairs of the People's Republic of China, "China and Venezuela," (n.d.), accessed May 24, 2015, http://www.fmprc.gov.cn/mfa_eng/wjb_663304/zzjg_663340/ldmzs_664952/gjlb_664956/3538_665158/.

21. Ministry of Foreign Affairs of People's Republic of China, "List of Agreements on Mutual Visa Exemption Between the People's Republic of China and Foreign Countries" August 5, 2014, accessed April 24, 2015, http://www.travelchinaguide.com/embassy/pdf/non-visa.pdf.

22. Ministry of Foreign Affairs of the People's Republic of China, "Xi Jinping and Nicolas Maduro Jointly Attend the Closing Ceremony of the 13th Meeting of the China-Venezuela High-level Mixed Committee," July 22, 2014, accessed August 20, 2016, http://www.fmprc.gov.cn/mfa_eng/wjb_663304/zzjg_663340/ldmzs_664952/gjlb_664956/3538_665158/3540_665162/t1177114.shtml.

23. Ministry of Foreign Affairs of the People's Republic of China, "Sino-Argentine Relations," (n.d.), accessed April 24, 2015, http://www.chinadaily.com.cn/english/focus/2004-11/11/content_390575.htm.

24. Jiao Wu, "China signs 12 deals with Venezuela," *ChinaDaily.com.cn*, September 23, 2013, accessed October 13, 2013, http://www.chinadaily.com.cn/world/2013-09/23/content_16985752.htm.

25. European Commission Directorate-General for Trade, "China: EU Bilateral Trade and Trade with the World," July 5, 2013, accessed October 13, 2013, http://trade.ec.europa.eu/doclib/docs/2006/september/tradoc_113366.pdf.

26. European Commission Directorate-General for Trade, "Venezuela: EU Bilateral Trade and Trade with the World," July 5, 2013, accessed October 13, 2013, http://trade.ec.europa.eu/doclib/docs/2006/september/tradoc_113462.pdf.

27. European Commission Directorate-General for Trade, "Venezuela: EU Bilateral Trade and Trade with the World," April 10, 2015, accessed May 3, 2015, http://trade.ec.europa.eu/doclib/docs/2006/september/tradoc_113462.pdf.

28. United Nations, United Nations Commodity Trade Statistics Database, accessed August 15, 2015, http://comtrade.un.org/db/default.aspx.

29. Ibid.

30. United Nations Conference on Trade and Development (UNCTAD FDI/TNC) Database, *Bilateral FDI Statistics 2014*, accessed April 19, 2015, http://unctad.org/Sections/dite_fdistat/docs/webdiaeia2014d3_CHN.pdf.

31. Inter-American Dialogue, "China-Latin America Finance Database," accessed October 13, 2013, http://thedialogue.org/map_list.

32. Guozheng Lu, "Post-Financial Crisis Trade Relations: A New Phase of China–Latin America Cooperation," in Shuangrong Hu, ed., *China–Latin America Relations Review and Analysis (Volume 1)* (Reading, UK: Path International Ltd.), 2012, 65.

33. United Nations, United Nations Commodity Trade Statistics Database, accessed July 22, 2016, ibid.

34. International Trade Centre, Directory of Trade Promotion Organizations and Other Trade Support Institutions, accessed April 19, 2015, http://www.intracen.org/itc/trade-support/tsi-directory.

35. Bartke, ibid., 204.

36. Ibid.

37. Ibid.
38. Ministry of Foreign Affairs of the People's Republic of China, "China Venezuela Bilateral Relations," ibid.
39. Ibid.
40. Ibid.
41. Ibid.
42. Ibid.
43. Ibid.
44. Ibid.
45. Ministry of Foreign Affairs of People's Republic of China, "Venezuela Recognizes China's Full Market Economy Status," December 24, 2004, accessed May 26, 2014, http://www.fmprc.gov.cn/mfa_eng/wjb_663304/zzjg_663340/ldmzs_664952/gjlb_664956/3538_665158/3539_665160/t176893.shtml.
46. Ministry of Foreign Affairs of the People's Republic of China, "President Hu Jintao Holds Talks with Venezuelan President Hugo Rafael CHAVEZ Frías," December 24, 2004, accessed August 20, 2016, http://www.fmprc.gov.cn/mfa_eng/wjb_663304/zzjg_663340/ldmzs_664952/gjlb_664956/3538_665158/3540_665162/t176888.shtml.
47. Ibid.
48. Ministry of Foreign Affairs of People's Republic of China, "Great Achievements Obtained in Zeng Qinghong's Visit to Venezuela: 19 Cooperation Documents Signed Between the Two Countries," ibid.
49. Ibid.
50. Ibid.
51. Ibid.
52. Ibid.
53. Ministry of Foreign Affairs of the People's Republic of China, "China and Venezuela," ibid., accessed November 17, 2014.
54. Ministry of Foreign Affairs of the People's Republic of China, "China and Venezuela," ibid.
55. Ibid.
56. Embassy of the Bolivarian Republic of Venezuela in the Republic of Belarus, "Signature of 24 New Agreements between Venezuela and China will benefit the Development of Both Nations," September 23, 2013, accessed May 25, 2015, http://www.embavenez.by/en/news/1159-firma-de-24-nuevos-acuerdos-entre-venezuela-y-china-beneficiaran-el-desarrollo-de-ambas-aciones?tmpl=component&print=1&layout=default&page=.
57. The Heritage Foundation and American Enterprise Institute, *China Global Investment Tracker Database*, accessed December 25, 2015, http://www.heritage.org/research/projects/china-global-investment-tracker-interactive-map.
58. Austin M. Strange, et al., "Tracking Underreported Financial Flows: China's Development Finance and the Aid–Conflict Nexus Revisited," *Journal of Conflict Resolution*, Volume 61, Issue 5 (2017): 935–963.
59. Strange, et al., ibid.

60. The Heritage Foundation and American Enterprise Institute, ibid.; and R. Evan Ellis, *China on the Ground of Latin America: Challenges for the Chinese and Impacts on the Region*, (New York, NY: Palgrave Macmillan), 2014, 60.

61. The Heritage Foundation and American Enterprise Institute, ibid.

62. Ibid.

63. Ellis, ibid., 60.

64. Ibid.

65. The Heritage Foundation and American Enterprise Institute, ibid.

66. Ibid.

67. Ibid.

68. Ellis, ibid., 18.

69. The Heritage Foundation and American Enterprise Institute, ibid.

70. Ibid.

71. Ellis, ibid., 122–123.

72. Ministry of Foreign Affairs of the People's Republic of China, "China Venezuela Bilateral Relations," ibid.

73. Ibid.

74. United States Department of Defense, Defense Intelligence Agency, *Directory of PRC Military Personalities* (Washington, DC), 2014, 22.

75. Stockholm International Peace Research Institute, SIPRI Arms Transfers Database, http://www.sipri.org/databases/armstransfers.

76. R. Evan Ellis, *China-Latin America Military Engagement: Good Will, Good Business, and Strategic Position* (Carlisle, PA: Strategic Studies Institute), August 2011, 22.

77. Ministry of Foreign Affairs of the People's Republic of China, "China Venezuela Bilateral Relations," ibid.

78. Zheng, Sun, and Yue, ibid.

79. William Ratliff, *China in Latin America's Future*,(n.d.), 5, Paper presented at CEAS China Brown Bag Series, the Center for Latin American Studies, Stanford University, Spring 2009-2010.

80. Bartke, ibid., 204; Ministry of Foreign Affairs of the People's Republic of China, "China Venezuela Bilateral Relations," ibid.; Ministry of Foreign Affairs of People's Republic of China, "Great Achievements Obtained in Zeng Qinghong's Visit to Venezuela: 19 Cooperation Documents Signed Between the Two Countries," ibid; and Embassy of the Bolivarian Republic of Venezuela in the Republic of Belarus, "Signature of 24 New Agreements between Venezuela and China will benefit the Development of Both Nations," ibid.

81. Ministry of Foreign Affairs of the People's Republic of China, "China Venezuela Bilateral Relations," (n.d.), accessed December 25, 2015, ibid.; and Ministry of Foreign Affairs of People's Republic of China, "China and Venezuela," (n.d.), accessed May 26, 2014, ibid.

82. Ministry of Foreign Affairs of the People's Republic of China, "China Venezuela Bilateral Relations," (n.d.), ibid.

83. Ibid.

84. Confucius Institute Online, Worldwide Confucius Institutes, accessed December 25, 2015, http://english.hanban.org/node_10971.htm.

85. Evan Ellis, "China's Cautious Economic and Strategic Gamble in Venezuela," *China Brief* (Jamestown Foundation), Volume XI, Issue 18, September 30, 2011, 9, accessed December 26, 2015.

86. Javier Corrales, "China and Venezuela's Search for Oil Markets," in Alex E. Fernandez Jilberto and Barbara Hogenboom, eds., *Latin America Facing China: South-South Relations beyond the Washington Consensus* (New York, NY: Berghahn Books), 2012, 124.

87. Ibid.

88. Bartke, ibid., 204; and Ministry of Foreign Affairs of the People's Republic of China, "China Venezuela Bilateral Relations," ibid.

89. Ministry of Foreign Affairs of the People's Republic of China, "China Venezuela Bilateral Relations," ibid.

90. Ibid.

91. Ibid.

92. Ibid.

93. Ibid.

94. Ibid.

95. Ministry of Foreign Affairs of People's Republic of China, "Great Achievements Obtained in Zeng Qinghong's Visit to Venezuela: 19 Cooperation Documents Signed Between the Two Countries," ibid.

96. China National Petroleum Company, "CNPC in Venezuela, Oil and Gas Operations," accessed January 5, 2016, http://www.cnpc.com.cn/en/Venezuela/country_index.shtml.

97. Ibid.

98. Ellis, *China on the Ground of Latin America: Challenges for the Chinese and Impacts on the Region*, 28; and Ministry of Foreign Affairs of the People's Republic of China, "China and Venezuela," (n.d.), accessed November 17, 2014, ibid.

99. The Heritage Foundation and American Enterprise Institute, ibid.

100. Embassy of the Bolivarian Republic of Venezuela in the Republic of Belarus, "Signature of 24 New Agreements between Venezuela and China will benefit the Development of Both Nations," ibid.

101. China National Petroleum Company, "CNPC in Venezuela, Major Events," accessed January 5, 2016, http://www.cnpc.com.cn/en/Venezuela/country_index.shtml.

102. Kevin P. Gallagher and Margaret Myers, "China-Latin America Finance Database," ibid.

103. Ellis, *China on the Ground of Latin America: Challenges for the Chinese and Impacts on the Region*, 98; and China National Petroleum Company, "CNPC in Venezuela, Oilfield Services Engineering," accessed January 5, 2016, http://www.cnpc.com.cn/en/Venezuela/country_index.shtml.

104. Strange, et al., ibid.

105. Ibid.

106. Strange, et al., ibid.

107. Strange, et al., ibid.

108. The Heritage Foundation and American Enterprise Institute, ibid.

109. Strange, et al., ibid.

110. The Heritage Foundation and American Enterprise Institute, ibid.

111. *Energy China News*, "Two Power Grid Projects in Venezuela Signed," December 29, 2014, accessed January 8, 2016, http://en.ceec.net.cn/art/2014/12/29/art_138_285931.html.

112. Ministry of Foreign Affairs of the People's Republic of China, "China Venezuela Bilateral Relations," (n.d.), accessed April 12, 2015, ibid.

113. Ibid.

114. "Venezuela, China: 38 years of diplomatic relations," *ChinaDaily.com.cn*, ibid.; and Ministry of Foreign Affairs of People's Republic of China, "China-Venezuela: Activities," ibid.

115. Corrales, ibid., 124.

116. China National Petroleum Company, "CNPC in Venezuela, Oilfield Services Engineering," accessed January 5, 2016, http://www.cnpc.com.cn/en/Venezuela/country_index.shtml.

117. Ellis, *China on the Ground of Latin America: Challenges for the Chinese and Impacts on the Region*, 98.

Conclusion

The fourteen chapters of this book examined China's relations with its principal energy suppliers on a bilateral level. It highlighted China's involvement in these countries based on a five-dimensional approach: political-diplomatic relations, economic-trade relations, military-security relations, cultural relations, and energy-petroleum relations. An examination of these criteria reveals that these countries are strategically significant to China's national security, economic prosperity, vital interests, sovereignty, and regime survival. In terms of national security, the Middle East and Central Asia are critical to Chinese stability in Xinjiang, Ningxia, and other majority Muslim regions in northwestern China.[1] In this respect, China needs the support of six countries, each of which has influence on Muslims in China: Iran, Kuwait, Oman, Saudi Arabia, the United Arab Emirates, and Kazakhstan. Saudi Arabia is the dominant country of the Islamic world.[2] It is home to Mecca and Medina, respectively, the birth place of Islam and the birth place of the prophet Mohammed.[3] To maintain sovereignty over Xinjiang, China needs Saudi Arabia's religious and political support.[4] To support China's sovereignty over Xinjiang, China also needs Iran's support because it has religious and historical ties to East Turkestan and Central Asia.[5] China also needs Kazakhstan's political support to combat extremism, terrorism, and separatism in the regions sharing their common borders. Kazakhstan hosts the region's largest Uyghur diaspora community while China is home to 1 million Kazakhs.[6] Both countries rely on each other's military and security cooperation as ongoing instability in the region, particularly from Afghanistan, threatens their stability, national security, and regional security.[7] Russia also factors in China's national security and vice versa because it is a member of the SCO. As an SCO member, Russia contributes not only to China's national security in battling extremism, terrorism, and separatism but also to the security of Central Asia as a border state to China and Kazakhstan. Iraq, Kuwait, Oman, and the United Arab Emirates figure in China's national security in terms of combating international terrorism. Specifically, Arab-Islamic support helps China to deal with the East Turkestan Islamic Movement seeking Xinjiang Province's independence. This movement is a threat to China's stability, security, and economic development.[8]

In addition to gathering support for China's national security such as dealing with Xinjiang, China needs the unwavering support of its key energy suppliers for its territorial claims over Taiwan, Tibet, and other newly made claims in the South China Sea. In this respect, it is essential for any state seeking diplomatic recognition from China honor the One-China policy and the peaceful reunification of Taiwan. This means that any country seeking diplomatic relations with China must break official relations with Taiwan and vice versa. China has the support of its principal energy suppliers in this regard; only twenty-one countries and the Holy See have official diplomatic relations with Taiwan and do not recognize the One-China Principle. China's claims in the South China Sea are highly disputed and even more so after the Permanent Court of Arbitration in The Hague ruled on July 12, 2016 ruled that China has no legal basis for its historical claim over the nine-dash line in a case brought on by the Philippines. According to this court, China's claim of the Paracel and Spratly Islands is unlawful. The Chinese government has rejected the ruling and continues to occupy and militarize them. Nevertheless, China's territorial claim, that includes their occupation and militarization, has alarmed its neighbors, especially those that also have claims over islands. Potentially, China's illegal occupation may strain its relations with United States if the crisis is not resolved. In the interim, countries may be forced to choose sides and China possibly may incorporate into its One-China Principle demanding that countries seeking continued diplomatic recognition recognize its territorial claims in the South China Sea.

China's energy needs are intricately linked to its national security. In this respect, China views its energy cooperation from a security prospective, for it seeks energy security rather than engaging in conflicts to defend its oil concessions.[9] It has done everything possible to date to ensure its energy security, including equity share exploration ventures, pipeline construction, increasing its storage capacity, and increasing its domestic production.[10] China has even shaped its foreign policy to ensure the steady supply of oil as manifested by its participation in peacekeeping missions in Africa and the Middle East.[11] China's principal energy suppliers are critical to its energy security because they supply approximately 93 percent of China's annual imports. Some states have even finalized agreements with China to set up new or upgrade China's existing refineries or build or route pipelines into China from Eurasia: Kazakhstan, Kuwait, Oman, Russia, Saudi Arabia, the United Arab Emirates, and Venezuela. China is becoming increasingly reliant on the Eurasia and the Middle East for its energy needs particularly from countries like Russia, Kazakhstan, Saudi Arabia, Iran, Iraq, Kuwait, and the United Arab Emirates not just because these countries have large proven oil reserves but because continently connected. In other words, crude petroleum and gas fuels can be transported over land to China using existing pipelines running through Eurasia. This mode of transit contributes significantly to China's energy security because it bypasses the sea lines of communication (SLOCs) and any interdiction from the U.S. Navy. Oman and the United Emirates contribute to China's energy security because both countries provide port services to Chinese warships conducting anti-piracy patrols in the Gulf of Aden, Horn of Africa, and Indian Ocean. These patrols contribute not only to China's energy security at sea but also to the maritime security of the SLOCs.

China is breaking ground in Africa and South America in countries like Angola, Sudan, South Sudan, Brazil, and Venezuela in terms of energy security, but the vast geographical distance and separation by water makes it tenuous and expensive. These countries also help China's energy diversification strategy in that it does not rely solely on one region such as the Middle East for its energy needs. Beyond oil and gas, China has invested in the energy futures of some of its principal oil suppliers. China has been involved in the construction of oil refineries, windmills, and solar panels across the Middle East.[12] China has also been involved in developing nuclear energy in the Middle East through offering consultations, training, designs, and reactor construction and operation in countries like Saudi Arabia, Iran, and the United Arab Emirates.[13] China sold nuclear reactors, boilers, machinery, and mechanical appliances, and parts thereof to all of its principal energy suppliers. They are in the top five commodities traded with China. China has also agreed to jointly mine for uranium in Kazakhstan, and China and Russia agreed to build a nuclear power plant in Jiangsu province using Russian-designed reactors. In Sudan, Chinese companies have agreed to build the country's first nuclear reactor by 2021.[14]

Beyond the nuclear sector, China has been involved in its key energy supplier's thermoelectric, hydroelectric, wind, and solar sectors. In Brazil, Chinese companies have acquired shares in thermoelectric plants, jointly agreed to build hydroelectric plants, and agreed to invest in a wind farm. In Kazakhstan, China has agreed to build a hydroelectric plant. In Russia, Chinese and Russian companies are in a joint venture to develop hydro and thermal power projects in Russian Siberia and the Far East.[15] In Sudan, Chinese companies jointly agreed to build the $1.8 billion, 1,250-megawatt Merowe Dam, which was commissioned in March 2009, which supplies not only electricity but water for farms. In the UAE, China is providing solar and wind energy technology.[16] In Venezuela, Chinese companies jointly agreed or built thermoelectric plants and renovate hydroelectric facilities and power transmission lines.

In conclusion, China's energy-petroleum relations are global today and have grown significantly since it opened its economy to trade and investment in the early 1980s. China's dependence on crude petroleum and other liquid fuels has grown in tandem with its energy-petroleum needs and resulted in China surpassing the United States as the world's largest net importer of petroleum and other liquid fuels as of March 2014. Nevertheless, China's growing energy needs is a matter of national security forcing it to take extraordinary measures to ensure the flow of energy from disparate parts of the world, including but not limited to employing soft power tools like investment, infrastructure development, and technical expertise to developing countries and developed countries traditionally allied to the United States.

China's growing economic-trade relations with its principal energy suppliers is a key indicator of its economic prosperity. China actually relies on fruitful bilateral relations to maintain its economic growth. In many cases, China established economic-trade relations with its energy suppliers long before it established diplomatic ties. In this respect, China established conducted trade talks and traded with many of its principal energy suppliers: Brazil, Iran, Iraq, Kazakhstan, Kuwait, Oman, Russia, Saudi Arabia, Sudan, and the United Arab Emirates. In many cases, China's ancient Silk Road paved the way for contemporary economic-trade relations. Additionally, Iraq, Kazakhstan, Oman, Russia, Saudi Arabia and the United Arab Emirates are part of China's Belt and Road Initiative-Silk Road Economic Belt and Twenty-First Century Maritime Silk Road, a development strategy and framework unveiled in September and October 2013, respectively, which focuses on connectivity and cooperation between China and Eurasia and underlines China's push to take a bigger role in global affairs.

The chief indicator of China's economic prosperity has been the level of bilateral trade that has expanded since 2000. In this respect, China's economy has grown exponentially in the last fifteen years through global trade, which is remarkable for a communist country. To illustrate, China's bilateral trade with the world was $474.29 billion in 2000. In 2015, China's bilateral trade with the world was $3.96 trillion. China's bilateral trade increased more than eightfold in fifteen years. In 2000, China's bilateral trade with its principal energy suppliers was $28.8 billion, approximately 6 percent of China's total bilateral trade. In 2015, China's bilateral trade with its principal energy suppliers was $378.5 billion, approximately 9.5 percent of China's total bilateral trade. China's bilateral trade with its principal energy suppliers has increased thirteen-fold.

In tandem with increased bilateral trade, China has become a top trading partner for many countries since 2000. More importantly, China ranked as a top five trading partner to almost all its principal energy suppliers in 2015: Angola (No. 1), Brazil (No. 2), Congo (No. 2), Iran (No. 2), Iraq (No. 2), Kazakhstan (No. 3), Kuwait (No. 2), Oman (No. 2), Russia (No. 2), Saudi Arabia (No. 2), Sudan (No. 1), the United Arab Emirates (No.2), and Venezuela (No.2).[17] Moreover, in 2015, mineral fuels, which includes crude petroleum, petroleum gas products, and liquid natural gas, has been one of the top five commodities imported by China from its principal energy suppliers: Angola (No. 1), Brazil (No. 3), Congo (No. 1), Iran (No. 1), Iraq (No. 1), Kazakhstan (No. 1), Kuwait (No. 1), Oman (No. 1), Russia (No. 1), Saudi Arabia (No. 1), Sudan (No. 1), the United Arab Emirates (No.1), and Venezuela (No.1). These countries were also China's top energy suppliers by supplying China with 89 percent of its imported oil in 2015: Angola (No.3/11.5 percent), Brazil (No.9/4.1 percent), Congo (No. 13/1.75 percent), Iran (No. 6/7.93 percent), Iraq (No.4/9.5 percent), Kazakhstan (No. 14/1.49 percent), Kuwait (No.8/4.3 percent), Oman (No. 5/9.56 percent), Russia (No.2/12.65 percent), Saudi Arabia (No. 1/15 percent), Sudan (No. 12/2.38 percent), the United Arab Emirates (No. 10/3.75 percent), and Venezuela (No. 7/4.77 percent). These countries are clearly important to China in terms of overall trading but also in oil trading.[18]

Another indicator of China's growing economic relations with its principal energy suppliers is the number of strategic partnerships China has formed since it opened its economy to the world. China has formed strategic partnerships with principal energy suppliers in Africa, Europe, the Near East, Central Asia, and South America: Angola, Brazil, Kazakhstan, Russia, Saudi Arabia, Sudan, the United Arab Emirates, and Venezuela.[19] China has also formed additional partnerships with Russia to further not only economic relations but strengthen political ties: the 1994 constructive partnership featuring good neighborliness and mutually beneficial cooperation; the 1996 partnership of strategic coordination based on equality and mutual benefit and oriented toward the twenty-first century; and the 2011 comprehensive strategic partnership.[20]

China's strategic partnerships have benefited not only its economic development and prosperity but also its principal energy suppliers. In this respect, China has provided loans, capital investment, financial assistance, infrastructure development, or debt relief: Angola–$28 billion, Brazil–$9.7 billion, Congo–$4.4 billion, Iran–$7.2 billion, Iraq–$4 billion, Kazakhstan–$6.2 billion, Kuwait–$1.7 billion, Oman–$310 million, Russia–$13.82 billion, Saudi Arabia–$18.5 billion, South Sudan–$1.76 billion, Sudan–$6.7 billion, the United Arab Emirates–$6.2 billion, and Venezuela–$46.2 billion. In some cases, China has made loans for oil such as Angola, Brazil, Russia, and Venezuela. Nevertheless, Chinese funding has helped develop many sectors: telecommunications, technology, motor and railway transportation, storage, automobiles, emergency response, utilities, agriculture, banking and finance, health, education, agriculture, fisheries, mining, solar energy, sports, seaport and airport development, power plant construction, seawater desalination, water supply, sanitation, general construction, infrastructure, and public works. Clearly, China's economic presence has been felt across the world, especially in those countries that supply its hydrocarbons.

Another important indicator of China's partnerships and growing global reach is its expanding military-security relations with its principal energy suppliers. Although China has been historically a modest supplier of weapons and equipment, it has rapidly expanded its military-security relations worldwide, especially with principal energy suppliers, since the beginning of the twenty-first century, as part of its "Go Out" or "Going Global" strategy. Whereas China's Cold War military-security relations served to expand communist ideology and influence such as employing Chinese military advisers and technicians in support of liberation movements in the Near East, Sub-Saharan Africa, and Southeast Asia, China's modern military-security relations, which include arms sales, security cooperation, and military-diplomatic presence in the form of defense attachés, is a strategic-level activity in support of a larger diplomatic, economic, and security agenda established by China's leadership.[21] David H. Shinn opined that:

> The PLA does not engage in freestanding military initiatives conducted by military professionals for military reasons. In other words, the PLA is not an independent actor; it must coordinate its activities with the party and the state bureaucracy. The PLA maintains an ambitious global program of military exchanges and training programs.[22]

Essentially, China's military-security relations today is part of a comprehensive foreign policy strategy designed to promote the Asian country diplomatically, economically, militarily, and culturally and not ideologically as it was in the Cold War.

China's modern military-security relations include arms sales, military-diplomatic exchanges, formal military-diplomatic representation, security consultations, port visits, joint training/joint exercises, educational exchanges, technical assistance, peacekeeping operations, and formal organizations. Arms sales range from non-existent, episodic, and recurring transfers of military weapons or equipment. China does not currently export weapons and equipment to Brazil, Kazakhstan, or Russia. Russia has consistently been China's principal arms supplier in the Cold War and post-Cold War. According to SIPRI, China has sporadically exported weapons to Angola (1975, 2013), Congo (1971, 1978, 2006–2007, and 2009), Iraq (1982–1989, 2004), Kuwait (2000–2003), Oman (2002–2003), Saudi Arabia (1987–1989,

2008–2009), South Sudan (2014), Sudan (1968–1973, 1978, 1981, 1987, 1989, 1991–1992, 1997, 1999, and 2001–2014), and the United Arab Emirates (1993–1994). China has regularly exported arms and equipment to Iran and Venezuela, respectively, since 1981 and 2006. In tandem with arms sales, China provided technical assistance to military personnel.

Bilateral military-diplomatic exchanges occurred on an episodic basis in the twenty-first century. Episodic exchanges include: Angola (2004, 2005, 2009, 2010, 2013, and 2014), Brazil (2002–2010 and 2013–2015), Congo (2003, 2005, 2010, and 2013), Iran (2003, 2005, and 2014), Kazakhstan (2003, 2005, 2006, 2009, 2010, and 2012), Kuwait (2003, 2007, 2010, and 2011), Oman (2008–2011, and 2014), Russia (2002–2010, 2014–2015), Saudi Arabia (2008, 2009, 2013–2014), Sudan (2002–2007, 2009, and 2014), the United Arab Emirates (2004, 2008–2010, and 2014), and Venezuela (2002, 2004–2008, 2010, and 2015). China has conducted the most military-diplomatic exchanges with Russia (45), Brazil (29), and Kazakhstan (12) since 2000.

Another indicator of China's growing military-security relations is its formal military representation. In this respect, China has assigned military attachés in the capitals of each country that principally supplies it crude petroleum except Iraq and South Sudan. However, not all of China's principal energy suppliers have stationed military attachés in Beijing. Oman is the only country of China's principal energy suppliers that does not have military-diplomatic representation in Beijing.

Beyond military-diplomatic exchanges and formal military representation, China has conducted numerous multilateral security consultations since 2000. China's principal energy suppliers include: Brazil, Kazakhstan, Russia, and Venezuela. More importantly, China, Kazakhstan, and Russia are also members of the six-member political, economic, and military organization Shanghai Cooperation Organization.

In the twenty-first century China has conducted numerous port visits to promote military-security cooperation. Chinese ships visited Angola, Brazil, Oman, Russia, and the United Arab Emirates. China also plans to establish a naval base in Luanda, Angola, by 2024, and port facility arrangements with Oman and the United Arab Emirates to service Chinese warships operating in the Gulf of Aden, the Horn of Africa, and western Indian Ocean.

An important aspect of China's growing military-security relations is joint training/joint exercise participation involving one or more its principal energy suppliers. In this respect, China participated in joint military training and exercises with Brazil (2013), Iran (2014), Kazakhstan (2003, 2007, 2009–2012, and 2014), Oman (2007, 2009, 2011, and 2013), Russia (2005, 2007, 2009, 2010, 2012, 2013, 2014, 2015, and 2016), the United Arab Emirates (2007, 2009, 2011, and 2013), and Venezuela (2011). Russia and Kazakhstan participated in Peace Mission exercises in Central Asia and Oman and the United Arab Emirates participated in AMAN sponsored by Pakistan.

China has provided military training to some of its principal energy suppliers: Angola, Brazil, Congo, Kazakhstan, Saudi Arabia, Sudan, and Venezuela. Brazil provided carrier take-off and landing training to Chinese navy pilots. In tandem with military training, China conducted educational exchanges with Brazil, Iraq, Russia, and Saudi Arabia. Beyond military training and educational exchanges, China has supplied peacekeeping forces in Darfur, Sudan and South Sudan.

China's military-security relations are extensive and have grown since its formation as a communist state on October 1, 1949. More importantly, China's bilateral military-security ties have expanded rapidly since 2000 in almost every aspect from arms sales to peacekeeping operations. China is also expected to establish permanent military bases abroad in support of its foreign policy objectives which include recognition of its One-China Policy, bilateral trade and investment, and securing and protecting vital energy resources such as oil and gas and other gas products from its point of origin to its destination in China.

China's cultural relations are useful in promoting its positive image globally and serve as a soft power tool for building ties with other countries especially with those which supply it with critical energy resources. Cultural relations have been and continue to be a part of China's foreign policy whether under Mao or post-Mao. Historically, China's cultural relations have typically preceded political-diplomatic relations and can be traced back to the Silk Road two millennia ago.[23] Since the founding of the PRC, China formed cultural ties before diplomatic ties were established with many countries, including those which are energy resource abundant. These include cultural ties with Brazil, Oman, and the United Arab Emirates. In some instances, China established cultural ties with the majority of its energy suppliers after diplomatic relations were established. Nevertheless, China established cultural ties with Iran, Iraq, Kazakhstan, Oman, Russia, and Saudi Arabia in ancient times because of the Silk Road trade routes on land and at sea.

China's modern cultural relations are manifested in many forms from agricultural aid and assistance to space and technology cooperation. Agricultural aid and assistance was provided to: Angola, Brazil, the Congo, South Sudan, Sudan, and Venezuela. China also provided medical aid and dispatched medical teams to: Angola, the Congo, South Sudan, Sudan, and the United Arab Emirates. Educational cooperation or academic scholarships were provided to its principal energy suppliers. Journalism or media cooperation occurred between China and Angola, Brazil, Iran, Iraq, Russia, South Sudan, Sudan, the United Arab Emirates, and Venezuela. Sports cooperation is also important. To date, China promoted sports cooperation with Angola,

Brazil, the Congo, Kazakhstan, Russia, and Venezuela. Each country except South Sudan participated in the 2008 Summer Olympic Games in Beijing, China. China also established air travel links with Angola, Brazil, Iran, Russia, Sudan, and the United Arab Emirates. Space and technology cooperation occurred between China and Brazil, Kazakhstan, Russia, the United Arab Emirates, and Venezuela. China jointly developed satellites with Brazil and helped launched them into space and sold satellites to Venezuela. China also established Confucius Institutes or Classrooms in each principal energy-supplying country except Iraq, Kuwait, Oman, Saudi Arabia, and South Sudan. Confucius Institutes are designed to promote the Chinese language and culture. China also hosted the 2010 Shanghai International Expo in its business capital. Each principal energy-supplying country except Kuwait and South Sudan participated and established either individual or national pavilions to promote their culture, music, traditions, and folklore.

THE ROAD FORWARD

Since economic reforms were implemented in 1978, China has rapidly grown into a global economic power. It has become a regional military power in the twenty-first century and is expected to be a global military power by 2025. It will also continue to engage energy-producing countries to meet its growing demand for oil and gas resources. It will use the elements of national power (political-diplomatic, economic-trade, military-security, and information-social) not only to satisfy its insatiable appetite for energy resources, but also to sustain its economic growth and achieve full military parity with United States.

Critics have argued that China's inevitable rise translates into United States decline as a world power. Much will depend on whether or not the United States remains globally engaged. Should United States become less engaged, China will likely fill the strategic void and economic competition for energy resources will result. Nevertheless, China will continue to forge strategic partnerships globally especially with those countries that supply its oil and gas and provide security guarantees either against potential American threats or a substitute of potential U.S. withdrawal for such guarantees.[24] In this respect, China has quietly engaged in a strategy of military and economic cooperation with Pakistan, Myanmar, Bangladesh, Sri Lanka, and the Maldives in Indian Ocean region in order to build and/or have access to ports and airbases to support not only a future tanker fleet but also a blue-water navy capable of projecting power not only in the Indian Ocean region but in the Persian Gulf. It is also building a base in Djibouti to support anti-piracy and naval patrols in the Gulf of Aden and the Horn of Africa. China is also exploring the idea of building future naval bases in the coastal countries of Sub-Saharan Africa that exit to the Atlantic Ocean or Indian Ocean.

Overall, China's strategic engagement and rising geopolitical influence in tandem with its adroit pursuit and development of scarce energy resources cause it to be a strategic energy resource competitor, politically, economically, and militarily, to the United States in those countries where both nations obtain their petroleum products. China will likely alter the status quo within the next 50 to 100 years and surpass the United States as a global power unless it can find a way to reduce its energy dependence on hydrocarbon-based fuels. It has already surpassed United States in terms of net crude oil imports as of March 2014.

RESEARCH ISSUES

Oil, gas, and trade volume data are relatively available through the United Nations Comtrade-International Trade Statistics Database. Oil and gas volume data can be obtained by converging kilograms to thousands of barrels per day or millions of cubic feet, respectively. Unfortunately, United Nations data on bilateral foreign direct investment flows and bilateral foreign direct investment stock both in the host economy and abroad by partner country is over four years old and therefore outdated. Further, similar data by partner country are either scarce or unavailable.

Energy data on Chinese acquisitions, joint partnerships, and other deals can be found by researching the International Energy Agency Internet website under publications. The IEA typically provides free publications. Similar information can also be researched in oil and gas trade magazines like the *Oil and Gas Journal*. Another good research source is the CNPC Internet website. This website has dropdown menus of the oil and gas company's global operations. CNPC is the only major oil and gas company that provides detailed public information about its worldwide operations. The Sinopec Internet website contains a map of global operations but provides no details. The CNOOC Internet website offers no detailed information on its global operations.

As China research sources may be unavailable regarding global project financing, AidData, Inter-American Dialogue, and the Heritage Foundation-the American Enterprise Institute provide some the best research data on Chinese financing worldwide by projects.

Arms transfer data and military expenditure by partner country are free and can be obtained electronically at the Stockholm International Peace Research Institute (SIPRI) Internet website. Chinese bilateral military interactions can be obtained by researching articles on the China Ministry of National Defense internet website.

Political-diplomatic and cultural data can be found by researching Chinese embassy Internet websites or the China Ministry of Foreign Affairs international website under country. Typically, information regarding bilateral agreements, memoranda of understanding, communiques, treaties, and protocols can be found at the same Internet websites under the respective country or by searching using keywords.

FURTHER RESEARCH

The purpose of this book was to examine China's bilateral relations with its principal energy suppliers using a five-dimensional framework. The target audience is scholars and students of China's comparative politics and energy security. The objective is to inspire them to conduct further research on China's bilateral relations using a five-dimensional approach. Typically, research studies in comparative politics are solely focused on single country-to-country analysis or regional analysis between one country and one or more regions. More often than not, these studies concentrate on the political-diplomatic and economic-trade dimensions and marginalize or exclude the military-security, cultural, or energy-petroleum dimensions. Contemporary bilateral relations studies should include those dimensions (military-security, cultural, and energy-petroleum) which have been historically relegated to the fringes of comparative studies.

With China rising in the twenty-first century and the availability of more open source information and statistical data, it behooves researchers to examine China's comparative politics on a bilateral scale using a comprehensive approach especially when geopolitics and energy security come into play. Using a bilateral five-dimensional framework, studies of Chinese comparative politics should be conducted on countries in those regions of the world which are more likely to influence or play a significant role in shaping global geopolitics in the twenty-first century: South Asia, Southeast Asia, Sub-Saharan Africa, South America, and Europe. The countries in these regions are important because they are politically, economically, and militarily significant not only to China but to the United States and the West. They are either abundant in natural resources or vital to the economic supply chain by sea or land. Militarily, these countries are key not only to ensuring resource security but to the combating non-state actors which threaten global stability.

The Arctic Circle cannot be ignored, especially since there is untapped potential in terms of natural and animal resources, which makes it geopolitically significant. The Arctic Circle is estimated to contain 22 percent of the world's oil and natural gas according to the United States Geological Survey; large quantities of minerals, including phosphate, bauxite, iron ore, copper and nickel; sub-Arctic fish stocks; and 10 percent of the world's fresh water reserves. A detailed analysis of China's bilateral relations with the Arctic Five (Canada, Norway, Denmark, Russia, and the United States) bordering the Arctic Circle would help illuminate the geopolitics of the region. Detailed comparative bilateral relations studies have been published on the Middle East, North Africa, and Central Asia thanks to Muhamad Olimat but more needs to be done. The challenge for scholars and students of Chinese comparative politics is to go further and examine those countries in regions of the world which have been intellectually marginalized using a five-dimensional approach.

NOTES

1. Muhamad S. Olimat, *China and the Middle East Since World War II* (Lanham, MD: Lexington Books), 2014, 293.
2. Ibid., 294.
3. Ibid.
4. Ibid.
5. Ibid.
6. Muhamad S. Olimat, *China and Central Asia in the Post-Soviet Era* (Lanham, MD: Lexington Books), 2015, 121.
7. Ibid.
8. Olimat, *China and the Middle East Since World War II*, 258.
9. Muhamad S. Olimat, *China and North Africa Since World War II* (Lanham, MD: Lexington Books), 2014, 194.
10. Ibid., 194–195.
11. Ibid., 195.
12. Olimat, *China and the Middle East Since World War II*, 295.
13. Ibid.
14. Stephen Stapczynski and Aibing Guo, "China's CNNC Seeking to Build Sudan's First Nuclear Reactor," *Bloomberg*, May 23, 2016, accessed July 23, 2016, http://www.bloomberg.com/news/articles/2016-05-24/china-s-cnnc-seeking-to-build-sudan-s-first-nuclear-reactor.
15. Nandan Unnikrishnan and Uma Purushothaman, *Trends in Russia-China Relations: Implications for India* (New Delhi, India: Observer Research Foundation), 2015, 46.
16. Olimat, *China and the Middle East Since World War II*, 254.
17. European Commission Directorate-General for Trade, "Kazakhstan: EU Bilateral Trade and Trade with the World," June 21, 2016, accessed July 23, 2016, http://trade.ec.europa.eu/doclib/docs/2006/september/tradoc_113406.pdf; European Commission Directorate-General for Trade, "Iran: EU Bilateral Trade and Trade with the World," June 21, 2016, accessed July 23, 2016, http://trade.ec.europa.eu/doclib/docs/2006/september/tradoc_113392.pdf; European Commission Directorate-General

for Trade, "Iraq: EU Bilateral Trade and Trade with the World," June 21, 2016, accessed July 23, 2016, http://trade.ec.europa.eu/doclib/docs/2006/september/tradoc_113405.pdf; European Commission Directorate-General for Trade, "Kuwait: EU Bilateral Trade and Trade with the World," June 21, 2016, accessed July 23, 2016, http://trade.ec.europa.eu/doclib/docs/2006/september/tradoc_113408.pdf; European Commission Directorate-General for Trade, "Oman: EU Bilateral Trade and Trade with the World," June 21, 2016, accessed July 23, 2016, http://trade.ec.europa.eu/doclib/docs/2006/september/tradoc_113430.pdf; European Commission Directorate-General for Trade, "Saudi Arabia: EU Bilateral Trade and Trade with the World," June 21, 2016, accessed July 23, 2016, http://trade.ec.europa.eu/doclib/docs/2006/september/tradoc_113442.pdf; European Commission Directorate-General for Trade, "United Arab Emirates: EU Bilateral Trade and Trade with the World," June 21, 2016, accessed July 23, 2016, http://trade.ec.europa.eu/doclib/docs/2006/september/tradoc_113458.pdf; European Commission Directorate-General for Trade, "Angola: EU Bilateral Trade and Trade with the World," June 21, 2016, accessed July 23, 2016, http://trade.ec.europa.eu/doclib/docs/2006/september/tradoc_112456.pdf; European Commission Directorate-General for Trade, "Sudan: EU Bilateral Trade and Trade with the World," June 21, 2016, accessed July 23, 2016, http://trade.ec.europa.eu/doclib/docs/2006/september/tradoc_147395.pdf; European Commission Directorate-General for Trade, "Russia: EU Bilateral Trade and Trade with the World," June 21, 2016, accessed July 23, 2016, http://trade.ec.europa.eu/doclib/docs/2006/september/tradoc_113440.pdf; European Commission Directorate-General for Trade, "Brazil: EU Bilateral Trade and Trade with the World," June 21, 2016, accessed July 23, 2016, http://trade.ec.europa.eu/doclib/docs/2006/september/tradoc_113359.pdf.; European Commission Directorate-General for Trade, "Venezuela: EU Bilateral Trade and Trade with the World," June 21, 2016, accessed July 23, 2016, http://trade.ec.europa.eu/doclib/docs/2006/september/tradoc_113462.pdf; and European Commission Directorate-General for Trade, "Congo: EU Bilateral Trade and Trade with the World," June 21, 2016, accessed July 23, 2016, http://trade.ec.europa.eu/doclib/docs/2006/september/tradoc_147253.pdf.

18. United Nations, United Nations Commodity Trade Statistics Database, accessed August 28, 2016, http://comtrade.un.org/db/default.aspx.

19. Olimat, *China and North Africa Since World War II*, 159; and Zhongping Feng and Jing Huang, "China's Strategic Partnership Diplomacy: Engaging with a Changing World" (Fride and ESPO), Working Paper No. 8, June 2014, accessed August 17, 2014, http://www.fride.org/descarga/WP8_China_strategic_partnership_diplomacy.pdf.

20. Feng and Huang, ibid.

21. David H. Shinn, "Military and Security Relations: China, Africa, and the Rest of the World" in Robert I. Rotberg, ed., *China into Africa: Trade, Aid, and Influence* (Washington, DC: Brookings Institution Press), 2008, 162.

22. Ibid.

23. Olimat, *China and North Africa Since World War II*, 196.

24. Olimat, *China and the Middle East Since World War II*, 298.

Bibliography

Ahmed, Javaid. "45 Years of China-Kuwait Diplomatic Relations." *Kuwait Times*, March 16, 2016. Accessed August 13, 2016. http://news.kuwaittimes.net/website/45-years-china-kuwait-diplomatic-relations/.

Allen, Kenneth. "Trends in PLA International Initiatives Under Hu Jintao." Paper presented at The National Bureau of Asian Research and Strategic Studies Institute of the U.S. Army War College Conference "Assessing the People's Liberation Army in the Hu Jintao Era," October 19–21, 2012.

Al Maimani, Jamal Bin Ramadan. "Economic Relations Between the Sultanate of Oman and China and India." *International Economy*, Volume 154, August/September 2005: 13–15.

Almasri, Mohammed. "Oman: BankMuscat, Bank of China join Hands to Tap Bilateral Trade & Investments." *Global Arab Network*, March 27, 2010. Accessed August 14, 2016. http://www.english.globalarabnetwork.com/201003275296/Economics/oman-bankmuscat-bank-of-china-join-hands-to-tap-bilateral-trade-a-investments.html.

Al-Suwaidi, Jamal S. "Introduction." In *China, India and the United States: Competition for Energy Resources.* Abu Dhabi, UAE: Emirates Center for Strategic Studies and Research, 2008. 3–27.

Al-Tamimi, Naser. "China–Saudi Relations: Booming Trade." *Al Arabiya News*, February 22, 2013. Accessed October 8, 2013. http://english.alarabiya.net/views/2013/02/22/2676 70.html.

Al-Tamimi, Naser. *China–Saudi Arabia Relations: Economic Partnership or Strategic Alliance?* Durham, UK: Al Sabah Number 2, June 2012. Accessed August 31, 2014. https://www.dur.ac.uk/resources/alsabah/China-SaudiArabiaRelations.pdf.

Alterman, Jon B. "China's Soft Power in the Middle East." In *Chinese Soft Power and Its Implications for the United States,* edited by Carola McGiffert, 63–76. Washington, DC: CSIS Press, March 2009.

Alterman, Jon. B. and John W. Garver. *The Vital Triangle: The United States and the Middle East.* Washington, DC: CSIS Press, 2008.

Alves, Ana Cristina. *The Oil Factor in Sino-Angolan Relations at the Start of the 21st Century*. Johannesburg, South Africa: South African Institute of International Affairs, February 2010. http://www.voltairenet.org/IMG/pdf/Sino-Angolan_Relations.pdf.

Andrews-Speed, Philip, Xuanli Liao and Roland Dannreuther. *The Strategic Implications of China's Energy Needs*. New York, NY: Oxford University Press, 2002.

Arab Times. (June 3, 2014). "Kuwait, China Ink Deals." Accessed September 21, 2014. http://www.arabtimesonline.com/NewsDetails/tabid/96/smid/414/ArticleID/206579/reftab/96/t/Kuwait-China-ink-deals/Default.aspx.

Arabian Industry. (May 13, 2013). "Dubai International Convention Centre Hosts Showcase of Chinese Building Wares." Accessed October 11, 2014. http://arabianindustry.com/construction/news/2013/may/13/dubai-international-convention-centre-hosts-showcase-of-chinese-building-wares-4307225/.

Aweti, Y. and A. Rodgers. "China—Doing Business with the UAE." *Zawya*, July 31, 2013. Accessed October 10, 2014. http://www.zawya.com/story/China_Doing_business_with_the_UAE-ZAWYA20130812055249/.

Azer News. (August 17, 2016). "China's EXIM Bank, Iran ink Finance Deal." Accessed August 19, 2016. http://iranoilgas.com/news/details?id=16425&title=China%E2%80%99s+ EXIM+Bank%2c+Iran+ink+finance+deal.

Bahrain News Agency. (December 8, 2003). "Kuwait, China sign Cooperation Agreement." Accessed August 13, 2016. http://bna.bh/portal/en/news/364544?date=2011-04-7.

Barbosa, Rui C., "200th Long March Rocket Launches CBERS-4 for Brazil." NASA Spaceflight.com, December 6, 2014. Accessed November 11, 2015. http://www.nasaspaceflight.com/2014/12/200th-long-march-launches-cbers-4-brazil/.

Bariyo, Nicholas. "South Sudan Signs Agreement with China's CNPC to Boost Oil Production." *The Wall Street Journal*, December 22, 2014. Accessed February 7, 2015. http://www.wsj.com/articles/south-sudan-signs-agreement-with-chinas-cnpc-to-boost-oil-production-1419242796.

Bartke, Wolfgang. *The Agreements of the People's Republic of China with Foreign Countries 1949–1990*. Munchen, Germany: K.G. Saur, 1992.

Berman, Ilan. "The Impact of Sino-Iranian Strategic Partnership," testimony, September 14, 2006, before U.S.–China Economic and Security Review Commission.

Blanchard, Christopher M., Nicolas Cook, Kerry Dumbaugh, Susan B. Epstein, Shirley A. Kan, Michael F. Martin, Wayne M. Morrison, Dick K. Nanto, Jim Nichol, Jeremy M. Sharp, Mark P. Sullivan, and Bruce Vaughn. *Comparing Global Influence: China's and U.S. Diplomacy, Foreign Aid, Trade, and Investment in the Developing World*, CRS Report RL34620, Washington, DC: Library of Congress, Congressional Research Service, August 15, 2008.

Bradbury, Rose. "Sudan, the Hollow State: What Challenges to Chinese Policy." *Journal of Politics and International Studies*, Volume 8, 2012/2013, 362–410. http://www.polis.leeds.ac.uk/assets/files/students/student-journal/ug-winter-12/130227-win12-rose-bradbury-10.pdf.

Brazilian Ministry of Foreign Affairs. "Note 161: Acts Signed During the Visit to Brazil by the President of China, Xi Jinping." Accessed May 16, 2015. http://www.itamaraty.gov.br/index.php?option=com_content&view=article&id=5716:a

tos-assinados-por-ocasiao-da-visita-ao-brasil-do-presidente-da-republica-popular-da-china-xi-jinping-brasilia-17-de-julho-de-2014&catid=42:notas&Itemid=280&l ang=pt-BR.

Campos, Indira and Alex Vines. "Angola and China: A Pragmatic Relationship." Working paper presented at the CSIS Conference "Prospects for Improving U.S.-China-Africa Cooperation," Washington, DC, December 5, 2007.

CCTV. "China and Kazakhstan." Accessed March 7, 2015. http://www.cctv.com/lm/1039/20/3.html.

CCTV. "China and Russia." Accessed January 18, 2015, http://www.cctv.com/lm/1039/20/1.html.

China–Brazil Business Council. Bilateral Agreements: Acts in Force Signed Between Brazil and People's Republic of China. Accessed May 1, 2015. http://www.cebc.org.br/en/data-and-statistics/bilateral-agreements.

China Daily. (March 22, 2013). "Experience China' opens in the Republic of Congo." Accessed August 13, 2016. http://www.china.org.cn/world/2013-03/22/content_28327582.htm.

ChinaDaily.com.cn. (July 20, 2006). "China Announce U.S. $1.3 b Russian Real Estate Project." Accessed March 11, 2016, http://www.chinadaily.com.cn/china/2006-07/20/content 645 771.htm.

ChinaDaily.com.cn. (June 28, 2012). "Venezuela, China: 38 years of diplomatic relations." Accessed October 13, 2013. http://www.chinadaily.com.cn/cndy/2012-06/28/content _15528289.htm.

China Gas. (May 22, 2007). "China Gas and Oman Oil Form Joint Venture-Set to become Major Energy Importer in China." Accessed August 15, 2016, http://www.chinagasholdings .com.hk/uploadfiles/20120514094849411.pdf.

China Military Online. (September 23, 2014). "First China–Iran Joint Military Exercise Attracts Attention." Accessed February 1, 2015. http://eng.mod.gov.cn/DefenseNews/2014-09/23/content_4539380.htm.

China National Petroleum Company. "CNPC in Iraq, Oilfield Services Engineering." Accessed February 6, 2015. http://www.cnpc.com.cn/en/Iraq/country_index.shtml.

China National Petroleum Company. "CNPC in Iran, Oilfield Services, Engineering and Construction." Accessed February 6, 2015. http://www.cnpc.com.cn/en/Iran/country _index.shtml.

China National Petroleum Company. "CNPC in Kazakhstan, Oilfield Services, Engineering and Construction." Accessed February 21, 2015. http://www.cnpc.com.cn/en/Kazakhstan/country_index.shtml.

China National Petroleum Company. "CNPC in Russia, Oilfield Services, Engineering and Construction." Accessed July 6, 2016. http://www.cnpc.com.cn/en/Russia/country_ index.shtml.

China National Petroleum Company. "CNPC in Venezuela, Major Events." Accessed January 5, 2016. http://www.cnpc.com.cn/en/Venezuela/country_index.shtml.

China National Petroleum Company. "CNPC in Venezuela, Oil and Gas Operations." Accessed January 5, 2016. http://www.cnpc.com.cn/en/Venezuela/country_index.shtml.

China National Petroleum Company. "CNPC in Venezuela, Oilfield Services Engineering." Accessed January 5, 2016. http://www.cnpc.com.cn/en/Venezuela/country_index.shtml.

Chinese-Embassy.info. "China embassies and consulates in Russia." Assessed July 3, 2016. http://www.chinese-embassy.info/europe/rus.htm.

Cole, Bernard. *Oil for the Lamps of China-Beijing's 21st Century Search for Energy*. Washington, DC: Institute for National Strategic Studies, National Defense University, 2003.

Confucius Institute Online. Confucius Institute. 2016. http://www.chinesecio.com/m/cio_wci.

Corkin, Lucy. "Angola Brief." Norway: Chr. Michelsen Institute, Volume 1, Issue 1, January 2011: 1–4. Accessed November 2, 2014. http://www.cmi.no/publications/file/3938-china-and-angola-strategic-partnership-or-marriage.pdf.

Corkin, Lucy. *Uncovering African Agency: Angola's Management of China's Credit Lines*. Farnham, UK: Ashgate Publishing Limited, 2013.

Corrales, Javier. "China and Venezuela's Search for Oil Markets." In *Latin America Facing China: South–South Relations Beyond the Washington Consensus*, edited by Alex E. Fernandez Jillerto and Barbara Hogenboom, 115–133. New York, NY: Berghahn Books, 2012.

Daly, John C. K. "Kazakhstan Nervously Contemplates Possible Impact of Sanctions Against Russia." *Eurasia Daily Monitor*, Volume XI, Issue 95, May 21, 2014.

Dang, Wendy. "China, Kuwait Sign New Air Service Agreement." *China Aviation Daily*, June 5, 2014. Accessed August 13, 2016. http://www.chinaaviationdaily.com/news/35/35186. html.

De Pierrebourg, Fabrice and Michel Juneau-Katsuya. *Nest of Spies: The Startling Truth About Foreign Agents at Work Within Canada's Borders*. Canada: HarperCollins, 2009.

Devereux, Charlie. "China Development Bank Lends Venezuela $42.5 Billion Since 2007." *Bloomberg Business*, September 25, 2012. Accessed January 1, 2016, http://www. bloomberg.com/news/articles/2012-09-25/china-development-bank-lends-venezuela-42-5-billion-since-2007.

Dickey, Lauren. "China Takes Steps Toward Realizing Silk Road Ambitions." *China Brief*, Volume XIV, Issue 11, June 14, 2014. 3–4

Dominguez, Jorge I. *China's Relations with Latin America: Shared Gains, Asymmetric Hopes*. Washington: Inter-American Dialogue, June 2006.

Downs, Erica. *Inside China, Inc: China Development Bank's Cross-Border Energy Deals*. Washington, DC: The Brooking Institution Press, March 2011.

Dwivedi, Ramakant. "China's Central Asia Policy in Recent Times." *China and Eurasia Forum Quarterly*, Volume 4, Issue 4, November 2006: 139–159.

Economic and Commercial Counsellor's Office of the Embassy of the People's Republic of China in Iraq. (November 28, 2014). "Agreement on Cultural Cooperation between the Governments of the People's Republic of China and the Republic of Iraq." Accessed August 18, 2016. http://iq2.mofcom.gov.cn/article/bilateralcooperation/.

Ellis, R. Evan. "Advances in China–Latin America Space Cooperation." *China Brief*, Volume X, Issue 14, July 9, 2010.

Ellis, Evan R. "China's Cautious Economic and Strategic Gamble in Venezuela," *China Brief* (Jamestown Foundation), Volume XI, Issue 18, September 30, 2011, 9. Accessed December 26, 2015.

Ellis, R. Evan. *China-Latin America Military Engagement: Good Will, Good Business and Strategic Position.* Carlisle, PA: Strategic Studies Institute, August 2011. 7–11.

Ellis, R. Evan. *China on the Ground of Latin America: Challenges for the Chinese and Impacts on the Region.* New York, NY: Palgrave Macmillan, 2014.

Embassy of the Bolivarian Republic of Venezuela in the Republic of Belarus. (September 23, 2013). "Signature of 24 New Agreements between Venezuela and China will benefit the Development of Both Nations." Accessed May 25, 2015. http://www.embavenez.by/en/news/1159-firma-de-24-nuevos-acuerdos-entre-venezuela-y-china-beneficiaran-el-desarrollo-de-ambas-aciones?tmpl=component&print=1&layout=default&page=.

Embassy of the People's Republic of China in the State of Kuwait. "China and Kuwait." Accessed October 8, 2013 and September 21, 2014. http://kw.china-embassy.org/eng/sbgx/t580302.htm.

Embassy of the People's Republic of China in the United Arab Emirates. "China and the United Arab Emirates." Accessed October 11, 2014. http://ae.china-embassy.org/eng/sbgx/t 150466.htm.

Embassy of the People's Republic of China in South Sudan. (November 23, 2012). "Sino-South Sudan Cultural and Educational Exchanges." Accessed February 7, 2015. http://ss.chines eembassy.org/eng/sbgx/whjw/.

Embassy of the People's Republic of China in South Sudan. (November 23, 2012). "Sino–South Sudan Economic & Trade Cooperation." Accessed February 5, 2015. http://ss.chinese embassy.org/eng/sbgx/jmwl/.

Embassy of the People's Republic of China in South Sudan. (November 23, 2012). "Sino–South Sudan Political Exchanges." Accessed February 5, 2015. http://ss.Chineseembassy.org/eng/sbgx/zjjw/.

Embassy of the People's Republic of China in Sudan. (June 7, 2012). "CCTV and Sudan State Television Signed a Cooperation Agreement." Accessed February 13, 2015. http://sd. china-embassy.org/eng/whjl/t939073.htm.

Energy China News. (December 29, 2014). "Two Power Grid Projects in Venezuela Signed." Accessed January 8, 2016. http://en.ceec.net.cn/art/2014/12/29/art_138_285931.html.

Ersan, Yagmur. "China and Venezuela strengthen bilateral relations." *Turkish Weekly,* October 2, 2013. Accessed October 13, 2013. http://www.turkishweekly.net/news/157211/china-and-venezuela-strengthen-bilateral-relations.html.

European Commission Directorate-General for Trade. (April 10, 2015). "Angola: EU Bilateral Trade and Trade with the World." Accessed May 3, 2015. http://trade.ec.europa.eu/doclib/docs/2006/september/tradoc_112456.pdf.

European Commission Directorate-General for Trade. (June 21, 2016). "Angola: EU Bilateral Trade and Trade with the World." Accessed July 23, 2016. http://trade.ec.europa.eu/doclib/docs/2006/september/tradoc_112456.pdf.

European Commission Directorate-General for Trade. (April 10, 2015). "Brazil: EU Bilateral Trade and Trade with the World." Accessed August 15, 2015. http://trade.ec.europa.eu/doclib/docs/2006/september/tradoc_113359.pdf.
European Commission Directorate-General for Trade. (June 21, 2016). "Brazil: EU Bilateral Trade and Trade with the World." Accessed July 23, 2016. http://trade.ec.europa.eu/doclib/docs/2006/september/tradoc_113359.pdf.
European Commission Directorate-General for Trade. (July 5, 2013). "China: EU Bilateral Trade and Trade with the World." Accessed October 13, 2013. http://trade.ec.europa.eu/doclib/docs/2006/september/tradoc_113366.pdf.
European Commission Directorate-General for Trade. (April 10, 2015). "China: EU Bilateral Trade and Trade with the World." Accessed May 3, 2015. http://trade.ec.europa.eu/doclib/docs/2006/september/tradoc_113366.pdf.
European Commission Directorate-General for Trade. (April 10, 2015). "Congo: EU Bilateral Trade and Trade with the World." Accessed May 3, 2015. http://trade.ec.europa.eu/doclib/docs/2006/september/tradoc_147253.pdf.
European Commission Directorate-General for Trade. (June 21, 2016). "Congo: EU Bilateral Trade and Trade with the World." Accessed July 23, 2016. http://trade.ec.europa.eu/doclib/docs/2006/september/tradoc_147253.pdf.
European Commission Directorate-General for Trade. (April 10, 2015). "Iran: EU Bilateral Trade and Trade with the World." Accessed May 3, 2015. http://trade.ec.europa.eu/doclib/docs/2006/september/tradoc_113392.pdf.
European Commission Directorate-General for Trade. (June 21, 2016). "Iran: EU Bilateral Trade and Trade with the World." Accessed July 23, 2016. http://trade.ec.europa.eu/doclib/docs/2006/september/tradoc_113392.pdf.
European Commission Directorate-General for Trade. (April 10, 2015). "Iraq: EU Bilateral Trade and Trade with the World." Accessed May 3, 2015. http://trade.ec.europa.eu/doclib/docs/2006/september/tradoc_113405.pdf.
European Commission Directorate-General for Trade. (June 21, 2016). "Iraq: EU Bilateral Trade and Trade with the World." Accessed July 23, 2016. http://trade.ec.europa.eu/doclib/docs/2006/september/tradoc_113405.pdf.
European Commission Directorate-General for Trade. (April 10, 2015). "Kazakhstan: EU Bilateral Trade and Trade with the World." Accessed May 3, 2015. http://trade.ec.europa.eu/doclib/docs/2006/september/tradoc_113406.pdf.
European Commission Directorate-General for Trade. (June 21, 2016). "Kazakhstan: EU Bilateral Trade and Trade with the World." Accessed July 23, 2016. http://trade.ec.europa.eu/doclib/docs/2006/september/tradoc_113406.pdf
European Commission Directorate-General for Trade. (April 10, 2014). "Kuwait: EU Bilateral Trade and Trade with the World." Accessed May 3, 2015. http://trade.ec.europa.eu/doclib/docs/2006/september/tradoc_113408.pdf.
European Commission Directorate-General for Trade. (June 21, 2016). "Kuwait: EU Bilateral Trade and Trade with the World." Accessed July 23, 2016. http://trade.ec.europa.eu/doclib/docs/2006/september/tradoc_113408.pdf.
European Commission Directorate-General for Trade. (April 10, 2015). "Oman: EU Bilateral Trade and Trade with the World." Accessed May 3, 2015. http://trade.ec.europa.eu/doclib/docs/2006/september/tradoc_113430.pdf.

European Commission Directorate-General for Trade. (June 21, 2016). "Oman: EU Bilateral Trade and Trade with the World." Accessed July 23, 2016. http://trade.ec.europa.eu/doclib/docs/2006/september/tradoc_113430.pdf.

European Commission Directorate-General for Trade. (April 16, 2014). "Russia: EU Bilateral Trade and Trade with the World." Accessed May 3, 2014. http://trade.ec.europa.eu/doclib/docs/2006/september/tradoc_113440.pdf.

European Commission Directorate-General for Trade. (April 10, 2015). "Russia: EU Bilateral Trade and Trade with the World." Accessed May 3, 2015. http://trade.ec.europa.eu/doclib/docs/2006/september/tradoc_113440.pdf.

European Commission Directorate General for Trade. (June 21, 2016). "Russia: EU Bilateral Trade and Trade with the World." Accessed July 23, 2016. http://trade.ec.europa.eu/doclib/docs/2006/september/tradoc_113440.pdf.

European Commission Directorate-General for Trade. (April 10, 2015). "Saudi Arabia: EU Bilateral Trade and Trade with the World." Accessed May 3, 2015. http://trade.ec.europa.eu/doclib/docs/2006/september/tradoc_113442.pdf.

European Commission Directorate-General for Trade. (June 21, 2016). "Saudi Arabia: EU Bilateral Trade and Trade with the World." Accessed July 23, 2016. http://trade.ec.europa.eu/doclib/docs/2006/september/tradoc_113442.pdf.

European Commission Directorate-General for Trade. (April 16, 2014). "Sudan: EU Bilateral Trade and Trade with the World." Accessed February 13, 2015. http://trade.ec.europa.eu/doclib/docs/2006/september/tradoc_147395.pdf.

European Commission Directorate-General for Trade. (June 21, 2016). "Sudan: EU Bilateral Trade and Trade with the World." Accessed July 23, 2016. http://trade.ec.europa.eu/doclib/docs/2006/september/tradoc_147395.pdf.

European Commission Directorate-General for Trade. (April 10, 2015). "United Arab Emirates: EU Bilateral Trade and Trade with the World." Accessed May 3, 2015. http://trade.ec.europa.eu/doclib/docs/2006/september/tradoc_113458.pdf.

European Commission Directorate-General for Trade. (June 21, 2016). "United Arab Emirates: EU Bilateral Trade and Trade with the World." Accessed July 23, 2016. http://trade.ec.europa.eu/doclib/docs/2006/september/tradoc_113458.pdf.

European Commission Directorate-General for Trade. (July 5, 2013). "Venezuela: EU Bilateral Trade and Trade with the World." Accessed October 13, 2013. http://trade.ec.europa.eu/doclib/docs/2006/september/tradoc_113462.pdf.

European Commission Directorate-General for Trade. (April 10, 2015). "Venezuela: EU Bilateral Trade and Trade with the World." Accessed May 3, 2015. http://trade.ec.europa.eu/doclib/docs/2006/september/tradoc_113462.pdf.

European Commission Directorate-General for Trade. (June 21, 2016). "Venezuela: EU Bilateral Trade and Trade with the World." Accessed July 23, 2016. http://trade.ec.europa.eu/doclib/docs/2006/september/tradoc_113462.pdf.

Feng, Zhongping and Jing Huang. "China's Strategic Partnership Diplomacy: Engaging with a Changing World." Fride and ESPO: Working Paper No. 8, June 2014. http://www.fride.org/descarga/WP8_China_strategic_ partnership_diplomacy.pdf.

Fernandez Jilberto, Alex E. and Barbara Hogenboom. "Latin America and China: South–South Relations in a New Era." In *Latin America Facing China: South–South Relations Beyond the Washington Consensus,* edited by Alex E. Fernandez

Jillerto and Barbara Hogenboom, 1–32. New York, NY: Berghahn Books, 2012.

Fomichev, Mikhail. "Transneft to Boost Pacific Oil Pipeline Capacity to 67M tones," *Ria Novosti*, July 31, 2013. Accessed October 13, 2013. http://en.rian.ru/business/20130731/182511026.html.

Francis, Caroline, Pratheepan Madasamy, Sharif Sokkary, and Skamania You. *China and Sudan–South Sudan Oil Free Impasse: Implications of Chinese Foreign Aid, Diplomacy, and Military Relations*. Michigan: University of Michigan, April 24, 2012. http://sites.fordschool.umich.edu/china-policy/files/2012/09/China-and-the-Sudan_South-Sudan-Oil-Fee-Impasse.pdf.

Freeman, Duncan. Jonathan Holslag, and Rhys Jenkins. *Chinese Resources and Energy Policy in Latin America*. Brussels: European Parliament, June 2007.

Gabuev, Alexander. *A "Soft Alliance"? Russia–China Relations After the Ukraine Crisis*. London, UK: European Council on Foreign Relations, May 2015.

Gallagher, Kevin P. and Margaret Myers. "China–Latin America Finance Database." Washington: Inter-American Dialogue, 2014. http://www.thedialogue.org/map_list/.

Gallagher, Kevin P., Amos Irwin, and Katherine Kowalski. *The New Banks in Town: Chinese Finance in Latin America*. Washington, DC: Inter-American Dialogue, February 2012.

Gao, Xiaolin. *Repacking Confucius: PRC Public Diplomacy and the Rise of Soft Power*. Stockholm, Sweden: Institute for Security and Development Policy, January 2008.

Graphisoft. (November 16, 2010). "ARCHICAD-designed Russian Pavilion at World Expo 2010 in Shanghai Takes the Silver." Accessed March 27, 2016. http://www.graphisoft.com/info/news/press_releases/russian-pavilion-shanghai.html.

Guriev, Sergei and Andrei Rachinsky. *The Evolution of Personal Wealth in the Former Soviet Union and Central and Eastern Europe*. Helsinki, Finland: UNU World Institute for Development Economics Research, Research Paper No. 2006/120, October 2006, 10, footnote 14.

Habboush, Mahmoud. "Cosco Shipping Signs $738 Million Deal to Expand U.A.E. Port." *Bloomberg*, September 28, 2016. Accessed October 5, 2016. http://www.bloomberg.com/news/articles/2016-09-28/cosco-shipping-signs-738-million-deal-to-expand-u-a-e-port.

Hale, Benjamin A. "Arrighi on Sino-Sudanese Relations: Trade, Investment, and Diplomacy in Twenty-First Century." Bachelor of Arts Thesis, Edith Cowan University, 2013. http://ro.ecu.edu.au/cgi/viewcontent.cgi?article=1086&context=theses_hons.

Hamdan Bin Mohammed Smart University. "First China-UAE Conference on Islamic Banking & Finance concludes with Positive Outlook for Future of Islamic Economy," May 30, 2016. Accessed August 16, 2016. https://www.hbmsu.ac.ae/news/first-china-uae-conference-on-islamic-banking-finance-concludes-positive-outlook-for-future-of.

Harold, Scott and Alireza Nader. *China and Iran: Economic, Political and Military Relations*. Santa Monica, CA: RAND Corporation, 2012.

Hartman, Adam. "Chinese Naval Base for Walvis Bay." *The Namibian*, November 19, 2014. http://www.namibian.com.na/indexx.php?id=20409&page_type=story_detail&category_id=1.

Heritage Foundation and American Enterprise Institute. *China Global Investment Tracker Database.* 2016. http://www.heritage.org/research/projects/china-global-investment-tracker-interactive-map.

Holz, Heidi and Kenneth Allen. "Military Exchanges with Chinese Characteristics: The People's Liberation Army Experience with Military Relations." In *The PLA At Home and Abroad: Accessing the Operational Capabilities of China's Military*, edited by Roy Kamphausen, David Lai, and Andrew Scobell, 429–480. Carlisle, PA: Strategic Studies Institute, June 2010.

Holz, Heidi and Kenneth Allen. "Military Exchanges with Chinese Characteristics: The PLA Experience with Military Relations." Paper presented at The National Bureau of Asian Research, Strategic Studies Institute of the U.S. Army War College, and Texas A&M University's Bush School Conference "The PLA at Home and Abroad," Carlisle Barracks, PA, September 25–27, 2009.

Horta, Loro. "Brazil–China Relations." Singapore: S. Rajaratnam School of International Studies, RSIS Working Paper No. 287, March 10, 2015.

Horta, Loro. "China and Brazil: Commercial Success Amidst International Tensions." Oakland, California: Japan Policy Research Institute, Working Paper No. 113, November 2007. Accessed October 31, 2015. http://www.jpri.org/publications/workingpapers/wp113.html.

Hsiao, L.C. Russell. "PLAN Officers to Train on Brazilian Aircraft Carrier." *China Brief*, Volume IX, Issue 12, June 12, 2009: 1–2

Hsu, Jing-Yun and Jenn-Jaw Soong. "Development of China–Russia Relations (1949–2011): Limits, Opportunities, and Economic Ties." *The Chinese Economy.* New York, NY: M.E. Sharpe, Inc., Volume 47, Issue 3, May–June 2014, 70–87.

http://china.aiddata.org/projects/37442.

http://china.aiddata.org/projects/37459.

http://china.aiddata.org/projects/37538.

http://china.aiddata.org/projects/37807.

http://china.aiddata.org/projects/37838.

http://china.aiddata.org/projects/38141.

http://china.aiddata.org/projects/39099.

http://china.aiddata.org/projects/39539.

http://china.aiddata.org/projects/39556.

http://china.aiddata.org/projects/40232.

http://china.aiddata.org/projects/40264.

http://china.aiddata.org/projects?utf8=%E2%9C%93&search=&country_name%5B%5D=Sudan.

http://china.aiddata.org/projects?utf8=%E2%9C%93&search=&country_name%5B%5D=South+Sudan.

Inter-American Dialogue. "China-Latin America Finance Database." Accessed October 13, 2013. http://thedialogue.org/map_list.

International Crisis Group. *China's Central Asia Problem.* Crisis Group Asia Report No. 244, February 27, 2013. Accessed February 28, 2015. http://www.crisisgroup.org/~/media/files/asia/north-east-asia/244-chinas-central-asia-problem.pdf.

International Crisis Group. *China's New Courtship in South Sudan.* Crisis Group Africa Report No. 186, April 2012. Accessed February 8, 2015. http://www.

crisisgroup.org/~/media/Files/africa/horn-of-africa/sudan/186-chinas-new-courtship-in-south-sudan.pdf.

International Trade Centre, Directory of Trade Promotion Organizations and Other Trade Support Institutions. http://www.intracen.org/itc/trade-support/tsi-directory.

Iran's Book News Agency. (June 9, 2016). "Iran and China sign Memo to exchange Cultural, Scientific Documents." Accessed August 19, 2016. http://www.ibna.ir/en/doc/naghli/237338/iran-and-china-sign-memo-to-exchange-cultural-scientific-documents.

Iran Daily. (May 24, 2016). "Iran, China sign Seven Commercial Cooperation Documents." Accessed August 19, 2016. http://www.iran-daily.com/News/151976.html.

Iraqi Daily Journal. (September 13, 2014). "Iraq, China Sign Cooperation Agreement in the Fields of Culture, Education, Media and Sport." Accessed September 14, 2014. http://www.iraqdailyjournal.com/story-z9658635.

Jakobson, Linda, Paul Holtom, Dean Knox, and Jingchao Peng. *China's Energy and Security Relations with Russia: Hopes, Frustrations and Uncertainties.* Stockholm, Sweden: SIPRI, Policy Paper No. 29, October 2011. Accessed February 28, 2015. http://books.sipri.org/files/PP/SIPRIPP29.pdf.

Ji, You. "The Soviet Model and the Breakdown of the Military Alliance." *China Learns from the Soviet Union, 1949–Present,* edited by Thomas P. Bernstein and Hua-Yu Li, 131–149. Lanham, MD: Lexington Books, 2010.

Jiang, Julie and Chen Dang. *Update on Overseas Investments by Chinese National Companies: Achievements and Challenges Since 2011.* Paris, France: Organization for Economic Cooperation and Development/International Energy Agency, June 2014.

Jiang, Shixue. "A New Look at Chinese Relations with Latin America." *Nueva Sociedad*, Volume 203, May–June 2006, 62–78. Accessed October 2, 2015.

Jiang, Shixue. "Demystifying the China–Brazil Relations." China Institute of International Studies, September 29, 2014. Accessed November 9, 2015. http://www.ciis.org.cn/english/2014-09/29/content_7270603.htm.

Johnson, Cecil. *Communist China and Latin America 1959–1967.* New York, NY: Columbia University Press, 1970.

Kalis, Naseer Ahmed. "Chinese Energy Investment in Kazakhstan: Challenges and Future Prospects." *International Journal of Scientific Research and Education*, Volume 2, Issue 1, January 2014: 264–273.

Kemp, Geoffrey. *The East Moves West: India, China, and Asia's Growing Presence in the Middle East.* Washington, DC: Brookings Institution Press, 2010.

Khodzhaev, Ablat. "The Central Asian Policy of the People's Republic of China." *China and Eurasia Forum Quarterly*, Volume 7, Issue 1, February 2009: 9–28.

Kim, Alexander. "China and Kazakhstan: Inevitability of Beijing's Growing Influence." *Eurasia Daily Monitor*, Volume X, Issue 153, August 16, 2013.

Kong, Hanbing. "The Transplantation and Entrenchment of the Soviet Economic Model in China." In *China Learns from the Soviet Union, 1949–Present,* edited by Thomas P. Bernstein and Hua-Yu Lim, 153–166. Lanham, MD: Lexington Books, 2010.

Korablinov, Alexander. "Russia, China sign 30 Cooperation Agreements." *Russia Beyond the Headlines*, June 27, 2016. Accessed August 26, 2016. http://rbth.com/international/2016/06/27/russia-china-sign-30-cooperation-agreements_606505

Kostecka, Daniel J. "Places and Bases: The Chinese Navy's Emerging Support Network in the Indian Ocean." *Naval War College Review*, Volume 64, Issue 1, 59–80, 2011.

Kuwait News Agency. (June 12, 2005). "Oman, China sign Oil Supply Agreement." Accessed August 15, 2016. http://www.kuna.net.kw/ArticlePrintPage.aspx?id=1568404&language=en.

Lanteigne, Marc. "China's Central Asian Energy Diplomacy." In *Caspian Energy Politics: Azerbaijan, Kazakhstan, and Turkmenistan,* edited by Indra Overland, Stina Torjesen, and Heidi Kjaernet, 101–115. New York, NY: Routledge, 2011.

Large, Daniel. *Sudan's Foreign Relations with Asia: China and the Politics of "Looking East."* Philadelphia, PA: Institute for Security Studies, ISS Paper 158, February 2008. http://dspace.africaportal.org/jspui/bitstream/123456789/30875/1/PAPER158.pdf?1.

Large, Daniel and Luke Patey. *Riding the Sudanese Storm: China, India, Russia, Brazil and Two Sudans.* Johannesburg, South Africa: South African Institute of Foreign Affairs, Occasional Paper No. 197, July 2014.

Large, Daniel and Luke Patey. "Sudan Looks East." In *Sudan Looks East: China, India and The Politics of Asian Alternatives,* edited by Daniel Large and Luke Patey, 1–34. Rochester, NY: James Currey Ltd., 2011.

Lee, Scott J. "From Beijing to Baghdad: Stability and Decision-making in Sino-Iraqi Relations, 1958–2012." B.A. thesis, University of Pennsylvania, April 1, 2013. Accessed September 19, 2014, http://repository.upenn.edu/curej/159/.

Leverett, Flynt. "Resource Mercantilism and the Militarization of Resource Management: Rising Asia and the Future of American Primacy." In *Energy Security and Global Politics: The Militarization of Resource Management*, edited by Daniel Moran and James A. Russell, 211–242. New York, NY: Routledge, 2009.

Lo, Bobo and Andy Rothman. *Asian Geopolitics.* Hong Kong, China: CLSA, May 2006.

Lu, Guozheng. "Post-Financial Crisis Trade Relations: A New Phase of China–Latin America Cooperation," In *China–Latin America Relations Review and Analysis (Volume 1),* edited by Shuangrong Hu, 57–71. Reading, UK: Path International Ltd., 2012.

Macauhub. (October 3, 2007). "Angola and China's Eximbank sign New Infrastructure Agreement." Accessed August 12, 2016. http://www.macauhub.com.mo/en/2007/10/03/3816/.

Macauhub. (April 18, 2008). "Angola: China and Angola to sign New Partnership Agreement to Support Basic Infrastructures." Accessed August 12, 2016. http://www.macauhub.com.m o/en/2008/04/18/4900/.

Macauhub. (August 15, 2016). "China and Angola sign Agreement for Mutual Acceptance of National Currencies." Accessed August 12, 2016. http://www.macauhub.com.mo/en/2015/08/05/china-and-angola-sign-agreement-for-mutual-acceptance-of-national-currencies/.

Maglad, Nour Eldin A. *Scoping Study on Chinese Relations with Sudan.* Nairobi, Kenya: African Economic Research Consortium, February 2008. http://hdl.handle.net/10419/93162.

Mao, Yufeng. "Beijing's Two-Pronged Iraq Policy." *China Brief*, Volume V, Issue 12, May 24, 2005. Accessed September 14, 2014. http://www.jamestown.org/programs/chinabrief/sin gle/?tx_ttnews%5Btt_news%5D=30441&tx_ttnews%5BbackPid%5D=195&no_cache=1#.VBaHfZtWZhE.

Marketos, Thrassy N. *China's Energy Geopolitics: The Shanghai Cooperation Organization and Central Asia*. New York, NY: Routledge, 2009.

McAuley, Anthony. "China State Oil Company win Abu Dhabi Oilfield Contract." *The National Business*, May 18, 2015. Accessed August 16, 2016. http://www.thenational.ae/business/energy/china-state-oil-company-wins-abu-dhabi-oilfield-contract.

McCaffrey, Barry. "Iran, Nukes, & Oil: The Gulf Confrontation." PowerPoint presentation presented at a seminar for NBC Executives and Producers, January 12, 2012.

McElhanney, M. "China—Doing Business with the UAE." *Arabbrains*, August 13, 2013. Accessed October 11, 2014. http://arabbrains.com/2013/08/13/china-doing-business-with-the-uae/.

McGill, Bates and Matthew Oresman. *China's New Journey to the West: China's Emergence in Central Asia and Implications for U.S. Interests*. Washington, DC: Center for Strategic and International Studies, August 2003.

Medeiros, Evan S. *China's International Behavior: Activism, Opportunism, and Diversification*. Santa Monica, CA: RAND Corporation, 2009.

Ministry of Commerce of People's Republic of China. (November 28, 2004). "China–Oman Bilateral Relations." Accessed October 3, 2014, http://om2.mofcom.gov.cn/article/bilater alcooperation/inbrief/200411/20041100004112.shtml.

Ministry of Foreign Affairs of People's Republic of China. (November 23, 1985). "Agreement Between the Government of the People's Republic of China and the Government of the State of Kuwait for the Promotion and Protection of Investments." Accessed September 21, 2014. http://www.fmprc.gov.cn/mfa_eng/wjb_663304/zzjg_663340/xybfs_663590/g jlb_663594/2838_663666/2839_663668/t16369.shtml.

Ministry of Foreign Affairs of People's Republic of China. (December 5, 1989). "Agreement Between the Government of the People's Republic of China and the Government of the State of Kuwait for the Avoidance of Double Taxation and the Prevention of Fiscal Evasion with Respect to Taxes on Income and Capital." Accessed September 21, 2014. http://www.fmprc.gov.cn/mfa_eng/wjb_663304/zzjg_663340/xybfs_663590/gjlb_663594/2838_663666/2839_663668/t16370.shtml.

Ministry of Foreign Affairs of People's Republic of China. (June 5, 2002). "Agreement on Air Transport between the Government of the People's Republic of China and the Government of the Republic of Iraq." Accessed September 19, 2014. http://www.fmprc. gov.cn/mfa_eng/wjb_663304/zzjg_663340/xybfs_663590/gjlb_6635 94/2823_663636/2824_663638/t16330.shtml.

Ministry of Foreign Affairs of People's Republic of China. (June 5, 2002). "Agreement on Cultural Cooperation between the Governments of the People's Republic of China and the Republic of Iraq." Accessed September 19, 2014. http://www.fmprc.gov.cn/mfa_eng/wjb_663304/zzjg_663340/xybfs_663590/gjlb_663594/282 3_663636/2824_663638/t16331.shtml.

Ministry of Foreign Affairs of People's Republic of China. (June 5, 2012). "A Joint Cooperation Agreement Between the Saudi Press Agency and the Chinese Xinhua

News Agency." Accessed May 26, 2014. http://www.fmprc.gov.cn/mfa_eng/ wjb_663304/zzjg_663340/x ybfs_663590/gjlb_663594/2878_663746/2879_6637 48/t16424.shtml.
Ministry of Foreign Affairs of People's Republic of China. (October 10, 2006). "Angola." Accessed October 15, 2014. http://www.china.org.cn/english/features/ focac/183584.htm.
Ministry of Foreign Affairs of People's Republic of China. (April 14, 2011). "Assistant Foreign Minister Liu Zhenmin Meets UAE Ambassador to China and the Two Sides Exchange the Instruments of Ratification of the Treaty between China and UAE on Criminal Judicial Assistance." Accessed August 16, 2016. http://www. fmprc.gov.cn/mfa_eng/wjb_ 663304/zzjg_663340/xybfs_663590/gjlb_663594/29 03_663806/2905_663810/t816038.shtml.
Ministry of Foreign Affairs of People's Republic of China. "China and Angola." Accessed October 15, 2014. http://www.fmprc.gov.cn/mfa_eng/wjb_663304/ zzjg_663340/fzs _663828/gjlb_663832/2914_663834/.
Ministry of Foreign Affairs of People's Republic of China. "China-Angola: Activities." Accessed August 7, 2016. http://www.fmprc.gov.cn/mfa_eng/wjb_663304/ zzjg 663340/fzs_663828/gjlb_663832/2914_663834/2916_663838/.
Ministry of Foreign Affairs of the People's Republic of China. "China and Brazil." Accessed November 17, 2014. http://www.fmprc.gov.cn/mfa_eng/wjb_663304/ zzjg_663340/ldmzs _664952/gjlb_664956/3473_665008/.
Ministry of Foreign Affairs of People's Republic of China. "China and Iran." Accessed June 8, 2014. http://www.fmprc.gov.cn/mfa_eng/wjb_663304/zzjg_663340/xybfs _663590/gjlb _663594/2818_663626/.
Ministry of Foreign Affairs of People's Republic of China. "China and Iraq." Accessed September 14, 2014. http://www.fmprc.gov.cn/mfa_eng/wjb_663304/ zzjg_663340/xybfs _663590/gjlb_663594/2823_663636/.
Ministry of Foreign Affairs of People's Republic of China. "China and Kuwait." Accessed May 9, 2014. http://www.fmprc.gov.cn/mfa_eng/wjb_663304/ zzjg_663340/xybfs_663590/gjl b_663594/2838_663666/.
Ministry of Foreign Affairs of People's Republic of China. "China and Oman." Accessed October 3, 2014. http://www.fmprc.gov.cn/mfa_eng/wjb_663304/ zzjg_663340/xybfs 66 3590/gjlb_663594/2863_663716/.
Ministry of Foreign Affairs of People's Republic of China. (November 26, 2004). "China and Saudi Arabia." Accessed August 29, 2014, http://jeddah.china-consulate.org/eng/zsgx/t 172060.htm.
Ministry of Foreign Affairs of People's Republic of China. "China and Sudan." Accessed February 13, 2015. http://www.fmprc.gov.cn/mfa_eng/wjb_663304/zzjg 663340/xybfs_ 663590/gjlb_663594/2883_663766/.
Ministry of Foreign Affairs of People's Republic of China. "China and United Arab Emirates." Accessed October 7, 2014. http://www.fmprc.gov.cn/mfa_eng/ wjb_663304/zzjg_663340/xybfs_663590/gjlb_663594/2903_663806/.
Ministry of Foreign Affairs of the People's Republic of China. "China and Venezuela." Accessed May 24, 2015. http://www.fmprc.gov.cn/mfa_eng/wjb_663304/ zzjg_663340/ldmzs_664952/gjlb_664956/3538_665158/.

Ministry of Foreign Affairs of People's Republic of China. "China–Brazil: Activities." Accessed August 8, 2016. http://www.fmprc.gov.cn/mfa_eng/wjb_663304/zzjg_663340/ldmzs 66 4952/gjlb_664956/3473_665008/3475_665012/.

Ministry of Foreign Affairs of People's Republic of China. "China–Congo: Activities." Accessed August 8, 2016. http://www.fmprc.gov.cn/mfa_eng/wjb_663304/zzjg 663340/fzs 663828/gjlb_663832/2954_663914/2956_663918/.

Ministry of Foreign Affairs of People's Republic of China. "China–Iran: Activities." Accessed August 8, 2016. http://www.fmprc.gov.cn/mfa_eng/wjb_663304/zzjg_663340/xybfs _663590/gjlb_663594/2818_663626/2820_663630/default_2.shtml.

Ministry of Foreign Affairs of People's Republic of China. "China–Iraq: Activities." Accessed August 8, 2016. http://www.fmprc.gov.cn/mfa_eng/wjb_663304/zzjg_663340/xybfs _663590/gjlb_663594/2823_663636/2825_663640/.

Ministry of Foreign Affairs of People's Republic of China. "China–Kazakhstan: Activities." Accessed August 9, 2016. http://www.fmprc.gov.cn/mfa_eng/wjb_663304/zzjg_ 663340/dozys_664276/gjlb_664280/3180_664322/3182_664326/default.shtml.

Ministry of Foreign Affairs of People's Republic of China. (June 5, 2012). "China–Iran: Joint Communiqué Between the People's Republic of China and the Islamic Republic of Iran." Accessed June 8, 2014. http://www.fmprc.gov.cn/mfa_eng/wjb_663304/zzjg_663340/xybfs_663590/gjlb_663594/2818_663626/2819_663628/t16315.shtml.

Ministry of Foreign Affairs of People's Republic of China. "China–Kuwait: Activities." Accessed August 22, 2015. http://www.fmprc.gov.cn/mfa_eng/wjb_663304/zzjg _663340/xybfs_663590/gjlb_663594/2838_663666/2840_663670/.

Ministry of Foreign Affairs of People's Republic of China. "China–Oman: Activities." Accessed August 9, 2016. http://www.fmprc.gov.cn/mfa_eng/wjb_663304/zzjg_663340/xybfs _663590/gjlb_663594/2863_663716/2865_663720/.

Ministry of Foreign Affairs of People's Republic of China. "China–Russia: Activities." Accessed August 9, 2016. http://www.fmprc.gov.cn/mfa_eng/wjb_663304/zzjg_663340/dozys _664276/gjlb_664280/3220_664352/3222_664356/.

Ministry of Foreign Affairs of People's Republic of China. "China–Russia: Documents." Accessed January 10, 2016. http://www.fmprc.gov.cn/mfa_eng/wjb_663304/zzjg_663 340/dozys_664276/gjlb_664280/3220_664352/3221_664354/.

Ministry of Foreign Affairs of People's Republic of China. (August 22, 2011). "China–Saudi Arabia." Accessed October 8, 2013. http://www.fmprc.gov.cn/eng/wjb/zzjg/xybfs/gjlb/2878/.

Ministry of Foreign Affairs of People's Republic of China. "China–Saudi Arabia-Activities." Accessed August 9, 2016. http://www.fmprc.gov.cn/mfa_eng/wjb _663304/zzjg_663340/xybfs _663590/gjlb_663594/2878_663746/2880_663750/default_1.shtml.

Ministry of Foreign Affairs of People's Republic of China. "China–South Sudan: Activities." Accessed August 9, 2016. http://www.fmprc.gov.cn/mfa_eng/wjb_663304/zzjg 663340/xybfs_663590/gjlb_663594/sousu_663756/ssaa_663760/.

Ministry of Foreign Affairs of People's Republic of China. "China–Sudan: Activities." Accessed August 9, 2016. http://www.fmprc.gov.cn/mfa_eng/wjb_663304/zzjg_663340/xybfs_66 3590/gjlb_663594/2883_663766/2885_663770/.

Ministry of Foreign Affairs of People's Republic of China. "China–Venezuela: Activities." http://www.fmprc.gov.cn/mfa_eng/wjb_663304/zzjg_663340/ldmzs_664952/gjlb_664956/3538_665158/3540_665162/.

Ministry of Foreign Affairs of People's Republic of China. (January 20, 1985). "Civil Air Transport Agreement Between the Government of the People's Republic of China and the Government of the State of Kuwait." Accessed September 21, 2014. http://www.fmprc. gov.cn/mfa_eng/wjb_663304/zzjg_663340/xybfs_663590/gjlb_663594/2838_663666/2839_663668/t16371.shtml.

Ministry of Foreign Affairs of People's Republic of China. (August 22, 2011). "China–United Arab Emirates." Accessed October 8, 2013. http://www.fmprc.gov.cn/eng/wjb/zzjg/xyb fs/gjlb/2903/.

Ministry of Foreign Affairs of People's Republic of China. "China–United Arab Emirates: Activities." Accessed August 9, 2016. http://www.fmprc.gov.cn/mfa_eng/wjb_663304/zzjg_663340/xybfs_663590/gjlb_663594/2903_663806/2905_663810/.

Ministry of Foreign Affairs of the People's Republic of China. "China Venezuela Bilateral Relations." Accessed April 12, 2015. http://news.xinhuanet.com/english/2007-03/16/content_5857909.htm.

Ministry of Foreign Affairs of People's Republic of China. (May 13, 2015). "Commemorating Great Victory of World War II and Composing New Chapter of Silk Road Cooperation Foreign Minister Wang Yi's Remarks on President Xi Jinping's Attendance at Celebrations Marking 70th Anniversary of Victory of Great Patriotic War in Russia and His Visits to Russia, Kazakhstan and Belarus." Accessed August 21, 2016. http://www.fmprc.gov.cn/mfa_eng/wjb_663304/zzjg_663340/dozys_664276/gjlb_664280/3180_664322/3182_664326/t1263828.shtml.

Ministry of Foreign Affairs of People's Republic of China. (November 15, 2000). "Communiqué Concerning the Establishment of Diplomatic Relations Between the People's Republic of China and the Kingdom of Saudi Arabia." Accessed May 26, 2014. http://www.fmprc .gov.cn/mfa_eng/wjb_663304/zzjg_663340/xybfs_663590/gjlb_663594/2878_663746/2879_663748/t16422.shtml.

Ministry of Foreign Affairs of People's Republic of China. (June 26, 2016). "Declaration of the People's Republic of China and the Russian Federation on the Promotion of International Law." Accessed August 20, 2016. http://www.fmprc.gov.cn/mfa_eng/wjb_663304/zzjg_ 663340/dozys_664276/gjlb_664280/3220_664352/3222_664356/t1386141.shtml.

Ministry of Foreign Affairs of People's Republic of China. (January 18, 2016). "Foreign Ministry Holds Briefing for Chinese and Foreign Media on President Xi Jinping's State Visits to Saudi Arabia, Egypt and Iran." Accessed August 19, 2016. http://www.fmprc .gov.cn/mfa_eng/wjb_663304/zzjg_663340/xybfs_663590/gjlb_663594/2878_663746/2880_663750/t1333116.shtml.

Ministry of Foreign Affairs of People's Republic of China. (January 30, 2005). "Great Achievements Obtained in Zeng Qinghong's Visit to Venezuela: 19 Cooperation Documents Signed Between the Two Countries." Accessed May 26, 2014. http://www.fmprc.gov.cn/mfa_eng/wjb_663304/zzjg_663340/ldmzs_664952/gjlb_664956/3538_665158/3539_665160/t182097.shtml.

Ministry of Foreign Affairs of People's Republic of China. (June 21, 2007). "Hu Jintao Holds Talks with Iraqi President Talabani." Accessed August 18, 2016. http://

www.fmprc.gov. cn/mfa_eng/wjb_663304/zzjg_663340/xybfs_663590/gjlb_6635 94/2823_663636/2825_663640/t333372.shtml.

Ministry of Foreign Affairs of People's Republic of China. (July 4, 2005). "Hu Jintao Holds Talks with Nazarbayev and Announces the Establishment of Strategic Partnership between China and Kazakhstan." Accessed August 21, 2016. http://www.fmprc.gov.cn/mfa_eng/wjb_663304/zzjg_663340/dozys_664276/gjlb_664280/3180_664322/3182_664326/t202534.shtml.

Ministry of Foreign Affairs of People's Republic of China. (December 20, 2006). "Hu Jintao Holds Talks with His Kazakh Counterpart Nazarbayev." Accessed August 21, 2016. http://www.fmprc.gov.cn/mfa_eng/wjb_663304/zzjg_663340/dozys_664276/gjlb_664280/3180_664322/3182_664326/t285010.shtml.

Ministry of Foreign Affairs of People's Republic of China. (August 18, 2007). "Hu Jintao Holds Talks with His Kazakh Counterpart Nazarbayev." Accessed August 21, 2016. http://www.fmprc.gov.cn/mfa_eng/wjb_663304/zzjg_663340/dozys_664276/gjlb_664280/3180_664322/3182_664326/t353591.shtml.

Ministry of Foreign Affairs of People's Republic of China. (September 26, 2005). "Hu Jintao Holds Talks with President of the Republic of Congo Sassan." Accessed August 8, 2016. http://www.fmprc.gov.cn/mfa_eng/wjb_663304/zzjg_663340/fzs_663828/gjlb_663832/2954_663914/2956_663918/t214311.shtml.

Ministry of Foreign Affairs of the People's Republic of China. (June 5, 2012). "Hu Jintao Holds Talks with Russian President Putin." Accessed August 20, 2016. http://www.fmprc.gov .cn/mfa_eng/wjb_663304/zzjg_663340/dozys_664276/gjlb_664280/3220_664352/3222_664356/t939577.shtml.

Ministry of Foreign Affairs of People's Republic of China. (January 23, 2006). "Hu Jintao Holds Talks with Saudi Arabian King Abdullah." Accessed August 19, 2016. http://www.fmprc .gov.cn/mfa_eng/wjb_663304/zzjg_663340/xybfs_663590/gjlb_663594/2878_663746/2880_663750/t232890.shtml.

Ministry of Foreign Affairs of People's Republic of China. (April 24, 2012). "Hu Jintao Holds Talks with South Sudanese President Silva Kari Mayardit." Accessed August 13, 2016. http://www.fmprc.gov.cn/mfa_eng/wjb_663304/zzjg_663340/xybfs_663590/gjlb_663594/sousu_663756/ssaa_663760/t926468.shtml.

Ministry of Foreign Affairs of People's Republic of China. (November 15, 2000). "Iranian President Khatami Meets with Foreign Minister Tang Jiaxuan." Accessed August 19, 2016. http://www.fmprc.gov.cn/mfa_eng/wjb_663304/zzjg_663340/xybfs_663590/gjlb _663594/2818_663626/2820_663630/t16317.shtml.

Ministry of Foreign Affairs of People's Republic of China. (January 12, 1983). "Joint Communiqué on the Establishment of Diplomatic Relations Between the People's Republic of China and the People's Republic of Angola." Accessed May 26, 2014. http://www.fmprc.gov.cn/mfa_eng/wjb_663304/zzjg_663340/fzs_663828/gjlb_663832/2914_663834/2915_663836/t16465.shtml.

Ministry of Foreign Affairs of People's Republic of China. (May 25, 1978). "Joint Communiqué on the Establishment of Diplomatic Relations Between the People's Republic of China and the Sultanate of Oman." Accessed October 3, 2014. http://www.fmprc.gov.cn/mfa_ eng/wjb_663304/zzjg_663340/xybfs_663590/gjlb_6635 94/2863_663716/2864_663718/t16402.shtml.

Ministry of Foreign Affairs of People's Republic of China. (November 1, 1984). "Joint Communiqué on the Establishment of Diplomatic Relations Between the People's Republics of China and the United Arab Emirates." Accessed October 11, 2014. http://www.fmprc.gov.cn/mfa_eng/wjb_663304/zzjg_663340/xybfs_663590/gjlb_663594/2903_663806/2904_663808/t16458.shtml.

Ministry of Foreign Affairs of People's Republic of China. (August 31, 2015). "Joint Declaration on New Stage of Comprehensive Strategic Partnership Between the People's Republic of China and the Republic of Kazakhstan." Accessed August 21, 2016. http://www.fmprc. gov.cn/mfa_eng/wjb_663304/zzjg_663340/dozys_664276/gjlb_664280/3180_664322/3182_664326/t1293114.shtml.

Ministry of Foreign Affairs of People's Republic of China. (April 17, 2009). "Joint Statement Between the People's Republic of China and the Republic of Kazakhstan." Accessed February 27, 2015. http://www.fmprc.gov.cn/mfa_eng/wjb_663304/zzjg_663340/dozys _664276/gjlb_664280/3180_664322/3181_664324/t559688.shtml.

Ministry of Foreign Affairs of People's Republic of China. (December 14, 2015). "Li Keqiang and Prime Minister Karim Massimov of Kazakhstan Hold Talks, Stressing to Deeply Promote China-Kazakhstan Production Capacity Cooperation in Order to Better Realize Mutual Benefits and Win-win Results." Accessed August 21, 2016. http://www.fmprc. gov.cn/mfa_eng/wjb_663304/zzjg_663340/dozys_664276/gjlb_664280/3180_664322/3182_664326/t1324827.shtml.

Ministry of Foreign Affairs of People's Republic of China. (March 27, 2015) "Li Keqiang Holds Talks with Prime Minister Karim Massimov of Kazakhstan Deciding to Comprehensively Carry Out Cooperation in Production Capacity and Push for Important Results." Accessed August 21, 2016. http://www.fmprc.gov.cn/mfa_eng/wjb_663304/zzjg 663340/dozys_664276/gjlb_664280/3180_664322/3182_664326/t1250472.shtml.

Ministry of Foreign Affairs of People's Republic of China (December 14, 2014). "Li Keqiang Arrives in Astana to Pay an Official Visit to Kazakhstan and Attend the Prime Ministers' Meeting of the Shanghai Cooperation Organization." Accessed August 21, 2016. http://www.fmprc.gov.cn/mfa_eng/wjb_663304/zzjg_663340/dozys_664276/gjlb_664280/3180_664322/3182_664326/t1219581.shtml.

Ministry of Foreign Affairs of People's Republic of China. (December 22, 2015). "Li Keqiang Holds Talks with Prime Minister Haider al-Abadi of Iraq, Emphasizing to Enrich Connotations of China–Iraq Strategic Partnership and Build Upgraded Version of Mutually Beneficial Cooperation." Accessed August 18, 2016, http://www.fmprc.gov.cn/mfa_eng/wjb_663304/zzjg_663340/xybfs_663590/gjlb_663594/2823_663636/2825_663640/t1327531.shtml.

Ministry of Foreign Affairs of People's Republic of China. (May 9, 2014). "Li Keqiang Visits Chinese Medical Aid Unit to Angola, Urging Them to Feel Patients' Sufferings with Their Hearts and Heal the Wounded and Rescue the Dying with Their Excellent Skills." Accessed August 12, 2016. http://www.fmprc.gov.cn/mfa_eng/wjb_663304/zzjg663340/fzs_663828/gjlb_663832/2914_663834/2916_663838/t1155439.shtml.

Ministry of Foreign Affairs of People's Republic of China. (May 20, 2015). "Li Keqiang and President Dilma Rousseff of Brazil Hold Talks, Stressing to Enhance Industrial

Investment Cooperation and Upgrade China–Brazil Mutually Beneficial Cooperation." Accessed August 20, 2016. http://www.fmprc.gov.cn/mfa_eng/wjb_663304/zzjg663340/ldmzs_664952/gjlb_664956/3473_665008/3475_665012/t1266054.shtml.

Ministry of Foreign Affairs of People's Republic of China. (June 3, 2014). "Li Keqiang Holds Talks with Prime Minister Sheikh Jaber Al-Mubarak Al-Hamad Al-Sabah of Kuwait, Stressing to Deepen China-Kuwait Friendly Relationship and Mutually Beneficial Cooperation and to Promote China's Relations with the Gulf Cooperation Council (GCC) and with the Arab Countries." Accessed August 13, 2016. http://www.fmprc.gov.cn/mfa_eng/wjb_663304/zzjg_663340/xybfs_663590/gjlb_663594/2838_663666/2840_663670/t1162411.shtml.

Ministry of Foreign Affairs of People's Republic of China. (October 13, 2014). "Li Keqiang and Prime Minister Dmitry Medvedev of Russia Co–chair 19th Regular Meeting Between Chinese and Russian Prime Ministers." Accessed August 20, 2016. http://www.fmprc.gov.cn/mfa_eng/wjb_663304/zzjg_663340/dozys_664276/gjlb_664280/3220_664352/3222_664356/t1200657.shtml.

Ministry of Foreign Affairs of People's Republic of China. (November 28, 2004 and March 29, 2014). "List of Agreements on Mutual Visa Exemption Between the People's Republic of China and Foreign Countries." Accessed October 3, 2014, February 13, 2015, February 27, 2015 and March 5, 2016. http://cs.mfa.gov.cn/wgrlh/bgzl/P020140328398504621618.pdf.

Ministry of Foreign Affairs of People's Republic of China. (March 14, 2014). "Li Yuanchao Holds Talks with Crown Prince Salman Bin Abdulaziz Al Saud, the First Deputy Prime Minister and Defence Minister of Saudi Arabia." Accessed August 19, 2016. http://www.fmprc.gov.cn/mfa_eng/wjb_663304/zzjg_663340/xybfs_663590/gjlb_663594/2878_663746/2880_663750/t1138412.shtml.

Ministry of Foreign Affairs of People's Republic of China. (March 14, 2014). "Li Yunshan Holds Talks with Crown Prince Salman Bin Abdul-Aziz Al Saud, the First Deputy Prime Minister and Defense Minister of Saudi Arabia." Accessed August 19, 2016. http://www.fmprc.gov.cn/mfa_eng/wjb_663304/zzjg_663340/xybfs_663590/gjlb_663594/2878_663746/2880_663750/t1138412.shtml.

Ministry of Foreign Affairs of People's Republic of China. (April 9, 2007). "Li Zhaoxing Holds Talks with UAE Foreign Minister." Accessed August 16, 2016. http://www.fmprc.gov.cn/mfa_eng/wjb_663304/zzjg_663340/xybfs_663590/gjlb_663594/2903_663806/2905_663810/t310396.shtml.

Ministry of Foreign Affairs of People's Republic of China. (June 5, 2012). "Memorandum of Understanding on Petroleum Cooperation between the Government of the People's Republic of China and the Government of the Kingdom of Saudi Arabia." Accessed May 26, 2014. http://www.fmprc.gov.cn/mfa_eng/wjb_663304/zzjg_663340/xybfs_663590/gj lb_663594/2878_663746/2879_663748/t16423.shtml.

Ministry of Foreign Affairs of People's Republic of China. (December 12, 2014). "Ministry of Foreign Affairs Holds Briefing for Chinese and Foreign Media on Premier Li Keqiang's Visit to Kazakhstan and Holding of Second Regular Meeting with Prime Minister of Kazakhstan, Attendance at 13th Meeting of the Council of Heads of Government of the SCO Member States, Attendance at Third Meeting of Heads of Government of China and CEEC and Visit to Serbia, and

Attendance at Fifth Summit of the Greater Mekong Subregion Economic Cooperation Program." Accessed August 21, 2016. http://www.fmprc.gov.cn/mfa_eng/wjb_663304/zzjg_663340/dozys_664276/gjlb_664280/3180_664322/3182_664326/t1219578.shtml.

Ministry of Foreign Affairs of People's Republic of China. (June 22, 2012). "Premier Wen Jiabao Holds Talks with Brazilian President Dilma Rousseff." Accessed August 20, 2016. http://www.fmprc.gov.cn/mfa_eng/wjb_663304/zzjg_663340/ldmzs_664952/gjlb_664956/3473_665008/3475_665012/t945181.shtml.

Ministry of Foreign Affairs of People's Republic of China. (April 9, 2008). "Premier Wen Jiabao Holds Talks with Kazakh Prime Minister Masimov." Accessed August 21, 2016. http://www.fmprc.gov.cn/mfa_eng/wjb_663304/zzjg_663340/dozys_664276/gjlb_664280/3180_664322/3182_664326/t423831.shtml.

Ministry of Foreign Affairs of People's Republic of China. (July 6, 2004). "Premier Wen Jiabao Meets with the Joint Delegation of The Cooperation Council for the Arab States of the Gulf (GCC)." Accessed August 13, 2016. http://www.fmprc.gov.cn/mfa_eng/wjb 66330 4/zzjg_663340/xybfs_663590/gjlb_663594/2838_663666/2840_663670/t142366.shtml.

Ministry of Foreign Affairs of People's Republic of China. (October 22, 2013). "Premier Li Keqiang Co-Chairs with Dmitry Anatolyevich Medvedev the 18th Regular Meeting between Chinese and Russian Prime Ministers, Jointly Deciding to Fully Deepen China–Russia Cooperation in All Fields and Push Forward Bilateral Comprehensive Strategic Cooperative Partnership to a New High." Accessed August 20, 2016. http://www.fmprc.gov.cn/mfa_eng/wjb_663304/zzjg_663340/dozys_664276/gjlb_664280/3220_664352/3222_664356/t1092653.shtml.

Ministry of Foreign Affairs of People's Republic of China. (October 31, 2008). "Wen Jiabao Holds Talks with His Kazakh Counterpart Masimov in Astana." Accessed August 21, 2016. http://www.fmprc.gov.cn/mfa_eng/wjb_663304/zzjg_663340/dozys_664276/gjlb _664280/3180_664322/3182_664326/t520789.shtml.

Ministry of Foreign Affairs of People's Republic of China. (February 25, 2005). "President Denis Sassou-Nguesso of the Republic of Congo Meets with Zeng Peiyan." Accessed August 13, 2016. http://www.fmprc.gov.cn/mfa_eng/wjb_663304/zzjg_663340/fzs_663 828/gjlb_663832/2954_663914/2956_663918/t185167.shtml.

Ministry of Foreign Affairs of People's Republic of China. (May 25, 2004). "President Hu Jintao Holds Talks with President Luiz Inacio Lula da Silva of Brazil." Accessed August 20, 2016. http://www.fmprc.gov.cn/mfa_eng/wjb_663304/zzjg_663340/ldmzs_664952/gjlb _664956/3473_665008/3475_665012/t120311.shtml/.

Ministry of Foreign Affairs of People's Republic of China. (May 21, 2004). "President Hu Jintao Holds Talks with His Kazakh Counterpart." Accessed August 21, 2016. http://www. fmprc.gov.cn/mfa_eng/wjb_663304/zzjg_663340/dozys_664276/gjlb_664280/3180_664322/3182_664326/t115553.shtml.

Ministry of Foreign Affairs of the People's Republic of China. (August 20, 2016). "President Hu Jintao Holds Talks with Venezuelan President Hugo Rafael CHAVEZ Frías" Accessed August 20, 2016. http://www.fmprc.gov.cn/mfa_eng/wjb_663304/zzjg_663340/ldmzs_ 664952/gjlb_664956/3538_665158/3540_665162/t176888.shtml.

Ministry of Foreign Affairs of People's Republic of China. (April 22, 2002). "President Jiang Zemin Held Talks with Iranian President Mohammad Khatami." Accessed August 19, 2016. http://www.fmprc.gov.cn/mfa_eng/wjb_663304/zzjg_663340/xybfs_663590/gjlb_663594/2818_663626/2820_663630/t16325.shtml.

Ministry of Foreign Affairs of People's Republic of China. (August 31, 2015). "President Xi Jinping Hold Talks with President Nursultan Nazarbayev of Kazakhstan and Decide in Unanimity to Promote China-Kazakhstan Relations to Higher Level and Wider Space." Accessed August 21, 2016. http://www.fmprc.gov.cn/mfa_eng/wjb_663304/zzjg_663340/dozys_664276/gjlb_664280/3180_664322/3182_664326/t1293118.shtml.

Ministry of Foreign Affairs of the People's Republic of China. (September 1, 2015). "President Xi Jinping Meets with President Omar Hassan Ahmad al-Bashir of Sudan." Accessed August 20, 2016. http://www.fmprc.gov.cn/mfa_eng/wjb_663304/zzjg_663340/xybfs_663590/gjlb_663594/2883_663766/2885_663770/t1294136.shtml.

Ministry of Foreign Affairs of People's Republic of China. (February 26, 2005). "The President of Angola Meets with Zeng Peiyan." Accessed August 12, 2016. http://www.fmprc.gov.cn/mfa_eng/wjb_663304/zzjg_663340/fzs_663828/gjlb_663832/2914_663834/2916_663838/t185309.shtml.

Ministry of Foreign Affairs of People's Republic of China. (June 14, 2006). "Relations with the Republic of Congo." Accessed November 8, 2014. http://www.china.org.cn/english/features/wenjiabaoafrica/171414.htm.

Ministry of Foreign Affairs of the People's Republic of China. "Sino-Argentine Relations." Accessed April 24, 2015. http://www.chinadaily.com.cn/english/focus/2004-11/11/content_390575.htm.

Ministry of Foreign Affairs of the People's Republic of China. "Sino–Brazilian Relations." Accessed November 10, 2015. http://www.chinadaily.com.cn/english/doc/2004-11/11/content_390572.htm.

Ministry of Foreign Affairs of the People's Republic of China. (December 6, 2012). "The 16th Meeting of the Joint Commission for the Regular Meetings of Heads of Government of China and Russia Is Held in Moscow." Accessed August 20, 2016. http://www.fmprc .gov.cn/mfa_eng/wjb_663304/zzjg_663340/dozys_664276/gjlb_664280/3220_664352/3222_664356/t996119.shtml

Ministry of Foreign Affairs of People's Republic of China. (December 24, 2004). "Venezuela Recognizes China's Full Market Economy Status." Accessed May 26, 2014. http://www.fmprc.gov.cn/mfa_eng/wjb_663304/zzjg_663340/ldmzs_664952/gjlb_664956/3538_665158/3539_665160/t176893.shtml.

Ministry of Foreign Affairs of People's Republic of China. (June 20, 2006). "Wen Jiabao Holds Talks with President of the Republic of Congo Sassou-Nguesso." Accessed August 13, 2016. http://www.fmprc.gov.cn/mfa_eng/wjb_663304/zzjg_663340/fzs_663828/gjlb_663832/2954_663914/2956_663918/t259149.shtml.

Ministry of Foreign Affairs of People's Republic of China. (May 19, 2004). "Wu Bangguo and Wen Jiabao Meets Respectively with Kazakh President Nursultan Nazarbayev." Accessed August 21, 2016. http://www.fmprc.gov.cn/mfa_eng/wjb_663304/zzjg 663340/dozys_664276/gjlb_664280/3180_664322/3182_664326/t115558.shtml.

Ministry of Foreign Affairs of People's Republic of China. (August 31, 2006). "Wu Bangguo Meets with Brazilian President Lula." Accessed August 20, 2016. http://www.fmprc.gov .cn/mfa_eng/wjb_663304/zzjg_663340/ldmzs_664952/gjlb_664956/3473_665008/3475_665012/t270476.shtml.

Ministry of Foreign Affairs of People's Republic of China. (September 10, 2012). "Wu Bangguo Meets with Iranian First Vice President Rahimi." Accessed August 19, 2016. http://www.fmprc.gov.cn/mfa_eng/wjb_663304/zzjg_663340/xybfs_663590/gjlb_663594/2818_663626/2820_663630/t969867.shtml.

Ministry of Foreign Affairs of People's Republic of China. (November 17, 2000). "Vice-President Hu Jintao Met with Kazakh Prime Minister." Accessed August 21, 2016. http://www.fmprc.gov.cn/mfa_eng/wjb_663304/zzjg_663340/dozys_664276/gjlb_664280/3180_664322/3182_664326/t16664.shtml.

Ministry of Foreign Affairs of People's Republic of China (January 21, 2016). "Xi Jinping and King Salman bin Abdulaziz Al Saud of Saudi Arabia Together Attend the Launch Ceremony of the Yasref Oil Refinery." Accessed August 20, 2016. http://www.fmpr c .gov.cn/mfa_eng/wjb_663304/zzjg_663340/xybfs_663590/gjlb_663594/2878_663746/2880_663750/t1333960.shtml.

Ministry of Foreign Affairs of the People's Republic of China. (July 22, 2014). "Xi Jinping and Nicolas Maduro Jointly Attend the Closing Ceremony of the 13th Meeting of the China-Venezuela High-level Mixed Committee." Accessed August 20, 2016. http://www.fmprc. gov.cn/mfa_eng/wjb_663304/zzjg_663340/ldmzs_664952/gjlb_664956/3538_665158/3540_665162/t1177114.shtml.

Ministry of Foreign Affairs of People's Republic of China. (September 7, 2013). "Xi Jinping and Nursultan Nazarbayev Jointly Attend Founding Ceremony of China-Kazakhstan Entrepreneurs Committee, Wishing China-Kazakhstan Cooperation Makes Further Progress." Accessed August 21, 2016. http://www.fmprc.gov.cn/mfa_eng/wjb_663304/zzjg_663340/dozys_664276/gjlb_664280/3180_664322/3182_664326/t1075970.shtml.

Ministry of Foreign Affairs of People's Republic of China. (January 20, 2016). "Xi Jinping Holds Talks with King Salman bin Abdulaziz Al Saud of Saudi Arabia Two Heads of State Jointly Announce Establishment of China–Saudi Arabia Comprehensive Strategic Partnership." Accessed August 19, 2016. http://www.fmprc.gov.cn/mfa_eng/wjb_66330 4/zzjg_663340/xybfs_663590/gjlb_663594/2878_663746/2880_663750/t1333527.shtml.

Ministry of Foreign Affairs of People's Republic of China. (January 23, 2016). "Xi Jinping Holds Talks with President Hassan Rouhani of Iran." Accessed August 19, 2016. http://www.fmprc.gov.cn/mfa_eng/wjb_663304/zzjg_663340/xybfs_663590/gjlb_663594/2818_663626/2820_663630/t1335157.shtml.

Ministry of Foreign Affairs of People's Republic of China. (July 5, 2016). "Xi Jinping Holds Talks with President Denis Sassou-Nguesso of the Republic of Congo, Both Heads of State Decide to Uplift Bilateral Relations to a Comprehensive Strategic Partnership of Cooperation." Accessed August 13, 2016. http://www.fmprc.gov.cn/mfa_eng/wjb_663 304/zzjg_663340/fzs_663828/gjlb_663832/2954_663914/2956_663918/t1378212.shtml.

Ministry of Foreign Affairs of People's Republic of China. (June 12, 2014). "Xi Jinping Holds Talks with President Denis Sassou-N'guesso of the Republic of Congo, Stressing to Deepen Friendship, Strengthen Cooperation and Promote the All-round Development of the China-Congo Relations." Accessed August 13, 2016. http://www.fmprc.gov.cn/mfa_eng/wjb_663304/zzjg_663340/fzs_663828/gjlb_663832/2954_663914/2956_663918/t1166113.shtml.

Ministry of Foreign Affairs of People's Republic of China. (September 7, 2013). "Xi Jinping Holds Talks with President Nursultan Nazarbayev of Kazakhstan Promote Good-Neighbourly Friendship, Mutual Benefit and Win-win Outcomes to Deepen China-Kazakhstan Comprehensive Strategic Partnership." Accessed August 21, 2016. http://www.fmprc.gov.cn/mfa_eng/wjb_663304/zzjg_663340/dozys_664276/gjlb_664280/3180_664322/3182_664326/t1075414.shtml.

Ministry of Foreign Affairs of People's Republic of China. (December 14, 2015). "Xi Jinping Meets with Crown Prince Sheikh Mohammed Bin Zayed Al-Nahyan of Abu Dhabi Emirate of the UAE." Accessed August 16, 2016. http://www.fmprc.gov.cn/mfa_eng/wjb_663304/zzjg_663340/xybfs_663590/gjlb_663594/2903_663806/2905_663810/t1324821.shtml.

Ministry of Foreign Affairs of People's Republic of China. (September 5, 2013). "Xi Jinping Meets with Russian President Vladimir Putin." Accessed August 20, 2016. http://www.fmprc.gov.cn/mfa_eng/wjb_663304/zzjg_663340/dozys_664276/gjlb_664280/3220_664352/3222_664356/t1074364.shtml.

Ministry of Foreign Affairs of People's Republic of China. (May 20, 2014). "Xi Jinping Holds Talks with President Vladimir Putin of Russia, Stressing to Expand and Deepen Practical Cooperation, Promoting China–Russia Comprehensive Strategic Partnership of Coordination to Higher Level," May 20, 2014. Accessed August 20, 2016. http://www.fmprc.gov.cn/mfa_eng/wjb_663304/zzjg_663340/dozys_664276/gjlb_664280/3220_664352/3222_664356/t1158516.shtml.

Ministry of Foreign Affairs of People's Republic of China. (June 25, 2016). "Xi Jinping Holds Talks with President Vladimir Putin of Russia Both Heads of State Stress Unswerving Commitment to Deepening China–Russia Comprehensive Strategic Partnership of Coordination." Accessed August 20, 2016. http://www.fmprc.gov.cn/mfa_eng/wjb_663 304/zzjg_663340/dozys_664276/gjlb_664280/3220_664352/3222_664356/t1375791.shtml.

Ministry of Foreign Affairs of People's Republic of China. (December 22, 2015). "Xi Jinping Meets with Prime Minister Haider al-Abadi of Iraq." Accessed August 18, 2016. http://www.fmprc.gov.cn/mfa_eng/wjb_663304/zzjg_663340/xybfs_663590/gjlb_663594/2823_663636/2825_663640/t1327529.shtml.

Ministry of Foreign Affairs of People's Republic of China. (March 24, 2006). "Zeng Qinghong Holds Talks with Brazilian Vice President Alencar." Accessed August 20, 2016. http://www.fmprc.gov.cn/mfa_eng/wjb_663304/zzjg_663340/ldmzs_664952/gjlb_664956/3473_665008/3475_665012/t242612.shtml.

Ministry of Foreign Affairs of People's Republic of China. (July 20, 2016). "Yang Jiechi Holds Meeting and Jointly Attends First Meeting of Council of Cooperation Between the Upper and Middle Reaches of the Yangtze River and the Volga Federal District with Plenipotentiary Representative of the Russian President in the

Volga Federal District Mikhail Babich." Accessed August 20, 2016. http://www.fmprc.gov.cn/mfa_eng/wjb_ 663304/zzjg_663340/dozys_664276/gjlb_664280/3220_664352/3222_664356/t1383610.shtml.

Ministry of Foreign Affairs of People's Republic of China. (October 16, 2013). "Zhang Dejiang Holds Talks with Nurlan Nigmatulin, Speaker of the Kazakh Parliament's Lower House." Accessed August 21, 2016. http://www.fmprc.gov.cn/mfa_eng/wjb_663304/zzjg_663340/dozys_664276/gjlb_664280/3180_664322/3182_664326/t1090479.shtml.

Murphy, Dawn. "China and the Middle East," testimony, June 6, 2013, before U.S.-China Economic and Security Review Commission.

Niazi, Khizar. "Kuwait Looks Towards the East: Relations with China." *Inter-Disciplinary Journal of Asian and Middle Eastern Studies*, Volume 26, September 2009. Accessed September 21, 2014: 1–13. http://idjames.org/2012/06/kuwait-looks-towards-the-east-relations-with-china/.

Nojonen, Matti. "Introduction: Adjusting to the Great Power Transition." In *Russia–China Relations: Current State, Alternative Futures, and Implications for the West*, edited by Arkady Moshes and Matti Nojonen, 7–21. Helsinki, Finland: The Finnish Institute of Foreign Affairs, 2011.

Obi, Cyril. "African Oil in the Energy Security Calculations of China and India" In *The Rise of China and India in Africa: Challenges, Opportunities and Critical Interventions,* edited by Fantu Cheru and Cyril Obi, 181–192. New York, NY: Zed Books, 2010.

Ogunsanwo, Alaba. *China's Policy in Africa 1958–1971.* London, UK: Cambridge University Press, 1974.

Oil and Gas Journal. (January 21, 2016). "Aramco, Sinopec move to expand Cooperation." Accessed August 19, 2016. http://www.ogj.com/articles/2016/01/aramco-sinopec-move-to-expand-cooperation.html.

Olimat, Muhamad S. *China and Central Asia in the Post-Soviet Era.* Lanham, MD: Lexington Books, 2015.

Olimat, Muhamad S. *China and the Middle East Since World War II.* Lanham, MD: Lexington Books, 2014.

Olimat, Muhamad S. *China and North Africa Since World War II.* Lanham, MD: Lexington Books, 2014.

Oliveira, Henrique Altemani de. "Brazil and China: From South–South Cooperation to Competition?" In *Latin America Facing China: South–South Relations Beyond the Washington Consensus,* edited by Alex E. Fernandez Jillerto and Barbara Hogenboom, 33–53. New York, NY: Berghahn Books, 2012.

Orange, Richard. "Kazakhmys gets $1.5bn loan from China." *The Telegraph*, June 14, 2011. Accessed December 21, 2014. http://www.telegraph.co.uk/finance/newsbysector/industry/mining/8573834/Kazakhmys-gets-1.5bn-loan-from-China.html.

Overland, Indra, Stina Torjesen, and Heidi Kjaernet. "Introduction: China and Russia: Partners or Firewalls for the Caspian Petro-States?" In *Caspian Energy Politics: Azerbaijan, Kazakhstan, and Turkmenistan,* edited by Indra Overland, Stina Torjesen, and Heidi Kjaernet, 93–100. New York, NY: Routledge, 2011.

Paik, Keun-Wook. *Sino-Russian Gas and Oil Cooperation: Entering into a New Era of Strategic Partnership?* Oxford, UK: The Oxford Institute for Energy Studies, OIES Paper WPM 59, April 2015.
Panapress.com. (September 4, 2012). "Congo, China Sign Cooperation Agreements." Accessed November 8, 2014. http://www.panapress.com/Congo-China-sign-cooperation-agreements-13-841438-0-lang2-index.html.
PetersburgCity.com. (March 24, 2006). "Construction Begins of 'Baltic Pearl' Project." Accessed March 23, 2016. http://petersburgcity.com/news/city/2006/03/24/baltic_pearl/.
Peyrouse, Sebastien. "Chinese Economic Presence in Kazakhstan: China's Resolve and Central Asia's Apprehension." *China Perspectives*. France: French Centre for Research on Contemporary China, March 2008, 34–39.
President of the Islamic Republic of Iran. (January 23, 2016). "Iran, China sign 17 Documents, MoUs." Accessed August 19, 2016. http://www.president.ir/en/91427.
Radio Free Europe/Radio Liberty. (January 24, 2016). "China, Iran agree to $600 Billion Trade Deal after Sanctions Lifted." Accessed August 19, 2016. http://en.trend.az/iran/business/2530745.html.
Rakhmat, Muhammad Zulfikar. "Exploring the China and Oman Relationship." *The Diplomat*, May 10, 2014. Accessed October 7, 2014. http://thediplomat.com/2014/05/exploring-the-china-and-oman-relationship/.
Rakhmetova, Klara. "Kazakhstan-China Oil Pipeline Project." *KazMunaiGas*. Accessed August 21, 2016. http://www.energycharter.org/fileadmin/DocumentsMedia/Presentations/CBP-KZ-CN.pdf.
Ratliff, William. *China in Latin America's Future*. Paper presented at CEAS China Brown Bag Series, the Center for East Asian Studies and the Stanford Center for Latin American Studies, Stanford University, Spring 2009–2010.
Reuters. (September 14, 2015). "China's SEPCO set to win gas booster contract from Saudi Aramco." Accessed August 26, 2016. http://www.reuters.com/article/sepco-saudi-aramco-gas-idUSL5N10Y0NR20150914.
Reuters. (May 23, 2016). "Chinese Investors to build Industrial Park at Oman's Duqm Port." Accessed August 16, 2016. http://www.reuters.com/article/oman-china-industry-idUSL5N18K32D.
Rigzone. (January 6, 2016). "China's Honghua Secures $25M Rig Supply Contract from Kuwait Drilling Co." Accessed August 13, 2016. http://www.rigzone.com/news/oil_gas/a/142342/Chinas_Honghua_Secures_25M_Rig_Supply_Contract_from_Kuwait_Drilling_Co.
Rousseau, Richard. "Kazakhstan: Continuous Improvement or Stalemate in its Relations with China?" *Strategic Analysis*, Volume 37, Issue 1, January–February 2013, 40–51.
Russia Beyond the Headlines. (June 24, 2016). "Russia–China Agreement on Grain Hub calls for investing $1.1 billion." Accessed August 26, 2016. http://rbth.com/business/2016/06/24/russia-china-agreement-on-grain-hub-calls-for-investing-11-bln_605857.
Ryan, Kevin. "Russo–Chinese Defense Relations: The View from Moscow." In *The Future of China–Russia Relations*, edited by James Bellacqua, 179–202. Lexington, KY: The University Press of Kentucky, 2010

Said, Summer. "Saudi Arabia, China Sign Nuclear Cooperation Pact." *The Wall Street Journal*, January 16, 2012. Web, April 20, 2012. Accessed May 26, 2014. http://online.wsj.com/article/SB10001424052970204468004577164742025285500.html.

Saurbek, Zhanibek. "Kazakh–Chinese Energy Relations: Economic Pragmatism or Political Cooperation?" *China and Eurasia Forum Quarterly*, Volume 6, Issue 1, February 2008: 79–93.

Schmidt, Peter. "At U.S. Colleges, Chinese-Financed Centers Prompt Worries About Academic Freedom." *The Chronicle of Higher Education*, October 22, 2010, A8. Accessed January 15, 2014. http://chronicle.texterity.com/chronicle/20101022a?pg=8#pg8.

Shi, Ze. *Building Strong China–Russia Energy Strategic Partnership*. Beijing, China: China Institute of International Studies, December 2, 2015. Accessed July 7, 2016. http://www.ciis.org.cn/english/2015-12/02/content_8422032.htm.

Shichor, Yitzhak. "China Means Business in Iraq." *China Brief*, Volume VII, Issue 21, November 20, 2007. Accessed September 14, 2014, http://www.jamestown.org/programs/chinabrief/single/?tx_ttnews%5Btt_news%5D=4542&tx_ttnews%5BbackPid%5D=197&no_cache=1#.VBaEWZtWZhE.

Shichor, Yitzhak. "Sudan: China's Outpost in Africa." *China Brief*, Volume V, Issue 21, October 13, 2005.

Shinn, David H. "Military and Security Relations: China, Africa, and the Rest of the World." In *China into Africa: Trade, Aid, and Influence,* edited by Robert I. Rotberg, 155–196. Washington, DC: Brookings Institution Press, 2008.

Shinn, David H. and Joshua Eisenman. *China and Africa: A Century of Engagement*. Philadelphia, PA: University of Pennsylvania Press, 2012.

Sputnik News. (December 23, 2015). "Iraq, China Sign Agreements on Defense, Silk Road Cooperation." Accessed August 19, 2016. http://sputniknews.com/politics/20151223/1032173543/silk-road-cooperation.html.

Stapczynski, Stephen and Aibing Guo. "China's CNNC Seeking to Build Sudan's First Nuclear Reactor." *Bloomberg*, May 23, 2016. Accessed July 23, 2016. http://www.bloomberg. com/news/articles/2016-05-24/china-s-cnnc-seeking-to-build-sudan-s-first-nuclear-reactor.

Stein, Matthew. *The Wariness in Kazakhstan of Chinese Economic Investments and Interests*. Fort Leavenworth, KS: U.S. Army, Foreign Military Studies Office, February 2013.

Stockholm International Peace Research Institute. SIPRI Arms Transfers Database. http://www.sipri.org/databases/armstransfers.

Strange, Austin M., Axel Dreher, Andreas Fuchs, Bradley Parks, and Michael J. Tierney. "Tracking Underreported Financial Flows: China's Development Finance and the Aid–Conflict Nexus Revisited." *Journal of Conflict Resolution,* Volume 61, Issue 5, 2017: 935–963.

Sudan Vision News Daily. (November 3, 2013). "The Sudanese Chinese Relations Glorious Past and Bright Future." Accessed February 16, 2015. http://news.sudanvisiondaily.com/details.html?rsnpid=228544.

Sutter, Robert G. *Chinese Foreign Relations: Power and Policy Since the Cold War*. Lanham, MD: Rowman & Littlefield, 2008.

Tania, Maxime. "China's Energy Security Towards Venezuela: Transnationalization and the Geopolitical Impact of the Sino-Venezuelan Relationship." Master's Thesis, University of Amsterdam, July 2012.

Tavares, Rodrigo Maciel and Dani K. Nedal. "China and Brazil: Two Trajectories of a Strategic Partnership," In *China Engages Latin America: Tracing the Trajectory*, edited by Adrian H. Hearn and Jose Luis Leon-Manriquez, 235–255. Boulder, CO: Lynne Rienner Publishers, Inc., 2011.

Thrall, Lloyd. *China's Expanding African Relations: Implications for U.S. National Security*. Santa Monica, CA: RAND, 2015.

Toumi, Habib. "Kuwait, China Sign 10 Cooperation Accords." *Gulf News*, June 4, 2014. Accessed September 21, 2014, http://gulfnews.com/news/gulf/kuwait/kuwait-china-sign-10-cooperation-accords-1.1342938.

Trend News Agency. (May 8, 2006). "Iran, China sign Document to boost Petro-Chemical Co-Op." Accessed August 19, 2016. http://en.trend.az/iran/business/2530745.html.

United Nations. United Nations Commodity Trade Statistics Database. http://comtrade.un.org/db/default.aspx.

United Nations Conference on Trade and Development (UNCTAD FDI/TNC) Database. *Bilateral FDI Statistics 2014*. Accessed November 1, 2014. http://unctad.org/Sections/dite_fdistat/docs/webdiaeia2014d3_CHN.pdf.

United Nations Conference on Trade and Investment. "The Rise of the BRICS FDI and Africa." March 25, 2013. Accessed October 13, 2013. http://unctad.org/en/PublicationsLibrary/webdiaeia2013d6_en.pdf.

United Nations Peacekeeping Website. Peacekeeping Statistics. *UN's Missions Detailed by Country*. December 31, 2014. Accessed January 6, 2015.

Unnikrishnan, Nandan and Uma Purushothaman. *Trends in Russia-China Relations: Implications for India*. New Delhi, India: Observer Research Foundation, 2015.

U.S. Army, Army Logistics University, ALU International Military Student Office, Country Notes-CENTCOM, *Oman*. Accessed October 4, 2014. http://www.alu.army.mil/ALU _INTERNAT/CountryNotes/CENTCOM/OMAN.pdf.

U.S. Central Intelligence Agency. *Communist China's Presence in Africa*. Washington, DC, June 20, 1969.

U.S. Department of Defense, Defense Intelligence Agency. *Directory of PRC Military Personalities*. Washington, DC, 2013, 2014.

U.S. Department of Defense. *Proliferation: Threat and Response*. Washington, DC, 1996.

U.S. Energy Information Administration, U.S. Department of Energy. Washington, DC. "Country Analysis Briefs: Angola." Last updated on September 17, 2014. http://www.eia.gov/countries/analysisbrie fs/Angola/angola.pdf.

U.S. Energy Information Administration, U.S. Department of Energy. Washington, DC. "Country Analysis Briefs: China." Last updated on May 14, 2015. https://www.eia.gov/beta/international/analysis_includes/countries_long/China/china.pdf

U.S. Energy Information Administration, U.S. Department of Energy. Washington, DC. "Country Analysis Briefs: Kazakhstan." Last updated on January 15, 2015. http://www.eia.gov/countries/analysis briefs/Kazakhstan/kazakhstan.pdf.

U.S. Energy Information Administration, U.S. Department of Energy. Washington, DC. "Country Analysis Briefs: Sudan and South Sudan," Last updated on September 3, 2014.

Vines, Alex, and Indira Campos. "China and India in Angola" In *The Rise of China and India in Africa: Challenges, Opportunities and Critical Interventions,* edited by Fantu Cheru and Cyril Obi, 193–207. New York, NY: Zed Books, 2010.

Visa House. "Russian Consulates around the World." Accessed July 3, 2016. http://www.russianconsulates .com/consulate.aspx?ConsulateID=1139.

Voloshin, George. "China Strengthens Its Hand in Kazakhstan After Xi Jinping's Visit." *Eurasia Daily Monitor,* Volume X, Issue 164, September 17, 2013.

Weitz, Richard. "China and Iraq: The Return." *Second Line of Defense,* June 22, 2012. Accessed September 15, 2014. http://www.sldinfo.com/china-and-iraq-the-return/.

Wenping, He. "The Darfur Issue: A New Test for China's Africa Policy." In *The Rise of China and India in Africa: Challenges, Opportunities and Critical Interventions,* edited by Fantu Cheru and Cyril Obi, 155–166. New York, NY: Zed Books, 2010.

Williams, Ogi. "Oil for Development: China's Investments in Angola and the Republic of Congo." *Consultancy African Intelligence,* July 29, 2014. Accessed November 8, 2014. http://www.consultancyafrica.com/index.php?option=com_content&view=article&id=1699:oil-for-development-chinas-investments-in-angola-and-the-republic-of-congo-&catid=58:asia-dimension-discussion-papers&Itemid=264.

Wishnick, Elizabeth. "Why a 'Strategic Partnership?' The View from China." In *The Future of China–Russia Relations,* edited by James Bellacqua, 56–80. Lexington, KY: The University Press of Kentucky, 2010.

Worden, Robert L., Andrea Matles Savada and Ronald E. Dolan, eds. *China: A Country Study.* Washington, DC: GPO for the Library of Congress, 1987.

Wu, Jiao. "China signs 12 deals with Venezuela." *ChinaDaily.com.cn,* September 23, 2013. Accessed October 13, 2013. http://www.chinadaily.com.cn/world/2013-09/23/content _16985752.htm.

Xinhua. (January 20, 2016). "China, Saudi Arabia Elevate Bilateral ties, Eye More Industrial Capacity Cooperation." Accessed May 12, 2017. http://news.xinhuanet.com/english/2016-01/20/c_135025406_2.htm.

Xinhua. (December 22, 2015). "China, Iraq sign Memo to promote Energy Partnership." Accessed August 19, 2016. http://news.xinhuanet.com/english/2015-12/22/c_134 942270.htm.

Xinhua. (November 6, 2011). "China, Oman to sign MOUs to boost Cooperation." Accessed August 14, 2016. http://www.chinadaily.com.cn/china/2010-11/06/content_11510675.h tm.

Yodogawa, Noriko and Alexander M. Peterson. "An Opportunity for Progress: China, Central Asia, and the Energy Charter Treaty." *Texas Journal of Oil, Gas, and Energy Law,* Volume 8, Issue 1, March 12, 2013, 111–142.

Yuan, Jing-Dong. "Sino-Russian Defense Ties: The View from Beijing." In *The Future of China–Russia Relations,* edited by James Bellacqua, 203–229. Lexington, KY: The University Press of Kentucky, 2010.

Zambelis, Chris. "China's Iraq Oil Strategy Comes into Sharper Focus." *China Brief*, Volume VIII, Issue 10, May 9, 2013: 10–13.
Zawya. (December 28, 2015). "UAE signs an MOU with People's Republic of China for Cooperation in Space Science." Accessed August 5, 2016. https://www.zawya.com/story/UAE_signs_MoU_with_China_for_cooperation_in_space_science-ZAWYA20151228061816/.
Zhao, Shengnan. "China and Angola sign Cooperation Deals." *China Daily*, June 10, 2015. Accessed August 12, 2016. http://www.chinadaily.com.cn/world/2015-06/10/content_ 20955887.htm.
Zheng, Bingwen, Hongbo Sun, and Yunxia Yue. "The Present Situation and Prospects of China–Latin American Relations: A Review of the History Since 1949." In *China–Latin America Relations Review and Analysis (Volume 1)*, edited by Shuangrong Hu, 1–21. Reading, UK: Path International Ltd., 2012.
Zhou, Hang. "China and South Sudan: Economic Engagement continues amid Conflict." *African Arguments*, September 12, 2014. Accessed August 13, 2016. http://africanarguments.org/2014/09/12/china-and-south-sudan-economic-engagement-continues-amid-conflict-by-zhou-hang/.
Zhou, Hang. "Testing the Limits: China's Expanding Role in the South Sudanese Civil War." *China Brief*, Volume XIV, Issue 19, October 10, 2014: 4–7.
Zhou, Zhiwei. "Analysis of Brazil and China's Rapid Development and Mutual Policy." In *China–Latin America Relations Review and Analysis (Volume 1)*, edited by Shuangrong Hu, 130–141. Reading, UK: Path International Ltd., 2012.

Index

Asian Infrastructure Investment Bank (AIIB), 147
Andrews-Speed, Philip and Roland Dannreuter:
   on China's corporate tactics to acquire oil and gas rights, xvi;
   on the description of oil, xiv;
   on gaining access to oil reserves, xvii
Angola:
   bilateral trade with China, 4;
   China's largest supplier of petroleum in Africa, 2, 9;
   Chinese support of liberation groups during the Cold War, 1, 43;
   Confucius Institute in, 8;
   cultural agreements with China, 8;
   cultural relations with China, 8–9;
   economic-trade agreements with China, 5;
   economic-trade relations with China, 3–7;
   energy cooperation with China, 9, 11;
   energy-petroleum agreements with China, 11;
   energy-petroleum relations with China, 9–11;
   largest trading partner in Africa, 3, 12;
   liquefied national gas exports to China, 10;
   loans for oil program with China, 2, 3, 5, 7, 12, 291;
   military-security relations with China, 7–8;
   military-security high level visits and exchanges with China, 7;
   petroleum exports to China, 10;
   petroleum gas exports to China, 10;
   political-diplomatic agreements with China, 1, 2–3;
   political-diplomatic high-level visits and exchanges with China, 2;
   political-diplomatic relations with China, 1–3;
   role of Chinese policy banks in Angola's infrastructure development, 2, 5, 6, 9, 12;
   second largest supplier of petroleum to China, 9;
   strategic partnership with China, 3, 291;
   weapon supplies from China, 7–8
Arab Spring, 97, 116, 117, 130, 191, 192, 196, 250

Bandung Conference, xix, 18, 58, 207, 224, 227
Brazil:
   banking and finance cooperation with China, 25;

bilateral trade with China, 21–22;
Confucius Institute in, 31,
cultural agreements with China,
    27–30;
cultural cooperation with China,
    30–31;
cultural relations with China, 26–31;
currency swap with China, 25, 35;
defense cooperation with China,
    25–26;
economic-trade agreements with
    China, 22–24;
economic-trade relations with China,
    21–25;
energy cooperation with China, 34;
energy-petroleum agreements with
    China, 34;
energy-petroleum relations with
    China, 31–34;
largest trading partner in South
    America, 21
loans for oil program with China, 33,
    291;
military-security agreements with
    China, 26;
military-security high level visits and
    exchanges with China, 25, 26;
military-security relations with
    China, 25–26;
petroleum exports to China, 32;
petroleum gas exports to China, 32;
political-diplomatic agreements with
    China, 17, 20;
political-diplomatic high-level visits
    and exchanges with China, 19–20;
political-diplomatic relations with
    China, 17–20;
role of Chinese policy banks
    in Brazil's infrastructure
    development, 25, 35;
strategic cooperation in space science
    and technology with China, 28,
    29, 30, 31;
strategic partnership with China, 19,
    20, 35, 291

Central Asian Republics:
    role in maintaining Xinjiang's
    security and regional
    security, 97
China:
    anti-piracy cooperation with Oman,
        134, 138;
    anti-terrorism cooperation with Saudi
        Arabia, 196–97;
    banking and finance cooperation with
        Brazil, 25;
    banking and finance cooperation with
        Kazakhstan, 95;
    banking and finance cooperation with
        Oman, 133;
    banking and finance cooperation with
        Russia, 156–57, 170;
    banking and finance cooperation
        with the United Arab Emirates,
        254–55;
    banking and finance cooperation with
        Venezuela, 266, 270;
    Belt and Road Initiative-Silk Road
        Economic Belt and Twenty-First
        Century Maritime Silk Road, 193,
        194, 290;
    bilateral trade with Angola, 4;
    bilateral trade with Brazil, 21–22;
    bilateral trade with Congo-
        Brazzaville, 44–45;
    bilateral trade with Iran, 59–60;
    bilateral trade with Iraq, 75–76;
    bilateral trade with Kazakhstan,
        92–93;
    bilateral trade with Kuwait, 117–18;
    bilateral trade with Oman, 131–32;
    bilateral trade with Russia, 149–51,
        179;
    bilateral trade with Saudi Arabia,
        192–93;
    bilateral trade with South Sudan,
        209–11;
    bilateral trade with Sudan, 228–29;
    bilateral trade with United Arab
        Emirates, 251–52;

bilateral trade with Venezuela, 267–68;
cultural agreements with Angola, 8;
cultural agreements with Brazil, 27–30;
cultural agreements with Congo–Brazzaville, 49–50;
cultural agreements with Iran, 64–65;
cultural agreements with Iraq, 79–80;
cultural agreements with Kazakhstan, 98;
cultural agreements with Kuwait, 122;
cultural agreements with Oman, 135;
cultural agreements with Russia, 167–71, 180;
cultural agreements with Saudi Arabia, 198;
cultural agreements with South Sudan, 217;
cultural agreements with Sudan, 239–40;
cultural agreements with United Arab Emirates, 256;
cultural agreements with Venezuela, 272–74;
cultural cooperation with Brazil, 30–31;
cultural cooperation with Iraq, 80;
cultural cooperation with Kazakhstan, 99–100;
cultural cooperation with Oman, 135–36;
cultural cooperation with South Sudan, 216;
cultural cooperation with Sudan, 238;
cultural cooperation with the United Arab Emirates, 256–57;
cultural cooperation with Venezuela, 274;
cultural exchanges with Russia, 165–66;
cultural relations with Angola, 8–9;
cultural relations with Brazil, 26–31;
cultural relations with Congo–Brazzaville, 49–50;
cultural relations with Iran, 64–65;
cultural relations with Iraq, 79–80;
cultural relations with Kazakhstan, 98–100;
cultural relations with Kuwait, 121–22;
cultural relations with Oman, 135–36;
cultural relations with Russia, 165–71;
cultural relations with Saudi Arabia, 197–98;
cultural relations with South Sudan, 215–17;
cultural relations with Sudan, 238–40;
cultural relations with United Arab Emirates, 256–57;
cultural relations with Venezuela, 272–74;
currency swap with Brazil, 25, 35;
currency swap with the United Arab Emirates, 254;
defense cooperation with Brazil, 25–26;
development of Sudan's oil sector, 242–43;
diversification strategies, xvi;
early cultural relations with Saudi Arabia, 197;
early relations with Sudan, 223, 224–26;
early relations with Russia, 143–44, 178–79;
early relations with United Arab Emirates, 249;
economic-trade agreements with Angola, 5;
economic-trade agreements with Brazil, 22–24;
economic-trade agreements with Congo-Brazzaville, 45–46;
economic-trade agreements with Iran, 60–61;

economic-trade agreements with Iraq, 76–77;
economic-trade agreements with Kazakhstan, 93–94;
economic-trade agreements with Kuwait, 119–20;
economic-trade agreements with Oman, 131–32, 133;
economic-trade agreements with Russia, 151–55;
economic-trade agreements with Saudi Arabia, 194;
economic-trade agreements with South Sudan, 211;
economic-trade agreements with Sudan, 229–30;
economic-trade agreements with United Arab Emirates, 253;
economic-trade agreements with Venezuela, 269–70;
economic-trade relations with Angola, 3–7;
economic-trade relations with Brazil, 21–25;
economic-trade relations with Congo-Brazzaville, 44–48;
economic-trade relations with Iran, 59–61;
economic-trade relations with Iraq, 75–78;
economic-trade relations with Kazakhstan, 92–96;
economic-trade relations with Kuwait, 117–20;
economic-trade relations with Oman, 131–34;
economic-trade relations with Russia, 149–57;
economic-trade relations with Saudi Arabia, 192–95;
economic-trade relations with South Sudan, 209–13;
economic-trade relations with Sudan, 227–35;
economic-trade relations with United Arab Emirates, 251–55;
economic-trade relations with Venezuela, 267–70;
energy cooperation with Angola, 9, 11;
energy cooperation with Brazil, 34,
energy cooperation with Congo-Brazzaville, 51–52;
energy cooperation with Iran, 66, 67;
energy cooperation with Iraq, 82;
energy cooperation with Kazakhstan, 104–7;
energy cooperation with Kuwait, 121–22;
energy cooperation with Oman; 137;
energy cooperation with Russia, 172, 180;
energy cooperation with Russia beyond oil and gas, 177, 180;
energy cooperation with Saudi Arabia, 199–201;
energy cooperation with South Sudan, 218–19;
energy cooperation with Sudan, 242–44;
energy cooperation with the United Arab Emirates, 258–60;
energy cooperation with Venezuela, 277–78, 279;
energy interest in Kazakhstan, 95–96;
energy-petroleum agreements with Angola, 11;
energy-petroleum agreements with Brazil, 34;
energy-petroleum agreements with Iran, 66, 67;
energy-petroleum agreements with Iraq, 81;
energy-petroleum agreements with Kazakhstan, 102–4;
energy-petroleum agreements with Kuwait, 123–124;
energy-petroleum agreements with Oman, 137;
energy-petroleum agreements with Russia, 173–77, 177–78, 180–81;

energy-petroleum agreements with Saudi Arabia, 200;
energy-petroleum agreements with South Sudan, 218;
energy-petroleum agreements with Sudan, 244;
energy-petroleum agreements with United Arab Emirates, 259;
energy-petroleum agreements with Venezuela, 276–77, 278, 279;
energy-petroleum relations with Angola, 9–11;
energy-petroleum relations with Brazil, 31–34;
energy-petroleum relations with Congo–Brazzaville, 51–52;
energy-petroleum relations with Iran, 65–67;
energy-petroleum relations with Iraq, 80–82;
energy-petroleum relations with Kazakhstan, 100–105;
energy-petroleum relations with Kuwait, 122–24;
energy-petroleum relations with Oman, 136–37;
energy-petroleum relations with Russia, 171–78;
energy-petroleum relations with Saudi Arabia, 198–201;
energy-petroleum relations with South Sudan, 217–19;
energy-petroleum relations with Sudan, 240–44;
energy-petroleum relations with United Arab Emirates, 257–60;
energy-petroleum relations with Venezuela, 275–78;
energy security, 288, 289;
green energy cooperation with United Arab Emirates, 260;
historical overview of oil energy dependency, xiv–xvii;
Import-Export Bank (EXIM), xvi, 11, 25, 33, 35, 61, 94, 104, 179, 270;
importance of cultural relations, xviii,
international security cooperation with South Sudan, 214–15;
involvement in Congo-Brazzaville's economic development, 44–46;
involvement in Kazakhstan's economic development, 94–95;
involvement in Kuwait's economic development, 120;
involvement in Oman's economic development, 132–34;
involvement in Russia's economic development, 155–56;
involvement in Saudi Arabia's economic development, 193–95;
involvement in South Sudan's economic development, 211–12;
involvement in Sudan's economic development, 230–34;
involvement in the United Arab Emirates' economic development, 253–54;
involvement in Venezuela's economic development, 270;
and the Iran-Iraq War, 59, 74, 130;
as Iran's principal supplier of WMD technology and assistance, 62;
liquefied natural gas imports from Angola, 10;
liquefied natural gas imports from Oman, 137;
liquefied natural gas imports from Russia, 173–74;
liquefied natural gas imports from United Arab Emirates, 258;
loans for oil program with Angola, 2, 3, 5, 7, 12, 291;
loans for oil program with Brazil, 33, 291;
loans for oil program with Russia, 177, 179, 291;
loans for oil program in Venezuela, 277, 279, 291;
as a major infrastructure developer in Iran, 59–60;

as a major infrastructure developer in Sudan, 224, 235, 244;
military-security agreements with Brazil, 26;
military-security agreements with Congo–Brazzaville, 49;
military-security agreements with Iraq, 79;
military-security agreements with Kazakhstan, 97–98;
military-security agreements with Kuwait, 121;
military-security agreements with Russia, 165;
military-security agreements with United Arab Emirates, 255;
military-security agreements with Venezuela, 272;
military-security cooperation with Russia, 158–64, 180;
military-security cooperation with Saudi Arabia, 195–97;
military-security cooperation with South Sudan, 214;
military-security cooperation with Sudan, 235–36, 237;
military-security cooperation with the United Arab Emirates, 255–56;
military-security cooperation with Venezuela, 270–272;
military-security high level visits and exchanges with Angola, 7;
military-security high level visits and exchanges with Brazil, 25, 26;
military-security high level visits and exchanges with Congo–Brazzaville, 48;
military-security high level visits and exchanges with Iran, 62;
military-security high level visits and exchanges with Iraq, 78;
military-security high level visits and exchanges with Kazakhstan, 96;
military-security high level visits and exchanges with Kuwait, 121;
military-security high level visits and exchanges with Oman, 134;
military-security high level visits and exchanges with Russia, 159;
military-security high level visits and exchanges with Saudi Arabia, 195–96;
military-security high level visits and exchanges with Sudan, 235–36;
military-security high level visits and exchanges with the UAE, 255;
military-security high level visits and exchanges with Venezuela, 271;
military-security relations with Angola, 7–8;
military-security relations with Brazil, 25–26;
military-security relations with Congo–Brazzaville, 48–49;
military-security relations with Iran, 61–64;
military-security relations with Iraq, 78–79;
military-security relations with Kazakhstan, 96–98;
military-security relations with Kuwait, 120–21;
military-security relations with Oman, 134–35;
military-security relations with Russia, 157–65;
military-security relations with Saudi Arabia, 195–97;
military-security relations with South Sudan, 213–15;
military-security relations with Sudan, 235–37;
military-security relations with United Arab Emirates, 255–56;
military-security relations with Venezuela, 270–72;
national security, 288;
naval modernization, xvi;

naval presence increase in the Indian Ocean and Persian Gulf, xiii;
nuclear energy cooperation with Iran, 67;
nuclear energy cooperation with Saudi Arabia, 200–201;
nuclear energy cooperation with Sudan, 244;
nuclear energy development, 288;
oil and gas acquisitions in Angola, 10–11;
oil and gas acquisitions in Brazil, 32–33;
oil and gas acquisitions in Congo–Brazzaville, 51;
oil and gas acquisitions in Iran, 66;
oil and gas acquisitions in Iraq, 81;
oil and gas acquisitions in Kazakhstan, 102–103;
oil and gas acquisitions in Kuwait, 123–24;
oil and gas acquisitions in Oman, 137;
oil and gas deals with Russia, 173–76;
oil and gas acquisitions in Saudi Arabia, 200;
oil and gas acquisitions in South Sudan, 217–18;
oil and gas acquisitions in Sudan, 241, 242–43;
oil and gas deals with the United Arab Emirates, 258–59;
oil and gas acquisitions in Venezuela, 275–76;
One-China Policy/Principle, 2, 17, 58, 97, 115, 116, 147, 251, 255, 265, 266, 288, 294;
P5+1 negotiations, 58, 117;
party-to-party relations with Sudan, 223, 226;
peacekeeping operations in South Sudan, 214–15;
petroleum gas imports from Angola, 10;
petroleum gas imports from Brazil, 32;
petroleum gas imports from Congo–Brazzaville, 51;
petroleum gas imports from Iran, 66;
petroleum gas imports from Iraq, 81;
petroleum gas imports from Kazakhstan, 101–102;
petroleum gas imports from Kuwait, 122–23;
petroleum gas imports from Oman, 137;
petroleum gas imports from Russia, 172–73;
petroleum gas exports from Saudi Arabia, 198–99;
petroleum gas exports from United Arab Emirates, 258;
petroleum imports from Angola, 10;
petroleum imports from Brazil, 32;
petroleum imports from Congo–Brazzaville, 51;
petroleum imports from Iran, 65;
petroleum imports from Iraq, 80–81;
petroleum imports from Kazakhstan, 100–101;
petroleum imports from Kuwait, 122–23;
petroleum imports from Oman, 136–37;
petroleum imports from Russia, 172–73;
petroleum imports with Saudi Arabia, 198–99;
petroleum imports from South Sudan, 217–18;
petroleum imports from Sudan, 240–41;
petroleum imports from United Arab Emirates, 257–58;
petroleum imports from Venezuela, 275;
political and ideological struggle with the Soviet Union, 144–46;

political-diplomatic agreements with Angola, 1, 2–3;
political-diplomatic agreements with Brazil, 17, 20;
political-diplomatic agreements with Congo–Brazzaville, 43;
political-diplomatic agreements with Iran, 58;
political-diplomatic agreements with Iraq, 73, 75;
political-diplomatic agreements with Kazakhstan, 87, 90–91;
political-diplomatic agreements with Kuwait, 117;
political-diplomatic agreements with Oman, 130;
political-diplomatic agreements with Russia, 143, 147, 148–49;
political-diplomatic agreements with Saudi Arabia, 191;
political-diplomatic agreements with South Sudan, 207;
political-diplomatic agreements with Sudan, 223;
political-diplomatic agreements with United Arab Emirates, 251;
political-diplomatic agreements with Venezuela, 265, 266–67;
political-diplomatic high-level visits and exchanges with Angola, 2;
political-diplomatic high-level visits and exchanges with Brazil, 19–20;
political-diplomatic high-level visits and exchanges with Congo–Brazzaville, 44;
political-diplomatic high-level visits and exchanges with Iran, 57;
political-diplomatic high-level visits and exchanges with Iraq, 75;
political-diplomatic high-level visits and exchanges with Kazakhstan, 90;
political-diplomatic high-level visits and exchanges with Kuwait, 117;
political-diplomatic high-level visits and exchanges with Oman, 130;
political-diplomatic high-level visits and exchanges with Russia, 147–48;
political-diplomatic high-level visits and exchanges with Saudi Arabia, 191;
political-diplomatic high-level visits and exchanges with South Sudan, 207;
political-diplomatic high-level visits and exchanges with Sudan, 227;
political-diplomatic high-level visits and exchanges with the UAE, 250–51;
political-diplomatic high-level visits and exchanges with Venezuela, 265, 266;
political-diplomatic relations with Angola, 1–3;
political-diplomatic relations with Brazil, 17–20;
political-diplomatic relations with Congo–Brazzaville, 43–44;
political-diplomatic relations with Iran, 57–59;
political-diplomatic relations with Iraq, 73–75;
political-diplomatic relations with Kazakhstan, 87–92;
political-diplomatic relations with Kuwait, 115–17;
political-diplomatic relations with Oman, 129–31;
political-diplomatic relations with Russia, 143–49;
political-diplomatic relations with Saudi Arabia, 189–92;
political-diplomatic relations with South Sudan, 207–9;
political-diplomatic relations with Sudan, 223–27;
political-diplomatic relations with United Arab Emirates, 249–51;

political-diplomatic relations with Venezuela, 265–67;
political, economic and military strategies, xv–xvii;
political party cooperation with South Sudan, 216;
role of Chinese policy banks in Angola's infrastructure development, 6–7, 9, 12;
role of Chinese policy banks in Brazil's infrastructure development, 25, 34, 35;
role of Chinese policy banks in Congo–Brazzaville's infrastructure development, 47–48;
role of Chinese policy banks in Kazakhstan's infrastructure development, 95;
role of Chinese policy banks in Russia's infrastructure development, 156, 179;
role of Chinese policy banks in South Sudan's infrastructure development, 211–12, 219;
role of Chinese policy banks in Sudan's infrastructure development, 233–35;
role of Chinese policy banks in Venezuela's infrastructure development, 266, 270;
as Russia's largest trading partner after the European Union, 149;
Sino-Russian arms trade, 158; 161–64;
Sino-Russian relations, 147–149;
Sino-Russian views on Pakistan, 147;
Sino-Soviet arms trade, 160–61;
Sino-Soviet relations, 144–46;
space cooperation with the United Arab Emirates, 257;
space technology cooperation with Venezuela, 274;
strategic consultations with Oman, 130–131;

strategic cooperation in space science and technology with Brazil, 28, 29, 30, 31;
strategic energy cooperation with Russia, 172;
strategic partnerships, xviii;
strategic partnership with Angola, 3, 291;
strategic partnership with Brazil, 19, 20, 35, 291;
strategic partnership with Iran, 58;
strategic partnership with Iraq, 82;
strategic partnership with Kazakhstan, 91, 92, 94, 99, 291;
strategic partnership with Russia, 143, 144, 149, 291;
strategic partnership with Saudi Arabia, 191, 291;
strategic partnership with Sudan, 223, 291;
strategic partnership with United Arab Emirates, 251, 291;
strategic partnership with Venezuela, 266, 291;
strategic relations with its principal and gas suppliers, xiii;
as Sudan's largest investor, 224;
support of Angolan liberation groups during the Cold War, 1, 43;
support of Left-Wing Movements in the Gulf Region (Saudi Arabia), 190;
support of the Dhofar Liberation Front (DLF) in the Gulf Region (Saudi Arabia), 190;
support of the Dhofar Liberation Front (DLF) in Oman's civil war, 58, 116, 129, 134, 249;
United Nations Peacekeeping Operations, 213–15, 227, 236, 288, 292, 294;
weapon supplies to Angola, 7–8;
weapon supplies to Congo-Brazzaville, 48–49;
weapon supplies to Iran, 63;

weapon supplies to Iraq, 78–79;
weapon supplies to Kuwait, 121;
weapon supplies to Oman, 134;
weapon supplies to Saudi Arabia, 196;
weapon supplies to South Sudan, 213–14;
weapon supplies to Sudan, 236–237;
weapon supplies to United Arab Emirates, 255;
weapon supplies to Venezuela, 271–72;
WMD assistance and technology to Iran, 62;
and Xinjiang, 96–97
Confucius Institutes: xviii, xxi, 8, 30, 31, 50, 65, 99, 136, 166–67, 238, 239, 257, 274, 295
Congo-Brazzaville:
as a base to conduct revolutionary activities in Central Africa, 43, 52;
bilateral trade with China, 44–45;
Confucius Institute in, 50;
cultural agreements with China, 49–50;
cultural relations with China, 49–50;
economic-trade agreements with China, 45–46;
economic-trade relations with China, 44–48;
energy cooperation with China, 51–52;
energy-petroleum relations with China, 51–52;
largest supplier of African oil after Angola, 52;
military-security agreements with China, 49;
military-security high level visits and exchanges with China, 48;
military-security relations with China, 48–49;
petroleum exports to China, 51;
petroleum gas exports to China, 51;
political-diplomatic agreements with China, 43;
political-diplomatic high-level visits and exchanges with China, 44;
political-diplomatic relations with China, 43–44;
weapon supplies from China, 48–49
Corkin, Lucy, 2, 3

Dhofar Liberation Front (DLF), 58, 129, 134, 190, 249

East Turkestan Islamic Movement (ETIM), 88, 97, 121, 196, 256, 288

GCC Trade Framework, 133, 253
Going-Global Strategy, xxii, 88, 292
Go-Out Policy, xxii, 88, 292

Iran:
bilateral trade with China, 59–60;
Confucius Institute in Iran, 65;
cultural agreements with China, 64–65;
cultural relations with China, 64–65;
economic-trade agreements with China, 60–61;
economic-trade relations with China, 59–61;
energy cooperation with China, 66, 67;
energy-petroleum agreements with China, 66, 67;
energy-petroleum relations with China, 65–67;
international terrorism cooperation with China, 62–64;
military-security high level visits and exchanges with China, 62;
military-security relations with China, 61–64;
nuclear energy cooperation with China, 67;
oil and gas as a pillar of the Sino-Iran relationship, 57, 65;

petroleum exports to China, 65;
petroleum gas exports to China, 66;
political-diplomatic agreements with China, 58;
political-diplomatic high-level visits and exchanges with China, 57;
political-diplomatic relations with China, 57–59;
strategic partnership with China, 58;
weapon supplies from China, 63;
WMD technology and assistance from China, 62

Iraq:
bilateral trade with China, 75–76;
Chinese investments in, 77–78;
cultural agreements with China; 79–80;
cultural cooperation with China, 80;
cultural relations with China, 79–80;
economic-trade agreements with China, 76–77;
economic-trade relations with China, 75–78;
energy cooperation with China, 82;
energy-petroleum agreements with China; 81;
energy-petroleum relations with China, 80–82;
international terrorism cooperation with China, 78;
military-security agreements with China, 79;
military-security high level visits and exchanges with China, 78;
military-security relations with China, 78–79;
political-diplomatic agreements with China, 73, 75;
political-diplomatic high-level visits and exchanges with China, 75;
political-diplomatic relations with China, 73–75;
petroleum exports to China, 80–81;
petroleum gas exports to China, 81;
strategic partnership with China, 82;

support of China for a permanent seat in the United Nations, 74;
weapon supplies from China, 78–79

Kazakhstan:
as China's largest supplier of petroleum in Central Asia, 100;
as part of the Russian Empire and Soviet Union, 87–89;
Baku-Tbilisi-Ceyhan (BTC) pipeline, 100;
banking and finance cooperation with China, 95;
bilateral trade with China, 92–93;
Confucius Institutes in, 99;
cultural agreements with China, 98;
cultural cooperation with China, 99–100;
cultural relations with China, 98–100;
economic cooperation with China, 94–95,
economic-trade agreements with China, 93–94;
economic-trade relations with China, 92–96;
energy cooperation with China, 104–105, 106–7;
energy-petroleum agreements with China, 102–104;
energy-petroleum relations with China, 100–105;
international terrorism cooperation with China, 96–97;
Kazakhstan-China oil pipeline, 101. 106;
military-security agreements with China, 97–98;
military-security high level visits and exchanges with China, 96;
military-security relations with China, 96–98;
petroleum exports to China, 100–101;
petroleum gas exports to China, 101–102;

political-diplomatic agreements with China, 87, 90–91;
political-diplomatic high-level visits and exchanges with China, 90;
political-diplomatic relations with China, 87–92;
role of policy banks in Kazakhstan's infrastructure development, 94–95;
strategic partnership with China, 91, 92, 94, 99;
Uzen-Atyrau-Samara (UAS) pipeline, 100;
and Xinjiang 96–97
Kuwait:
active involvement in Chinese companies, 120;
bilateral trade with China, 117–118;
cultural agreements with China, 122;
cultural relations with China, 121–22;
economic-trade agreements with China, 119–20;
economic-trade relations with China, 117–20;
energy cooperation with China, 123–24;
energy-petroleum agreements with China, 123–24;
energy-petroleum relations with China, 122–24;
international terrorism cooperation with China, 121;
military-security agreements with China, 121;
military-security high level visits and exchanges with China, 121;
military-security relations with China, 120–21;
petroleum exports to China, 122–23;
petroleum gas exports to China, 122–23;
political-diplomatic agreements with China, 117;
political-diplomatic cooperation, 116–17;
political-diplomatic high-level visits and exchanges with China, 117;
political-diplomatic relations with China, 115–17;
regional cooperation with China, 117;
weapon supplies from China, 121

Look East policy, 231

Medeiros, Evan S.:
On China's strategic partnerships, xviii
Murphy, Dawn:
on China's strategic partnerships, xviii

National Liberation Front of Angola (FNLA), 1, 43
National Oil Companies (NOCs): xvi, xvii, xxii, 193
National Union for the Total Independence of Angola (UNITA), 1, 2, 6, 43
New Silk Road Initiative, 88–89, 290
NOCs. See National Oil Companies

oil:
importance of, xiv
Oman:
anti-piracy cooperation with China, 134, 138;
banking and finance cooperation with China, 133;
bilateral trade with China, 131–32;
cultural agreements with China, 35;
cultural cooperation with China, 135–36;
cultural relations with China, 135–36;
economic-trade agreements with China, 131–33;
economic-trade relations with China, 131–34;
energy cooperation with China, 137;

energy-petroleum agreements with China, 137;
energy-petroleum relations with China, 136–37;
foreign direct investment in China, 133–34;
international cooperation, 130;
international terrorism cooperation with China, 135;
liquefied natural gas imports to China, 137;
military-security high level visits and exchanges with China, 134;
military-security relations with China, 134–35;
petroleum exports to China, 136–37;
petroleum gas exports to China, 137;
political-diplomatic agreements with China, 130;
political-diplomatic high-level visits and exchanges with China, 130;
Port of Salalah to rest and replenish PLAN ships, 134, 138;
political-diplomatic relations with China, 129–31;
strategic consultations with China, 130–31;
weapon supplies from China, 134

People's Movement for the Liberation of Angola (MPLA), 1, 2, 6, 43
Plan of the Book, xviii–xxiv
cultural relations, xxi–xxii;
economic-trade relations, xx;
energy-petroleum relations, xxii–xxiv;
military-security relations, xxi;
political-diplomatic relations, xix
Popular Front for the Liberation of the Occupied Arabian Gulf (PFLOAG), 116, 129, 190, 249, 250

Russia:
banking and finance cooperation with China, 156–57, 170;
bilateral trade with China, 149–51, 179;
Confucius Institutes in, 166–67;
cultural agreements with China, 167–71, 180;
cultural exchanges with China, 165–66;
cultural relations with China, 165–71;
early relations with China, 143–44, 178–79;
economic-trade agreements with China, 151–55;
economic-trade relations with China, 149–57;
energy cooperation with China, 172, 180;
energy cooperation with China beyond oil and gas, 177, 180;
energy-petroleum agreements with China, 173–78, 180–81;
energy-petroleum relations with China, 171–78;
liquefied natural gas exports to China, 173–74;
loans for oil program with China, 177, 179, 291;
military influence on China, 157–58;
military-security agreements with China, 165;
military-security cooperation with China, 158–64, 180;
military-security high level visits and exchanges with China, 159;
military-security relations with China, 157–65;
oil and gas deals with China, 173–76;
oil and gas pipelines, 171–72;
petroleum exports to China, 172–73;
petroleum gas exports to China, 172–73;
political-diplomatic agreements with China, 143, 147, 148–49;
political-diplomatic high-level visits and exchanges with China, 147–48;

political-diplomatic relations with China, 143–49;
Sino-Russian arms trade, 158; 161–64;
Sino-Russian relations, 147–49;
Sino-Russian views on Pakistan, 147;
Sino-Soviet arms trade, 160–61;
Sino-Soviet relations, 144–46;
strategic energy cooperation with China, 172;
strategic partnership with China, 143, 148, 149

Saudi Arabia:
anti-terrorism cooperation with China, 196–97;
as China's largest supplier of crude petroleum, 198;
bilateral trade with China, 192–93;
cultural agreements with China, 198;
cultural relations with China, 197–98;
early cultural relations with China, 197;
early diplomatic relations with China, 189;
early trade relations with China, 189;
economic-trade agreements with China, 194;
economic-trade relations with China, 192–95;
energy cooperation with China, 199–201;
energy-petroleum agreements with China, 200;
energy-petroleum relations with China, 198–201;
as a major investor of China, 192–93;
military-security high level visits and exchanges with China, 195–96;
military-security cooperation with China, 195–97;
military-security relations with China, 195–97;
nuclear energy cooperation with China, 200–1;
petroleum exports to China, 198–99;
petroleum gas exports to China, 198–99;
political-diplomatic agreements with China, 191;
political-diplomatic high-level visits and exchanges with China, 191;
political-diplomatic relations with China, 189–92;
and the Silk Road Economic Belt and the 21st Century Maritime Silk Road, 193, 194;
strategic partnership with China, 191;
weapon supplies from China, 196
Sea Lines of Communication (SLOC), xvi, 289
Shanghai Cooperation Organization (SCO), xxi, 64, 92, 96–97, 147, 159, 180, 287, 293
Shanghai International Expo, xxi, 8, 31, 49, 80, 99, 136, 167, 197, 239, 256, 257, 274, 295
Shinn, David H.:
on the use of the Chinese military to acquire oil, xvii
South Sudan:
bilateral trade with China, 209–11;
Chinese peacekeepers in, 214–15;
conflict with Sudan, 207–9;
cultural agreements with China, 217;
cultural cooperation with China, 216;
cultural relations with China, 215–17;
early diplomatic relations with China, 207;
economic-trade agreements with China, 211;
economic-trade relations with China, 209–13;
energy cooperation with China, 218–19;
energy-petroleum agreements with China, 218;

energy-petroleum relations with China, 217–19;
international security cooperation with China, 214–15;
military-security cooperation with China, 214;
military-security relations with China, 213–15;
petroleum exports to China, 217–18;
political-diplomatic agreements with China, 207;
political-diplomatic high-level visits and exchanges with China, 207;
political-diplomatic relations with China, 207–9;
political party cooperation with China, 216;
Sudan People's Liberation Movement (SPLM), 216;
weapon supplies from China, 213–14

Sudan:
bilateral trade with China, 228–29;
China's development of Sudan's oil sector, 242–43;
Confucius Institute in, 238;
cultural agreements with China, 239–40;
cultural cooperation with China, 238;
cultural relations with China, 238–40;
early relations with China, 223–26;
economic-trade agreements with China, 229–30;
economic-trade relations with China, 227–35;
energy cooperation with China, 242–44;
energy-petroleum agreements with China, 244;
energy-petroleum relations with China, 240–44;
military-security cooperation with China, 235–37;
military-security high level visits and exchanges with China, 235–36;
military-security relations with China, 235–37;
nuclear energy cooperation with China, 244;
party-to-party relations with China, 223, 226;
petroleum exports to China, 240–41;
political-diplomatic agreements with China, 223;
political-diplomatic high-level visits and exchanges with China, 227;
political-diplomatic relations with China, 223–27;
strategic partnership with China, 223;
weapon supplies from China, 236–37

Treaty of Nerchinsk, 144

United Arab Emirates:
banking and finance cooperation with China, 254, 255;
bilateral trade with China, 251–52;
cultural agreements with China, 256;
cultural cooperation with China, 256–57;
cultural relations with China, 256–57;
currency swap with China, 254;
Dragon Mart, 251, 260;
early relations with China, 249;
economic-trade agreements with China, 253;
economic-trade relations with China, 251–55;
energy cooperation with China, 258–60;
energy-petroleum agreements with China, 259;
energy-petroleum relations with China, 257–60;
green energy cooperation with China, 260;
international terrorism cooperation with China, 255–56;

liquefied natural gas exports to China, 258;
military-security agreements with China, 255;
military-security cooperation with China, 255–56;
military-security high level visits and exchanges with China, 255;
military-security relations with China, 255–56;
petroleum gas exports to China, 257–58;
political-diplomatic agreements with China, 251;
political-diplomatic high-level visits and exchanges with China, 250–51;
political-diplomatic relations with China, 249–51;
space cooperation with China, 257;
strategic partnership with China, 251;
weapon supplies from China, 255

Venezuela:
banking and finance cooperation with China, 266, 270;
bilateral trade with China, 267–68;
cultural agreements with China, 272–74;
cultural cooperation with China, 274;
cultural relations with China, 272–74;
economic-trade agreements with China, 269–70;
economic-trade relations with China, 267–70;
energy cooperation with China, 277–79;
energy-petroleum agreements with China, 276–79;
energy-petroleum relations with China, 275–78;
loans for oil program with China, 279, 291;
military-security agreements with China, 272;
military-security high level visits and exchanges with China, 271;
military-security cooperation with China, 270–72;
military-security relations with China, 270–272;
petroleum exports to China, 275;
political-diplomatic agreements with China, 265–67;
political-diplomatic high-level visits and exchanges with China, 265, 266;
political-diplomatic relations with China, 265–67;
space technology cooperation with China, 274;
strategic partnership with China, 266;
weapon supplies from China, 271–72

About the Author

George G. Eberling completed his PhD in Political Science from Claremont Graduate University in May 2010. *China's Bilateral Relations with Its Principal Oil Suppliers* is his third publication. He previously published *Chinese Energy Futures and Their Implications for the United States* in October 2011 and *Future Oil Demands of China, India, and Japan: Policy Scenarios and Implications* in July 2014.

China's Bilateral Relations with Its Principal Oil Suppliers was prepared by George Eberling in his personal capacity. The views expressed in the book are George Eberling's own and do not reflect the view of the U.S. Citizenship and Immigration Services, the U.S. Department of Homeland Security, or the U. S. government.